FIFTH EDITION

Research Methods in Psychology

David G. Elmes
Washington and Lee University

Barry H. Kantowitz
Battelle Memorial Institute

Henry L. Roediger III
Rice University

WEST PUBLISHING COMPANY
St. Paul ∎ New York ∎ Los Angeles ∎ San Francisco

Artist: Printing Arts, Inc.
Copyeditor: Kathleen Rae Pruno
Cover image: The Stock Market/Zefa, 1991
Composition: Parkwood Composition Services, Inc.
Index: Northwind Editorial Services
Text design: John Edeen

WEST'S COMMITMENT TO THE ENVIRONMENT

In 1906, West Publishing Company began recycling materials left over from the production of books. This began a tradition of efficient and responsible use of resources. Today, up to 95% of our legal books and 70% of our college texts and school texts are printed on recycled, acid-free stock. West also recycles nearly 22 million pounds of scrap paper annually—the equivalent of 181,717 trees. Since the 1960s, West has devised ways to capture and recycle waste inks, solvents, oils, and vapors created in the printing process. We also recycle plastics of all kinds, wood, glass, corrugated cardboard, and batteries, and have eliminated the use of Styrofoam book packaging. We at West are proud of the longevity and the scope of our commitment to the environment.

Production, Prepress, Printing and Binding by West Publishing Company.

 PRINTED ON 10% POST CONSUMER RECYCLED PAPER

LIBRARY OF CONGRESS CATALOGING-IN-PUBLICATION DATA

Elmes, David G.
    Research methods in psychology / David Elmes,
Barry Kantowitz, Henry Roediger.—5th ed.
        p.   cm.
    Includes bibliographical references and index.
    ISBN 0-314-04458-2
    1. Psychology—Research—Methodology.   2. Psychology,
Experimental.   I. Kantowitz, Barry H.   II. Roediger, Henry L.
III Title.
BF76.5.E44 1995   94-34602
150'.724—dc20   CIP

CONTENTS

CHAPTER 6
OBSERVATION IN PSYCHOLOGICAL RESEARCH   143

CHAPTER 11
ALTERNATE EXPERIMENTAL DESIGNS   269

PART 4
☐ FINISHING PSYCHOLOGICAL RESEARCH   303

CHAPTER 12
INTERPRETING THE RESULTS OF RESEARCH   305

CHAPTER 13
PRESENTING RESEARCH RESULTS   331

□ STATISTICAL APPENDIXES   365

APPENDIX A
DESCRIPTIVE STATISTICS   367

APPENDIX B
INFERENTIAL STATISTICS   381

APPENDIX C
STATISTICAL TABLES   415

PREFACE

We are pleased to present you with the fifth edition of our textbook, which was first published in 1981. The book you are holding now differs radically from the first edition. We have tried to revise each edition in response to numerous comments from students, professors, and reviewers, as well as our own changing ideas in teaching the Research Methods course. The popularity of the previous editions of the text have permitted us to present you with this fifth edition, which we hope you will find rewarding. As in the previous editions, this book presents the methods of psychological science necessary to permit a good understanding of valid and reliable research. Whether you as a student become a producer or consumer of research, you must be able to evaluate and appraise it.

TEXT ORGANIZATION

The text is divided into four parts or sections. The first part focuses on the basics of scientific investigation, including the philosophy of science. The first two chapters within this section provide the groundwork for the remainder of the material. The third chapter considers ethics in research, and the fourth chapter is about exploring the literature of psychology, including advice on how to read an article. The second part contains four chapters about techniques of scientific psychology. These include material about psychological measurement, descriptive observations, correlational research, and the basics of experimental research. The third part of the book contains three chapters about advanced topics in experimentation. These chapters are on experimental design, more complex experimental designs, small-n research, and quasi-experimental research. Finally, the fourth part contains two chapters on important issues in finishing psychological research. One is concerned with interpreting research results and the other explains how to present psychological research, both in written reports and in oral presentations. Finally, there are appendices on descriptive and inferential statistics.

Pedagogical Features

Each chapter contains several features designed to improve comprehension and enhance interest. The **Facing Page** provides a summary of the upcoming chapter. The facing page will alert you to important concepts and will provide a convenient aid for review. The **Overview** introduces the substance of each chapter. Within the chapter there are frequent **Concept Summaries,** which are designed to drive home important concepts and to assist in study and review. Most chapters include an **Application** section, which considers how some of the concepts discussed in that chapter can be used outside of the laboratory setting. At the end of each chapter are several features: a point-by-point **Summary**; a list of **Key Concepts**; thought-provoking **Exercises**; and **Suggested Readings**. These features will help you derive maximum benefit from the contents of the chapter—they will reinforce and extend your understanding. Most of the chapters are followed by a **Psychology in Action** section, which presents a project for you to undertake. These projects are intended to further your interest in scientific psychology.

As in earlier editions, many concepts are discussed more than once. The repeated discussion of important ideas in separate parts of the text is done to enhance understanding. We want to take advantage of the well-known benefits of distributed practice and varied rehearsal to maximize the efficiency of the learning process for our readers.

CHANGES FROM THE FOURTH EDITION

Users of the fourth edition will notice many changes in the current edition. The advice of our capable reviewers, the suggestions of readers, and our own experience have resulted in changes in organization and in content. The book has been greatly reorganized, with some chapters added and others reformulated. The first four chapters have been heavily revised. Chapter 1 introduces students to psychological research and considers the beginnings of a project. Students participate as subjects in an experiment, and then many of the basics of research are examined in the light of their experience in this experiment. Chapter 2 focuses on theory construction and hypothesis testing, with more information provided on the philosophy of science. Chapter 3 is about ethical issues in research, and Chapter 4 informs students about exploring the literature of psychology, including how to find information on topics in which they are interested and tips on how to read journal articles. On the advice of reviewers, the chapters on ethics and on how to read articles have been moved forward in the book for this edition. In particular, reviewers pointed out that it is valuable to have information on how to explore the literature of psychology early in the course.

The four chapters of the second part of the book also contain many changes. In particular, we now have a chapter called Measurement in Psychological Research (Chapter 5) concerned with many issues in psychological measurement. In our chapters on descriptive and correlational research we have tried to include many more examples to show the important types of research that can be conducted using these techniques. The last chapter introduces students to experimental research. The second part of the book, represents a new formulation for covering these topics, and we hope readers will agree that the progression through these chapters provides a good, logical introduction to the topics at hand. We recommend that the chapters in Part II be read in order.

The third part of the book, on advanced experimentation, includes two chapters on experimental design, a chapter on small-n experiments and a chapter on quasi-experiments. Once again, we have tried to show in the latter chapter how interesting and valid psychological research can be conducted without using the standard large-n designs practiced by many fields of psychology.

In the final part of the book we include new material on problems of interpreting psychological research and also devote an entire chapter to presenting research results. In past editions we have concentrated exclusively on production of written reports, but now we also include some tips on making oral presentations in classes or at conferences.

In many places we have chosen new examples to illustrate concepts and principles. Students intrigued by nearly any aspect of scientific psychology will find examples to challenge and to interest them. We have tried to take examples across the entire spectrum of psychology, but of course examples chosen often depend on the topic being discussed. Our goals in choosing examples were threefold: to illustrate the proper ways to conduct research, to convey the importance and tremendous scope of psychological science, and to impart a sense of fun and excitement that can be found in undertaking psychological investigations. We hope that we have been successful in attaining those goals.

ACKNOWLEDGMENTS

Writing a textbook is a cooperative effort among the authors, readers, and users of earlier editions; the editors and production staff; and the sage advice of several capable reviewers. Many readers of the fourth edition and the professors who assigned it have written us with valuable suggestions and comments, especially Erin D. Bigler, of the University of Utah, Bobbie Spellman of the University of Texas, and Edmond Vernator of Millsaps College. We thank them for their help and hope that new readers will help us devise a sixth edition. We appreciate the help of the production staff at West—a group of competent people who made our job easier and the product better. Amy Gabriel, our production editor, skillfully navigated the book through the many difficult steps from manuscript to the book you are holding. John Tuvey, our promotion manager, was again a pleasure to work with. Many Schiller, our editor, deserves special recognition for her organizational skill and wit and her unflagging enthusiasm for our book. Her advice and encouragement have kept us going. We also owe a debt to all our reviewers: Harry Avis, Albert Bartz, Steve Blankenship, Joan Bombace, Charles Brewer, Fred Bryant, Elizabeth Capaldi, Raymond Corteen, E. C. Dalrymple-Alford, Chris Davis, Morton Heller, Larry Hochhaus, David Hogberg, Phyllis Hornbuckle, John Jahnke, Lori Kolbet, Richard Lehman, John Limber, James McCroskery, Kenneth McIntire, Fred Meeker, Michael

Moore, Michael Perone, Alexander Pietrecicz, Tess Rottman, Michael Stadler, Therow Stimmel, Jeanette Ward, Royce White.

Others have provided invaluable technical help. It is pleasure to recognize the contributions of Kathleen B. McDermott and Jessica Antonich. They helped in many ways with such skill and efficiency that this edition would be in limbo without their fine assistance. The support of Washington and Lee University, especially its Department of Psychology, is gratefully acknowledged. Several authors and publishers have helped us reproduce important materials. We are grateful to the Literary Executor of the late Sir Ronald A. Fisher, F.R.S., to Dr. Frank Yates, F.R.S., and to Longman Group Ltd. London for permission to reprint Table C-5 from their book *Statistical Tables for Biological Agricultural and Medical Research* (6th edition, 1974).

Finally, we owe an incalculable debt to our teachers who encouraged us to pursue scientific psychology. We would like to dedicate this work to the memory of three outstanding individuals who shared the fun and excitement of experimental psychology with us: **David A. Grant, William M. Hinton,** and **L. Starling Reid.** Each, in his own way, encouraged students to engage in sound psychological research. Their enthusiasm led us into experimental psychology, and we hope that you find a similar model to lead you in the same direction.

David G. Elmes
Barry H. Kantowitz
Henry L. Roediger III

ABOUT THE AUTHORS

David G. Elmes is a Professor of Psychology and Head of the Department of Psychology at Washington and Lee University, where he has taught since 1967. He earned his B.A. with high honors from the University of Virginia and continued on to complete the M.A. and Ph.D. degrees there. Elmes was Adjunct Professor at Hampden-Sydney College, was a research associate for a year in the Human Performance Center of the University of Michigan, and was a Visiting Fellow of University College at the University of Oxford, England. At Washington and Lee he is a codirector of the Cognitive Science Program. Professor Elmes edited *Readings in Experimental Psychology* and is coauthor of the fifth edition of *Experimental Psychology* (with B. H. Kantowitz and H. L. Roediger III). He has published numerous articles concerned with human and animal learning and memory. He frequently referees papers submitted to technical journals and was a Consulting Editor for the *Journal of Experimental Psychology: Learning, Memory, and Cognition* for several years. In the Council on Undergraduate Research, he is Councilor of the Psychology Division, and he is Editor of the *Psychology Directory*.

Barry H. Kantowitz is Director of the Human Factors Transportation Center at Battelle Memorial Institute, Seattle, in the Center for Human Factors and Organizational Effectiveness. He received the Ph.D. degree in Experimental Psychology from the University of Wisconsin in 1969. From 1969 to 1987 he held positions as Assistant, Associate, and Professor of Psychological Sciences, at Purdue University, West Lafayette, Indiana. Dr. Kantowitz was elected a Fellow of the American Psychological Association in 1974. He has been a National Institute of Mental Health Postdoctoral Fellow at the University of Oregon, a Senior Lecturer in Ergonomics at the Norwegian Institute of Technology, Trondheim, Norway, and a Visiting Professor of Technical Psychology at the University of Lulea, Sweden. He has written and edited more than one dozen books. His research on human attention, mental workload, reaction time, human-machine interaction, and human factors has been supported by the Office of Education, the National Institute of Mental Health, the National Aeronautics and Space Administration, and the Air Force Office of Scientific Research. He served a five-year term on the editorial board of *Organizational Behavior and Human Performance*. He has published over seventy scientific articles and book chapters.

Henry L. Roediger III is the Lynette S. Autrey Professor of Psychology at Rice University, where he has taught since 1988. He received a B.A. degree in psychology from Washington and Lee University in 1969 and a Ph.D. in cognitive psychology from Yale University in 1973. He has previously been on the faculty at Purdue University (1973–1988) and spent three years as a visiting professor at the University of Toronto. His research interests lie in cognitive psychology, particularly in human learning and memory. He has published over eighty chapters, articles, and reviews as well as two other textbooks: *Psychology* (coauthored with E. D. Capaldi, S. G. Paris, J. Polivy, and P. Herman) and *Experimental Psychology* (with D. G. Elmes and B. H. Kantowitz). He also edited (with F. I. M. Craik) *Varieties of Memory and Consciousness: Essays in Honour of Endel Tulving*. Roediger serves as Editor of *Psychonomic Bulletin & Review*, and as a Consulting Editor for *Journal of Memory and Language*, *Memory*, and *Neuropsychology*. He served as Editor of the *Journal of Experimental Psychology: Learning, Memory, and Cognition*, from 1985 to 1989 and as its Associate Editor from 1981 to 1984. He was a member of the Governing Board of the Psychonomic Society for five years (Chair, 1989–1990) and was President of the Midwestern Psychological Association in 1992–1993. In 1994 he received a Guggenheim Fellowship and was elected a member of the Society of Experimental Psychologists.

BASICS OF SCIENTIFIC PSYCHOLOGY

Goals of Psychological Research

- ❏ Conducting sound research
- ❏ Critically evaluating research

Sources of Psychological Research

- ❏ Theories
- ❏ Practical problems

Sources of Research Ideas

- ❏ Observation
- ❏ Experts
- ❏ Journals

Steps in the Research Process

- ❏ Get an idea
- ❏ Formulate a testable hypothesis
- ❏ Review the literature
- ❏ Conduct pilot research
- ❏ Complete the research
- ❏ Conduct statistical tests
- ❏ Interpret the results
- ❏ Prepare an article

Be Sure to

- ❏ Consider ethical issues
- ❏ Guard against researcher bias
- ❏ Construct operational definitions

CHAPTER 1

BEGINNING PSYCHOLOGICAL RESEARCH

In this chapter you will participate in a demonstration experiment. Then you will discover that the focus of this book is on conducting sound research and critically evaluating the research of others. You will be introduced to the initial stages of the research process—getting ideas, formulating hypotheses, reviewing the literature, and conducting preliminary research.

Psychological research attempts to understand why people and animals behave as they do. Psychologists usually define **behavior** as overt activities, such as eating, recalling stories, and so on. What about covert psychological processes, such as thinking and feeling? Although thoughts and feelings are not directly observable, they influence such aspects of behavior as reaction time and blood pressure, which are often used to measure these covert processes.

Psychological research is very important. The astounding number of practical gains are too numerous to list, but include discoveries such as improved methods of treating psychologically disordered people, better designs of vehicles to make them easier and safer to use, and new ways of enhancing the performance and happiness of workers. Just as important are the scientific gains provided by psychological research. Scientific psychology is a relatively young science, having begun in earnest in the middle of the nineteenth century. Nevertheless, the 150 years of psychological research have resulted in a dramatic increase in the scientific understanding of behavior.

In this chapter you will first participate in an experiment. Then we examine how psychological research is begun by using the demonstration experiment as an example.

An Investigation of Reading

To start your study of psychological research, we want you to take part in an experiment. We hope that your participation in this project will elicit the kinds of questions about research that psychology students and experimental subjects often ask. We also will use the experiment to highlight many issues confronting researchers in psychology as they begin to study and use the methods of scientific psychology.

Introduction and Method

The design of the following demonstration experiment tries to decide whether aspects of reading and counting can occur automatically. You are a skilled reader, having spent a dozen or so years of your life practicing this skill. You probably believe that reading words and enumerating objects are rational, deliberate processes. Are they? Do you have to think about reading and naming while doing them, or do these processes occur automatically with little conscious effort? To find out whether reading can occur automatically, you will engage in a series of reading and naming tasks. The crucial part of the experiment is that the tasks differ in their requirements. The behavior you will measure is how fast you do each. One task is set up so that if reading occurs automatically, you will do that task more slowly than the others.

To participate in this experiment, you will need a clock or a watch with a second hand (a watch that records elapsed time in seconds will do), and you also will need a pen or a pencil. You might want to do this experiment with a classmate, so you can accurately time each other. Your task is to read or name a series of digits or symbols as quickly and as accurately as you can. The digits and symbols are in a single column. You should start at the top and go to the bottom of the column without skipping any items. You will go through three different columns on three different pages. Be sure to do them in order. At the top of each page are directions—read them carefully, because the directions on each page are different. The phase *Start Time* is also at the top of each page. If you are working alone and are using a clock or watch with a second hand, write down the exact time in minutes and seconds. Then start the task. If you are using a watch that records elapsed time, start the time and then begin the task. When you have finished the task on a particular page, either note your finishing time or stop your watch and write down the elapsed time. If you are doing this experiment with a classmate, have him or her time you as you go through each task. Your classmate then can serve as a subject, and you can do the timing for each task.

To begin the experiment, turn to page 25. Do not continue reading here until you have participated in the experiment.

Results and Discussion

What happened in the experiment? For each column of digits or symbols, figure out how long it took you to do the task. If you recorded elapsed time, this is straightforward. If you wrote down your start and finish times, calculate the time to go through the column by subtracting the start time from the finish time. When you compare the results of the three tests, you probably will find that naming the number of numbers (the last task you did) took the longest time, and reading the digits took the shortest time.

When we conducted this experiment, we obtained the results shown in Figure 1–1. Students in our classes took an average of about 2 seconds longer to enumerate the pluses (the second task) than to read the digits (the first task). In the final task of naming the number of numbers, our students averaged about 6 seconds longer than simply reading the digits. If you combine your results with those of your classmates, statistical procedures described in appendix B will allow you to decide whether the

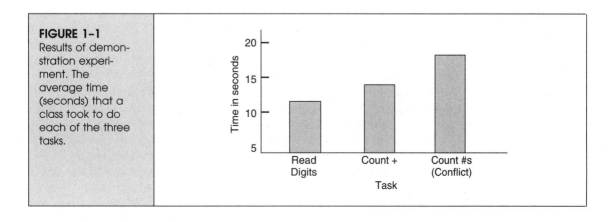

FIGURE 1–1
Results of demonstration experiment. The average time (seconds) that a class took to do each of the three tasks.

differences in completion time among the tasks are large enough to be considered real or reliable ones worth considering.

An alternative way to think about the results is to examine how long on average it took people to respond to each item. Because there were 32 items in each task, we can divide the mean time by 32 to find the average time per item. The students averaged .35 seconds to read a single digit, .43 seconds to count a row of pluses, and .57 seconds to count a row of numbers in the conflict task.

Time to read through the columns measures reading difficulty; the longer the time, the more difficult the task. Why is it difficult to name the number of digits when the response is different from the name of the digit? That is, why is it difficult to say "4" when you see 3 3 3 3?

To answer this question, we will outline a theory that seems to account for the results. Other researchers have found that people usually are slower in naming the quantity of digits when the names of those digits conflict with that quantity. Apparently, we automatically read the name of the digits as we are enumerating the quantity. So when we have to respond "2" when we see 3 3, we simultaneously have the responses "2" and "3" available, and because we cannot say two things at once, competition exists between the available responses.

You can think of this as a mental race between two processes that lead to different responses when you see 3 3. One process is naming the digits ("3"); the other is counting them and saying the number ("2"). Because the naming process is greatly practiced, it wins the race, and the naming response ("3") comes to mind before the correct counting response ("2"). Thus there is response competition, because you must inhibit the faster naming response to permit the slower counting response to be spoken. Even if you try to ignore the names of the digits completely, you will discover that you are slower in counting numbers than you were in counting pluses (check the results of the second test you took). This outcome can be interpreted as showing that reading is an automatic process, because even when you try to avoid reading the numbers 3 3, you cannot completely suppress the response "3." Put another way, you cannot not read. Try looking at a word and not reading it.

GOALS OF PSYCHOLOGICAL RESEARCH

You have just participated in a demonstration experiment that was supposed to show that reading occurs even when we do not want it to under some circumstances. You could ask at this point why people bother to engage in research, or why you are taking a course that focuses on research. A survey of over 650 departments of psychology in colleges and universities showed that 73 percent required some combination of courses in statistics and research design as part of their major program (A. J. Golden, personal communication, January 2, 1991), and an additional 20 percent of these departments have research methods and statistics courses as optional components of the psychology major. Why the emphasis on research in 93 percent of the programs?

Two important reasons for the research focus are to teach you how to conduct sound research and to teach you how to evaluate the results of research. We examine each of these purposes in turn.

Conducting Research

Science progresses when new facts lead to new theories. This progression begins with attempts to answer questions. Is reading a deliberate, reflective process? Not always, as our demonstration experiment shows. Scientific interest in reading is more than idle curiosity—it is curiosity guided by theories and data (facts). The finding that reading often does not require conscious attention must be considered by theories that attempt to explain some aspects of reading. For example, Cohen, Dunbar, and McClelland (1990) developed a theory of attention that tries to show how skilled reading develops. The theory predicts, for example, that highly practiced readers will be more disrupted by conflicts between reading and naming than will less fluent readers. Cohen and associates showed that this is the case, and their theory provides an account of the mechanisms underlying the effects of experience on automaticity. Thus, basic scientific research arises from curiosity and provides the data that allow the development of theoretical explanations.

Scientific progress is not only driven by basic questions and theories, but also motivated by practical problems. One aspect of the research by Cohen and his colleagues shows that automaticity in reading takes a substantial amount of practice. Some obvious practical questions include: How much practice leads to fluent reading? What is the best way to practice to become fluent? The application of scientific psychology to applied problems has had a tremendous impact on social welfare, and the development of improved ways to teach reading is no exception. The understanding of reading has benefited from attempts to determine its bases and solve some practical problems (Crowder & Wagner, 1992).

Obviously, psychological research is not exclusively practical or exclusively theoretical in its focus. Psychological research can have an impact on scientific explanation and the amelioration of applied problems. Many facets of human affairs involve psychological research, and a sample of careers using scientific psychology is summarized in the Application section.

CONCEPT SUMMARY

Research helps

- provide scientific understanding
- solve practical problems

APPLICATION

RESEARCH CAREERS IN PSYCHOLOGY

Many of you may view a course about psychological research as a necessary hurdle for a major in psychology, but of little intrinsic interest. We hope that this book will convince you that psychological research is important and exciting. One reason you may not be particularly interested in psychological research is that you are unaware of the variety of fields open to qualified researchers. You do not have to have a Ph.D. to do good psychological research, and good psychological research does not necessarily deal with esoteric theoretical problems. In fact, we believe there are many careers that demand sound psychological research.

The range of opportunities for a person with training in psychological research is surprisingly broad. Most of these areas require an advanced degree in psychology, but that is not always the case. In any event, almost all aspects of our life need and use psychological research. Here is a list of some of the less obvious careers involving psychological research.

1. A police psychologist who serves as an expert witness on a variety of topics. The psychologist may do work on eyewitness testimony, profiles of criminals, and incentive programs for the department members.

2. A psychologist who does library and laboratory research on the causes of traffic accidents and who evaluates

Evaluating Research

Although you have diverse opportunities for a career in psychological research, conducting sound research is not the only focus of a course concerned with research methods. The second focus of such a course and this book is to help you evaluate the results of psychological research. Because the same research methods are used in many disciplines, much of the information you learn in this book about the logic of research will generalize to other fields, such as biology, sociology, and medicine. As an involved member of society, you will be influenced by psychological research. To be a careful consumer of research findings, you need to be able to consider carefully the soundness of the research.

We hope that you will acquire the ideas necessary to think critically about research. A **critic** makes an informed or reasoned judgment about safety programs. Or, a psychologist who does the same kind of work but specializes in industrial or home accidents.

3. A research psychologist who specializes in population trends: migration, fertility, marriage, and the effects of population density. Federal, state, and local governments often need qualified psychologists to conduct such research.

4. A research psychologist who designs effective computer displays and user-friendly components and software. Such psychologists are in high demand throughout private industry.

5. A research psychologist who determines effective ways of increasing energy conservation. These researchers might study personality dynamics, or they might examine ways to teach people to conserve energy.

6. A research psychologist who tries to determine the brain mechanisms involved in alcoholism and drug addiction. Such a researcher is likely to work in a government hospital or hold an academic position.

7. A research psychologist in human-factors engineering who is interested in one or more of the following: urban transportation, military training, hijacking, equipment design, or the effects of fatigue on performance.

If you are interested in additional descriptions, the following book may be helpful: Woods, P. J. (1976). *Career opportunities for psychologists.* Washington, DC: American Psychological Association.

the value of something. So, a **critical thinker** does not just find fault or criticize unfavorably. Rather, a critical thinker exercises careful judgment. Critical thinking is difficult. You probably accepted the results of the demonstration experiment without a second thought. Unfortunately, the design of the experiment does not permit an unequivocal answer to the original question.

Let us outline the principles of a good experiment and see how our experiment fails to meet those principles. In an ideal experiment, something is manipulated or changed, potential sources of influence are held constant, and some behavior is measured. The factor varied is called the **independent variable,** and the behavior measured is called the **dependent variable. Control variables** are those held constant. The researcher manipulates or changes the independent variable so that the effects of the different values or levels of the independent variable can be determined by changes in the dependent variable. In the demonstration experiment, the three tasks were the levels of the independent variable, and your time to go through the lists was the dependent variable. The order in which you and your classmates went through the tasks was constant. The constancy of order is the problem. A summary of the variables in experiments is presented in Figure 1–2.

To see how the constant order presents difficulties, you need to recognize that another variable that could influence the dependent variable should not vary with or contaminate the independent variable in an experiment. Because order and task varied together, they are said to be confounded. **Confounding** here means that both the tasks and the order in which they were done varied together—order of the tasks and their nature were confused or confounded. The longer time required in the third task may have resulted from fatigue or boredom rather than from the nature of the task. More likely, people did the tasks better as they went through them, which would underestimate the effect of the independent variable. In either case the independent variable may not have caused changes in reading time, and the results of the experiment may not be interpretable.

A critical view of the experiment questions the soundness of the results. A more careful research design would have different people go through the tasks in different orders, resulting in an unconfounding of order and task. Alternatively, different groups of people would each be exposed to one task, so order of experiencing the tasks is not a consideration. When either is done, approximately the same results are obtained—the conflict task still takes longest to complete. Because you did not know that until now, you should have been skeptical of the results. As a general rule, you should carefully evaluate research procedures so that potential problems such as confounding may be identified.

An important time for you to think critically about research is when the results may have personal importance. Consider a hypothetical example. Suppose that in a few years Doris, your child, is in the first grade. Her teacher calls you in for a conference and informs you that Doris has difficulty learning to read. The teacher then tells you that the school has several ways to provide remedial help. You and the teacher will choose what seems the best alternative to help Doris' progress. Can you make an informed judgment about the remedial reading methods? You probably are not an expert in teaching reading. Yet, can you decide that one method shows more promise than another? What do you need to know? At least some parts of the answers to these questions require that you can critically assess the research and theory underlying the various programs.

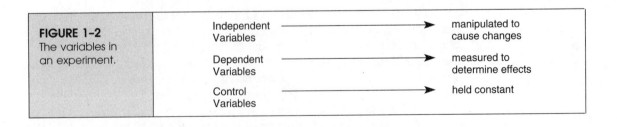

FIGURE 1–2
The variables in an experiment.

Independent Variables	→	manipulated to cause changes
Dependent Variables	→	measured to determine effects
Control Variables	→	held constant

Most of this book tries to help you identify problems associated with conducting sound research and to help you develop the skills necessary to make informed judgments about the research process. You need to be able to identify weaknesses and to rectify them. Choosing a poor remedial reading program for your daughter could have dramatic effects—much more dramatic than getting a mediocre grade in a required course. The need to understand psychological research will last your whole life not just a single term of your undergraduate career.

CONCEPT SUMMARY

Critical thinking about research involves

- making informed judgments
- looking for design flaws such as confounding

SOURCES OF RESEARCH IDEAS

We emphasize conducting and evaluating research. What constitutes a research project? The typical research project proceeds as follows: get the research idea, formulate a testable hypothesis, review the pertinent literature, conduct preliminary research, design the project, collect the data, analyze the results statistically, interpret the data, and write the report. It sounds easy and straightforward, but it is not. In this chapter we focus on the initial stages of a research project, and the rest of the book will try to complete the picture.

Observation

Science begins with observation—both as a source of data and as a source of ideas for further research. Look around with a critical eye, and you will likely generate a number of ideas for research. All you need to do is observe yourself, your classmates, your family, or even your pet. Then phrase your question so that you can make additional observations. Some typical questions might include: Do I study better in the library than in my dormitory room? Do students learn more in small classes than in large classes? Do students retain as much after studying with music on as without music? Do children work harder or less hard when given rewards such as candy? These and similar questions are easy to generate, and with some work they can be turned into manageable research projects. Your native curiosity or the need to solve a particular problem will serve you well in developing ideas for research.

Experts

Both people, such as your professor, and textbooks, such as this one or your introductory psychology text, are usually good sources of research ideas. Often an idea presented in class or one that you read about will produce an interesting idea. Once you are titillated by a problem, you should seek a consultant. Within a particular course, your instructor is the obvious choice. Beyond a particular course, you may try to get advice from someone whose competence and interest match what you are interested in exploring. Many faculty members will be delighted to discuss research with you. If you have read about an interesting research project, you can try writing to the author.

We designed this text to be a source of possible research projects. If you carefully answer the design-related questions that appear at the end of most chapters, the germ of a good research project may be lurking in one or more of your answers. Many of the questions derive from problems in actual research, so it is apparent that even experts do not conduct perfect research. Why not profit from their mistakes? Another source of ideas in this book are the exercises presented at the end of each chapter in the Psychology in Action section. These exercises are usually easy to carry out. If you think critically about them, you will likely devise additional research projects.

Journals

Ideas frequently come from reading journal articles. Chapter 4 of this book considers how to read a journal article carefully. If you are going to be reading journal articles soon, we suggest that you read that chapter before you get into the technical literature. After reading several journal articles, you will soon have a longer list of possible experiments than you could perform.

To keep track of ideas generated from your critical reading of journals or textbooks, you should keep records of your research ideas. Most psychologists have some sort of index file containing information about the articles they have read. On your file cards you should have several kinds of information: authors' names, journals, and article titles; and information about the procedure and results. It is probably best to supplement your article file with a file of research ideas. Most psychologists keep a file of such ideas, and you should too. Write down the reference that started you thinking, a short description of your idea for a project, and the date the idea occurred. You will find it interesting to go back through your files to see how your thinking about some topic has changed over time.

As your idea file gets larger because each article you read suggests at least one additional project to you, you are now confronted with another problem. At first an idea for any project was cause for celebration. Later the problem becomes one of deciding which of several ideas in your file should be tried. Some potential ideas will be eliminated because you do not have access to specialized equipment or special subject populations. Others will be too complicated or will take too long to carry out. After paring down your list, you probably still will have more than one alternative. Assuming that each idea is equally practical and feasible, given your resources, our advice is to tackle the project you think would be most fun. Psychological research is interesting, exciting, and often has important outcomes. However, interest, excitement, and importance will happen only if you do research (follow up on your idea file).

If you are unsure about what journals and other resources to examine for research ideas, you should refer to Chapter 4. For the moment you should know that the most important general resource is *Psychological Abstracts.* This publication contains brief abstracts of articles from almost all journals that publish psychologically related research. If you find an abstract of interest there, you can then read the entire article or send a note to the author requesting a reprint of the article or additional information.

CONCEPT SUMMARY

Sources of ideas include

- observation
- experts
- journals

DEVELOPING TESTABLE HYPOTHESES

After you have developed an idea, you need to frame it in the form of a testable hypothesis. A **testable hypothesis** makes a statement about a presumed or theoretical relation between two or more variables (Kerlinger, 1986). According to Kerlinger, a testable hypothesis either states or implies that the variables are measurable. It also specifies the relation among the variables. Specifying measurements and relations sets the stage for the research project, because research requires that something can be observed and measured. Therefore, if a hypothesis is not testable, research on it is impossible.

Consider one of the possible ideas generated from observation that was considered above: Do I study better in the library than in my dormitory room? Is this a testable hypothesis? A relation is implied—better study in the library—but measurements are not specified. So at this point the hypothesis is not testable. How can you measure better study? One way would be to assess the outcome of study; namely, your grades on a test could be determined. Grades are observable and measurable, so they fit one of Kerlinger's criteria for a testable hypothesis. The reformulated question might become: Do I get better grades on tests after studying in the library than after studying in my dorm room? Because you might be interested in the generality of the research outcome, you can modify the initial question to develop the following hypothesis: Higher grades are obtained after studying in the library than after studying in the dorms. This hypothesis follows

Kerlinger's guidelines, because it specifies both what will be measured and the expected relationship between study location and grades.

At this point you might want to practice developing testable hypotheses. Take some of the ideas or questions you have and see if you can put them in testable form. Any research that you undertake requires a testable hypothesis, so now is a good time to practice generating them. If you do not have many potential ideas to consider, several are available in one of the exercises at the end of this chapter.

Many hypotheses cannot be tested, because they either do not include variables that can be observed and measured or do not specify relations among variables. Thus, scientific research cannot be used to study many moral and religious issues. Research can be used to assess a person's attitude toward abortion, for example, but it cannot address the issue of whether abortion in principle is good or bad. The broad statement "Abortion is wrong" specifies neither what is to be measured nor relations among measurable variables. Testable hypotheses about the positive or negative impact of abortion in particular circumstances are possible, but encompassing hypotheses about the moral value of abortion are not. Many questions that you generate may not be testable, because they fail to include observable and measurable variables. Scientific research can be used to study how people respond to colors, but it cannot address the question of whether your experience of the color blue is the same as someone else's experience of the color blue. *Experience* in this context cannot be measured, but responding (behavior) can.

CONCEPT SUMMARY

Testable hypotheses specify

- how variables will be measured
- how variables will be related

REVIEWING THE LITERATURE

The next phase of the research process involves a review of the pertinent literature. Previously, we discussed using journals to obtain ideas. Now we will consider another important use of journals—determining what is known about your hypothesis. A literature review will reveal whether your research hypothesis has been tested, and it will indicate important things for you to consider in developing your research project.

You do not want to reinvent the wheel. The idea about the effects of study location on grades probably is not novel. So you must find out whether someone else has already tested your hypothesis. Thousands of research articles about psychological hypotheses are published each year, so you will probably find many articles related to your hypothesis. Even if those articles do not match your hypothesis precisely, you will probably discover many details that will allow you to devise your own research project more efficiently. Chapter 4 takes you through a literature search, so we will not provide all the details here. Two of the many valuable sources of information include *Psychological Abstracts,* mentioned earlier, and the article or articles that led to your research question. At the end of those articles you will find a reference list, which is a good place to start your search for additional information related to your hypothesis.

Suppose you wanted to test a hypothesis related to the demonstration experiment. We referenced an article concerned with the conflict effect by Cohen and others (1990). So, you might look up that article in the Reference section of this book, and then go to the library to read it. You can read about the research they did and the theory they proposed. You can use their reference list as a source of additional articles for your literature search (they reference over 70 research papers). One thing you will discover is that the conflict effect shown in the demonstration experiment is usually called the **Stroop effect** after the man who first demonstrated the phenomenon (Stroop, 1935). Generally, you should read the primary source of a research phenomenon, so examine Stroop's paper. If you are interested in the Stroop effect, you will find a recent review of 50 years of research on the Stroop effect by MacLeod (1991) to be very helpful. He cites about 400 studies, and he also summarizes them. For a person interested in the phenomenon, this journal article is an extremely important source of information.

Another efficient way to get background information is to examine the subject index of textbooks. If you look in the index of this book, you will find that the Stroop effect is discussed in two different places later in the text. In those discussions you will find additional references that might be valuable to read. A particularly important article is the one by Windes (1968). Windes apparently was the first researcher to use a task similar to the one used in the demonstration experiment.

CONCEPT SUMMARY

To begin a literature search use

- *Psychological Abstracts*
- reference lists of relevant articles
- textbooks

CONDUCTING PILOT RESEARCH

Before undertaking a full-scale research project, you should do some preliminary research, which is usually called **pilot research.** A thorough literature search will help you devise a reasonable research plan, as well as help you figure out what kinds of material and apparatus you may need.

However you will probably find it necessary to try out various parts of your project. This is the purpose of pilot research.

In pilot research you test a small number of participants to try to ensure that you have all the bugs out of your research procedure. You will find out whether your subjects understand the instructions. You will learn how much time the experiment requires and whether the tasks you chose are too easy or too hard. You will be able to practice using the equipment and materials, and you will be able to practice observing and measuring the behavior of interest.

Frequently, pilot research is used to assess the levels of the independent variable to make sure that they have an effect on the dependent variable. If one level of the independent variable is presenting the conflicting digits upside down, you should try this out on a few people to ensure that there is less conflict than when the digits are right-side up. Suppose you find that there is less conflict when the digits are presented upside down. Is that a foolproof sign that you have an independent variable that works? Probably, but it may not be the case. One difficulty with pilot research is that you test your procedure on just a few participants. For whatever reason, this small sample of people may not be representative of the population of people you are interested in testing. To find out whether your pilot data are a fluke, you need to conduct the full-blown project with a large number of observations under each level of the independent variable. Although the small test sample is a problem, pilot research plays an important role in developing a sound research project.

CONCEPT SUMMARY

Conduct pilot research to

- refine the research procedures
- test the levels of your independent variable

SOME PITFALLS TO AVOID

Several potential difficulties await the researcher. In addition to the possibility of confounding mentioned earlier, researchers need to worry about the ethicality of their research, whether they have inadvertently biased the results, and the reliability of their communication. Other potential pitfalls are detailed later.

Ethics

Ethical issues in psychological research receive a separate and detailed treatment in Chapter 3. The issues are so prominent, however, that we outline some of them here. The overarching issue involves the well-being of the research participants, whether human or animal. Scientists have an obligation to treat the objects of their work in an ethical fashion. Treating research participants ethically is a complex issue often involving pragmatic choices between the needs of the researcher and the needs of the participant. With human participants, the ethical questions seem to boil down to the so-called Golden Rule—the researcher should treat the participants as he or she would wish to be treated. Thus, physical and mental harm are avoided or minimized, confidentiality is not breached, and dishonesty and deception are not used.

Ethical issues surrounding the use of animals in research are complex and emotionally charged. A major governing body for psychological research, the American Psychological Association, specifically bans cruel or negligent treatment of animals. That association has detailed guidelines that define what constitutes humane treatment of animals used in research. Furthermore, many federal and state agencies also have regulations governing research with animals. Nevertheless, some people oppose using animals in research. We examine some of the pros and cons in Chapter 3. Ethical issues facing a researcher are among the most important ones that must be resolved while conducting a research project. You as an ethical person and scientist must consider these issues carefully.

CONCEPT SUMMARY

To conduct ethical research

- treat humans as you would be treated
- treat animals humanely

Biased Research

An ethical researcher does not present fraudulent results. Deliberate bias of this sort is uncommon in science. However, **inadvertent researcher bias** is a problem of unknown magnitude. Just how often unplanned researcher bias occurs is difficult to determine, because many parts of the research process may be inadvertently contaminated. A scientist's political beliefs, for example, could result in an incomplete survey that assesses some attitudes and not others. This does not necessarily indicate deliberate bias, but may merely represent the fallibility of the scientist. The scientist can think about only a limited number of things at a time, so the research designs will partially reflect his or her own preferences. A famous example of faulty research design is the case of Samuel G. Morton, a well-known physician and scientist in the early and middle 1800s. He collected over one thousand human skulls of people belonging to different races. He believed that skull volume was indicative of intelligence; hence, he used his collection of skulls to examine intelligence differences among races, reporting that Caucasians were the most intelligent, blacks were least intelligent, and Native Americans were in between, a conclusion in perfect agreement with the prejudices of the time. It was not until 1978 that Stephen Jay Gould, a Harvard paleontologist, concluded, from the very data reported by Morton, that there were no differences at all among races. Gould showed that Morton had chosen his skulls in line with his expectations: For one group of blacks, he used an all-female sample whereas for the comparison group of whites he used an all-male sample, ignoring the fact that male skulls tend to be larger than female skulls (Broad and Wade, 1982). One aspect of the Morton affair that should be kept in mind is that the scientific community of that time accepted his research as scientifically valid; only under the scrutiny of contemporary scientists with different social beliefs was the biased design exposed. Thus, the questions asked by a researcher and the method he or she uses to answer those questions may be the result of the researcher's preconceptions about the problem. There are two solutions to this dilemma: (1) Researchers should be aware of their own underlying preconceptions (these preexisting notions are what philosophers of science call "paradigms"; Kuhn, 1962); and (2) many scientists should undertake a variety of attacks on a problem.

Another source of researcher bias derives from treating participants in a project differently over and above any *planned* differences in treatment. A substantial amount of evidence indicates that how the researcher treats the subjects can have a profound effect on the results of the experiment (Barber, 1976). What measures can be taken to prevent a researcher from inadvertently influencing the outcome? Suppose you collected the data for Carver, Coleman, and Glass (1976) in their experiment concerned with fatigue suppression in hard-driving Type A personalities and more mellow Type B's. You know ahead of time that half your subjects (the A's) might be prone to coronary heart disease. You record the exercise time on a treadmill as the subjects are working at or beyond their maximum oxygen consumption. Would you treat Type A's and Type B's differently? Would subtle body movements or the tone of your voice clue the Type A's to take it easy so they do not overstress their hearts? (This is unlikely, because the Type A's were young—they supposedly had the *potential* for coronary problems later in life.)

There are two ways to minimize this type of researcher bias. In the first place, the researcher must conduct the project as uniformly as possible for all participants. There should be strict adherence to a **protocol.** The only differences in treatment should be those that are introduced deliberately— independent variables, different questions in a survey, different observing times, and so on. Type A's must be treated exactly like Type B's. This was done by Carver and coworkers, who even went so far as to eliminate the data on a subject who was acquainted with one of the data collectors.

A second way to minimize inadvertent differential treatment is to make the researcher *blind* with respect to potentially important attributes of the participants or the task. The experimenters in the study by Carver and associates did not know whether a subject was a Type A or a Type B, which diminished the chances of treating the Type A's differently on the treadmill. Furthermore, the subjects did not know that the experimenters were interested in how long the subjects stayed on the treadmill. When subjects' behaviors are recorded in some way for later analysis, the people who score the recorded behavior often are blind to the treatment administered to a particular subject. In this instance, being blind to the treatment condition increases the likelihood that the scorer of the results will be objective and not be biased by his or her expectations of what the results should be. If both the subject and the researcher are blind, we have what is called a **double-blind design.**

Double-blind designs are common in medical experiments that test the effectiveness of drugs. The experimental group is given the drug, and the control group is given a placebo substance. A **placebo** (the word is derived from a Latin word meaning "I shall please") is a pharmacologically inert substance (a "sugar pill") given to control subjects to deceive them. The controls, along with the experimental group, assume they are receiving a real drug, so the expectations are the same for the two groups. Not only are the placebo subjects blind, but so is the researcher. The researcher does not know who is receiving the placebo and who is getting the real drug. In the typical drug experiment, the substances have code numbers that cannot be deciphered by the person administering the drugs. However, someone knows who received the placebo and who received the drug. These precautions decrease the possibility of the control subjects being treated differently than the experimental subjects (apart from the drug, of course).

The personal attributes of a researcher may bias the actions of the participants. The age, sex, race, and authority of the researcher may determine how the subjects react. For example, a subject in an interview is more likely to report sexual thoughts when the interviewer is of the same sex (Walters, Shurley, and Parsons, 1962). This kind of problem is solved if there is more than one researcher and each one follows the research protocol exactly. In your own research, you may not be able to enlist assistance from others. Therefore, you should try to treat each subject identically.

Strict adherence to procedure is important to minimize inadvertent researcher bias. This advice is particularly true when considering how data is recorded. Barber (1976) discusses several studies which show that data-recording errors do occur and tend to bias the results in the direction desired by the experimenter. Hence, in every condition for every subject, we must record data in the same way. This means that before the project is begun, we must define exactly what constitutes an acceptable datum.

Another potential researcher bias occurs in research with animals. When working with animals, a researcher must guard against **anthropomorphizing.** This refers to the tendency to attribute human characteristics, especially thoughts and feelings, to animals. Anthropomorphism is sometimes obvious, as in "The dog loved and respected its master," and sometimes not so obvious, as in "The rat was hungry so it ate a lot." A similar problem arises in describing the thoughts and feelings of people belonging to technologically primitive cultures. An observer might attribute standard Western thought to such groups, as in "Their love of individual liberty conflicted with the socialist ideology of the tribal council." All of these examples are actually theoretical statements that may not be warranted on the basis of the data. How do we define "love" in a dog? Does it mean the dog wagged its tail or came when it was called? What is hunger for a rat? These sorts of issues are examined in the next section.

CONCEPT SUMMARY	

Control inadvertent researcher effects by using

- uniform treatment
- double-blind design

Reliability of Communication

We have discussed pitfalls in the research process resulting from ethical issues and experimenter bias. Assuming that you have effectively dealt with problems in these areas, another pitfall awaits you in conveying the results of your research to other scientists.

No serious discussion, scientific or otherwise, can progress very far unless the participants agree to define the terms they are using. Imagine that you and your date are having a friendly argument about who is the best athlete of the year. How do you define athlete? You both would agree about such common sports as tennis, swimming, and gymnastics. But what about more esoteric sports such as frisbee throwing, hang gliding, and hopping cross-country on a pogo stick? Should practitioners of these activities be considered for your athlete-of-the-year award? Until this question of definition is answered, your discussion may just go around in circles.

Similar problems can arise in scientific discussions. Let us imagine that scientists in psychophysical laboratories in West Lafayette, Indiana, and Clayton Corners, Arkansas, are studying tail-flicking responses of the horseshoe crab to flashes of light. One laboratory finds that crabs give tremendous tail flicks, whereas the other lab finds that crabs hardly move their tails at all. The scientists are very concerned and they exchange terse letters and autographed pictures of their respective crabs. Eventually they discover the reason for the discrepancy. They were each defining the flash of light differently (their flashes were of different durations), even though the brightness of the two flashes was similar. When they adjusted their flashes to be the same, both labs obtained the same results. This example is a little farfetched since, as we all know, crabs cannot autograph their pictures. Furthermore, all good psychologists know the importance of defining the stimulus exactly, so this confusion would probably not have occurred in the first place. But this example does show what *could* happen if scientists were not very careful about defining their terms.

Although social conversation and scientific discourse both require definitions, the requirements for scientific definition are more stringent. Terms that are perfectly adequate for ordinary conversation are usually too vague for scientific purposes. When you state that someone has a pleasant personality, other people have a good idea of what you mean. But when a psychologist uses the term *personality* in a technical sense, a great deal of precision is necessary. This important distinction between technical usage and common usage occurs frequently in psychology. It is all too easy to slip and use technical language imprecisely, especially in psychology. Words such as *information, anxiety,* and *fluency* have broad everyday meanings, but they must be precisely limited when they are used in a technical sense. The most common way of providing such technical meaning is by using an **operational definition.**

An operational definition is a formula for building a construct in a way that other scientists can duplicate. "Take the eye of a newt, the leg of a frog, three oyster shells, and shake twice" is an operational definition, although we may not know what is being defined. This recipe can be duplicated and so meets the major criterion for an operational definition. You can tell from this example that an operational definition does not have to make any sense, as long as it is clear and can be copied. In general terms, something is operationally defined when the procedures or operations used to produce and measure it are clearly specified. For instance, we might operationally define a construct called *centigrams* as the product of your height in centimeters and your weight in grams. Any scientist can easily determine the centigram score, so this is an operational definition. Of course, it probably could not be used for any important scientific purpose, but the potential utility of an operational definition is a separate issue from its clarity.

FINISHING THE RESEARCH PROJECT

After completing the preliminary stages outlined above and considering the pitfalls, you can now conduct the research, analyze and interpret the data, and then write a research paper. The remainder of this book focuses on these aspects of the research process. We hope you will be a critical reader and thinker, using the information we convey to conduct sound psychological research and to evaluate carefully the research of others.

Neither the practice nor the use of science is easy. The benefits that can be derived from scientific knowledge and understanding depend on critical and well-informed citizens and scientists. Unless you plan to hibernate or drop out of society in some other way, you are going to be affected by psychological research. As a citizen you are a consumer of the results of psychological research, and we hope that the material discussed in this book will help to make you a more intelligent consumer.

Some of you, we hope, will become scientists. We also hope that some of you budding scientists will focus on why people and animals think and act as they do. We wish you future scientists good fortune. Your scientific career will be exciting, and we hope that your endeavors will be positively influenced by the principles of psychological research presented in this text.

About a hundred years ago, T. H. Huxley, a British scientist, said: "The chessboard is the world, the pieces are the phenomena of the universe, the rules of the game are what we call the laws of Nature. The player on the other side is hidden from us. We know that his play is always fair, just, and patient. But we also know, to our cost, that he never overlooks a mistake, or makes the smallest allowance for ignorance."

SUMMARY

1. One goal of psychological research is to provide scientific understanding about why people and animals behave as they do.

Another goal of psychological research is to solve practical problems.

2. The goals of this book (and, likely, your course) are to help teach you how to conduct sound research and to help you learn how to evaluate critically the research of others.

3. An experiment involves manipulating or changing the levels of an independent variable while trying to minimize the effects of confounding variables that may vary with the independent variable. Those factors that are held constant are called control variables. The behavior that is measured is called the dependent variable.

4. Research begins with observation, which is a source of data and ideas for research projects. Other sources of research ideas are journal articles and experts, such as your professor or your textbook.

5. Numerous journals report the results of psychological research. One of the better sources for research ideas and background information is *Psychological Abstracts.*

6. A testable hypothesis makes a statement about a presumed or theoretical relation between two or more variables. A testable hypothesis implies or specifies how the variables are measured.

7. Prior to undertaking a research project, you should do a literature search to find out whether your hypothesis has been studied. Becoming acquainted with the literature also will help you to design your project carefully and efficiently.

8. Preliminary research, called pilot research, usually is done before conducting a research project. The pilot research will help you refine your procedure, and it may help you to choose appropriate levels of your independent variable.

9. An ethical scientist treats research participants fairly and humanely.

10. Good research is often clouded by inadvertent researcher bias. A scientist's beliefs, attitudes, and scientific approach may bias the outcome of a research project. A careful researcher attempts to overcome this problem by strict adherence to a research protocol and other design tactics, such as the double-blind design.

11. A careful researcher operationally defines concepts by noting how they are produced and measured.

■ KEY CONCEPTS

anthropomorphizing
confounding
control variable
critic
critical thinker
dependent variable
double-blind design
ethical issues

inadvertent researcher bias
independent variable
operational definition
pilot research
placebo
protocol
Psychological Abstracts
Stroop effect
testable hypothesis

■ EXERCISES

1. [*Special Exercise.*] (Some of the exercises at the end of chapters ask that you critique a research project in some way. You are provided with enough information in the question to answer it. If some procedural detail is omitted—for example, the time of day the research was conducted—you may assume that the detail is irrelevant. Base your discussion on the information provided.) Do you listen to music as you are studying? A large percentage of college students do. A substantial amount of research concerns the effects of music on people's ability to learn and remember. The research has generated an interesting controversy. Some researchers find that listening to music disrupts learning, and others report that music does not disrupt learning. Generate several testable hypotheses as to why music might or might not have a negative effect on learning. One thing you might consider is the type of music. One of the authors of this book never studied in his dorm room as a freshman because his roommate regularly played Ravel's *Bolero* during the evening.

2. Look up the term *aggression* in the index of a recent issue of *Psychological Abstracts*, then read several of the abstracts. Note how articles with various emphases are organized in the *Abstracts*. Articles about animal aggression are grouped together and in a different section than those concerned with aggression in children.

3. Transform each of the following problems or statements into at least two testable hypotheses:
    a. You can't teach an old dog new tricks.
    b. Eating junk food lowers your grade point average.
    c. A penny saved is a penny earned.
    d. The best way to study is cramming the night before an exam.
    e. Out of sight, out of mind; or—Absence makes the heart grow fonder.

■ SUGGESTED READINGS

The following two books contain additional information about the preliminary stages of a research project: Alsip, J. E., & Chezik, D. D. (1974). *Research guide in psychology*. Morristown, NJ: General Learning Press. Leedy, P. D. (1985). *Practical research: Planning and design* (3rd ed.). New York: Macmillan.

Psychology in Action
The Stroop Effect

The original version of the Stroop test used color words such as *red* and *blue* printed in mismatching colors of ink. You could see if the same sorts of results occur in the color Stroop effect as occur in the number Stroop done in this chapter. You will need some index cards, colored markers, and a watch with a second hand (or some other way of measuring response times).

Suppose you have markers of four different colors (for example, red, blue, green, and yellow). Take 16 index cards and put a bold line of color on each one—four cards should have a red stripe, four a blue one, four a green one, and four a yellow one. Next, right the words *blue, red, yellow,* and *green* with a black marker on index cards—four cards with each word. Finally, write the color words in a mismatching color (that is, *blue* in red ink); have four cards for each color word in mismatching ink. Your stimuli are now completed. The three decks you made correspond, respectively, to the naming, reading, and conflict tasks used in the number version of the Stroop task.

Shuffle each deck, and see how long it takes you to go through each one. You might want to do a careful mini experiment. Test three different people with three different orders of the tasks: one gets *naming, reading,* then *conflict*; one gets *reading, conflict,* then *naming*; and one gets *conflict, naming,* then *reading.* Doing the experiment this ways gets rid of the confounding of order with task that was present in the version of the Stroop test done in the chapter. If the entire class conducts this experiment, you could use all possible orders of three tasks several times, which would also mean that each task preceded and followed the other ones equally often. The relative difficulty of the three conditions should have been the same as in the number Stroop test.

Now you might consider some additional experiments that could be done using either version of the task. The Psychology in Action section for a later chapter also suggests variants of the Stroop task. Try to think of some interesting research to do without peeking at the later chapter. One thing you may have noticed when you did the number Stroop is that some mismatches between digits and quantity were more likely to slow down your naming time than were others. Is this true for everybody or just you? Do most people have difficulty with the same mismatches, or do the difficult ones differ from person to person?

THE EXPERIMENT   DIRECTIONS: Name the numbers below aloud as fast as you can.

START TIME

_____

2
1
4
3
3
2
4
1
4
1
3
2
2
1
3
4
3
1
4
2
4
3
2
1
1
3
2
4
2
3
4
1

FINISH TIME   To continue the experiment, please go to the next page.

_____

ELAPSED TIME

_____

THE EXPERIMENT   DIRECTIONS: Count the number of + s aloud in each row as fast as you can.

START TIME

_____

FINISH TIME   To continue the experiment, please go to the next page.

_____

ELAPSED TIME

_____

```
+
+ + + +
+ + +
+ +
+ + + +
+ +
+ + +
+
+
+ +
+ + +
+ + + +
+ +
+ + + +
+
+ + +
+ + + +
+ + +
+
+ +
+ +
+ + +
+
+ + + +
+
+ + + +
+ +
+ + +
+ + +
+ + + +
+
+ +
```

THE EXPERIMENT   DIRECTIONS: Count the number of digits aloud in each row as fast as you can.

START TIME

_____

FINISH TIME   You are through participating in the experiment. Please return to page 5.

_____

ELAPSED TIME

_____

2
1111
444
33
3333
222
44
11
4
11
3333
222
2222
11
3
444
3333
111
2
44
33
444
2
1111
3
1111
44
222
444
3333
2
11

EXPLANATION IN SCIENTIFIC PSYCHOLOGY

Why do people and animals behave as they do?

Research
- ❏ Arises from curiosity
- ❏ Solves basic and applied problems

Sources of Belief
- ❏ Authority
- ❏ Tenacity
- ❏ A priori assumptions
- ❏ Empiricism

Scientific Procedures
- ❏ Induction
- ❏ Deduction
- ❏ Strong inference

Scientific Theories
- ❏ Organize and predict
- ❏ Are: parsimonious
  precise
  testable

Scientific Data
- ❏ Illustrate psychological processes
- ❏ Demonstrate what can happen in controlled settings

CHAPTER 2

EXPLANATION IN SCIENTIFIC PSYCHOLOGY

How does science differ from other modes of understanding? What are some of the assumptions underlying the scientific method? How do psychologists use theory and data to explain behavior? We pursue these questions in this chapter by examining a social psychological phenomenon called social loafing. Because the answers to the questions provide a framework for the rest of the text, you need to understand what is meant by scientific explanation.

A scientist wants to discover how and why things work. In this desire he or she does not differ from anyone else who is also curious about the world we inhabit. The casual observer may not feel terribly frustrated if some observation cannot be explained. For example, the nonscientist may simply accept that water always goes down a sink drain counterclockwise or that individuals tend to work less hard in groups than when alone. However, the professional scientist has a strong desire to pursue an observation until an explanation is available or a problem is solved. By being unwilling to tolerate unanswered questions and unsolved problems, scientists use several techniques for obtaining relief from curiosity and developing explanations. Careful application of these techniques distinguishes scientific understanding from everyday understanding.

In this chapter we introduce scientific explanation from the viewpoint of a working scientist—in particular, an experimentally oriented psychologist. To do so we examine a series of research studies on social loafing. The purpose of the research is to understand why people work less hard in groups than when they work alone. Our discussion of scientific explanation leads to a consideration of aspects of the philosophy of science used for an understanding of behavior. Because abstract principles of science do not always make much sense when removed from specific topics, we relate the philosophy of science to research on social loafing. We intend to show how psychologists undertake to explain why people and animals behave as they do.

MAKING SENSE OF THE WORLD

Social Loafing

A common observation—one you probably have made yourself on many occasions—is that people working in a group often seem to "slack off" in their effort. Many people in groups seem willing to let a few do the work. Bibb Latané, a social psychologist, noticed this tendency and decided to study it experimentally. Initially, Latané examined the research literature to see if any evidence existed for this phenomenon of people's working less hard in groups, which he named **social loafing.** One of the earliest studies of social loafing was conducted by a French agricultural engineer (Ringelmann, 1913; Kravitz and Martin, 1986), who asked people to pull on a rope as hard as they could. The subjects pulled by themselves or with one, two, or seven others. A sensitive gauge was used to measure how strongly they pulled the rope. If people exert as much effort in groups as when alone, then the group performance should be the sum of the efforts of all individuals. Ringelmann discovered that groups of two pulled at only 95 percent of their capacity, and groups of three and eight sank to 85 percent and 49 percent, respectively. So, it is probably not just our imaginations when we notice others (and ourselves?) putting forth less effort when working in groups: Ringelmann's research provides us with a good example of social loafing.

Latané and his colleagues then performed a systematic series of experiments on the phenomenon of social loafing (Latané, 1981; Latané, Williams, and Harkins, 1979). They first showed that the phenomenon could be obtained in other experimental situations besides that of rope pulling. They also demonstrated that social loafing occurs in several different cultures (Gabrenya, Latané, and Wang, 1983) and even holds for young children. Thus social loafing is a pervasive characteristic of working in groups.

Latané related this work to a more general theory of human social behavior (Latané, 1981). The evidence from the experimental studies points to **diffusion of responsibility** as a possible reason for social loafing. People working by themselves think they are responsible for completing the task; when they work in groups, however, this feeling of responsibility diffuses to others. The same idea accounts for behavior in other group situations: if one of your professors asked a question in a class containing only two other people, you would probably feel responsible for trying to answer. However, if there were 200 other people in the class, you would likely feel much less responsible for answering. Similarly, people are more likely to help in an emergency when they feel the burden of responsibility than when there are several others about who could help.

One possible benefit of such basic research into a phenomenon is that the findings may be applied later to solve some practical problem. A problem in American society is the declining productivity of the work force. Although social loafing is, at best, only one factor involved in this complicated issue, Marriot (1949) showed that factory workers working in large groups produce less per individual than do those working in small groups. Thus, basic research that would show a way to overcome the problem of social loafing may be of great practical import. In fact, Williams, Harkins, and Latané (1981) found conditions that eliminated the effect of social loafing in their experimental situation. When individual performance (rather than just performance of the entire group) was monitored within the group situation, the individuals worked just as hard as they did when they worked alone. Certainly more research must be done, but simply measuring individual performance in group situations could help eliminate social loafing and increase productivity. The proposed solution may seem simple, but many jobs measure only group performance, not individual performance.

Research on social loafing by Latané and others shows how an interesting problem can be studied scientifically and be understood. The research will, when carefully conducted, promote a better explanation of the phenomenon of interest than will simple observation of events and reflection about them. Let us now examine the nature of scientific explanations.

SOURCES OF UNDERSTANDING

Fixation of Belief

Science and scientific psychology in particular are valid ways to acquire knowledge about the world around us. What characteristics of the scientific approach make it a desirable way to learn about and arrive at beliefs about the nature of things? Perhaps the best way to answer this question is to contrast science with other modes of fixing belief, since science is only one way that understanding is obtained.

More than a hundred years ago, the American philosopher Charles Sanders Peirce (1877) compared the scientific way of knowing with three other methods of developing beliefs He called these the *authority, tenacity,* and *a priori* methods. According to Peirce, the simplest way of fixing belief is to take someone else's word on faith. A trusted authority tells you what is true and what is false. Young children believe what their parents tell them simply because Mommy and Daddy are always right. As children get older they may discover, unhappily, that Mom and Dad are not always correct when it comes to astrophysics, macroeconomics, computer technology, and other specialized fields of knowledge. Although this may cause children to doubt some of their parents' earlier proclamations, they may not completely reject this method of fixing belief. Instead, some other authority may be sought. Religious beliefs are formed by the **method of authority.** Long after children have rejected their parents as the source of all knowledge, they may still believe that the pope is infallible insofar as religious doctrine is concerned. Believing the evening news means that one accepts Dan Rather or some other news commentator as authority. You may believe your professors because they are authorities. Because people lack the resources to investigate everything they learn, much knowledge and many beliefs are fixed by the method of authority. Provided nothing happens to raise doubts about the competence of the authority setting the beliefs, this method offers the advantages of minimum effort and substantial security. It is most pleasant in a troubled world to have complete faith in beliefs handed down to you.

Another method of fixing belief is one in which a person steadfastly refuses to alter acquired knowledge, regardless of evidence to the contrary. The **method of tenacity,** as it was termed by Peirce, is commonly seen in racial bigots who rigidly cling to a stereotype even in the presence of a good counterexample. Although this method of maintaining a belief may not be entirely rational, we cannot say it is completely without value. Bigots are still around and somehow manage to find a few others to share their beliefs. The method of tenacity allows people to maintain a uniform and constant outlook on things, so it may relieve them from a certain amount of stress and psychological discomfort. For people who have difficulty handling stress, the method of tenacity may be a reasonable way to try to understand the world.

The third nonscientific method discussed by Peirce fixes belief a priori. In this context the term *a priori* refers to something that is believed without prior study or examination. In the **a priori method** propositions that seem reasonable are believed. This is an extension of the method of authority. However, no one particular authority is being followed blindly in this method; rather, the general cultural outlook fixes belief a priori. People once believed the world was flat; and it did seem reasonable to suppose that the sun revolved around the earth as does the moon. Indeed, the world does look flat if you are not in a spacecraft.

The last of Peirce's methods, the **scientific method,** fixes belief on the basis of experience. If we define scientific psychology (as well as science in general) as a repeatable, self-correcting undertaking that seeks to understand phenomena on the basis of empirical observation, then we can see several advantages to science over the methods just outlined. Let us see what we mean by **empirical** and **self-correcting,** and examine the advantages associated with those aspects of science. First, none of those other methods relies on data (observations of the world) obtained by systematic observation. That is, the other methods do not have an empirical basis for fixing belief. The word *empirical* is derived from an old Greek word meaning *experience.* Having an empirical basis for beliefs means that experience rather than faith is the source of knowledge. Having one's beliefs fixed by authority carries no guarantee that the authority obtained data before forming an opinion. By definition, the method of tenacity refuses to consider data, as does the a priori method. Facts that are considered in these other modes of fixing belief are not ordinarily obtained by systematic procedures. For example, casual observation was the "method" that led to the ideas that the world was flat and that frogs spontaneously generated from the mud each spring, as Aristotle believed.

The second advantage of science is that it offers procedures for establishing the superiority of one belief over another. Persons holding different beliefs not based on science will find it difficult to reconcile their opinions. Science overcomes this problem. In principle, anyone can make an empirical observation, which means that scientific data can be public and can be repeatedly obtained. Through public observations, new beliefs are compared with old beliefs, and old beliefs are discarded if they do not fit the empirical facts. This does not mean that each and every scientist instantaneously drops outmoded beliefs in favor of new opinions. Changing scientific beliefs is usually a slow process, but eventually incorrect ideas are weeded out. Empirical, public observations are the cornerstone of the scientific method, because they make science a self-correcting endeavor and lead to scientific understanding.

CONCEPT SUMMARY

Methods of fixing belief include

- authority
- tenacity
- a priori
- scientific (empirical)

THE NATURE OF SCIENTIFIC EXPLANATION

Empirical observation and self-correction are the hallmarks of the scientific method. In this section we examine how these work in science and scientific psychology.

Let us first step back and look at the social loafing research in a general way. Casual observation and some applied work suggested the problem area to be investigated. Laboratory experiments indicated some characteristics of social loafing and tested some predictions about its nature. Eventually, the data from the experiments suggested a solution to the practical aspects of social loafing. The same data also were related to diffusion of responsibility, a more general theory in social psychology. This summary captures how science typically works: empirical observations made on the basis of either casual observations or more formal theories reveal something about those theories, which in turn can lead to further empirical work.

According to Harré (1983), this cyclical and self-correcting nature of science was first recognized by Francis Bacon (1561–1626). Bacon is credited with being the leading force in the scientific revolution that began in the seventeenth century (Jones, 1982). Although Bacon's analysis seems somewhat primitive today, he anticipated several important aspects of modern science that we explore in detail.

Induction and Deduction

All approaches to science share certain basic elements. The most important of these are **data** (empirical observations) and **theory** (organization of concepts that permit prediction of data). Science needs and uses both data and theory, and our outline of research on social loafing indicates that they can be interlinked in a complex way. However, in the history of science, individual scientists have differed about which is more important and which comes first. Trying to decide this is a little like trying to decide whether the chicken or the egg comes first. Science attempts to understand why things work the way they do, and, as we will argue, understanding involves both data and theory.

Although Bacon recognized the importance of both data and theory, he believed in the primacy of empirical observations. Modern scientists also emphasize data and view progress in science as working from data to theory. Such an approach is an example of **induction,** in which reasoning proceeds from particular data to a general theory. The converse approach, which emphasizes theory predicting data, is called **deduction.** With deduction, reasoning proceeds from a general theory to particular data. Because many scientists and philosophers of science have argued for the primacy of one form of reasoning over the other, we will examine induction and deduction in some detail.

Because empirical observations distinguish science from other modes of fixing belief, many have argued that induction must be the way that science should work. As Harré (1983) states it, "observations and the results of experiments are said to be 'data,' which provide a sound and solid base for the erection of the fragile edifice of scientific thought" (p. 6). In the case of social loafing, the inductive position would be that the facts of social loafing derived from experimentation produced the theory of diffusion of responsibility.

One problem with a purely inductive approach has to do with the finality of empirical observations. Scientific observations are tied to the circumstances under which they are made. This means that the laws or theories that are induced from them also must be limited in scope. Subsequent experiments in different contexts may suggest another theory or modifications to an existing one. So, theories that are induced on the basis of particular observations can (and usually do) change when other observations are made. This, of course, is a problem only if one takes an authoritarian view of ideas and believes in clinging tenaciously to a particular theory. Theories induced from observations are tentative ideas not final truths. Changes in understanding that occur as a result of continued empirical work exemplify the self-correcting nature of science.

According to the deductive view, which emphasizes the primacy of theory, the important scientific aspect of the social loafing research is the empirical guidance provided by the formal theory of social loafing. Further, the more general theory, diffusion of responsibility, provides understanding of social loafing. The deductive approach holds well-developed theories in high regard. Casual observations, informal theories, and data take second place to broad theories that describe and predict a substantial number of observations.

From the standpoint of the deductive approach, scientific understanding means, in part, that a theory will predict that certain kinds of empirical observations should occur. In the case of social loafing, the theory of diffusion of responsibility suggests that monitoring individual performance in a group should reduce the diffusion of responsibility. In turn, measuring individual effort should reduce the amount of social loafing that is observed. Experimental tests of this prediction confirm it, as we have seen.

But what do correct predictions reveal? If a theory is verified by the results of experiments, a deductive scientist might have increased confidence in the veracity of the theory. However, empirical observations are not final and can change. The tentative nature of scientific understanding means that verifying or confirming a theory is not enough. Popper (1961), a philosopher of science, has suggested that good theories, like good hypotheses (see Chapter 1), must be testable. The empirical predictions must be capable of tests that could show them to be false. This suggestion of Popper's has been called the **falsifiability view.** According to the falsifiability view, the temporary nature of induction makes negative evidence more important than positive support. If data confirm a prediction, one cannot say that the theory is true. However, if a theory leads to a prediction that is not supported by the data, then Popper would argue that the theory must be false, and it should be rejected. According to Popper, a theory can never be proven; it can only be disproven. The importance of falsification is discussed in the Application section.

One problem with the deductive approach has to do with the theories themselves. Most theories include many assumptions about the world that are difficult to test and may be wrong. In Latané's work one assumption underlying the general theory is that measuring a person's behavior in an experimental context does not change the behavior in question. Although this often is reasonable to assume, we will show later that people can react to being observed in unusual ways, which means that this assumption is sometimes wrong. If the untested assumptions are wrong, then a particular experiment that falsifies a theory may have falsified it for the wrong reasons. That is, the test of the theory may not have been fair or appropriate.

APPLICATION
THE IMPORTANCE OF FALSIFICATION

Most students find the philosophical idea of falsifiability a difficult one to understand. Why is it important to try to disconfirm a hypothesis rather than simply confirm that it is correct? The primary reason is because confirming evidence could be consistent with any number of hypotheses or theories, but disconfirming evidence will rule out some. Negative evidence usually provides more meaningful information than does confirming evidence.

To see how this works, consider the following problem from an experiment by Wason (1977). Wason presented his subjects with the series 2 4 6, which was supposed to illustrate a particular rule. The people in Wason's experiment were to discover the rule by generating sequences that Wason would confirm or deny as being consistent with the rule he had in mind. One plausible hypothesis is that the rule is any series of even numbers increasing by two. Wason observed that people showed a persistent bias in selecting sequences confirming that hypothesis. They generated sequences such as: 8 10 12, 300 302 304, 620 622 624, and so on. Unfortunately, there are an infinite number of such strings, and although they confirm the theory of even numbers increasing by two, they are also consistent with other hypotheses. Could the rule be any numbers increasing by two, such as 3 5 7? Could the rule be even more general, such as any three ascending numbers? To test the last hypothesis, the subjects would have to suggest a sequence such as 6 7 8. Participants rarely generated sequences like the last one, even though it would rule out the previous two hypotheses. Furthermore, any three ascending numbers was the rule.

In ordinary human reasoning, the bias to confirm hypotheses is striking even though it is not very productive. In scientific reasoning, the confirmation bias would limit scientific progress, because the bias would make self-correction unlikely. Why is there such a strong bias toward confirming hypotheses? Johnson-Laird (1988) notes that some confirmation is necessary, and he also notes that seeking ways to disconfirm a hypothesis is often difficult. Apparently, therefore, people take the easy way out and simply seek confirming evidence. If you are interested in pursuing this topic, Best (1989) reviews the large literature on reasoning and faulty reasoning.

One conclusion, then, is that the deductive approach by itself cannot lead to scientific understanding.

At this point you may be wondering whether scientific understanding is possible if both induction and deduction are not infallible. Do not despair. Science is self-correcting, and it can provide answers to problems, however temporary those answers may be. Scientific understanding changes as scientists ply their trade. We have a better understanding of social loafing now than we did before Latané and his coworkers undertook their research. Through a combination of induction and deduction science progresses toward a more thorough understanding of its problems. Figure 2–1 illustrates how induction and deduction join to produce understanding.

By way of concluding this section, let us reexamine social loafing. Initially, positive experimental results bolstered our confidence in the general notion of social loafing. These results, in turn, suggested hypotheses about the nature of social loafing. Is it a general phenomenon that would influence even group-oriented individuals? Does it occur in the workplace as well as the laboratory? Positive answers to these questions are consistent with a diffusion-of-responsibility interpretation of social loafing.

In the next phase of the research, Latané and his colleagues attempted to eliminate other explanations of social loafing by falsifying predictions made by these alternative theories. In earlier work they tested a particular person's effort both when alone and when in a group. They subsequently reasoned that under these conditions a person might rest during the group test so he or she could allocate greater effort to the task when tested alone. To eliminate the possibility that allocation of effort rather than diffusion of responsibility accounted for social loafing, they conducted additional experiments in which a person was tested either alone or in a group—but not in both situations. Contrary to the allocation-of-effort hypothesis, the results showed that social loafing occurred when a person was tested in just that one condition of being in a group (Harkins, Latané, and Williams, 1980). Therefore, they concluded that diffusion of responsibility was a more appropriate account of social loafing than was allocation of effort.

Note the course of events here. Successive experiments pitted two possible outcomes against each other in the hopes that one possibility

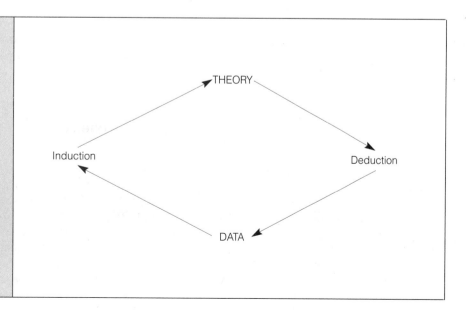

FIGURE 2-1
A theory organizes and predicts data. By means of deduction, particular observations (data) may be predicted. By means of induction, the data suggest organizing principles (theories). This circular relationship indicates that theories are tentative pictures of how data are organized.

would be eliminated and one supported by the outcome of the research. As Platt (1964) has noted, this eliminative procedure, which he calls **strong inference,** should, in the ideal case, yield one remaining theory (if the procedure of strong inference is used repeatedly). Of course, subsequent tests of the diffusion-of-responsibility theory might contradict it or add to it in some way. Thus, the theory might be revised or, with enough contradictions, rejected for an alternative explanation, itself supported by empirical observations. In any event, where we stand now is that we have constructed a reasonable view of what social loafing entails and what seems to cause it. The mixture of hypotheses induced from data and experimental tests deduced from testable hypotheses resulted in the theory that diffusion of responsibility leads to social loafing.

CONCEPT SUMMARY

The scientific method involves

- deduction—reasoning from general to specific cases
- induction—reasoning from specific to general cases
- strong inference—eliminating possible alternative explanations

---

What Is a Theory?

Thus far we have argued that scientific understanding is tentative: incorrect theories are modified and additional information is gathered through empirical tests about the problem at hand. In this section we focus on explaining theories.

A theory can be crudely defined as a set of related statements that explains a variety of occurrences. The more the occurrences, and the fewer the statements, the better the theory. The law of gravity explains falling apples, the behavior of roller coasters, and the position of bodies within the solar system. With a small number of statements about the mutual attraction of bodies, it explains a large number of events. It is therefore a powerful theory. (This does not necessarily mean it is a correct theory, because there are some events it cannot explain.)

Theory in psychology performs two major functions—**organization** and **prediction.** First, it provides a framework for the systematic and orderly display of data—that is, it serves as a convenient way for the scientist to organize data. Even the most dedicated inductive scientist will eventually have difficulty remembering the outcomes of dozens of experiments. Theory can be used as a kind of filing system to help experimenters organize results. Second, it allows the scientist to generate predictions for situations in which no data have been obtained. As noted in Chapter 1, these testable hypotheses guide research. The greater the degree of precision of these predictions, the better the theory. With the best of intentions, scientists who claim to be testing the same theory often derive from the theory different hypotheses about the same situation. This unfortunate circumstance is relatively more common in psychology, where many theories are stated in a loose verbal fashion, than in physics, where theories are more formal and better quantified through the use of mathematics. Although psychologists are rapidly becoming equipped to state their theories more precisely through such formal mechanisms as mathematics and computer simulations, the typical psychological theory still is not as precise as theories in other sciences.

Let us see how the theory devised by Latané to account for social loafing stacks up with regard to organization and prediction. The theory of diffusion of responsibility organizes a substantial amount of data about social loafing. More important, the theory seems to account for a remarkable variety of other observations. For example, Latané (1981) notes that the size of a tip left at a restaurant table is inversely related to the number of people in the dinner party. Likewise, proportionately more people committed themselves to Christ at smaller Billy Graham crusades than at larger ones. Finally, work by Latané and Darley (1970) shows that the willingness of people to help in a crisis is inversely related to the number of other bystanders present. The entire pattern of results can be subsumed under the notion of diffusion of responsibility, which asserts that people feel less responsibility for their own actions when they are in a group than when they are alone. So, people in groups are less likely to help in an emergency, they are less likely to leave a large tip, and so on. Latané's theory also makes rather precise predictions about the impact of the presence of other people on a person's actions. In fact, one version of the theory (Latané, 1981) presents its major assumptions in terms of mathematical equations.

Theories are devised to organize concepts and facts into a coherent pattern and to predict the results of future research. Sometimes the two functions of theory—organization and prediciton—are called *description* and *explanation,* respectively. Unfortunately, formulating the roles of theory in this manner often leads to an argument about the relative superiority of deductive or inductive approaches to science—a discussion we have already dismissed as fruitless. According to the deductive scientist, the inductive scientist is concerned only with description. The inductive scientist defends against this charge by retorting that description is explanation. If a psychologist could correctly predict and control all behavior by referring to properly organized sets of results, then that psychologist would also be explaining behavior. The argument is futile because both views are correct. If all the necessary data were properly organized, predictions could be made without recourse to a formal body of theoretical statements. Because all the data are not properly organized as yet, and perhaps never will be, theories are required to bridge the gap between knowledge and ignorance. Remember, however, that theoretical explanation is tentative, because all the data will never be in. So, we have merely recast the argument between inductive and deductive views about which approach will more quickly and surely lead to truth. Ultimately, description and explanation may be equivalent. The two terms describe the path taken more than the eventual theoretical outcome. To avoid this pitfall, we refer to the two major functions of theory as organization and prediction rather than as description and explanation.

CONCEPT SUMMARY

A theory
- organizes data
- predicts new research

Intervening Variables

Theories often use constructs that summarize the effects of several variables. Variables are discussed at greater length in later chapters. Recall that in Chapter 1 we discussed independent and dependent variables. Independent variables are those manipulated by the experimenter. For example, not allowing rats to have any water for several hours would create an independent variable called hours of deprivation. Dependent variables are those observed by the experimenter. For example, one could observe how much water a rat drinks.

Science tries to explain the world by relating independent and dependent variables. **Intervening variables** are abstract concepts that link independent variables to dependent variables. Gravity is a familiar construct that accomplishes this goal. It can relate an independent variable, how many feet of height an object is dropped, to a dependent variable, the speed of the object when it hits the ground. Gravity also summarizes the effects of height on speed for all manner of objects. Gravity explains falling apples as well as falling baseballs. Science progresses when a single construct, such as gravity, explains outcomes in many different environments. By connecting concepts to independent and dependent variables, scientists attempt to make their theories empirical and testable. Diffusion of responsibility is an intervening variable connected to group size on the one hand and individual behavior, such as work effort, on the other. If diffusion of responsibility were not measurable and producible, it would be a useless theoretical concept. Testable predictions concerning diffusion of responsibility can be made only if it can be varied (it is tied to an independent variable) and observed (it is tied to a dependent variable). The importance of testable concepts is considered further in the Psychology in Action section at the end of this chapter.

Kantowitz and Caspar (1988) have explained how a single intervening variable, workload, organizes experimental results efficiently. **Workload** is an intervening variable that relates the demands of the work environment to the capability of the human operator. People perform best at moderate levels of workload. A study of truck driver workload, being conducted for the U.S. Department of Transportation by the Battelle Human Factors Transportation Center, will be used to explain the benefits of intervening variables. This study compares the driver workload when a tractor pulls a single trailer versus the same tractor and driver pulling triples (three trailers connected to each other). It is being conducted on the road with professional drivers over a 400-mile course centered on Portland, Oregon.

Figure 2–2 shows a direct and an indirect way to relate an independent variable, road geometry, to a dependent variable, tachometer reaction

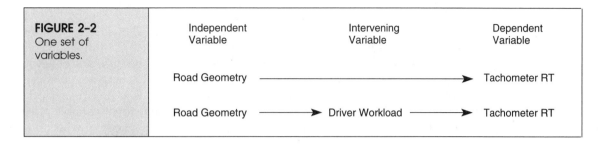

FIGURE 2-2
One set of variables.

time (RT). Research conducted in a laboratory truck simulator (Kantowitz, 1994) showed that when professional truck drivers are required to read their engine tachometer, RT is influenced by road geometry (Radius of curvature) and traffic density. Tight curves and dense traffic result in longer RT to read the tachometer. The direct relationship uses only one arrow to link road geometry to tachometer RT. The results of the experiment could be used to build a mathematical formula that relates road curvature to RT. The indirect method uses two arrows. The first arrow relates degree of highway curvature to driver workload, an intervening variable. When curvature increases, so does driver workload. The second arrow relates the intervening variable, driver workload, to tachometer RT. When workload increases, so does RT. Because the indirect method is more complicated, requiring an extra arrow, you might expect the scientist to prefer the direct method of explanation. Indeed, if the only scientific goal were to relate radius of road curvature to tachometer RT, you would be correct because science prefers simple explanations to complex explanations. However, as we shall explain, the scientific goal is more general.

Figure 2–3 relates two independent variables, road geometry and number of trailers being towed, to two dependent variables, tachometer RT and heart rate variability. As workload increases, heart rate variability decreases (Kantowitz & Caspar, 1988). Again both direct and indirect explanations are shown. In Figure 2–3 direct and indirect explanations are equally complex. Each requires four distinct arrows.

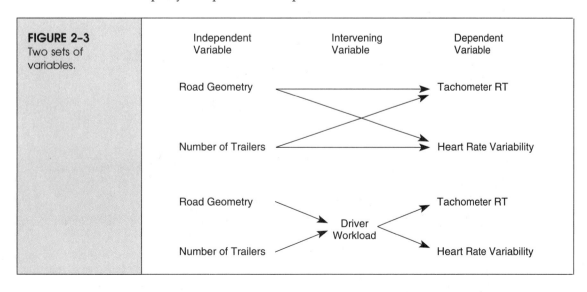

FIGURE 2-3
Two sets of variables.

Figure 2–4 relates four independent variables to four dependent variables. Type of dolly is an independent variable in the Battelle study. In the United States most trucks use a type A dolly to connect the trailers. But in Canada a more expensive dolly (type C) is often used because it is believed to offer superior control. Another goal of the study is to compare the effects of these two types of dolly and the level of traffic density on driver workload and driver behavior. Subjective ratings are a dependent variable often used to measure workload (Kantowitz & Caspar, 1988). Steering wheel rate is also a dependent variable that refers to driver control movements of the steering wheel. Again both direct and indirect explanations are shown. Now it is obvious that the indirect method is less complicated. It requires 8 separate arrows, whereas the direct method requires 16 arrows. So as science tries to relate more independent and dependent variables, intervening variables become more efficient.

Intervening variables have yet another advantage. Workload, no matter how produced, should have the same effect on all dependent variables. This can be tested in experiments. If it is not true, we can modify the idea of a single intervening variable. Later chapters discuss this under the topic of converging operations.

Evaluating Theories

The sophisticated scientist does not try to determine if a particular theory is true or false in an absolute sense. There is no black-and-white approach

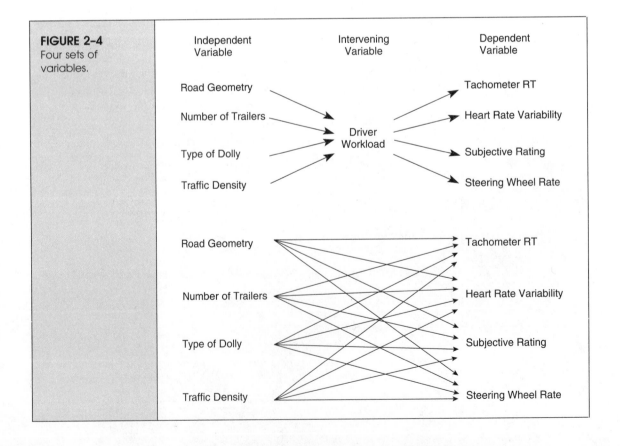

FIGURE 2–4
Four sets of variables.

to theory evaluation. A theory may be known to be incorrect in some portion and yet continue to be used. In modern physics, light is represented, according to the theory chosen, either as discrete particles called quanta or as continuous waves. Logically, light cannot be both at the same time. Thus, you might think that at least one of these two theoretical views must necessarily be false. The physicist tolerates this ambiguity (although perhaps not cheerfully) and uses whichever representation—quantum or wave—is more appropriate. Instead of flatly stating that a theory is true, the scientist is much more likely to state that it is supported substantially by data, thereby leaving open the possibility that new data may not support the theory. Although scientists do not state that a theory is true, they must often decide which of several theories is best. As noted earlier, explanations are tentative; nevertheless, the scientist still needs to decide which theory is best for now. To do so, there must be explicit criteria for evaluating a theory. Three such criteria are **parsimony, precision,** and **testability.**

One criterion was hinted at earlier when we noted that the fewer the statements in a theory, the better the theory. This criterion is called parsimony, or sometimes Occam's razor, after William of Occam. If a theory needs a separate statement for every result it tries to explain, clearly no economy has been gained by the theory. Theories gain power when they can explain many results with few explanatory concepts. Thus, if two theories have the same number of concepts, the one that can explain more results is a better theory. If two theories can explain the same number of results, the one with fewer explanatory concepts is to be preferred. Here you can see the relationship between theories and intervening variables. Constructs, such as diffusion of responsibility and workload, are intervening variables tied to several independent and dependent variables. The theoretical notion of diffusion of responsibility is parsimonious because it accounts for substantial amounts of data, as seen in our previous discussion.

Precision is another important criterion, especially in psychology, where it is often lacking. Theories that involve mathematical equations or computer programs are generally more precise, and hence better, than those that use loose verbal statements (all other things being equal, of course). Unless a theory is sufficiently precise so that different investigators can agree about its predictions, it is for all intents and purposes useless.

Testability goes beyond precision and is the most important aspect of a good theory, as we have emphasized in this chapter and the previous one. A theory can be very precise and yet not able to be tested. For example, when Einstein proposed the equivalence of matter and energy ($E = MC^2$), nuclear technology was not able to test this relationship directly. The scientist places a very high value on the criterion of testability, because a theory that cannot be tested can never be disproved. At first you might think this would be a good quality because it would be impossible to demonstrate that such a theory was incorrect. The scientist takes the opposite view, as we noted in the discussion of falsifiability. For example, consider ESP (extrasensory perception). Some believers in ESP claim that the presence of a disbeliever is sufficient to prevent a person gifted with ESP from performing, because the disbeliever puts out "bad vibes" that disrupt ESP. This means that ESP cannot be evaluated, because only believers can be present when it is demonstrated. The scientist takes a dim view of this logic, and most scientists, especially psychologists, are skeptical about ESP. Belief in a theory increases as it survives tests that could reject it. Because some future test possibly may find a flaw, belief in a theory is never absolute. If a theory cannot logically be tested, it cannot be evaluated; hence, it is useless to the scientist. If it is logically possible but not yet technically feasible, as was once the case with Einstein's theory, then evaluation of a theory is deferred.

CONCEPT SUMMARY

Good theories are

- parsimonious
- precise
- testable

THE SCIENCE OF PSYCHOLOGY

Some students find it difficult to think of psychology as a science in the same sense that physics and chemistry are sciences. They believe that there are aspects of human experience, such as the arts, literature, and religion, that defy scientific analysis. How can the beauty of a Klee lithograph, a Beethoven sonata, a Cartier-Bresson photograph be reduced to cold scientific equation? How can the tender feelings of a first romance, the thrill of driving a sports car at 100 miles per hour, and the agony of a defeated football team be captured in the objective, disinterested fashion required by science?

Some psychologists, known as humanists, would answer these questions in the negative. These humanists, most often clinical and counseling psychologists, claim that to evaluate and test human feelings and experience objectively by traditional scientific methods is impossible. Even tough, "brass-instrument" experimental psychologists concur that the domain of science is limited. We cannot establish or refute the existence of God by scientific means any more than we could test gravity by theological methods. Science operates where it can test hypotheses (see Chapter 1). This does not mean that knowledge cannot be gained wherever science fears to tread—that is, by nonscientific means. Many important fields of human endeavor have yet to benefit from extensive scientific analysis—ethics, morals, law, to name but a few.

However, most scientists believe that scientific analysis eventually might be usefully applied to many such areas. Much of contemporary psychology was regarded as the sole property of philosophy at one time. As psychological techniques improved, these aspects of human expertise and behavior moved into the realm of science. And now most psychologists believe that virtually all facets of human experience are fair game for the science of psychology. If testable hypotheses can be made, then scientific psychology can be used. Deriding scientific progress in psychology, as did one U.S. senator who criticized the National Science Foundation for supporting research on romantic love (Elmes, 1988), will not halt efforts to expand psychological knowledge. Although concern for the proper and ethical use of such knowledge is valid and important, ignorance is no solution.

Hard Science as a Model for Experimental Psychology

Psychologists can be arranged along a continuum according to how well they think physics and chemistry serve as a model for psychology to emulate. The "hard-shelled" psychologists think these older sciences are perfect models, whereas the "soft-shelled" psychologists believe that social sciences must find another model. Because we are experimental psychologists by trade, and because this book is intended as an experimental-psychology text, we tend to sample more from the hard-boiled end of the continuum.

All science has data and theory. What distinguishes among the different sciences, and among the subspecialties within a science like psychology, is the different techniques used. Astronomers do not need Skinner boxes any more than animal-learning psychologists need telescopes. Yet both practice science. A learning theorist's memory drum is not intrinsically superior to a social psychologist's "aggression machine." Even the modern microcomputer of an information-processing psychologist does not guarantee better science, although it may improve the odds. Most of this text is devoted to explaining the techniques needed in psychological research today. Although the hard-shelled psychologist does have more refined techniques, this is in part because of selection of problems that are amendable to sophisticated analysis. As psychology subjects more and more of human experience and behavior to scientific analysis, it is only natural that initial techniques may be crude. At one time this was true of hard-shelled psychology, too. Having a hard shell should not preclude one from having an open mind.

Psychology and the Real World

Scientists in general, and psychologists in particular, have many reasons for pursuing their profession. We think it rather easy to prove that psychological research does serve humankind (see the Application section in Chapter 1). We would like to stress that we do not find service to humankind the only, or necessarily the major, justification for a career as a research psychologist. Many scientists investigate certain problems simply because they find them interesting. We have complete sympathy with a colleague who might state that he or she studies gerbils just because gerbils provoke his or her curiosity. It is true that certain studies are performed on animals because they are unethical or impractical to perform on humans—for example, studies of long-term crowding, punishment, drugs, and so on—but it is equally true that the behavior of animals is interesting in its own right.

As noted in Chapter 1, ideas for research come from both theoretical predictions and practical problems, and scientific research is often divided into two categories: basic and applied. **Applied research** aims at solving a specific problem—such as how to cure bedwetting—whereas **basic research** has no immediate practical goal. Basic research establishes a reservoir of data, theoretical explanations, and concepts that can be tapped by the applied researcher. Without this source, applied research would soon dry up and sputter to a halt, unless applied researchers became of necessity basic researchers. It takes quite a while for a concept developed by basic research to find some useful application in society. Adams (1972) traced five socially important products to discover the impact, if any, of basic research. Although basic research accounted for 70 percent of the significant events, these events occurred 20 to 30 years before the ultimate use of the product. This long time lag obscures the crucial role of basic research so that many persons incorrectly believe that basic research is not very useful to society. Often it is difficult to tell what basic research being done today will have an impact 30 years from now. But this inability to predict does not mean that we should stop doing basic research (Elmes, 1988).

Although the scientific quest for knowledge may be for one purpose only, usually basic and applied interests eventually intermingle in interesting ways as demonstrated by the various kinds of research done on social loafing. Ringelmann's early observations of social loafing in the laboratory were also documented in the workplace (Marriot, 1949). A potentially useful way to improve group productivity then arose from the laboratory work of Latané and his colleagues, who found that individual performance assessment can reduce social loafing.

The division of research into basic and applied categories is common, but a far more important distinction is between good and bad research. The principles and practices covered in this text apply with equal force to basic and applied research. You can and should use them to evaluate all the psychological research you encounter, whether as a student, a professional psychologist, or an educated person reading the daily newspaper.

Are Experiments Too Far from Real Life?   Students of psychology typically demand a higher level of relevance in their psychology courses than they expect from other sciences. Students who are not at all dismayed that their course in introductory physics did not enable them to repair their automobile are often disturbed that their course in introductory psychology did not give them a better insight into their own motivations, did not cure their neuroses, and failed to show them how to gain eternal happiness. If you did not find such information in introductory psychology, we doubt that you will find it in this text either. If this seems unfair, read on.

The data that psychologists gather may at first seem unimportant, because an immediate relationship between basic psychological research and pressing social or personal problems may be difficult to establish. Naturally, people then doubt the importance of this research and wonder why the federal government, through various agencies, funds researchers to watch rats press bars or run through mazes.

The difficulty, however, is not with the research but with the expectations as to how "useful" research should be conducted. As noted by Sidman (1960), people expect progress to occur by the establishment of laboratory situations that are analogous to real-life situations: "In order to study psychosis in animals we must learn how to make animals psychotic." This is off the mark. The psychologist tries to understand the underlying *processes* rather than the physical situations that produce these processes. The physical situations in the real world and the laboratory need not be at all similar, provided that the same processes are occurring.

Suppose we would like to know why airplane accidents occur, or more specifically, what the relationship is between airplane accidents and failure of attention on the part of the pilot and/or the air traffic controller. A basic researcher might approach this problem by having college sophomores sit in front of several lights that turn on in rapid succession. The sophomore has to press a key as each light is illuminated. This probably seems somewhat removed from mid-air collisions of aircraft. Yet although the physical situations are quite different, the processes are similar. Pressing a key is an index of attention. Psychologists can overload the human operator by presenting lights faster than he or she can respond. Thus, this simple physical situation in a laboratory allows the psychologist to study failure of attention in a carefully controlled environment. In addition to the obvious safety benefits of studying attention without having to crash airplanes, we will show in later chapters that there are many scientific advantages to the laboratory environment. Because failures of attention are responsible for many kinds of industrial accidents (DeGreene, 1970, chapters 7 and 16), studies of attention by use of lights and buttons can lead to improvements outside the laboratory.

By the same token, establishing similar physical situations does not guarantee similarity of processes. One can easily train a rat to pick up coins in its mouth and bury them in its cage. But this does not necessarily mean that the "miserly" rat and the miserly human who keeps coins under his or her mattress do so because the same psychological processes are controlling their behaviors.

You also should be aware of two important reasons for doing research, the purposes of which (at least initially) may not be directly related to practical affairs (Mook, 1983). One reason that basic research aids understanding is that it often demonstrates what *can* happen. Thus under controlled conditions, it can be determined whether social loafing does occur. Furthermore, the laboratory affords an opportunity to determine the characteristics of social loafing more clearly than does the workplace, where a number of uncontrolled factors, such as salary and job security, could mask or alter the effects of social loafing (see Chapter 3).

A second reason for the value of basic research is that the findings from a controlled, laboratory setting may have more force than similar findings obtained in a real-life setting. Showing that the human operator can be overloaded in a relatively nonstressful laboratory task suggests that attentional factors are crucial for performance. Individuals could be even more likely to be overloaded under the stressful conditions of piloting large passenger planes in crowded airspaces.

If a researcher wants to test a theoretical prediction or apply a laboratory result in an applied setting, then real-life tests are required (Kantowitz, 1992a). There are strong limitations on applying basic research directly to a practical setting (Kantowitz, 1990). For example, despite the large amount of basic knowledge about workload, several cautions need be observed before applying this knowledge to truck drivers on the road (Kantowitz, 1992b). Similarly, installing a way of assessing individual performance to reduce social loafing in a group manufacturing situation without first testing in a manufacturing environment would be foolhardy.

There are two morals to this section. First, basic research is often closer to real life than may appear at first glance. Second, although applied research benefits from previous basic research, gaining this benefit in a practical situation is seldom easy. Additional testing and evaluation in the applied setting is usually needed.

CONCEPT SUMMARY

Good laboratory research

- examines psychological processes
- shows what can happen in a controlled setting
- may have more force than real-life research

One way to summarize the material presented in this chapter is to say that engaging in experimental psychology can be stimulating and enjoyable. The attempt to understand why people and animals behave as they do arises out of curiosity and the search for solutions to basic and applied problems. Although empirical procedures that rely on induction and deduction offer advantages over other methods of fixing belief, the advantages come with a cost. The cost is that theoretical explanations are always tentative because alternative theories lead to the search for new data, and new data provide the bases for modifications of existing theories. Paradoxically, the cost provides the scientific psychologist with a payment by helping to satisfy curiosity, at least temporarily, and by stimulating that curiosity into additional research and theory. Trying to answer questions about ourselves and animals is an exciting challenge. We hope that you are spurred by this challenge and are gratified by the application of sound psychological science to the understanding of behavior.

SUMMARY

1. Scientific psychology is concerned with the methods and techniques used to explain why people and animals behave as they do. This curiosity may be satisfied by basic or applied research, which usually go hand in hand to provide understanding.

2. Our beliefs are often established by the method of authority, the method of tenacity, or the a priori method. The scientific method offers advantages over these other methods because it relies on systematic, empirical observation and is self-correcting.

3. Scientists use both inductive and deductive reasoning to arrive at explanations of thought and action.

4. A theory organizes sets of data and generates predictions for new situations in which data have not been obtained.

5. A good theory is parsimonious, precise, and testable.

6. Laboratory research is concerned with the processes that govern behavior and with showing the conditions under which certain psychological processes can be observed.

■ KEY CONCEPTS

a priori method	organization
applied research	parsimony
basic research	precision
data	prediction
deduction	scientific method
diffusion of responsibility	self-correcting
empirical	social loafing
falsifiability view	strong inference
intervening variable	testability
induction	theory
method of authority	workload
method of tenacity	

■ EXERCISES

1. Make a list of five statements that might be considered true. Include some controversial statements (for example, men have lower IQs than women), as well as some you are sure are correct. Survey some of your friends by asking if they agree with these statements. Then, ask their justifications for their opinions. Classify their justifications into one of the methods of fixing beliefs discussed in this chapter.

2. Compare and contrast inductive and deductive approaches to science. Clarify your answers by referring to at least one branch of science outside experimental psychology.

3. Discuss social loafing research from the standpoint of strong inference.

4. Is it necessary (or even desirable) for experimental psychologists to justify their research in terms of applied benefits to society?

5. [*Special Exercise.*] In 1983, a researcher studied how three age groups felt about war. One group contained 10-year-olds, a second group consisted of 35-year-olds, and the last group was made up of 60-year-

olds. Marked differences in their attitudes about war were observed. There is an important confounding variable in this study. What is it? Speculate on the effects of this confounding with regard to the attitudes of each age group. (Hint: You might think about this question in terms of the generation gap.)

■ SUGGESTED READINGS

Further information about the nature of science and scientific psychology may be found in: Kantowitz, B. H., and Roediger, H. L., III, and Elmes, D. G. (1994). *Experimental psychology: Understanding psychological research* (5th ed.). St. Paul: West.

Excellent discussions about the nature and importance of scientific psychology appear in these publications: Broadbent, D. E. (1973). *In defense of empirical psychology.* London: Methuen. Hebb, D. O. (1974). What psychology is about. *American Psychologist, 29,* 71–79. Sidman, M. (1960). *Tactics of scientific research.* New York: Basic Books.

For those of you who are particularly interested in the philosophy of science, we recommend these two books: Kendler, H. H. (1981). *Psychology: A science in conflict.* New York: Oxford. Mayr, E. (1982). *The growth of biological thought.* Cambridge, MA: Belknap Press.

Psychology in Action
Intervening Variables and Testability

One way to gauge the value of a theory is to determine its testability. Theories are testable to the extent that the concepts can be manipulated and observed. Hence, connecting intervening variables to independent and dependent variables is crucial for scientific progress. You can assess theories in psychology by how well they define their intervening variables. If you examine a dictionary of psychology such as the one by Chaplin (1968), you can assess a theory. For example, Freud defines *personality* as "the integration of the id, the ego, and the superego." The crux of the definition of the *id* is "that division of the mind, or psyche, which is the seat of the libido. From it (the id) arise the animalistic, chaotic impulses which demand gratification." Are the Freudian notions of *personality* and the *id* formulated as intervening variables? What are the independent variables? What are the dependent variables? Can you generate testable hypotheses from Freud's ideas?

Dollard and Miller (1950) and many other experimentally oriented psychologists believe that Freud's theories do not allow testability. The primary reason is because most Freudian concepts are hard to connect to independent and dependent variables. Dollard and Miller tried to rephrase many of Freud's concepts so that they were intervening variables that could be studied in an objective way.

To assess the scientific value of other theories, you might try examining some other concepts in a dictionary of psychology. *Aggression* and *Sheldon's constitutional theory of personality* are two entries worth exploring for intervening variables.

CONDUCTING ETHICAL RESEARCH

Follow the APA's guidelines for research with humans and animals

Ethical Considerations in Research

❏ Is my project designed in accordance with contemporary ethical standards?

❏ Will my human subjects be treated in a dignified fashion without having their personal freedom violated or their physical or emotional health damaged?

❏ Will I treat my animal subjects in a humane fashion?

❏ Do I understand the ethical principles behind drug research?

❏ Have I read and understood the ethical principles espoused by the American Psychological Association?

❏ Am I an honest scientist?

CHAPTER 3

CONDUCTING ETHICAL RESEARCH

The scientific enterprise creates ethical dilemmas. Scientific knowledge and techniques that can be used for human betterment can be turned to manipulative and exploitative purposes as well. Just as results of research in atomic physics can be used for the treatment of cancer as well as for destructive weapons, so methods discovered to reduce prejudice toward minority groups, to eliminate troublesome behavior problems, or to facilitate learning in school may also be used to manipulate political allegiance, to create artificial wants, or to reconcile the victims of social injustice to their fate. The double-edged potentiality of scientific knowledge poses ethical problems for all scientists. To the extent that psychological research deals with important problems and potent methods, psychologists must recognize and alert others to the fact that the potential for misuse of research increases its potential for constructive application. (American Psychological Association, 1982, p. 16)

RESEARCH WITH HUMAN PARTICIPANTS

The quotation introducing this chapter is from a publication of the American Psychological Association (APA). It comes from a preamble to a lengthy discussion of ethical principles covering all aspects of psychology and is presented in abbreviated form here to emphasize the ethical obligations of researchers in all areas of science. These obligations are straightforward in principle but difficult to implement. We examine both the ethical principles and the problems associated with putting them into practice in psychology. Psychologists worry about the ethics of research involving both human participants and animals. Although some of this concern is selfish, owing to fear of restriction of research funds and loss of access to subject populations, most psychologists are ethical persons who have no desire to inflict harm on anyone. The mad researcher, who will do anything to obtain data, is largely fictional.

An experimenter cannot be completely impartial and objective in judging the ethical issues concerning his or her own research, so most universities and research institutions have peer committees that judge the ethicality of proposed research. Indeed, any federally funded research must be approved by such a committee before any funding is granted.

Various ethical issues become obvious in the context of an actual research project. Imagine you are a psychologist interested in determining to what extent depressive feelings influence how well people remember. One very important reason why you want to study this topic is that depression is a fairly common emotional problem among college students, and you would like to determine how this problem could affect academic performance. You decide to do a tightly controlled laboratory experiment to determine the effects of depression on memory. You want to induce depression in some of your subjects, and then compare their memory to that of other subjects who were not induced to be depressed. You induce depression in your subjects by a procedure devised by Velten (1968). In this procedure subjects read aloud sixty self-referent statements associated with the mood in question. In this case, the participant reads statements that are supposed to induce depression, beginning with relatively mild ones, such as "Today is neither better nor worse than any other day," and progressing to more extreme ones, such as "I feel so bad that I would like to go to sleep and never wake up." Velten's procedure induces a mild, temporary depression; participants report feeling depressed, and their behavior suffers on a variety of tasks.

Many details of this experiment have not been specified, but it should be obvious that the welfare of the research participants in this study could be jeopardized (for complete details of this experiment, see Elmes, Chapman, and Selig, 1984). Inducing a negative mood (such as depression) in college students could have disastrous effects on their social and intellectual functioning. How can you as an ethical researcher try to preserve and protect the fundamental human rights of your participants? What would you do to protect their welfare and at the same time conduct an internally valid experiment?

In a review of research on mood and memory, Blaney (1986) listed a number of studies in which depression was induced in college students. In some experiments, a happy mood was induced in subjects. Do the ethical considerations depend on the kind of mood—happy or sad—that is induced in a subject? Also, researchers have used several different mood-induction procedures in their experiments. Besides the Velten (1968) procedure described above, hypnosis and music have been used to induce a depressed or happy mood. Do ethical considerations depend on the mood-induction technique? These questions concerning mood-induction research illustrate how ethical issues associated with psychological research may vary according to the specific circumstances in the experiment.

The APA (1981a, 1987, 1989) has provided ethical guidelines for researchers. The association outlined ten general principles governing the conduct of research with human participants. To consider how the welfare of the students was protected in those studies, we examine the principles that guide research involving human participants. *You should read and understand these ethical principles before you conduct a research project with human participants.*

> The decision to undertake research rests upon a considered judgment by the individual psychologist about how best to contribute to psychological science and human welfare. Having made the decision to conduct research, the psychologist considers alternative directions in which research energies and resources might be invested. On the basis of this consideration, the psychologist carries out the investigation with respect and concern for the dignity and welfare of the people who participate and with cognizance of federal and state regulations and professional standards governing the conduct of research with human participants.

1. In planning a study, the investigator has the responsibility to make a careful evaluation of its ethical acceptability. To the extent that the weighing of scientific and human values suggests a compromise of any principle, the investigator incurs a correspondingly serious obligation to seek ethical advice and to observe stringent safeguards to protect the rights of human participants.

2. Considering whether a participant in a planned study will be a "subject at risk" or a "subject at minimal risk," according to recognized standards, is of primary ethical concern to the investigator.

3. The investigator always retains the responsibility for ensuring ethical practice in research. The investigator is also responsible for the ethical treatment of research participants by collaborators, assistants, students, and employees, all of whom, however, incur similar obligations.

4. Except in minimal-risk research, the investigator establishes a clear and fair agreement with research participants, prior to their participation, that clarifies the obligations and responsibilities of each. The investigator has the obligation to honor all promises and commitments included in that agreement. The investigator informs the participants of all aspects of the research that might reasonably

be expected to influence willingness to participate and explains all other aspects of the research about which the participants inquire. Failure to make full disclosure prior to obtaining informed consent requires additional safeguards to protect the welfare and dignity of the research participants. Research with children or with participants who have impairments that would limit understanding and/or communication requires special safeguarding procedures.

5. Methodological requirements of a study may make the use of concealment or deception necessary. Before conducting such a study, the investigator has a special responsibility to (i) determine whether the use of such techniques is justified by the study's prospective scientific, educational, or applied value; (ii) determine whether alternative procedures are available that do not use concealment or deception; and (iii) ensure that the participants are provided with sufficient explanation as soon as possible.

6. The investigator respects the individual's freedom to decline to participate in or to withdraw from the research at any time. The obligation to protect this freedom requires careful thought and consideration when the investigator is in a position of authority or influence over the participant. Such positions of authority include, but are not limited to, situations in which research participation is required as part of employment or in which the participant is a student, client, or employee of the investigator.

7. The investigator protects the participant from physical and mental discomfort, harm, and danger that may arise from research procedures. If risks of such consequences exist, the investigator informs the participant of that fact. Research procedures likely to cause serious or lasting harm to a participant are not used unless the failure to use these procedures might expose the participant to risk of greater harm, or unless the research has great potential benefit and fully informed and voluntary consent is obtained from each participant. The participant should be informed of procedures for contacting the investigator within a reasonable time period following participation should stress, potential harm, or related questions or concerns arise.

8. After the data are collected, the investigator provides the participant with information about the nature of the study and attempts to remove any misconceptions that may have arisen. Where scientific or humane values justify delaying or withholding this information, the investigator incurs a special responsibility to monitor the research and to ensure that there are no damaging consequences for the participant.

9. Where research procedures result in undesirable consequences for the individual participant, the investigator has the responsibility to detect and remove or correct these consequences, including long-term effects.

10. Information obtained about a research participant during the course of an investigation is confidential unless otherwise agreed upon in advance. When the possibility exists that others may obtain access to such information, this possibility, together with the plans for protecting confidentiality, is explained to the participant as part of the procedure for obtaining informed consent.

Principles 9 and 10 are the ones most relevant to protecting welfare, and they can be summarized by noting that the experimenter has an obligation to minimize harm to the participant. The subject should be warned ahead of time if there is potential harm, the subject should be able to withdraw if he or she chooses, and deception should be used carefully. The experimenter is obligated to undo any harm, and the results should remain confidential with regard to a particular participant unless agreed otherwise. These principles need to be reckoned with in any research project.

Informed Consent and Deception

The ethical researcher informs subjects, prior to participation, of "all aspects of the research that might reasonably be expected to influence willingness to participate and explains all other aspects of the research about which participants inquire." This means that the participants must be forewarned about those aspects of the research that may have detrimental effects. In most psychological research, participants receive complete information about what they will be asked to do during the research project, so that they can give **informed consent** about their understanding of the possible problems associated with participation. Participants are rarely misled as to the nature of the experiences they will have during the experiment. Furthermore, an experimenter usually states the purpose of the experimental procedure truthfully. Nonetheless, experimenters sometimes mislead participants about the true purpose of an experiment. This false description is often referred to as a "cover story." This kind of **deception** is usually done to control subject reactivity. For instance, a researcher interested in whether people behave more assertively in same-gender groups than in mixed-gender groups tells people that they will be working on problems that require group cooperation. They are also told that the purpose of the experiment is to evaluate the difficulty of these tasks. The researcher was concerned that participants' behavior might change if they knew the real purpose of the experiment. In this case, information regarding the hypothesis under test probably will not change anyone's decision to participate, but this information might change performance on the task. Deception of this sort, although usually harmless, must be considered carefully because the participant's consent is not fully informed. A person might choose not to participate in a particular experiment because he or she does not approve of the purpose of the experiment.

Even more rare than deception concerning the purpose of an experiment is deception concerning the experiences that the participant will have during the experiment. Such deception is, unfortunately, necessary to answer some research questions. For example, if an investigator wants to see how well people recall information that they are not actively trying to remember, he or she might not inform participants that the experiment requires a memory test. Obviously, the omission of information prevents participants from giving fully informed consent.

Thus, whenever a research question requires deception, the ethical researcher faces a dilemma. Obviously, people must be warned if the procedure will place them in serious danger of physical or psychological harm. Deception in such cases is clearly unethical. When a procedure involves only minor risks, on the other hand, the decision regarding full disclosure to participants is more difficult. In all cases, the potential benefits of the research must be weighed against the actual and potential costs to the participant. Only when the potential benefits of the experiment far exceed any risks to the participant can deception be justified. Even then, participants should always receive as much information as possible, and they should know that they can end their participation at any time without negative consequences.

Let us reexamine the depression and memory experiment we discussed earlier, focusing on the question of informed consent. The people who signed up to participate were told that some of the things they were going to do in the experiment might make them feel unhappy, and they were given the opportunity to refuse to participate. The specific nature of the manipulation, such as the Velten technique and who was going to serve in the experimental group, was not disclosed ahead of time. People may have reacted unusually if they knew all the details. Because the effects of the mood induction were known to be temporary, the researchers believed that partial information was enough to permit informed consent. Here, although some information was omitted, participants were not misled about what to expect in the experiment.

The issues surrounding informed consent and deception often require considerable thought and deliberation to arrive at ethical solutions. Individual researchers are seldom left to their own devices to make these decisions. Supposedly, every research institution in this country has a standing committee that must approve any experimental procedure involving human subjects. These committees try to ensure the ethical treatment of experimental participants. We discuss these boards in more detail later.

In sum, fully informed consent is the norm in most areas of psychology. Occasionally, some information is withheld or participants are misled so as to prevent subject reactivity. In such cases, the experimenter, as well as members of institutional review boards, take great care in deciding whether the benefits of the procedure outweigh the risks to the participants.

Freedom to Withdraw

As mentioned briefly in the previous section, participants should be allowed to decline to participate or to withdraw at any time. Everyone would agree that the mad scientist who straps participants to the chair is unethical. Moreover, few people would deny that people who are unhappy about participating should have the **freedom to withdraw**. Where, then, is the ethical dilemma? The major problem revolves around the definition of a willing volunteer participant. Consider the subject pool for the depression and memory experiment: undergraduate students (mostly freshmen and sophomores) taking introductory psychology. They sign up to participate in experiments, and they usually receive some sort of course credit for their service. Are they volunteering when they sign up, or are they under some sort of coercion that they have inferred from the situation? If the students actually receive extra credit, they are likely to be acting on their own volition. If they must participate as part of a course requirement, then the freedom to participate or not is less obvious. When students are required to participate, they should have some optional way of fulfilling the requirement, such as writing a paper or attending a special lecture. The point, then, is to provide freedom to the potential subjects, so they can participate or not as they choose.

Generally, when the pool of potential participants is a captive audience, such as students, prisoners, military recruits, and employees of the experimenter, the ethical researcher considers the individual's freedom to withdraw or to participate. In the depression and memory experiment, volunteer students were recruited with the lure of extra credit (participation was not mandatory). When they signed up, they were forewarned about the possibility of unhappiness (they could agree to participate or not). The instructions at the beginning of the experiment informed them that they had the option of quitting at any time and still receive full extra credit (they were free to withdraw).

Protection from Harm and Debriefing

The APA suggests an additional safeguard to provide research participants with **protection from harm.** The subjects should have a way to contact the investigator following participation in the research. Even the most scrupulously ethical project of the minimal-risk sort may have unintended aftereffects. Thus, the participant should be able to receive help or advice from the researcher if problems should arise. We have had participants cry (out of frustration and embarrassment) during what was supposed to be a standard, innocuous memory experiment. Those subjects may have carried away from the experiment a negative self-image or strong feelings of resentment toward the experimenter in particular or research in general.

Because of such unintended effects, the prudent researcher provides detailed **debriefing,** which means that the investigator explains the general purposes of the research. Furthermore, the researcher completely describes the manipulations so that any questions or misunderstandings may be removed.

Let us apply the principles of debriefing and protection from harm to the depression and memory experiment. At the end of that project, the participants were given a list of phone numbers of people who could be contacted in the unlikely event that the subjects felt depressed following the experiment. The list of contacts included the principal investigator, a counselor, and the dean of student affairs and his assistant. Also, the day after participation, each subject who had read the depression-inducing statements was phoned by one of the experimenters, who tried to determine whether the participant was having any negative aftereffects.

The participants received thorough debriefing. They were told about the mood-induction procedure and how its effects were temporary. In addition, other details of the experimental design and rationale were outlined, and any questions the participants had were answered.

Removing Harmful Consequences

Debriefing subjects and giving them phone numbers may not be sufficient in a risky project. If a participant could suffer long-term consequences as a result of serving in a research project, the investigator has the responsibility for **removing harmful consequences.** The feelings of resentful subjects may be difficult to reverse, because the resentment may be unintended and undetected. However, where the risks are known, the ethical investigator must take steps to minimize them.

Prior to the debriefing in the depression and memory experiment, the participants read a series of self-referent statements designed to induce elation. This exercise was supposed to counteract the effects of the negative mood induced earlier. Then the participants were questioned about their current feelings, and they were also asked to sign a statement that said they left the experiment feeling no worse than when they began it. All participants signed the statement, but had they not, a contingent plan was to keep them in the laboratory under the supervision of one of the experimenters until they felt better.

Confidentiality

What a subject does in an experiment should be confidential unless otherwise agreed. An ethical researcher does not run around saying things like: "Bobby Freshman is stupid; he did more poorly than anyone else in my experiment." Also, personal information about particular participants, such as their attitudes toward premarital sex or their family income, should not be revealed without their permission. The principle of **confidentiality** seems straightforward, but a researcher can be faced with an ethical dilemma when trying to uphold confidentiality.

This dilemma arose in the depression and memory experiment. The experimenter was confronted with an ethical problem, because he believed it was necessary to violate the principle of confidentiality in order to uphold the principle of protection from harm. How did this dilemma develop? One of the first tasks of the participants was to answer some questions concerning their mental health. They indicated whether they were currently seeking professional help for a personal problem. If they were, they provided some details about the problem and the therapeutic procedure. The participants were assured that their answers were confidential. Then the subjects completed a clinical test that assessed their current level of depression. If a participant indicated that he or she was being treated for depression and scored high on the test, the experiment was discontinued at that point. The researchers wanted to minimize harm and maximize frank, open responding by assuring the students of the confidential nature of their responses and by using the depression test to prevent a depressed person from becoming even more depressed by the mood-induction procedure. Nevertheless, an ethical dilemma arose. In the course of the experiment, two students scored very high on the depression test, and one of them was not undergoing therapy. Because the test was known to be a reliable and valid predictor of clinically serious depression, the principal investigator believed that it was necessary to warn one of the college's counselors about the two students who appeared to have very high levels of depression. Then, under the guise of a routine interview, the counselor talked to these students.

This type of dilemma occurs frequently in research. To adhere to one ethical principle may necessitate violating another. Easy choices vanish when this happens. In the case we mentioned, if the highly depressed students had suspected that the investigator had betrayed their confidence, permanent resentment and mistrust could have resulted. On the other hand, the investigator could not ignore the fact that these students, particularly the one not undergoing therapy, were in severe distress. At the time, ensuring that the students received help seemed much more important than upholding their right to confidentiality.

As our example illustrates, ethical decisions must sometimes be made on the basis of pragmatic concerns. In other words, people involved in making decisions about a research project must focus on how best to protect the participants and at the same time conduct a meaningful, valid project. To see how difficult some ethical decisions can be, examine the Application.

Research involving humans rarely offers a completely clear glimpse of what is ethical. The responsibility for ethical practice rests on the researcher, review boards, and journal editors who review research for publication. In limited instances a researcher might justify deception, concealment, and breaches of confidentiality. However, such questionable ethical practices must be avoided if possible. Ethical violations are not prerequisites of good research.

CONCEPT SUMMARY

When conducting research with human subjects, an ethical researcher

- ensures that participants are fully informed as to the experimental procedure and give their consent before beginning the experiment.
- uses deception only when there is no other way to answer the research question and only when the potential benefit of the experiment far exceeds any risk to the participants.
- ensures that participants feel free to withdraw from the experiment at any time without fear of penalty.
- removes any harmful consequences resulting from the experiment, including long-term consequences.
- maintains confidentiality regarding information about participants acquired during the course of the experiment.

ETHICS IN RESEARCH WITH ANIMALS

Although the majority of research in contemporary psychology focuses on humans, an appreciable number of studies focus on animals (Miller, 1985).

APPLICATION

Ethical Research Projects

Imagine you direct an ethics review board, and you must decide whether to allow the following examples of proposed research:

1. An environmental psychologist sits in a crowded library and keeps detailed records of seating patterns.

2. An environmental psychologist takes videotapes of seating patterns in a library. These tapes are maintained indefinitely, and library patrons do not know they have been filmed.

3. An experimental psychologist tells students that she is interested in their reading comprehension when in reality she is recording the speed of their responses rather than their comprehension.

4. A social psychologist is studying bystander intervention in a liquor store. Permission has been obtained from the store manager. In clear view of a patron, an experimenter ''steals'' a bottle of liquor. A second experimenter approaches the patron and asks, ''Did you see him steal that bottle?''

5. A social psychologist connects surface electrodes to male participants, with their prior approval. These subjects are told that the electrodes are connected to a meter in front

Animals are often used to answer questions that would be impossible or impractical to answer by using human beings. Some people believe, however, that animals should not be used in various kinds of research (Bowd, 1980). For example, Rollin (1985) argued that if the concept of legal and moral rights can be applied to human research, it can also be applied in the same way to animal research. He suggested that the status of research with animals needs elevation to that of human subjects, with many of the same rules that govern human research applied to animals. Recently, reports in the media have discussed the purported mistreatment of laboratory animals and the attempts of animal-rights advocates to limit the use of animals in research. Therefore, a consideration of why animals are used in research is important, and an understanding of the ethical safeguards for animals is necessary.

Animals are also the subjects of research because they are interesting and because they form an important part of the natural world. The number of bird-watchers, amateur naturalists, and comparative psychologists and of them that measures sexual arousal. In reality, the meter is controlled by the experimenter. Participants are then shown slides of nude males and females. The meter gives high readings for pictures of males, leading the participants to believe they have latent homosexual tendencies.

People do not agree about which of these examples constitutes ethical or unethical research, and we will not presume to give you definitive answers. Informal discussion with our colleagues reveals that only the first example received unequivocal clearance as an ethical project. Because the psychologist merely observed strangers, informed consent did not seem necessary. Any individual, psychologist or not, could easily observe these same people in the library. Our colleagues rated the potential harm as extremely small.

Some people raised objections to every other example. Number 2 invaded personal privacy, because the tapes were not erased after data analysis. Most colleagues accepted number 3 only if the experimenter carefully debriefed participants by explaining the nature and reasons for the deception. Example number 4 describes an actual project, in which a patron denied seeing the theft and then called the police as soon as she left the store. The investigator had to go to the police station and bail out the experimenters. Number 5 describes another real experiment, and our colleagues did not think it was ethical, even with debriefing. Even immediate, extensive debriefing probably could not remove the potential psychological harm of making a participant believe that he had hidden homosexual tendencies. Devising an ethical research project can be difficult.

ethologists readily attest to the interest. More important in terms of ethical concerns, however, is that animals serve as convenient, highly controlled models for humans *and* other animals.

Arguments against Research with Animals

Ethics prohibit experimentally induced brain damage in human beings, preclude deliberate separation of a human infant from its parents, forbid testing of unknown drugs on human beings, and generally exclude dangerous and irreversible manipulations on human beings. Animal-rights advocates believe that research on animals should have the same prohibitions. According to the animal-rights advocates, researchers need to uphold the rights of both human beings and animals because, for example, they believe that experimental destruction of a monkey's brain is as ethically reprehensible as the destruction of the brain of a human being. Three points summarize the animal-rights advocates' position: (1) animals feel pain and their lives can be destroyed, as is true of humans (Roberts, 1971); (2) destroying or harming any living thing is dehumanizing to the human scientist (Roberts, 1971); and (3) claims about scientific progress being helped by animal research are a form of racism and, like interracial bigotry, are completely unwarranted and unethical. Neglecting the rights and interests of other species has been called **speciesism** by Singer (1978). Most experimental psychologists, especially psychobiologists, have strong reservations about the validity of these points. Let us consider each in turn.

Arguments for Research with Animals

The first point is that animals feel pain and suffering. Certainly, this is true, but ethical standards exist in all scientific disciplines that use animals as research subjects. A major portion of these principles concerns the proscription of undue pain and inhumane treatment. No ethical psychologist would deliberately mistreat research animals, nor would an ethical psychologist deliberately inflict undue harm on an animal. When pain and suffering are inflicted on an animal, it is only after considerable deliberation by the scientist and the appropriate ethics review boards. Such deliberations weigh the suffering of the animal against the potential benefits of the experiment. Only when the benefits far exceed the harm is the experiment approved and conducted. Finally, an important point to make about behavioral research on animals is that much of it does not involve pain or physical harm to the animals being studied.

The second plank of the animals-rights platform is that the destruction of any living thing is dehumanizing to the human scientist. Presumably, plants are not meant to be included here, for as human beings, we must destroy plants, if not animals, to survive. Even if this proscription against killing living things is limited to animals, it has a number of serious implications beyond eliminating animal research. If one uses this argument against animal research, then one should not eat meat of any kind. Likewise, one should not use any products derived from the destruction of animals (e.g., leather). Finally, if the destruction of animals is dehumanizing, then is it not also dehumanizing to benefit from the destruction of animals? If so, then a true believer in animal rights should forsake most of the wonders of modern medicine because virtually all of it benefited from animal research. However, consistent adherence to a belief in animal rights is often difficult. Plous (1991) illustrated the difficulty in a survey of activists who attended a large rally in support of animal rights. Plous reports that a substantially higher percentage of activists claim to be vegetarians or vegans (people who eat no animal products, including milk and eggs) than do people in general. Many activists say they do not use leather goods. Nevertheless, a majority of animal-rights activists (53 percent) report they buy leather goods, ingest animal flesh, or both.

Finally, there is the charge that scientific progress at the expense of animals is simply speciesism, the belief that the sacrifice of members of other species is justified if our species is benefited. As a criticism against animal research, this argument ignores the fact that a significant amount of animal research benefits the welfare of animals. For example, Miller (1985) points out that research on learned taste aversion in rats has led to new, nonlethal means of keeping coyotes away from sheep and crows away from crops. Similarly, research on how hatchling ducks imprint on human care-takers has been used to better prepare artificially incubated condor chicks for the wild.

In any case, even if using animals for the benefit of human beings is a form of speciesism, it is doubtful that many people would give up the benefits already achieved or even give up the possible future benefits to be derived from animal research. Consider this quote from Robert J. White, an eminent neuroscientist and neurosurgeon, who conducted research on monkeys that involved removing the brain of the animal: "As I write this article, I relive my vivid experiences yesterday when I removed at operation a large tumor from the cerebellum and brain stem of a small child. This was a surgical undertaking that would have been impossible a few decades ago, highly dangerous a few years ago, but is today thanks to extensive experimentation on the brains of lower animals, routinely accomplished with a high degree of safety" (1971, p. 504).

In addition to the benefits of experimental neurosurgery, numerous benefits are derived from behavioral research with animals. Miller (1985) notes that psychological experiments with animals have led directly to benefits in the treatment of such diverse psychological problems as bedwetting, phobias, compulsive disorders such as anorexia nervosa, and depression. Moreover, animal experiments have given rise to behavioral technologies such as biofeedback that have been used to help individuals with neuro-muscular disorders regain control over their bodies. Psychological research with animals has also demonstrated experimentally the link between psychological stress and physical health. Other studies have demonstrated that the detrimental effects of physically separating an infant from its parents—as is necessary when a newborn must be placed in an incubator to sustain its life—can be largely reversed simply by stroking the infant during three 15-minute periods during the day. Miller describes a variety of other benefits that have arisen from behavioral research on animals, his point being that the benefits of psychological experimentation on animals are substantial, contrary to the claims made by some animal-rights activists (Plous, 1991).

Gallup and Suarez (1985) reviewed the rationale, extent, and use of animals in psychological research. They considered the possible alternatives and concluded that in many cases, there is no viable alternative to the use of animals in psychological research.

Guidelines for the Use of Animals in Research

Psychologists have focused on the humane and ethical treatment of animals used in research for a long time (Greenough, 1992). For example, one early statement of humane treatment (Young, 1928) asserted that animals used as research subjects "... shall be kindly treated, properly fed, and their surroundings kept in the best possible sanitary condition" (p. 487). This concern is echoed in the modern guidelines of APA (1981a) governing research with animals, which state as a general principle that

> An investigator of animal behavior strives to advance understanding of basic behavioral principles and/or to contribute to the improvement of human health and welfare. In seeking these ends, the investigator ensures the welfare of

animals and treats them humanely. Laws and regulations notwithstanding, an animal's immediate protection depends upon the scientist's own conscience.

As in virtually any human enterprise, abuses of humane treatment sometimes occur in the use of animals in research. However, these abuses go against the standard practice of animal researchers. Ethical researchers treat animals humanely. When people uncover unethical treatment of animals, they should seek to punish the researchers in question. Just because some abuses occur, it does not follow that all animal research should be prohibited. The typical view of animal-rights activists (Plous, 1991) derives from a philosophical position that prohibits the use of animals for human benefit as a general rule, not just for research. You must decide for yourself what attitude to take toward animal research, but the importance of the issue necessitates that you critically consider each side of the debate and its implications.

The five primary considerations for researchers using animal subjects are listed below.

1. The acquisition, care, use, and disposal of all animals are in compliance with current federal, state or provincial, and local laws and regulations.

2. A psychologist trained in research methods and experienced in the care of laboratory animals closely supervises all procedures involving animals and is responsible for ensuring appropriate consideration of their comfort, health, and humane treatment.

3. Psychologists ensure that all individuals using animals under their supervision have received explicit instruction in experimental methods and in the care, maintenance, and handling of the species being used. Responsibilities and activities of individuals participating in a research project are consistent with their respective competencies.

4. Psychologists make every effort to minimize discomfort, illness, and pain of animals. A procedure subjecting animals to pain, stress, or privation is used only when an alternative procedure is unavailable and the goal is justified by its prospective scientific, educational, or applied value. Surgical procedures are performed under appropriate anesthesia; techniques to avoid infection and minimize pain are followed during and after surgery.

5. When it is appropriate that the animal's life be terminated, it is done rapidly and painlessly.

The above guidelines were designed for experienced researchers. The APA (1981b) has also provided guidelines for the student researcher, which follow.

■   ■   ■

Guidelines for the Use of Animals in School Science Behavior Projects

1. In the selection of science behavior projects, students should be urged

to select animals that are small and easy to maintain as subjects for research.

2. All projects *must* be preplanned and conducted with humane considerations and respect for animal life. Projects intended for science fair exhibition must comply with these guidelines as well as with additional requirements of the sponsor.

3. Each student undertaking a school science project using animals *must have a qualified supervisor.* Such a supervisor shall be a person who has had training and experience in the proper care of the species and the research techniques to be used in the project. The supervisor *must* assume the primary responsibility for all conditions of the project and must ensure that the student is trained in the care and handling of the animals as well as in the methods to be used.

4. The student shall do relevant reading about previous work in the area. The student's specific purpose, plan of action, justification of the methodology, and anticipated outcome for the science project shall be submitted to and approved by a qualified person. Teachers shall maintain these on file for future reference.

5. No student shall inflict pain, severe deprivation, or high stress levels or use invasive procedures such as surgery, the administration of drugs, ionizing radiation, or toxic agents *unless* facilities are suitable both for the study and for the care and housing of the animals and *unless* the research is carried out under the extremely close and rigorous supervision of a person with training in the specific area of study. These projects must be conducted in accordance with the APA *Principles for the Care and Use of Animals.*

6. Students, teachers, and supervisors *must* be cognizant of current federal and state legislation and guidelines for specific care and handling of their animals (e.g., the Animal Welfare Act). Copies of humane laws are available from local or national humane organizations. A recommended reference is the *Guide for the Care and Use of Laboratory Animals,* available from the Superintendent of Documents, U.S. Government Printing Office, Washington, D.C. 20402, Stock Number 017-040-00427-3.

7. The basic daily needs of each animal shall be of prime concern. Students *must* ensure the proper housing, food, water, exercise, cleanliness, and gentle handling of their animals. Special arrangements *must* be made for care during weekends, holidays, and vacations. Students must protect their animals from sources of disturbance or harm, including teasing by other students.

8. When the research project has been completed, the supervisor is responsible for proper disposition of the animals. If it is appropriate that the animal's life be terminated, it shall be rapid and painless. *Under no circumstances should students be allowed to experiment with such procedures.*

9. Teachers and students are encouraged to consult with the Committee on Animal Research and Experimentation of the American Psychological Association for advice on adherence to the guidelines. In cases where facilities for advanced research by qualified students are not available, the Committee on Animal Research and Experimentation will try to make suitable arrangements for the students.

10. A copy of these guidelines shall be posted conspicuously wherever

animals are kept and projects carried out, including displays at science fairs.

■   ■   ■

Both sets of guidelines emphasize decent care and treatment. Both also mention additional regulations. Before using animal subjects, you should understand the contents of both sets of guidelines, and you should become familiar with relevant state and local humane regulations. *An ethical psychologist does not mistreat animal subjects, nor does an ethical psychologist submit animal subjects to undue pain or harm.*

CONCEPT SUMMARY

When deciding whether to engage in research with animals, you should consider

- whether you accept the proposal that animals deserve to be treated as equivalent to humans and the full implications of this philosophical position.

When conducting research with animal subjects, an ethical researcher

- ensures that the research is supervised by a trained psychologist.
- subjects animals to pain or discomfort only when no alternative procedure is available and the knowledge to be gained justifies the suffering of the animal.
- makes every effort to minimize any pain or discomfort associated with the experiment.

ETHICS IN DRUG RESEARCH

The APA guidelines for the use of drugs in research involving both humans and animals are printed below. We want to discourage most undergraduate research on drugs, especially projects using human beings. Special government permits are required for research with controlled substances (including marijuana), and most student projects neglect to include appropriate **aftercare** for their human participants. You are responsible for accidents, antisocial behavior, and worse yet, addiction that could result from an experimentally induced high. If you are compelled to engage in drug research, use animals as your subjects and use legal substances. Be sure also that you understand the following rules as well as the other legal documents that are mentioned therein.

■ ■ ■

APA Guidelines for Psychologists on the Use of Drugs in Research

General Principle: A psychologist or psychology student who performs research involving the use of drugs shall have adequate knowledge and experience of each drug's action or shall work in collaboration with or under the supervision of a qualified researcher. Any psychologist or psychology student doing research with drugs must comply with the procedural guidelines below. Any supervisor or collaborator has the responsibility to see that the individual he supervises or collaborates with complies with the procedural guidelines.

Definition of a Qualified Researcher

1. A qualified researcher possesses a Ph.D. degree based in part upon a dissertation that is experimental in nature and in part upon training in psychology, pharmacology, physiology, and related areas, and that is conferred by a graduate school of recognized standing (listed by the United States Office of Education as having been accredited by a recognized regional or national accrediting organization).
2. A qualified researcher has demonstrated competence as defined by research involving the use of drugs which has been published in scientific journals; or continuing education; or equivalent experience ensuring that the researcher has adequate knowledge of the drugs, their actions, and of experimental design.

Definition of a Drug

In these Guidelines, the term drug includes (a) all substances as defined by the term drug in the ``Federal Food, Drug, and Cosmetic Act'' (21 USC 321) and (b) all substances, Schedules I-V, as listed in the ``Comprehensive Drug Abuse Prevention and Control Act of 1970'' (21 USC 812; PL 91-513, Sec. 202) in its present form or as amended (Federal Food, Drug, and Cosmetic Act, 21 USC, Sec. 201 (g), Appendix A). Copies of these acts are available from the Superintendent of Documents, United States Government Printing Office, Washington, D.C. 20402.

Procedural Guidelines

1. All drugs must be legally obtained and used under conditions specified by state and federal laws. Information concerning these laws should be obtained from federal or state authorities.
2. Proper precautions must be taken so that drugs and drug paraphernalia that are potentially harmful are available only to authorized personnel. All such drugs used in experiments should be kept in locked cabinets and under any additional security prescribed by law.
3. All individuals using or supervising the use of drugs in research must be familiar with PL 91-513, the ``Comprehensive Drug Abuse Prevention and Control Act of 1970,'' and its implementing regulations as well as all amendments to the act and other drug laws relevant to their research.
4. The use of drugs must be justified scientifically.

5. All individuals using or supervising the use of drugs in research must familiarize themselves with available information concerning the mode of action, toxicity, and methods of administration of the drugs they are using.
6. In any experiment involving animals, the welfare of the animal should be considered as specified in APA's ``Precautions and Standards for the Care and Use of Animals.''
7. Research involving human subjects is governed by additional guidelines as set forth in APA's ``Ethical Standards for Psychological Research.''
8. The present Guidelines should be brought to the attention of all individuals conducting research with drugs.
9. The present Guidelines should be posted conspicuously in every laboratory in which psychologists use drugs.

Source: American Psychological Association Ad Hoc Committee on Guidelines for the Use of Drugs and Other Chemical Agents in Research. From *American Psychologist* Vol. 27, 1972. Copyright 1972 by the American Psychological Association. Reprinted by permission of the publisher.

■ ■ ■

SCIENTIFIC FRAUD

In Chapter 1 we discussed inadvertent researcher bias. Here, in the context of ethics, we consider deliberate bias by scientists—**fraud.** When scientists engage in research, they expend substantial time and effort, and their prestige and career advancement often depend on the success of their research. Under these pressures, some scientists are not completely honest in their treatment of their experiments and their data. Instances of deliberate falsification can range from "fudging" or "cooking" data—results are manipulated so as to make them look better—to "forging" data—observations are reported that were never in fact made (Kohn, 1986).

A frequently cited example of fudging is the case of Sir Cyril Burt. He was a well-respected psychologist who studied the role of heredity in intelligence. He published several papers reporting data collected on identical twins, some reared together, others reared apart. The data were collected in the period 1913–1932. In three papers, he reported a correlation in IQ scores of .944 for twins reared together and of .771 for twins reared apart. Although the correlations were identical for the three papers, each reported an appreciably different number of subjects. That the correlations remained unchanged despite the addition of new subjects is extremely improbable. This evidence, along with other suspicious facts, led some scientists and historians to conclude that Burt's data were not completely honest (Kohn, 1986; Broad and Wade, 1982).

There are a number of examples of forging data. A famous case is that of the "Piltdown Man" discovered in England in 1912. The Piltdown Man consisted of a skull of humanoid appearance and an apelike jawbone. The bones supposedly represented the "missing link" between apes and humans. The finding was widely, although not universally, accepted for fifty-seven years until suspicious scientists used a variety of dating methods to show that the jaw was of modern origin whereas the skull was substantially older. The scientists discovered that the jaw identical to that of an orangutan. Piltdown Man was a hoax, and although there are a number of theories as to who perpetrated the fraud, the evidence is inconclusive.

Deliberate researcher bias can be more subtle than forging or even fudging data. A researcher can choose not to report results that are incompatible with a personal theory or even with his or her political or social beliefs. Similarly, a biased scientist may design projects such that negative or ideologically bad results are unlikely.

How do we detect fraud? Science is self-correcting. The truth will win out. When an important finding is published, the scientific community takes it seriously and pursues the implications of the reported data. When other scientists try to repeat the fraudulent experiment, they will fail to get the reported results, and such failures will eventually lead scientists to conclude that the findings were not real. Thus, the repetition of experiments is important to detecting scientific fraud (Barber, 1976). Direct, specific repetitions are called **replications.** It may take many failed replications and years of effort, however, before the entire scientific community agrees that the fraudulent results should be discarded, a fact that illustrates the serious consequences of scientific fraud.

Most ethical review boards, which are discussed in the next section, monitor the scientific practices that could lead to scientific fraud. Moreover, individuals guarantee federal granting agencies that they have not engaged in fraudulent practices. Upon discovering fraud, the granting agencies suspend the grant and may attempt to recover funds that have been expended. Researchers who are guilty of fraud will not receive additional grants. Thus, institutions and granting agencies also play a role in containing fraud.

CONCEPT SUMMARY

Fraud is discovered by

- replication of research

Fraud is contained by

- institutional boards
- granting agencies

MONITORING ETHICAL PRACTICES

The American Psychological Association provides ethical guidelines for psychological research. Acceptance of membership in the association commits the member to adherence to these principles. The principles are also intended for nonmembers, including students of psychology and others who work on psychological research under the supervision of a psychologist.

The American Psychological Association established an Ethics Committee that fulfills a number of purposes. Through publications, educational meetings, and convention activities, the Ethics Committee educates psychologists and the public about ethical issues related to psychological research. The committee also investigates and adjudicates complaints concerning unethical research practices. Examples of these cases can be found in an APA (1987) publication titled *Casebook on Ethical Issues.* The Ethics Committee also publishes an annual report in *American Psychologist.*

In addition to the ethical guidelines established by APA, any institution that receives money from the federal government—which means virtually every U.S. institution that engages in research—must have an **institutional review board** (IRB) that oversees the protection of human subjects and an institutional animal care and use committee that oversees the protection of animal subjects. All experiments must be approved by the members of these committees. Federal regulations require that each IRB have at least five members who are qualified to review the kind of research typically conducted within the institution. Furthermore, if an IRB regularly reviews research involving vulnerable individuals (e.g., children, prisoners, the mentally disabled), the committee should include at least one member whose area of expertise deals with such individuals. There must be at least one member whose primary concern is in a scientific area and one member whose primary concern is in a nonscientific area. There must also be someone on the committee, usually an attorney, who can ascertain whether proposed research violates any laws or federal regulations. Finally, regulations require that at least one member of the committee be otherwise free from affiliation with the institution. This diversity in membership helps to ensure that the rights of individuals participating in research are protected.

How does an IRB make its decision regarding the ethicality of a particular research project? First, it assesses the level of risk involved in the procedure. Many psychological experiments are classified as involving only "minimal risk." Minimal risk means that the experimental procedures involve no greater risk than is associated with daily activities. If greater than minimal risk is deemed necessary for research purposes, then the IRB must decide whether these risks are reasonable in relation to the benefits that would be gained from the research. The IRB also ensures that participants are fully informed prior to the experiment and that their safety and confidentiality are safeguarded.

An acquaintance with the institutional review process should help to reassure you that ethical research in psychology, and in other sciences, is the rule, not the exception. Because of safeguards built into the structure of research institutions, scientists cannot simply rely solely on their own judgment to protect the humans and animals participating in their experiments. Further, the boards help to emphasize honesty in research, which helps to reduce fraudulent practices.

SUMMARY

1. An ethical investigator protects the welfare of research participants by following the ethical standards of the American Psychological Association.

2. Informing the participant about the experiment prior to participation and minimal use of deception on the part of the investigator allow the participant to make a reasoned judgment about whether to participate.

3. The participant has the right to decline to serve in an experiment or to withdraw from an experiment at any time.

4. In an ethical investigation, the participant is protected from physical and mental harm.

5. After the data have been collected, participants should be carefully debriefed to remove any misconceptions that may have arisen.

6. Any harmful consequences resulting from an experiment should be removed by the investigator.

7. Unless the participant otherwise agrees, information relating to his or her participation is confidential.

8. Attempts to uphold ethical principles sometimes lead to a dilemma in that adherence to one principle may violate another.

9. When animal subjects are used, care should be taken to minimize their pain and discomfort.

10. Research with drugs poses special welfare problems, especially those involving the aftercare of participants.

11. Ethical scientists are honest. They do not engage in activities that misrepresent the conduct and outcome of research.

12. Scientific fraud can be detected by replications of research, and it is monitored by institutional boards and granting agencies.

13. Institutional review boards help monitor ethical practices in research and ensure the ethical treatment of participants.

■ KEY CONCEPTS

aftercare
confidentiality
debriefing
deception
fraud
freedom to withdraw
informed consent

institutional review board
protection from harm
removing harmful consequences
replication
speciesism

■ EXERCISES

Reconsider the ethical principles presented in this chapter and read the list of ethical principles published by American Psychologist Association (1981a, 1981b, 1987).

1. Read selections from the *Casebook on Ethical Issues* published by the American Psychological Association (1987), which is probably available in your library. This book describes the background of different ethical complaints, how the complaints came to be sent to the Ethics Committee, and how the cases were adjudicated. Select two cases and consider the ethical principles involved in the case. Describe why you agree or disagree with the adjudication of the Ethics Committee.

2. Read two of the articles listed below. These articles describe the ethical issues associated with different types of psychological research. Consider the general ethical principles that apply in both cases. Describe how the ethical issues differ between the two types of research discussed in the articles.

■ SUGGESTED READINGS

Bowd, A. D. (1980). Ethical reservations about psychological research with animals. *Psychological Record, 30,* 201–210.

Devenport, L. D., & Devenport, J. A. (1990). The laboratory animal dilemma: A solution in our backyards. *Psychological Science, 1,* 215–216.

Hoff, C. (1980). Immoral and moral uses of animals. *New England Journal of Medicine, 302,* 115–118.

Imber, S. D., Glanz, L. M., Elkin, I., Sotsky, S. M., Boyer, J. L., & Leber, W. R. (1986). Ethical issues in psychotherapy research: Problems in a collaborative clinical study. *American Psychologist, 41,* 137–146.

Melton, G., & Gray, J. (1988). Ethical dilemmas in AIDS research: Individual privacy and public health. *American Psychologist, 43,* 60–64.

Milgram, S. (1977). Ethical issues in the study of obedience. In S. Milgram (Ed.), *The individual in a social world* (pp. 188–199). Reading, MA: Addison-Wesley.

Miller, N. E. (1985). The value of behavioral research on animals. *American Psychologist, 40,* 423–440.

Scarr, S. (1988). Race and gender as psychological variables: Social and ethical issues. *American Psychologist, 43,* 56–59.

Sieber, J. E., & Stanley, B. (1988). Ethical and professional dimensions of socially sensitive research. *American Psychologist, 43,* 49–55.

Smith, C. P. (1983). Ethical issues: Research on deception, informed consent, and debriefing. In L. Wheeler & P. Shaver (Eds.), *Review of personality and social psychology* (Vol. 4, pp. 297–328). Beverly Hills, CA: Sage.

HOW TO CONDUCT A LITERATURE REVIEW

Use . . .

❑ Psychological Abstracts

❑ Social Science Citation Index

❑ PSYCLit

HOW TO READ RESEARCH REPORTS

What to Look for in the . . .

❑ Abstract: What was done to whom, and what was found

❑ Introduction: What the author proposes; the hypotheses tested

❑ Method: Dependent, independent, subject, and control variables; does the method test the hypothesis?

❑ Results: Do the results support or reject the hypothesis?

❑ Discussion: What conclusions are stated?

❑ References: Other reports you might read: Are citations complete?

CHAPTER 4

EXPLORING THE LITERATURE OF PSYCHOLOGY

Suppose you developed an interest in the Stroop effect after participating in the demonstration at the end of chapter 1. You have developed a testable hypothesis about reading based on this demonstration experiment. Because the experiment showed that it is difficult not to read words, you reasoned that the conflict might disappear if reading were made difficult, say, by printing the materials upside down. Your hypothesis is: The time required to read lists with a conflict between the number of digits and their name will be less if the digits are presented upside down rather than right-side up. However, when you have a research idea, it is always possible that someone else has had the same idea and already has done the experiment that you are considering. For this reason, you should do a literature search before running the experiment. A literature search will allow you to discover (a) whether the experiment has been done and (b) any ``tricks of the trade'' that might help you in designing your own experiment.

How to do a Literature Search

If you are unsure about what resources you should examine to help you refine your research ideas, you can refer to Table 4–1 (p. 80) to help you along. The table lists several general sources of information as well as journals with particular topical emphases. Perhaps the most important general resource is **Psychological Abstracts,** which contains brief abstracts of articles from almost all journals that publish psychological research. More will be said about abstracts later in the chapter, but typically they are short (150 words or less) summaries of the experiments in the article. After you have found an abstract of interest there, you can then find the entire article in your library or send a note to the author requesting a reprint of the article or additional information. The other resources listed in Table 4–1 have a variety of purposes, and we recommend that you familiarize yourself with each of the first seven general-purpose resources and as many of the research journals as seem to be of interest to you. We have included only a small number of research journals in the table, but the ones we have included are among the most widely read in psychological research. Others emphasizing education, clinical problems, sociology, law, and industrial concerns can be ferreted out of your school's library.

Many libraries have a **computerized literature search** available. You provide the topic, and the computer scans standard abstracting sources (such as the *Psychological Abstracts*) as well as government documents and technical reports that often are not abstracted. Computer searches can be quick and thorough, but they also can be expensive. However, a computer search is much less costly than the value of time needed to accomplish the same search manually. It is possible for one hour of computer-search time to yield the same number of useful references as three to five days of intensive manual searching. Furthermore, some databases (such as Knowledge Index) have special low rates on nights and weekends that allow even students on tight budgets to afford computer services.

An excellent method for discovering new findings uses the **Social Science Citation Index,** which can be searched either by computer or manually. By entering a critical or key reference, you can obtain a list of more recent articles that have cited your critical reference. Because these articles contain a discussion of your key reference, it is very likely that they are directly related to your topic of interest. This is an extremely efficient way to bring yourself up to date in some specific content area. For an example of a literature search, see the Psychology in Action section at the end of this chapter.

Once you have done your literature search and obtained the articles relevant to your research interest, the next step is to read the articles.

Trying to read a psychology journal article for the first time can be a challenging experience. Researchers write articles for other researchers, so they use jargon and a terse writing style. These features aid communication among scholars in a particular field, because they can read short reports and understand them. But such writing can be difficult to comprehend for students beginning their study of a field. The following section is designed to prepare you for your first encounter with the literature of experimental psychology. Because psychology is a science, progress is measured by the cumulation of knowledge in the various fields. Researchers spend a great deal of their time reading and writing journal articles in an effort to contribute to this cumulation of knowledge. Even if your career in psychology extends no further than this course, you will discover that critical thinking and writing skills are invaluable for living in a world that revolves around information. To help you become fluent in the art of reading research reports, we will describe the format and style most often used in journal articles. Then, hints will be provided to help you become a critical reader, skilled at objectively evaluating an article. With some practice, you will be able to read psychology articles with relative ease.

THE PARTS OF AN ARTICLE

The basic psychology article consists of seven parts: title and author(s), abstract, introduction, method, results, discussion, and references. Each part has an important function and is a necessary component of the article.

Title and Author(s)

The **title** gives you an idea of the contents of an article. Because titles must be short, the most common type of title states only the dependent and independent variables—for example, ''Rate of bar pressing as a function of quality and quantity of food reward.'' Although this title is not particularly appealing, it conveys important information. The title and author(s) of each article typically occupy a prominent place in a given journal issue, such as the inside front cover, back cover, or first page.

As you continue to gain knowledge in a particular content area, you will become familiar with many researchers. You may start to pay attention to the authors first and then look at the titles. After you have read several articles published by the same **author,** you will grow in understanding of that writer's viewpoints and how they differ from those of other researchers.

So many psychology articles are published each month that no one has the time to read all of them. The table of contents is a first step to selecting those articles relevant to your own interests. But an even better decision can be made by consulting the abstract and the references of an article.

Abstract

The **abstract** is a short paragraph (100 to 150 words) that summarizes the key points of an article. According to the *Publication Manual of the American Psychological Association* (1994), it should be ''. . . dense with information but also readable, well organized, brief, and self-contained'' (p. 8). The abstract is the best way to discover quickly what an article is about. A well-written journal abstract will convey the problem under investigation, the

TABLE 4–1
Some Important Resources for Psychological Research

TOPIC AREA	TITLE OF RESOURCE	COMMENT
Article titles	*Current Contents*	Several specialty areas
Author citations	*Social Science Citation Index*	
Article abstracts	*Science Citation Index*	
	Biological Abstracts	
	Ergonomics Abstracts	
	Index Medicus	
	Psychological Abstracts	
Review articles	*American Psychologist*	
	Annual Review of Psychology	Book with chapter-length reviews
	Psychological Bulletin	
	Psychological Review	Often contains original studies
	Psychological Science	Contains research articles, too
	Psychonomic Bulletin & Review	
Empirical articles	*American Journal of Psychology*	Contains research articles, too.
	Animal Learning and Behavior	Some field studies
	Behavior Therapy	
	Behavioral Neuroscience	
	Canadian Journal of Experimental Psychology	
	Child Development	
	Cognitive Psychology	
	Cognitive Science	
	Developmental Psychology	
	Developmental Psychobiology	
	Journal of Abnormal Psychology	
	Journal of Applied Behavioral Analysis	
	Journal of Applied Psychology	
	Journal of Comparative Psychology	
	Journal of Educational Psychology	
	Journal of Experimental Child Psychology	Some field studies
	Journal of Experimental Psychology: Animal Behavior Processes	
	Journal of Experimental Psychology: General	

TABLE 4-1		
Some Important Resources for Psychological Research- *Continued*		
TOPIC AREA	**TITLE OF RESOURCE**	**COMMENT**
	Journal of Experimental Psychology: Learning, Memory, and Cognition	
	Journal of Experimental Psychology: Human Perception & Performance	
	Journal of Experimental Social Psychology	
	Journal of the Experimental Analysis of Behavior	Small-*n* experiments
	Journal of Memory and Language	
	Journal of Personality and Social Psychology	
	Learning and Motivation	
	Memory & Cognition	
	Neuropsychology	
	Perception & Psychophysics	
	Psychobiology	
	Quarterly Journal of Experimental Psychology	
Various research methods	*Behavior Research Methods, Instrumentation and Computers*	Notes on apparatus and computers
	Psychological Methods	

procedure used to explore the problem, the results, the conclusions, and the implications or applications of the research findings. This information provided in brief allows you to discover quickly if a particular article warrants further reading. As you gain experience and become familiar with authors in the field, you will want to consult the references as well before making this decision.

Introduction

The **introduction** specifies the problem to be studied and tells why it is important. The author also reviews the relevant research literature on the topic. A good introduction also specifies the hypotheses to be tested and gives the rationale behind the predictions.

Method

The **method** section describes in detail the operations performed by the experimenter. It is usually printed in smaller type to conserve space, but this does not mean it is an unimportant part of the article to be quickly skimmed. The method section should contain enough information that another experimenter could replicate the study.

It is customary to divide the method section into subsections that cover subjects, apparatus or materials, and procedure. The **subject** section tells how many subjects there were, how they were selected (randomly, haphazardly, only the investigator's relatives, etc.) and who they were (college undergraduates taking introductory psychology, paid volunteers obtained by an ad in a newspaper, a particular strain of rats purchased from a supply house). The **apparatus** section describes any equipment used to test the subjects. This section might include such details as the model number of a computer or the size of a conditioning chamber. This section is referred to as the **materials** section when questionnaires, written or videotaped sketches, and other similar means are used to test subjects. If they are long, special materials may be placed in an appendix section, usually set in smaller type. The **procedure** section explains what happened to the subjects and includes instructions (for human subjects), statistical design features, and so forth.

Results

The **results** section tells what happened in the experiment. It is unusual to find raw data or individual subjects' scores reported in a journal article; instead, descriptive statistics are presented that summarize the data. Inferential statistics present the probability of whether the observed differences between the various experimental conditions have been produced by random, or chance, factors. This information helps both the researcher and the reader determine how confident to be that the independent variable(s) produced a change in the dependent variable. (See Appendixes A and B for further explanation and review.) Both kinds of statistics are important and help psychologists understand the outcome of an experiment.

Either tables or graphs may be used to describe and summarize data. In the typical **table**, such as Table 4–2, data and summarized data appear under various headings. These data are taken from an experiment designed to determined whether instructions given to subjects during a recognition test influence their test performance (Roediger & McDermott, 1994). Based on research in the animal-learning literature, the authors hypothesized that when given pairs of items to choose from (*chair phone*), in which one item

---

TABLE 4–2
Proportion of Items Correctly Recognized as a Function of Study and Test Orientation

	TEST ORIENTATION	
Study	Old	New
Shallow	.77	.80
Deep	.85	.94

had appeared earlier in the study phase and one had not, people would be more accurate at choosing the "new" item (i.e., the one they had not studied) than choosing the "old" item even though in both cases the underlying task is to discriminate the studied from nonstudied item. Additionally, these researchers manipulated the level of processing at study; for some items subjects answered questions pertaining to the semantic nature of items (e.g., how pleasant is this item?), and for others they answered questions regarding the structural aspects of words (e.g., how many letters in the word?) Before you look at the data, you should first read the title of the table (the title generally appears immediately under or next to the words Table n, where n refers to the number of the table). The title of the table should be explicit enough to tell you what sorts of data appear in the table. The title of Table 4–2 tells you that it contains information about recognition performance as a function of study and test conditions. Next, you should examine the headings and subheadings carefully. These will tell you about the conditions or variables that are relevant to the data in the table. For example, in Table 4–2 the headings include study and test orientation. So, you should look for data that show the proportion correct in each of the four conditions. We see from these data that subjects are generally better at picking "new" items ($M = .87$) than "old" items ($M = .81$). Additionally, these researchers replicated a finding that has been well documented in the memory literature: items encoded with respect to meaning are better remembered than those encoded with respect to their surface features (*the levels of processing effect*; Craik & Lockhart, 1972). Finally, you should note that the effect of test orientation is greater at the deep level of processing (.09) than the shallow level (.03). This phenomenon is called an *interaction* and is an important aspect of experimental data. Later in the text, we will spend a considerable amount of time discussing interactions.

You have not encountered any **figures** containing data in this chapter. Some data are shown in Figure 4–1. These are the results of an experiment conducted in one of our classes. The experiment concerned conflict resolution, which was tested by having the students read through a series of questions that asked them to choose between two personal characteristics. The characteristics the students chose from were wealth, health, happiness, intelligence, popularity, talent, and attractiveness. Each characteristic was paired with each other one, and the students read through two series of 21 questions. One series had questions such as "Which would you rather be, more healthy or more wealthy than you are now?" The other series of questions substituted the word *less* for the word *more* (that is, less healthy or less wealthy). The conflict questions containing the word *more* are called approach-approach conflicts, and the conflict questions with the word *less* in them are called avoidance-avoidance conflicts. The students had to circle the characteristic in each pair that they either wanted more of or less of, and their time to go through each set of questions was measured. In Figure 4–1, we see the mean resolution time per conflict scaled on the vertical axis in seconds. The vertical axis is called the **ordinate.** On the horizontal axis, which is called the **abscissa,** we have the two types of conflict. Inside the figure are the results of the experiment. Nearly all figures from any type of psychological research have a scale of the dependent variable (what is measured) on the ordinate. In figures from experiments, the independent

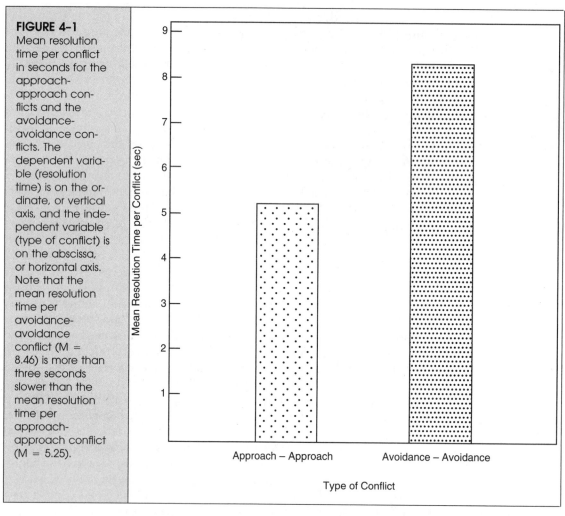

FIGURE 4-1
Mean resolution time per conflict in seconds for the approach-approach conflicts and the avoidance-avoidance conflicts. The dependent variable (resolution time) is on the ordinate, or vertical axis, and the independent variable (type of conflict) is on the abscissa, or horizontal axis. Note that the mean resolution time per avoidance-avoidance conflict (M = 8.46) is more than three seconds slower than the mean resolution time per approach-approach conflict (M = 5.25).

variable (what is manipulated) is on the abscissa. In correlational research, another dependent variable is on the abscissa. Be sure to examine the labels on the ordinate and abscissa so you know what data are plotted in the figure; then you can examine the data. In figure 4–1 the heights of the bars tell you the mean resolution time per condition, and you can see that it took the students about three seconds longer on average to resolve avoidance-avoidance conflicts than it did to resolve approach-approach conflicts.

Figure 4–1 is a bar graph, and data from an experiment are plotted as bars when the levels of the independent variable are defined at the nominal level. (That is, the conditions are qualitatively different and have different names, but cannot be ordered on a quantitative dimension). A different way to plot data is shown in Figure 4–2. There the data appear as points (circles or triangles) connected by lines (solid or broken). Curves such as these are drawn when the independent variable is measured on a scale other than a nominal scale, one in which an ordering of the measures is possible. In Figure 4–2, the abscissa represents the number of steps apart in desirability that two personal traits were for a subject. In the original experiment, students had to choose between all combinations of seven

FIGURE 4-2
Mean resolution time per conflict (the dependent variable on the ordinate) as a function of the number of steps apart in the desirability of the trait given up in an avoidance-avoidance conflict (the independent variable on the abscissa) for freshmen (triangles with broken lines) and seniors (filled circles and solid lines). Note that the freshmen and seniors do about the same for the first three steps, but that the freshmen have much more difficulty resolving the conflicts for the final three steps. Thus, the two curves diverge (they are not parallel).

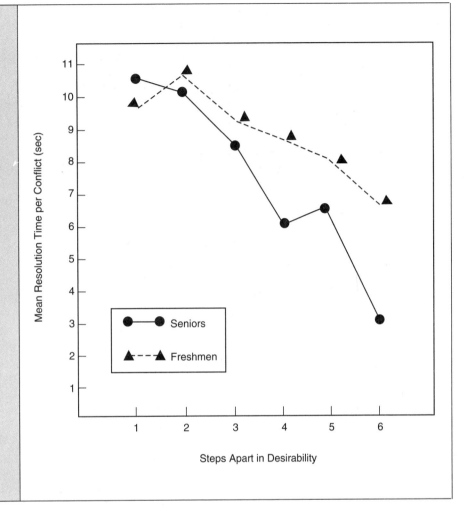

traits: talent, intelligence, wealth, health, happiness, popularity, and attractiveness. The experimenter could have the students rank these traits in importance and then could see if the time to resolve a conflict depended on whether the comparison was between two traits that were close in desirability or between two traits that were very different in desirability. If the traits were ranked in the order in which they are listed here, we might find that the students had more difficulty choosing between less intelligence or less wealth than choosing between less talent and less attractiveness. (As far as we know, precisely that experiment has not been done. The data shown in Figure 4–2 are fictitious.)

The abscissa in Figure 4–2 is at the ordinal level, so the data are plotted as points within the figure. A line graph like this is used when the independent variable is ordered along a dimension. This figure has two sets of points, one for freshmen and one for seniors. It is conventional to use different symbols for different curves within a graph, as is done with circles and triangles in Figure 4–2. It is also conventional to connect data points with straight lines, unless you actually determine the equation for the curve that could pass through those points. After you have examined the ordinate and abscissa, the parameters within the graph (that is, the labels for the different conditions—in this case, freshmen and seniors), and any legend under the figure, you can then study the data. Two aspects of the fictional data in Figure 4–2 are noteworthy. First, freshmen take longer to resolve conflicts than do seniors. Second, freshmen and seniors take about the same amount of time to resolve the difficult conflicts (at steps 1 through 3), but the seniors become progressively faster than the freshmen as they go from step 4 to step 5 to step 6. The second feature means that the curves diverge (they are not parallel) and as mentioned previously, this divergence is called an interaction.

When you are trying to understand the data in a figure, be sure that you pay close attention to the scale of the dependent variable on the ordinate. Sometimes the scale can be misleading: An abbreviated scale with widely spaced numbers will tend to make differences appear more impressive, and a scale with numbers jammed close together will tend to make differences appear smaller. To see how this works, consider the following example.

Suppose that the number of murders in a city increased from 72 to 80 to 91 over three years. The next year, the mayor is running for reelection and is eager to show that the city has been safe for the last three years under her administration. So her campaign workers draw up the graph shown in the left of Figure 4–3. By making the scale on the ordinate very long, they create the impression that the murder rate is fairly steady. In the same year, the city police are arguing that they need higher staffing levels. They want to show that the city is becoming more unsafe, so they depict the murder rate as increasing steeply by changing the scale, as in the right-hand graph of Figure 4–3.

The facts are shown accurately in both groups. However, the left graph gives the impression that the murder rate is increasing very gradually, hardly worth worrying about. (Hasn't the mayor done a good job leading the city?) The right graph, on the other hand, creates the impression that the murder rate is increasing dramatically. (Don't we need more police?)

These graphing techniques are common. In fact, there are exaggerated scales used in some of the graphs in this book to show patterns of results more clearly. You should always look carefully to see what the scale is in a graph. With experimental data, it is more important to determine whether a difference is statistically reliable than to determine whether the difference appears "large" when graphed.

There is no fixed rule for setting an appropriate level of significance—.05 (or 5 in 100) as opposed to .001 (or 1 in 1,000) for instance. It is up to the researcher to decide whether the odds are just right, too high, or too low. Depending on the import of your conclusions, you may require more (e.g., .001 or 1 in 1,000) or less certainty (e.g., .10 or 10 in 100) that what happened has not happened by chance.

But which way of graphing the results is right? In a sense, both are, because both can be argued to portray matters accurately. However, if statistical tests have shown a difference to exist between the two measures, then the graph on the right more accurately captures the relation between measures.

FIGURE 4–3
Variation in scales. Exactly the same data are presented in the two panels of Figure 4-3, but the variation in scales on the ordinate causes the graph at the left to seem to show the murder rate to be increasing only slightly, whereas the one at the right seems to show the rate going up dramatically. Yet,
both graphs actually show the murder rate accurately—the difference is in the scale on the y-axis. It is
important to examine a graph carefully and note the scale of measurement, because scale changes
can make small differences look large and vice versa.

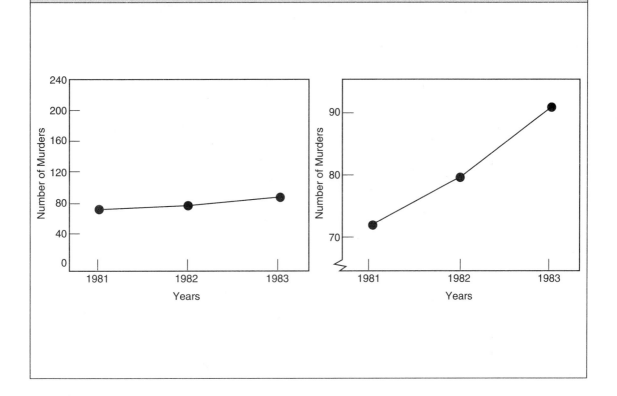

Inferential statistics permit the assessment of whether differences that
appear in the results, as on the right are real and not due to chance factors.
Inferential statistics about the data appear in statements such as
"$F(4,60) = 2.03, p < .05$." All this means is that the odds for obtaining by
chance an F-statistic at least as large as 2.03 would be 5 percent if the
experiment were repeated. That is, if the experiment were conducted 100
times, the results would be similar in at least 95 out of the 100 repetitions.

Imagine the problem of a graduate-student admissions officer who has
been told that resources at the university are extremely limited. It has been
suggested that she discriminate against women in accepting students into
the program, because they are believed to be less likely to finish. She would
like to put such unsubstantiated notions to rest and so commissions a statistical analysis to test this hypothesis. Here, odds of 5 in 100 to reject the
null hypothesis that women are less likely than men to finish are too high,
because the import is so great. A level of significance of 1 in 1,000 would
be more appropriate.

Or take the case of a breakfast-cereal company that wishes to include a "prize" inside the box. It performs a statistical analysis to decide which of five potential prizes, all of which cost the same, is preferred by consumers. If there is any difference among prizes, the company wants to be sure to find the best one. If the firm is wrong and incorrectly selects one, when in fact all are equally attractive, no great harm is done, because each prize costs the same. Here, odds of 5 in 100 are too low. A level of significance of 50 in 100 might be more appropriate. The situation determines what the level of significance should be. Additional discussion of inferential statistics and the level of significance can be found in appendix B.

In the results section, the author's specific choice of words is important. Beware of such statements as this: "Although the data just barely missed reaching the proposed level of significance, it appears that a trend in the predicted direction did occur." This kind of statement should be approached with caution for several reasons. First, the word *trend* is a technical term: existence of a trend can be determined only by an appropriate statistical test. Second, it implies that results that are significant go beyond a trend—that is, they are true and utterly reliable—and that failure to reach a prescribed level only means that "truth" is latent rather than explicit. This implication is false: even significant results are reliable only in a probabilistic sense—for example, 95 times in 100.

Discussion

The **discussion** is the most creative part of an article. Here, an author is permitted to restate what the data show (if he or she so desires) and to draw theoretical conclusions. Most editors have firm standards for both method and results sections, but the author is given greater latitude in the discussion. In the words of the *APA Publication Manual* (1994): "You are free to examine, interpret, and qualify the results, as well as to draw inferences from them" (p. 18). Keep in mind that research results are not incontestable truths and that experimental findings are relative to the context in which they are found. Freedom for the author requires caution from the readers.

References

References are found at the end of the article. In contrast to journals in other disciplines, psychology journals list full titles of referenced articles. This practice helps to tell the reader what the article is about. Furthermore, the references are valuable as a guide for related information. They can also be used as an index of the merit of the article. Articles should refer to the most recently published works in the area, as well as to the most important previous publications. Furthermore, only articles cited in text should be included in the reference section. This is different from a bibliography, which includes as many relevant citations as a feasible.

CHECKLIST FOR THE CRITICAL READER

In this section, we offer some hints that have helped us to become better consumers of the information presented in psychological journals. Our major suggestion is to avoid rushing through an article. Instead, you might deliberately stop after each section and write down the answers to the questions we shall list here. This can be difficult at first, but with practice, this process becomes automatic and requires little extra time.

Introduction

1. *What is the author's goal?* The introduction explains the reasons behind the research and reviews the prior literature on the phenomena of interest. If one or more theories are related to the research, the introduction gives the predictions the theories make. As with scientists in other areas, psychologists do not necessarily agree as to the underlying mechanisms and theoretical interpretations of behavior. The author may present a particular theory that he or she thinks provides a useful explanation of behavior. Although the author may present more than one theory in the introduction, he or she will proceed later on to demonstrate that they do not all help equally to predict and explain the obtained results. Try to figure out which of the several theories the author believes and which are slated for subsequent rejection.

2. *What hypothesis will be tested in the experiment?* The answer to this should be obvious and stated directly within the introduction section.

3. *If I had to design an experiment to test this hypothesis, what would I do?* This is the key question for the introduction. You must try to answer this *before* continuing on to the method section of the article. Many experiments are done within the context of a systematic investigation of behavior to test and support a particular theoretical framework developed by the author. If the author has any skill as a wordsmith, once you have finished the next section, you are likely to agree with the method that the author has advocated in the article. A clever author will plant the seeds to this answer in the introduction itself; this practice makes it harder for you to state a method independently. Write down the major ideas for your method of testing the hypothesis.

Method

Compare your answer to question 3 with that of the author of the article. They probably will differ, if you have not peeked. Now answer questions 4a–c.

4a. *Is my proposed method better than the author's?* Regardless of who has the better method, you or the author, this forced comparison will make you think about the method section critically, instead of passively accepting it.

4b. *Does the author's method actually test the hypothesis?* The hypothesis is sometimes the first casualty, disappearing between the introduction and method sections. Always check that the method used is adequate and relevant to the hypothesis at hand.

4c. *What are the independent, dependent, and control variables?* This is an obvious question and can be answered quickly. Listing the variables helps you avoid passive reading of the method section. After you have resolved differences between your proposed method and the author's, answer the next question.

5. *Using the subjects, apparatus, materials, and procedures described by the author, what results would I predict for this experiment?* You must answer this on your own before reading the results section. To help yourself, review the hypotheses and the independent and dependent variables. You may find it impossible to predict a single outcome. This is not really a problem, since the author probably also had more than one prediction originally. He or she may have done some preliminary investigations to narrow down possible outcomes; alternatively, he or she may have been surprised by the results and had to rethink the introduction once the results were in. Draw a rough sketch illustrating the most likely outcomes you have predicted.

Results

Compare the results with your predictions. If they are the same, go on to questions 7a and 7b. If not, answer question 6.

6. *Did the author get unexpected results?* After some thought, you will reach one of two conclusions: either your prediction was wrong, or the results are hard to believe. Perhaps the method the author selected was inappropriate and did not adequately test the stated hypotheses or introduced sources of uncontrolled variance. Or perhaps these results would not be obtained again if the experiment were repeated. You might even try your own experiment. See if you can replicate the reported results.

7a. *How would I interpret these results?*

7b. *What applications and implications would I draw from my interpretation of the results?* Try to answer this question and question 7a on your own, before reading the discussion.

Discussion

As mentioned earlier, the discussion section includes the author's interpretation of the data in the form of conclusions. A good discussion section brings the reader full circle in that it provides a narrative response to the question posed in the introduction. In addition, the author expands on his or her conclusions by offering insight regarding the applications and implications of the experimental results.

As a critical reader, you have constructed your own interpretation of the results. Compare the merits of your interpretation with the merits of the author's. Which one do you prefer? Answer questions 8a and 8b to help you critically assess yours and the author's interpretation of the results.

8a. *Does my interpretation or the author's best represent the data?* Because authors are allowed more latitude in the discussion section than in other sections of a report, it is possible to find that an author has drawn conclusions that may not be warranted by the data. In other cases, authors draw conclusions that are largely appropriate and then proceed to extend these conclusions beyond what the data can support. The latter situation typically occurs when a researcher fails to recognize the limitations of the dependent variable.

8b. *Do I or does the author offer the most cogent discussion of the applications and implications of the results?* This question is secondary to the question posed in 8a. Nonetheless, you can gain valuable insight regarding the overall integrity of the research by considering this question. A researcher's responsibilities extend beyond that of conducting a tightly controlled experiment; he or she must also consider the rationale and theory that underlie the research. The extent to which an author demonstrates wisdom in identifying applications and implications of the results provides a good indication of the overall integrity of the research.

Checklist Summary

As you are reading your first article carefully, try to write down the answers to all eight questions. It is hard work the first several times, so do not be discouraged. The following is a typical psychological article. It has been analyzed according to the checklist summarized in Table 4–3.

A SAMPLE JOURNAL ARTICLE

In this section, we have reprinted a short article from the *Journal of Applied Psychology* with sample answers to the checklist questions. The article is about an experiment asking whether individuals who are innocent of a crime but have crime-relevant knowledge will appear guilty on a polygraph (lie-detector) test called the Guilty Knowledge Test.

Most articles are written for experts in a particular area, so the authors of a report assume that their readers have some knowledge of the topic under investigation. In addition, most journals set page limitations on articles, which means that some information may be missing or presented very tersely. The assumptions made by the authors and the brevity of many

---

TABLE 4-3
Questions for Critical Readers

Introduction
1. What is the author's goal?
2. What hypothesis will be tested in the experiment?
3. If I had to design an experiment to test this hypothesis, what would I do?

Method
4a. Is my proposed method better than the author's?
4b. Does the author's method actually test the hypothesis?
4c. What are the independent, dependent, and control variables?
5. Using the subjects, apparatus, materials, and procedures described by the author, what results would I predict for this experiment?

Results
6. Did the author get unexpected results?
7a. How would I interpret these results?
7b. What applications and implications would I draw from my interpretation of the results?

Discussion
8a. Does my interpretation or the author's best represent the data?
8b. Do I or does the author offer the most cogent discussion of the applications and implications of the results?

---

articles pose a problem for the novice reader. The novice may have to read other articles or textbooks in order to understand a particular report. To help you understand the following report, we present some background information.

Bradley and Rettinger (1992) were interested in determining whether a revised version of the Guilty Knowledge Test (GKT) could accurately determine the guilt or innocence of suspects who were innocent of a crime but had crime-related knowledge (i.e., innocent-aware suspects). The original GKT was designed simply to reflect suspects' awareness of crime-relevant knowledge. Bradley and Rettinger reasoned that innocent-aware suspects might appear guilty on the original GKT and so decided to revise it to examine suspects' *knowledge plus actions,* rather than mere *knowledge,* related to the crime.

The revised GKT includes crime-relevant questions with several alternatives (e.g., "Did you murder the man in a house? a hotel? a bank? a store?") and crime-irrelevant questions with several alternatives (e.g., "Did you eat lunch in a restaurant? a house? a park? a school?"). The subject is instructed to respond "no" to each alternative for every question. A polygraph examiner measures the subject's skin resistance levels during the GKT. Skin resistance is measured by attaching electrodes to the subject's skin. As general arousal (e.g., anxiety, stress, fear) increases, skin resistance decreases. The assumption for developing the revised GKT was that a subject who is guilty and answers "no" to an action question would experience some level of anxiety or stress (i.e., low skin resistance), whereas an innocent subject with crime-relevant knowledge would not, but would show normal skin resistance. Bradley and Rettinger (1992) manipulated the guilt of student volunteers in a mock crime situation to determine whether their assumption regarding the accuracy of the revised GKT was a valid one.

Bradley and Rettinger (1992) also studied the effects self-monitoring—a subject variable—on the determination of guilt or innocence in the GKT. Self-monitoring is a personality dimension on which individuals differ. Self-monitoring refers to the extent to which an individual monitors his or her environment in order to display appropriate behavior (see Schneider, 1988). "High self-monitors" are very much concerned with behaving in a manner that is appropriate to a given social environment. For this reason, Bradley and Rettinger believed that guilty, high self-monitors would identify and concentrate on crime-relevant questions more readily than would guilty, low self-monitors. This would cause guilty, high self-monitors to experience higher levels of general arousal and facilitate a guilty classification. The researchers had no reason to believe that self-monitoring would result in any differences for innocent subjects. In other words, the effect of guilt was predicted to depend on whether the subject was a high versus low self-monitor.

Bradley and Rettinger's (1992) report is brief. Now that you have some background information, you are ready to approach this article as a critical reader. To help you, we have placed checklist items at various, strategic locations.

■ ■ ■

Awareness of Crime-Relevant Information and the Guilty Knowledge Test

M. T. Bradley and J. Rettinger
Division of Social Science,
University of New Brunswick,
Saint John, New Brunswick, Canada

The effects of awareness of crime-relevant information on the detection of deception with the Guilty Knowledge Test were examined. Student subjects were assigned to 1 of 3 groups: a guilty group, members of which committed a mock crime; an innocent group aware of details about the crime; or an innocent group unaware of such information. After following instructions, subjects were tested on the polygraph with a 10-item Guilty Knowledge Test and were offered $20.00 for an innocent test outcome. Skin resistance response scores of guilty subjects lying about crime-relevant information were higher than the scores of innocent informed subjects, whose scores in turn were higher than those of innocent unaware subjects. This replicated findings of an earlier study in which similar procedures were used and supported the view that subjects aware of crime-relevant information can appear less deceptive than subjects lying about crime-relevant information.

Portions of this study were supported by Grant A7B66 from the Natural Sciences and Engineering Research Council of Canada.
Correspondence concerning this article should be addressed to M. T. Bradley, Division of Social Science, University of New Brunswick, P.O. Box 5050, Saint John, New Brunswick, Canada, E2L4L5.

The purposes of the present study were to replicate earlier findings (Bradley & Warfield, 1984) indicating that innocent subjects with crime-relevant information can be found innocent on a guilty-knowledge detection-of-deception polygraph test and to examine an individual-differences factor, self-monitoring (Snyder, 1974), in the detection context.

The Guilty Knowledge Test (GKT; Lykken, 1981) includes the assumption that suspects aware of crime-relevant information will be physiologically more reactive to questions about that information than to similar but crime-irrelevant items. If only guilty suspects are aware of information and innocent suspects are not, then the test should be optimally effective in discriminating between the two types of suspects. A recent review by Iacono and Patrick (1988) of laboratory studies showed that, under the above conditions, the median of accurate classifications of guilty subjects was at the 90% level and that the median of accurate classifications of innocent subjects was at the 100% level.

Bradley and Warfield (1984) examined the theoretical basis of the GKT. In the GKT, subjects are questioned about whether they know if particular items among sets of related items are associated with a specific crime or not. If they are aware of the information but respond with a ``No,'' then a differential physiological response to the particular item could be due to the subjects' untruthful denial, to their awareness of the relevance of the item, or to a combination of the two factors. Bradley and Warfield, to understand the influence of awareness with and without lying, changed the format of the test questions. Instead of asking if subjects were aware of certain items, they asked if the subjects did various actions involving the key items. In this way, guilty subjects denying those activities were aware and lying, whereas innocent subjects who knew information were aware but truthful in saying no because they did not do the actions. The addition of subjects who knew nothing of the crime created a group whose members were not lying and who were unaware. All of the guilty and innocent-unaware subjects and 75% of the innocent but aware subjects were correctly classified. Memory tests showed no differences in memory between the guilty and innocent-aware groups. Therefore, though guilty knowledge was a necessary condition for detection, without an attempt at deception that knowledge did not necessarily result in a suspect's appearing guilty.

The modification of the GKT from a test based on knowledge to one based on knowledge plus actions (Bradley & Warfield, 1984) was done for theoretical reasons, but the result is a test that may have some value in applied settings. The modified test, which could more appropriately be called a Guilty Actions Test (GAT), has potential, by its wording, to solve problems that arise for the standard form of the GKT when innocent suspects in a real criminal investigation have crime-relevant information. If, for example, potential test information has been reported in the newspaper, all suspects, including the guilty, may admit to knowing that information, with the consequence that a GKT in standard format would not be appropriate because neither type of suspect has anything to deny. If, however, the results with the modified form of the test reported by Bradley and Warfield can be replicated and if they generalize to the field, innocent suspects denying guilty actions, if found innocent, could in all likelihood be considered innocent. In another situation, innocent-aware suspects may attempt to deny knowledge because they have been threatened by the real criminal. A standard GKT would find such a suspect deceptive and, by inference, that suspect could be considered guilty. Testing with a GAT would allow the suspect to not lie even though he or she was aware of the information and thereby could afford the possibility of a judgment of nondeceptive and innocent. Of course, until this test is better understood, it is premature to regard this possibility as anything more than speculation to direct further studies.

An objective of the present study was, in part, to replicate the work of Bradley and Warfield (1984). The original study included five groups. Subjects in one group were guilty, and subjects in another were innocent and unaware of crime-relevant information. Three groups were made up of subjects who were innocent but aware of crime-relevant information, because they had witnessed the crime, because they had read about the crime in complete detail, or because they had received crime-relevant information in a noncrime context.

We considered the most important conditions to be the guilty condition, an innocent-aware condition in which subjects had read of the items, and the innocent-unaware condition. The guilty and innocent groups represent the ideal ones for the test. The innocent-aware group was meant to simulate the situation in which suspects in the field have learned information from newspaper reports, other suspects, or the police themselves.

Bradley and Warfield (1984) could be criticized for having fairly small incentives for their groups. Greater amounts of money were used in the present experiment. With more at stake, subjects who know key terms, regardless of whether they attempt deception or not, may be more reactive to questions and would be more likely to appear deceptive.

Individual differences, such as extraversion (Bradley & Janisse, 1981; Steller, Haenert, & Eiselt, 1987) and Machiavellianism (Bradley & Klohn, 1987), can influence detection such that individuals scoring high on either of these measures are more readily detected than are those scoring low. For high extraverts, it was speculated that their general familiarity and relative comfort in social situations would result in a more ready identification of and concentration on crime-relevant questions. In a similar fashion, the shrewdness of high Machiavellians should result in the identification of and concentrated attention on crime-relevant questions. Such awareness may allow these individuals to adopt a facade to deceive an observer about their behavior, but their autonomic responsivity should reflect the underlying effort associated with deliberate impression-management attempts. Self-monitoring (Snyder, 1987), although not correlated with Machiavellianism, and only mildly correlated with extraversion, shares characteristics related to awareness of and sensitivity to social situations with the goal of impression management. If these are important elements related to differential detectability, then deceptive high self-monitors may also be more detectable than deceptive low self-monitors. Differences were not expected for the innocent subjects because members of these groups were not attempting deception. Overall, it was predicted that guilty subjects would receive scores most indicative of guilt. Innocent-unaware subjects would appear innocent, and innocent-aware subjects would generally score as innocent but with some tendency to score toward the guilty end of the spectrum. The self-monitoring effects were expected in the guilty and innocent-aware groups but theoretically could not appear in the scores of innocent but unaware subjects.

■ ■ ■

Question 1. What are the authors' goals? The authors propose to replicate an earlier study (Bradley & Warfield, 1984) indicating that innocent subjects who had knowledge of a crime could be found innocent on a revised version of the GKT. They were also interested in examining whether a person's self-monitoring tendencies would alter the accuracy of the GKT.

Question 2. What hypotheses will be tested? The hypotheses are listed as questions to be answered before one can accept the validity of the GKT: (1) Is it possible for innocent-aware subjects to appear innocent on the GKT? (2) Does the GKT accurately discriminate among guilty, innocent-aware, and innocent-unaware subjects? (3) Does the effect of actual guilt on the classification of guilt versus innocence depend on whether a subject is a high or a low self-monitor?

Question 3. How would I test these hypotheses? For the first and second hypotheses, you could create three "guilt" conditions: guilty, innocent-aware, and innocent-unaware. Guilty subjects could receive detailed instructions about a mock crime and then commit the crime. You could give the innocent-aware subjects the details of the mock crime but not have them commit the crime. Innocent-unaware subjects could serve as a control group since they would neither commit the mock crime nor be given any crime-relevant details. You could then administer the GKT along with a polygraph, because you would not want to rely on subjects' verbal or self-reports. With respect to the first hypothesis, you could look at whether the innocent-aware subjects were found to be innocent using the GKT. For the second hypothesis, you could determine whether the GKT classifications agreed with the subjects' assigned condition (i.e., guilty, innocent-aware, innocent-unaware). You could pretest your group of subjects using a self-monitoring questionnaire and include only the subjects who were definitely high or low self-monitors. You could then create trios of subjects that were matched on self-monitoring scores and randomly assign each trio member to one of the three guilt conditions (see chapter 9 for more detailed information on matching). This would ensure equivalent groups on the self-monitoring variable. Finally, you could adopt a 99 percent confidence level (i.e., 1-in-100 chance that an observed treatment effect is due to random or chance factors) for all statistical analyses, given the serious nature of the problem.

■ ■ ■

Method

Subjects

Forty-eight men who volunteered for course credit were selected from a larger pool of 69 introductory psychology students on the basis of their scores on the revised Self-Monitoring Scale (Lennox & Wolfe, 1984). They were divided into high and low self-monitoring groups on the basis of the 24 highest scores (M = 49.4) and the 24 lowest scores (M = 34.6). In turn, these groups were randomly sorted into guilty, innocent-aware, and innocent-unaware with the restriction that there be an equal number of high and low self-monitors in each condition. Subjects included in the study signed a consent form that told them they would be interrogated for a mock crime that they might or might not have committed. The form indicated that subject participation was voluntary and that they could withdraw from the experiment at any time without penalty. Male subjects were chosen because men are more often suspects in criminal investigations.

Apparatus

A Lafayette model 760-566 polygraph was used to record skin resistance responses, thoracic respiration, and abdominal respiration. The polygraph has fitted with a stimulus marker to record question onset. Skin resistance was measured by standard Lafayette zinc-zinc chloride electrodes. After the skin had been cleaned with a cotton swab dipped in alcohol, the electrodes were attached to the medial phalanges of the first and second fingers. Respiration was measured with a standard Lafayette pneumatic chest assembly. Baseline and sensitivity levels were adjusted individually.

Procedure

Subject instructions and procedural details, except for some changes to accommodate a different laboratory setting and a larger amount of money, were similar to those reported by Bradley and Warfield (1984). The procedure given in brief here along with any changes should provide an understanding of the study, but for replication purposes readers ought to refer to the more detailed description reported by Bradley and Warfield.

Subjects arrived at the laboratory individually at a predetermined time. They were met by an assistant who directed their attention to a folder that contained instructions appropriate for each individual's particular condition.

Guilty subjects were instructed to commit a mock crime. They were told to go to a storeroom, where they used a metal revolver (hidden on a window ledge) to shoot and murder a medical mannequin. They stole $15.00 from the victim, wrapped the gun in a cloth, placed it in the wastebasket, and hid the money in their footwear. When finished, they returned to the laboratory for the remainder of the 10 min.

Both the innocent-aware and unaware groups were given instruction sheets that told them they were murder suspects and that, although they had no convincing alibis to account for what they were doing at the time of the murder, they would have a chance to demonstrate their innocence in a polygraph test. The instructions then differed for innocent-aware subjects by continuing and giving all the details of the crime that the guilty subjects committed. Members of both innocent groups of subjects waited in the laboratory alone for 10 min. while reading their instructions. All subjects were told that if the guilty subjects were found innocent they would be given $20.00 and that if the innocent subjects were found innocent they would also receive $20.00.

After the 10 min. interval, the laboratory assistant returned and accused each subject of murder. Subjects were told they would have the opportunity to demonstrate their innocence in a polygraph examination given by an examiner completely unaware of their actual guilt or innocence. They were reminded of the incentive conditions and the importance of appearing innocent throughout the entire procedure. Just before meeting the examiner, subjects were asked to estimate how effective, from 0% to 100%, the polygraph would be in discovering their actual guilt or innocence.

Subjects were taken to the polygraph room, where they were introduced to the examiner. The examiner prepared subjects and attached the physiological devices for measurement of responses during the test.

The test consisted of a GKT with 10 sets of alternatives. The critical alternatives were those outlined earlier in the procedure. Subjects were instructed to answer *no* to all question alternatives. These included the critical ones, and thus guilty subjects would be lying, whereas innocent subjects would be telling the truth. An example of a question set with alternatives follows: ``You murdered the man in a: house? bank? store? hotel? service station?'' The questions were worded such that a guilty subject denying, as in the example, that he murdered the man in a hotel would be lying, whereas innocent subjects would be telling the truth even if they knew the man was murdered in the hotel.

All 10 sets of questions were delivered in such a way as to minimize vocal inflections. The questions were spaced 20 s apart, and it took 17 min. to give the test.

At the end of the examination, subjects were told that their charts would be scored and the results given in about 15 min. Subjects were sent back to the laboratory assistant. The assistant gave them two memory tests, with strict assurance that the results of the memory tests would not be available to the polygraph examiner before he judged their charts. The first memory test was on recall of crime-relevant items. Subjects attempted to answer questions such as the following: ``In what part of the body was the man shot?'' and ``What was the name of the man who was murdered?''. The second test was a recognition memory test. In this test, subjects were to circle the correct crime-relevant alternative on a copy of the GKT that had been used in their polygraph examination. If they were guilty or innocent-aware subjects, they were attempting to recall or recognize the crime-relevant items. Innocent-unaware subjects were asked to make their best guess as to the items involved in the crime. Money, 50¢ per correct item in each test, was used as an inducement to respond correctly. Thus, subjects could gain $10.00 with correct recall and recognition of the 10 items on both tests. Once these activities were completed, subjects were paid and debriefed.

Data Quantification and Analysis

Skin resistance responses were found for the final four alternatives in each of the 10 question sets on the GKT. This was done by measuring the maximum upward pen displacement within 10 s after the beginning of the questions. Pen displacement reflects resistance changes, and relatively large amplitudes in this context are associated with knowledge and, inferentially, deception (Lykken, 1959). The response to the first alternative in each question set was excluded from measurement and served instead as a buffer item to at least partially habituate the orienting responses expected with the introduction of new question sets. The response to the critical alternative was assigned a score 2, 1, or 0, depending on its magnitude relative to the other responses in the set. If the response to the critical alternative was largest, it received a rank of 2; if second largest, it received a rank of 1. A rank of 0 was assigned for any other response magnitude. With 10 sets of alternatives, the scoring ranged from 0 to 20.

Respiration scores were derived through the use of a contour map wheel. The wheel was used to follow the curvilinear tracings that represent inhalation and exhalation; it gave distance readings in millimeters. Measures were taken for 10 s of chart time following question onset. Timm (1982) found respiratory suppression associated with deception. If the shortest response was to the critical item, it received a rank score of 2; if the response was the second smallest, it received a rank score of 1. A rank score of 0 was given for any other response magnitude. The response for the first alternative in each question set served as an orienting response buffer item and was excluded from analysis.

After these scores were obtained, they were analyzed in a 2 × 3 analysis of variance (ANOVA). The first factor was the two levels of self-monitoring, and the second factor was the three subject conditions. All measures, including memory scores, estimates of polygraph effectiveness, thoracic and abdominal respiration, and skin resistance responses, were analyzed in this design.

■ ■ ■

Question 4a. Is my proposed method better than the authors'? Our methods are essentially the same except that we used a matching technique to ensure equivalent groups in terms of subjects' self-monitoring scores. In that respect, ours is more tightly controlled. However, the authors' method is fine.

Question 4b. Does the authors' method actually test the hypotheses? Yes, although we may be concerned that the authors tested only male subjects. Their reasoning was that "men are more often suspects in criminal investigations" (p. 56). Even so, women are sometimes suspects. It is important to determine whether the GKT is equally accurate with men and women. Otherwise, the independent and subject variables seem appropriate, and the ultimate classification of guilt versus innocence (based on skin resistance, thoracic respiration, and abdominal respiration) is straightforward.

Question 4c. What are the variables (independent, subject, dependent, control)? Independent variable: guilt condition (guilty, innocent-aware, innocent-unaware). Subject variable: self-monitoring (high versus low). Dependent variables: skin resistance, thoracic respiration, abdominal respiration, subjects' estimates of polygraph effectiveness, recognition memory, and recall memory. Control variable: gender (held constant by testing only male subjects), interval between entering the lab and GKT polygraph test (10 minutes).

Question 5: What do we predict? On the basis of Bradley & Warfield (1984), we can predict that innocent-aware subjects will be found innocent at a greater-than-chance level. In addition, we might predict that the GKT will correctly classify subjects in the three guilt conditions at a greater-than-chance level. Finally, on the basis of past theory and research on self-monitoring, the effect of guilt should vary depending on whether the subject is a high or a low self-monitor.

■ ■ ■

Results

Detection scores for skin resistance responses, $F(2, 42) = 39.03$, thoracic respiration scores, $F(2, 42) = 4.09$, polygraph accuracy estimates, $F(2, 42) = 4.90$, recognition memory scores, $F(2, 42) = 187.54$, and recall memory scores, $F(2, 42) = 191.89$, differed across the three conditions (see Table 1). There were, however, no differences on any of the variables associated with self-monitoring, either as main effects or in interaction with group factors. Abdominal respiration scores showed no significant differences.

The guilt condition differences were examined with Tukey's honestly significant difference test with alpha set at .05. The examination of detection scores based on skin resistance showed that guilty subjects scored as more reactive than did innocent-unaware and innocent-aware subjects. Innocent-aware subjects scored as more guilty than did innocent-unaware subjects. With regard to respiration scores, guilty subjects scored as more guilty than did innocent-unaware subjects but did not score as more guilty than innocent-aware subjects.

The estimates of polygraph effectiveness were identical for the innocent-unaware and guilty groups, but these estimates were higher than those made by the innocent-aware group. For the innocent-aware group, estimates of polygraph accuracy were correlated with thoracic respiration scores such that higher detection scores were associated with higher accuracy estimates ($r = .50$). Using the effectiveness estimates as a covariate in the original analysis of detection scores resulted in only trivial changes in F values: $F(2, 41) = 40.65$ for skin resistance; $F(2, 41) = 4.56$ for thoracic respiration. The results were essentially the same as in the initial analysis.

TABLE 1
Means and Standard Deviations of Physiological Scores, Accuracy Estimates, and Memory Scores in Each Experimental Condition

	ESTIMATES OF									
Subjects	**Skin resistance**		**Thoracic respiration**		**Polygraph accuracy**		**Recognition memory**		**Recall memory**	
	M	SD	M	SD	M	SD	M	SD	M	SD
Innocent-unaware	5.75	1.6	6.50	2.8	74.06	24.6	1.81	1.6	1.44	1.7
Innocent-aware	10.06	3.5	7.50	3.5	50.00	29.3	9.37	1.5	9.12	1.6
Guilty	13.81	2.1	9.87	3.6	74.06	20.4	9.87	0.3	9.87	0.3

Recall and recognition memory scores for both the guilty and innocent-aware groups were significantly higher than the memory scores for the innocent-unaware group. There were no significant differences between the guilty and innocent-aware groups with regard to either memory test.

In field work, a cutoff value on detection scores would be imposed to decide guilt or innocence. Ten was selected as a cutoff point for this study because it had resulted in an optimal level of classification of guilty and innocent subjects in an earlier and very similar study (Bradley & Warfield, 1984). Table 2 shows the classification results.

Chi-square analyses of the data in Table 2 showed that the frequencies of classification as guilty or innocent differed depending on the conditions to which subjects were assigned: for skin resistance, $\chi^2(2, N=48)=32.0$; for thoracic respiration, $\chi^2(2, N = 48)=9.8$; and for abdominal respiration, $\chi^2(2, N=48)=6.6$.

Correlations between skin resistance scores and thoracic and abdominal respiration scores were significant ($r=.31$ and $r=.33$, respectively), as was the correlation between the two respiration measures ($r=.61$). A classification based on the weighted linear combination of these scores, derived through discriminant analysis, resulted in 13 of the 16 guilty subjects, 12 of the 16 innocent-aware subjects, and 16 of the 16 innocent-unaware subjects being classed correctly in the respective groups. A chi-square analysis, $\chi^2(2, N = 48)=24.2$, showed a difference across the three conditions.

Because the three conditions were essentially the same as those used by Bradley and Warfield (1984), an analysis was conducted between the skin resistance scores obtained in the current and earlier experiments. The only difference of note between each experiment was that Bradley and Warfield used $5 as an incentive to appear innocent, whereas in the present study $20 was used. The data were analyzed in a 2 (experiment) $\times$ 3 (guilt condition) ANOVA. The scores among the three conditions differed, $F(5, 66)=77.53$,

---

TABLE 2
Classification of Subjects as Guilty or Innocent on the Basis of Skin Resistance and Respiration Scores

	ASSIGNED CONDITION		
Classification	Guilty	Innocent-aware	Innocent-unaware
Skin resistance			
Guilty	16	8	0
Innocent	0	8	16
Thoracic respiration			
Guilty	9	4	1
Innocent	7	12	15
Abdominal respiration			
Guilty	7	3	1
Innocent	9	13	15

but there were no differences between experiments, and the interaction of conditions and experiments was not significant.

■ ■ ■

Question 6. Did the author get unexpected results? Yes. Two, in particular. One, the accuracy of the classification of innocent-aware subjects was somewhat discouraging. A "false alarm" rate—the proportion of innocent-aware subjects classified as guilty—of 25 percent, or 4 of 16, seems high. Also, using the same linear combination of skin resistance, thoracic respiration, and abdominal respiration resulted in 19 percent, or 3 of 16, guilty subjects being classified as innocent—"misses". With regard to self-monitoring, there were no significant effects or interactions. With null results, it is impossible to determine whether self-monitoring, in truth, has no effect or the selection of high and low subjects was not extreme enough.

Question 7a. How would we interpret the results? Having knowledge of a crime is sufficient for a nontrivial percentage of innocent subjects (25 percent) to appear guilty on a revised GKT. This occurred despite the fact that subjects' actions, rather than their knowledge, were the primary focus of investigation. It is difficult to interpret the lack of main effects or interactions for the self-monitoring variable in the light of the null findings. Perhaps Bradley and Rettinger's (1992) initial pool of subjects did not vary along the full range of self-monitoring values (see chapter 7 on restriction of range). If this was the case, then the two self-monitoring groups formed from this initial pool would not have been as dissimilar as one would expect or hope. It is difficult to determine from their report whether this was the case, because Bradley and Rettinger do not describe either the range of self-monitoring scores for their initial pool of subjects or the possible range of values for the self-monitoring scale. Also, it is not clear whether mean differences between high and low self-monitors were equal across the three guilt conditions. This is something that could have been ensured through random assignment of matched trios of subjects to the three conditions.

7b. What applications and implications would we draw from our interpretation of the results? We would be hesitant to use the revised Guilty Knowledge Test to determine the guilt or innocence of suspects in an actual criminal investigation. A nontrivial percentage of innocent-aware (25 percent) and guilty (19 percent) subjects were misclassified. More research needs to be conducted before the GKT is used in actual criminal investigations.

■ ■ ■

Discussion

Guilty knowledge is necessary for detection. This was demonstrated by the fact that none of the innocent-unaware subjects were incorrectly detected by either the skin resistance scores alone or by the linear combination of scores from all three measures. Guilty knowledge alone, however, is not necessarily a sufficient condition for detection. Innocent-aware subjects did not differ in memory from guilty subjects but had scores less indicative of guilt. Because lying or attempting deception is a major factor differentiating the two groups, it could be argued that the act of deception results in a significant augmentation of physiological responding to critical items. In addition, as suggested by the work of Lang (1979), because guilty subjects read and carried out their actions, whereas innocent-aware subjects only read of them, the greater physiological responsiveness of the guilty subjects could be due to the richer and more complex memory codes associated with the key items.

Innocent-aware subjects made lower estimates of polygraph accuracy than did subjects in either the guilty or innocent-unaware groups. It could appear that these estimates were related to the less accurate polygraph classification results found with the innocent-aware group. This interpretation presents some difficulties. Because estimates were taken after subjects had carried out their instructions, the low estimates and inaccurate classification of the innocent-aware group could both be related to the assigned condition but not necessarily to each other. The analysis in which estimates were used as a covariate with detection scores made essentially no difference to the outcome, and testing for correlations within each group produced only the one result with thoracic respiration in the innocent-aware group. Furthermore, the correlation was positive, meaning that the innocent-aware subjects who believed the polygraph would find them innocent were instead more likely to be found guilty. Saxe, Dougherty, and Cross (1985), in their review of the relationship between effectiveness and detection scores, found some evidence supporting a relationship between estimates of effectiveness and actual test outcome effectiveness, but other evidence cited by them showed no relationship. Our current findings of an effect, but in the opposite direction of that usually hypothesized, do not clarify what the potential relation might be. A study with effectiveness ratings obtained before subjects are assigned to conditions may be more informative.

Levels of self-monitoring were not related to detection scores of guilty subjects. This result calls into question speculations by Bradley and Janisse (1981) and Bradley and Klohn (1987) that the shared characteristics involving attention and expressive self-control among high self-monitors, extraverts, and Machiavellians accounted for differential detection rates in their studies. Perhaps it is the more specific characteristics of each personality type, such as the manipulativeness of the high Machiavellians and the insensitivity to trivial items (control questions) of the extraverts, that account for earlier results. Alternatively, physiological reactivity may be somewhat equivalent in both high and low self-monitors but for different reasons. For example, responsivity in high self-monitors may be reflective of cognitive effort, whereas with low self-monitors reactivity may reflect emotionality due to lying or to the negative tone of the events.

Given the simplicity of method in the present study, the results are of both theoretical and applied interest. The finding that subjects who were simply aware of key information did not obtain detection scores as high as guilty subjects, who were aware and deceptive, suggests that lying augments physiological responsivity, at least with the skin resistance measure in the GKT. The reasons why such a result might occur are wide ranging. For example, factors related to acts of deception, more complex memory codes due to acting out the crime, or motivational reasons may all play some role. Any of these factors and potential interactions can be readily investigated because the paradigm, involving items of the same type that differ only in crime relevance, and subjects differing in knowledge, is quite basic compared with other lie detection tests, which include complex questions of different types.

Because the data were available, we attempted to ascertain the role of motivation by comparing the present results with those obtained in an earlier study by Bradley and Warfield (1984), who used the same procedures but different incentive levels. No differences were found. Incentives could not, of course, affect the innocent-unaware group but could theoretically be expected to differentially augment responses to key items in the innocent-aware group and the guilty group. It is difficult to know what to make of this failure to find significant differences between the studies, especially with regard to field applications. The groups in Bradley and Warfield's study were small, and as a consequence power for statistical analysis was low. Although the experimental procedures for each study were very similar, they were done almost 4 years apart. It could be argued, because of this time factor, that comparison of the two studies is not fully justified. Finally, and arguably the most important point because of its relevance to external validity, small monetary rewards contingent on avoiding detection in the laboratory may be so different from the severe consequences involved in actual lie detection tests that the current results about motivation may not be generalizable to field situations.

If the results of the present experiment do generalize to field situations, they raise some interesting questions. At present the GKT is ignored, whereas the assumption-laden Control Question Test is favored by field workers (Lykken, 1981). Part of the rationale for not using the GKT is that innocent subjects aware of information will respond as guilty. This study of the modified GKT partially supports that assumption and justifies field workers' caution because 50% of the innocent-aware group was misclassified as guilty. That said, however, it will be unfortunate if the test continues to be ignored. The test could be used as a screening tool for suspects because the data, at least with skin resistance scores, suggest that a high degree of confidence can be placed in an innocent outcome.

References

Bradley, M. T., & Janisse, M. P. (1981). Extraversion and the detection of deception. *Journal of Personality and Individual Differences, 2,* 99–103.

Bradley, M. T., & Klohn, K. I. (1987). Machiavellianism, the Control Question Test and the detection of deception. *Perceptual and Motor Skills, 64,* 747–757.

Bradley, M. T., & Warfield, J. F. (1984). Innocence, information, and the Guilty Knowledge Test in the detection of deception. *Psychophysiology, 21,* 683–689.

Iacono, W. G., & Patrick, C. J. (1988). Assessing deception: Polygraph techniques. In R. Rogers (Ed.), *Clinical assessment of malingering and deception* (pp. 205–233). New York: Guilford.

Lang, P. J. (1979). A bio-informational theory of emotional imagery. *Psychophysiology, 16,* 495–512.

Lennox, R. D., & Wolfe, R. N. (1984). Revision of the Self-Monitoring Scale. *Journal of Personality and Social Psychology, 46,* 1349–1364.

Lykken, D. T. (1959). The GSR in the detection of guilt. *Journal of Applied Psychology, 43,* 385–388.

Lykken, D. T. (1981). *A tremor in the blood: Uses and abuse of the lie detector.* New York: McGraw-Hill.

Saxe, L., Dougherty, D., & Cross, T. P. (1985). The validity of polygraph testing: Scientific analysis and public controversy. *American Psychologist, 40,* 355–366.

Snyder, M. (1974). Self-monitoring of expressive behavior. *Journal of Personality and Social Psychology, 30,* 526–537.

Snyder, M. (1987). *Public appearances, private realities: The psychology of self-monitoring.* New York: W. H. Freeman.

Steller, M., Haenert, P., & Eiselt, W. (1987). Extraversion and the detection of information. *Journal of Research in Personality, 21,* 334–342.

Timm, H. W. (1982). Effect of altered outcome expectancies stemming from placebo and feedback treatments on the validity of the guilty knowledge technique. *Journal of Applied Psychology, 67,* 391–400.

Received August 21, 1989
Revision received August 27, 1991
Accepted August 28, 1991

■ ■ ■

8a. Does our interpretation or the author's best represent the data? It appears that we differ from the authors in terms of adopting a "glass half full" versus "glass half empty" approach to the data, respectively. We were more stringent or conservative in judging the utility of the Guilty Knowledge Test for assessing the guilt or innocence of suspects. Given the serious consequences of misclassifying suspects, the authors might have focused more on the incidence of misclassification and less on the incidence of correct classifications.

8b. Do we or does the author offer the most cogent discussion of the applications and implications of the results? Putting aside the fact that we arrived at different interpretations and conclusion for the experimental results, the applications and implications offered by the authors are as good or better then ours.

In summary, when you read a research report, you should read actively and critically. The checklist for the critical reader is designed to get you into the habit of actively asking questions about the reports you read: Why hypotheses are being tested? How are they being tested? Does the method test the hypotheses? Do the results apply to the hypotheses? How does the author relate the results to the purposes of the research? What interpretations and inferences are made by the author?

SUMMARY

1. Before embarking on a research project, it is wise to do a literature search to detect what other researchers have done that is related to your proposed experiment.

2. There are seven parts to psychological journal articles: title and author(s), abstract, introduction, method, results, discussion, and references.

3. The abstract is a short (150-word) description of the article.

4.   The introduction describes the rationale behind the experiment.

5.   The method section describes the subjects, materials, design, and procedures used by the experimenter.

6.   The results section contains a summary of the data collected in the experiment.

7.   Proper interpretation of tables and figures is crucial to understanding the results of experiments reported in journal articles. The vertical axis of a figure is called the ordinate, on which the dependent variable is scaled. The horizontal axis of a figure is called the abscissa, and in experiments the independent variable appears on the abscissa.

8.   The discussion section is the part of the article in which the author can state the implications of his or her findings.

9.   The reference section contains a list of all papers referenced in the article.

10. The critical reader is able to answer such question as: What hypothesis does this experiment test? How might this experiment have been done differently? What results would I predict for this experiment? How would I interpret the author's results?

■ KEY CONCEPTS

abscissa
abstract
apparatus
author
computerized literature search
discussion
figures
introduction
materials

method
ordinate
procedure
PSYCLit
Psychological Abstracts
results
Social Science Citation Index
subjects
tables
title

Psychology in Action
A Literature Search

Suppose you became interested in the effects of hypnosis on memory. Many people believe that hypnosis is a viable way to remember events that might otherwise not be retrieved, yet many courts will not let people who have been hypnotized testify as witnesses. Why is this? Are our memories susceptible to change when we are under hypnosis? Or does hypnosis help memory? These are the types of questions in which you are interested.

To obtain answers to these questions, you will do a literature search. Because you are not particularly knowledgeable in this area, you do not know the names of any researchers who have done work on the effects of hypnosis on memory. Therefore, the best place to start is probably *Psychological Abstracts* or *PSYCLit*. *PSYCLit* is the electronic equivalent of the printed reference source *Psychological Abstracts*; *PSYCLit* is usually preferable because electronic searches are more efficient than manual searches. You do not have to be a librarian or a computer expert to use electronic databases such as *PSYCLit*. Help screens are available as well as printed instructions; additionally, the reference staff at your library can answer questions and help you plan your search strategy.

To find out about the effects of hypnosis on memory, you might begin by looking up a "keyword"; to do this, you simply type in a word that captures the topic in which you are interested (e.g., *hypnosis*). However, a recent search turned up 1,413 journal articles written about the subject of hypnosis since 1987; clearly, this is too many to work with. A search of *memory* turns up even more articles: over 11,000! In this situation, you will want to combine keywords to pare down the numbers; because you are interested in the *susceptibility* of *memory* to *hypnosis*, you can type in all three words at once; the result is a list of all the articles that contain information about all three concepts. You have now narrowed the field down to a workable list of 31 references, each accompanied by a brief abstract. You now skim the titles and abstracts and determine which articles look especially interesting; you will probably want to go to the journals after this step and read the articles that look most relevant to your interests. Review articles are especially helpful at this stage because they summarize and evaluate many empirical articles.

Now suppose you have found an article that contains a theory about hypnosis and memory that is particularly interesting to you; you would like to know about the implications of this theory and whether it has generally held up under experimental scrutiny. One way to do this would be to find out what more recent articles have cited this article. To do this, you would use the *Social Science Citation Index (SSCI)*; like *Psychological Abstracts,* it exists in both printed and electronic form. Again, the electronic form is generally preferable in that it is more efficient. *SSCI* allows you to enter an article's reference and find out who has cited that article. That way, you can find out the recent developments in that area.

Often, libraries will have printers that allow you to print out any interesting references you might discover when using electronic searches. Additionally, you can sometimes download the references onto your own floppy disk. Ask your reference librarian what types of options you have at your library.

TECHNIQUES OF SCIENTIFIC PSYCHOLOGY

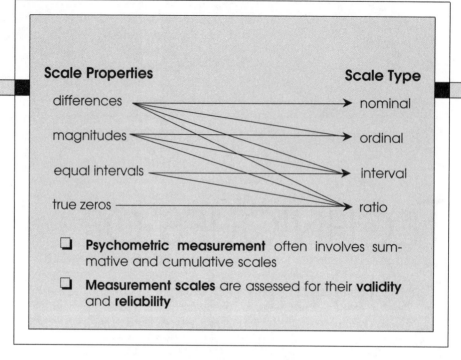

Scale Properties

differences

magnitudes

equal intervals

true zeros

Scale Type

nominal

ordinal

interval

ratio

❏ **Psychometric measurement** often involves summative and cumulative scales

❏ **Measurement scales** are assessed for their **validity** and **reliability**

CHAPTER 5

MEASUREMENT IN PSYCHOLOGICAL RESEARCH

Measurement is one hallmark of science. In this chapter we consider the properties of measurement scales and the types of measurement scales used in psychology. One class of scales we discuss are psychometric ones, which assess human characteristics such as intelligence and depression. We will examine how the validity and reliability of measurement scales are determined.

A brief summary of the previous chapters might go like this: theories and observations result in hypotheses that are testable by empirical observations. The new observations then provide the bases for theoretical development and new testable hypotheses. To complete the background necessary for a detailed examination of research methods, we need to consider the measurement of behavior. According to Edwin G. Boring (1961), the eminent historian of psychology, a science grows and progresses to the extent that it uses measurement. As noted earlier, testable hypotheses imply that the predicted outcomes can be measured. Furthermore, empirical observations in psychology are based on the measurement of dependent variables. Measurement then is an important aspect of scientific psychology.

What is measurement? **Measurement** is a systematic way of assigning numbers or names to objects and their attributes. It is a dictum in psychology that anything that exists, be it alarm calls of chickadees or emotional reactions to earthquakes, exists in some amount. Anything that exists in some amount can be measured. The scientific study of behavior demands that we be able to measure it and its attributes. Otherwise, we will be unable to generate adequate hypotheses and precise theories. In this chapter we first consider the types of measurement scales used by psychologists. Then we examine ways of evaluating measurements and developing measurement scales.

MEASUREMENT SCALES

When we assign names or numbers to objects and their attributes, we need a measurement scale. When we measure temperature, for example, we usually use either the Fahrenheit scale or the Centigrade scale, and weight can be measured in pounds or kilograms. Measurement scales differ in the information they provide, because different scales, say weight and temperature, result from different measurement operations.

Properties of Measurement Scales

There are four properties of measurement scales that we need to consider (see McCall, 1990, for additional information). All measurement scales require that objects and their attributes have instances that are different from each other. This fundamental property, **difference,** means that some temperatures must be hotter (or colder) than others. One detectable difference among people is sex, and we can sort people into two piles: female and male. All measurement scales have this characteristic, but not all have the other properties, which we now discuss.

Some measurement scales can determine the **magnitude** of attributes. This means that the scale can show that one attribute is greater than, less than, or equal to another instance of that attribute. The Mohs' scale determines the hardness of minerals. Diamonds are harder than quartz crystals, and quartz crystals are harder than pieces of mica. A person surveyed about the amount of fear generated by the San Francisco earthquake (none at all, some, or very much) would have his or her magnitude of fear assessed. Using such a survey could reveal that some people were more fearful than others.

Another property of attributes that some scales can determine is whether there are **equal intervals** between magnitudes of the attributes. Both temperature scales have equal intervals, because a one-degree change in temperature is the same magnitude regardless of whether we are considering very hot temperatures or very cold ones. The typical intelligence test assesses magnitudes of intelligence with equal intervals between them. The difference between an intelligence test score, say the familiar IQ measure, of 125 and a score of 120 is believed to represent the same difference that exists between scores of 85 and 90.

A final property of some measurement scales is a **true zero** point on the scale. The true zero is when nothing of the attribute being measured exists. Fahrenheit and Centigrade scales do not have a true zero point. For both scales the zero point does not reflect zero temperature. To detect zero temperature—so-called *absolute zero*—the Kelvin scale must be used.

Types of Measurement Scales

Psychologists use four types of measurement scales, called nominal, ordinal, interval, and ratio, although other types exist. These scale types are determined by which of the four properties of measurement they possess. The four scale types are listed here according to the increasing informativeness of the scales, with each scale type having the properties of the preceding types in addition to new properties. One thing this means is that data obtained using a ratio scale could be statistically analyzed by methods appropriate to any of the three lesser scales, but statistics appropriate only for a ratio scale would not fit the lesser scales (see the statistical appendixes). A second thing this means is that scales with more properties provide more information.

Nominal Scales.   A **nominal scale** measures just the property of difference and nothing else. A nominal scale merely sorts objects or attributes into different categories. Your ZIP code is a nominal number because it puts you into a particular (geographical) category, but it does not reveal much else about you. Nominal scales are weak ones in the sense that you cannot legitimately perform many mathematical operations on nominal numbers. You might have a use for the average Scholastic Aptitude Test (SAT) score in your class. The SAT scale is considered to have at least interval scale properties (see below). But, what would the average ZIP code of your class tell you? Not much, because the assignment of numbers to geographical area is not based on magnitudes in any obvious way. Likewise, sex is measured at the nominal level, and you cannot average category labels. Even if the category labels were numbers, say male = 1 and female = 2, the assignment of numbers is arbitrary and not based on magnitudes. Thus, statistics such as the arithmetical average (the mean, which is the sum of the scores divided by the number of scores) are inappropriate for nominal numbers. Putting a person into a particular category, such as giving the person a name, merely tells us that the person is different from other people. A nominal number does not assist us in measuring the person's attributes with much depth.

Ordinal Scales.   **Ordinal scales** measure differences in magnitude. An ordinal scale can be achieved by having people rank order a set of objects. You would obtain an ordinal scale if you rank ordered all your friends of the opposite sex according to their attractiveness. The first person in your ranking is the most attractive, the second person on your scale is the next most attractive, and so on. If you try ranking your friends this way, one of the first things you will notice is that the differences between adjacent scale values are not equal for all the people you ranked. The first two people may be nearly equal in attractiveness, but the sixth and seventh people may differ substantially. So, ordinal scales do not have equal intervals, which means that you probably should not add them or perform many other mathematical operations on them. You know from your ranking that the third person is more attractive than the seventh, but you do not know how much more.

Interval Scales.   You can add and subtract numbers from interval scales, because the intervals between adjacent values are equal throughout the scale. **Interval scales** possess the scale properties of difference, order, and equal intervals. A temperature rise of one degree produces the same change from 35° to 36° as it does from 22° to 23°. As noted above many psychologists treat IQ scores as interval level numbers, which means that mean IQ scores can be calculated. It is very difficult to substantiate that IQ differences are equal throughout the scale. Thus, psychologists taking a conservative view would treat IQ scores as ordinal data. If IQ scores are ordinal, then we cannot assume that the difference between a hypothetical IQ score of 120 and 124 represents the same difference that exists between a score of 100 and 104. All we can say if we are conservative is that 124 represents a higher IQ than does 120, and, in turn, 104 is more than 100.

Ratio Scales.   **Ratio scales** have all four of the properties of measurement scales: difference, magnitude, equal intervals, and a true zero. As such, a ratio scale provides the most information and is usually considered the most powerful form of psychological measurement. Because ratio scales have a true zero, they allow us to determine the ratios of the scale values (hence, the name, ratio scale). Even if IQ were measured at the interval level, it is not sensible to assert that an IQ of 120 is twice that of 60 or half again bigger than an IQ of 80. A typical ratio scale used in psychology is the time it takes someone to complete a task. Zero time truly means no time was spent on the task. Also, four minutes spent on a task bears the same relation to one minute as does twenty minutes to five, because the ratio of the two time periods is 4:1 in both instances.

Importance of Measurement Scales

Some of the previous discussion of scales may have seemed too abstract to assist in understanding behavior. The examples we provided should have indicated that the different scales yield different kinds of information. The more of the four properties (difference, magnitude, equal intervals, and a true zero) possessed by a scale, the more the information provided. You might expect that psychologists should always strive for ratio measurement of behavior, because a ratio scale provides the most information. Unfortunately, deriving a ratio scale for important psychological phenomena is often very difficult. A substantial amount of psychological measurement is at the ordinal and interval level. What does that mean to you? First, as noted above, it will determine the kinds of mathematical and statistical operations that you can use on the numbers. Second, and perhaps more important, it means that when you evaluate the assertions of a researcher, you should be able to identify the measurement scale underlying the assertions. You should recognize that it is invalid to say that "Betty is twice as smart as Tom," unless the measure of smartness is at the ratio level. Furthermore, scale type will also play an important part in your own research. If, for example, you determine that Betty is lazier than Tom but you do not know how much more (an ordinal scale), then you are constrained about what you can say about the differences between Betty and Tom. You are limited further if all you determine is that Tom is witty but Betty is not (a nominal scale). The kinds of conclusions we can draw rests, in part, on the measurement scale. Behavioral data derived from different scales tell us different things.

CONCEPT SUMMARY

Measurement scales can have the properties of difference, magnitude, equal intervals, and a true zero.

MEASUREMENT PROCEDURES

Recall that in the first chapter we discussed *operational definitions*, which define concepts by describing the operations used to produce and measure them, and in the second chapter we considered *intervening variables*, which characterize abstract concepts by linking several independent variables (the inputs that produce the intervening variable) and dependent variables (the outputs used to measure the intervening variable). The two types of definitions clearly specify scientific terminology. How do they differ? An important way in which the two concepts differ relates to the number of inputs and outputs used in each case. Intervening variables usually are more complex than operationally defined concepts, because the former rely on several variables. The complexity associated with intervening variables leads to them often being called **theoretical constructs.** This designation derives from the idea that the theory constructs the observed relationships among the several independent and dependent variables involved in determining the intervening variables. In this section we examine some ways in which theoretical constructs are measured.

Schematic drawings of two theoretical constructs appear in Figure 5–1. The top portion has well-specified inputs, lights of differing intensities, and outputs, statements concerning whether the light is perceived. We might call this construct *brightness.* The bottom portion of the figure illustrates a construct with less well-specified inputs, previous experience and genetics, but has precise outputs, statements regarding feelings of depression. We might call this construct *depression.* Scaling of concepts such as brightness is called **psychophysical scaling.** Concepts that receive psychophysical scaling usually relate psychological judgments to inputs with a known physical dimension. For example, a typical psychophysical experiment might relate what a person says about the detection of lights to the intensity of those lights. We can contrast psychophysical scaling to **psychometric scaling,** which applies when concepts, such as depression, are measured but usually do not have clearly specified inputs. Ordinarily, psychometrically measured constructs are only assessed and not produced. We assess a person's feelings of depression or his or her level of intelligence. This assessment contrasts to manipulating the conditions under which they occur so that we can produce variations in them, as we can by changing brightness judgments by manipulating light intensity.

Before we examine some scaling techniques, we should note that less precise theories result from assessment than production. Thus, many scientific psychologists try to specify the independent variables that produce psychometrically determined constructs. Substantial progress has been

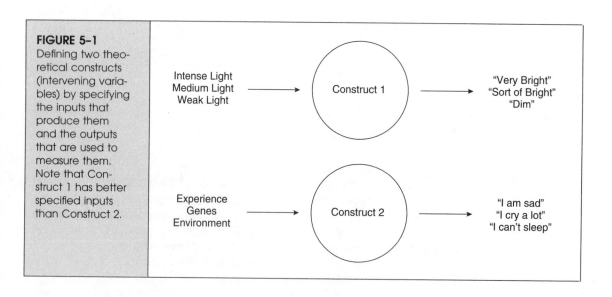

FIGURE 5-1
Defining two theoretical constructs (intervening variables) by specifying the inputs that produce them and the outputs that are used to measure them. Note that Construct 1 has better specified inputs than Construct 2.

made in doing this for some constructs (for example, *learning, memory,* and *social loafing*), and less progress has been made on others (including concepts such as *depression, schizophrenia,* and *intelligence*).

CONCEPT SUMMARY

- **Theoretical constructs** are intervening variables. Several independent and dependent variables define the construct.
- **Psychophysical scaling** is used to measure constructs that have well-specified inputs and outputs.
- **Psychometric scaling** is used to measure concepts that are assessed, which means that the independent variables usually are not well specified.

Psychophysical Scaling

Psychophysics involves determining psychophysical scales—the psychological reactions to physical events having a known dimension. Boring (1950) claims that scientific psychology began with the development of procedures to measure the relation between internal impressions, such as brightness judgments, and the external world, for example light intensity. The early scientists, led by Gustav Fechner (1860, republished in 1966) who developed psychophysical scaling methods, formulated the first mathematical laws of psychological phenomena. Fechner and other early psychophysicists concluded that private, internal judgments could be measured accurately. Just as physicists could measure light intensity, sound intensity, and weight, so too could psychophysicists measure the corresponding psychological attributes of brightness, loudness, and heaviness.

Determining how loud a sound seems or how painful a shock feels is difficult because there is rarely a one-to-one relation between physical values and psychological values. If a rock band turned up its amplifiers to produce twice as much energy, this twofold increase would not result in listeners hearing music twice as loud. To double the loudness requires nearly a ten-fold increase in energy, which means that radios, telephones, and other devices that convey sound must be calibrated so that manipulating their energy output is done proportionately to increments in perceived loudness.

Psychophysical Scales.   The early work by Fechner involved very laborious experiments in which he determined the minimal energy needed to detect the presence of a stimulus, which he called the **absolute threshold.** Typically, the observer in his experiments might hear (or see or weigh) sequences of stimuli of increasing or decreasing intensity, to which the observer says "Yes" when the stimulus is detected and "No" when it is not. The absolute threshold is operationally defined as the mean of the intensities at which the observer switches from "Yes" to "No" (or from "No" to "Yes").

In a variation of this procedure, the experimenter wants to determine how different two stimuli must be before they can be reliably distinguished. Consider such an experiment in which heavier and lighter stimuli are compared against a standard weight of 300 grams. Decreasingly lighter or decreasing heavier stimuli are compared to the standard. The observer says "Heavier" or "Lighter" as appropriate. As the comparison stimuli approach the standard and detecting differences becomes more difficult, the observer will switch from saying "Heavier" or "Lighter" to "Equal". This procedure permits a determination of the **difference threshold,** which is half of the average difference between stimuli that can be reliably distinguished as heavier than the standard and those that can reliably distinguished as lighter than the standard. For example, an observer might be asked to determine whether lifted weights differ from a 300-gram standard weight. On average the observer might switch from saying "Heavier" to "Equal" at 310 grams and from "Lighter" to "Equal" at 290 grams. Half of this 20-gram difference defines the difference threshold.

E. H. Weber, whose pioneering work in psychophysics preceded Fechner's by about twenty years, discovered some important properties of the difference threshold. One property that Weber determined was that the magnitude of the difference threshold increases with increases in the magnitude of the standard stimulus. This means that if 10 grams is the difference threshold when 300 grams is the standard, the corresponding value for a 600-gram standard stimulus would be a difference threshold of 20 grams. A familiar example will illustrate this psychophysical finding. In a room lit by a single candle, the addition of another lit candle will make the room noticeably brighter. However, in a room illuminated by several intense lamps, adding a single lit candle will not noticeably increase the brightness of the room.

Weber is famous for determining a second property of the difference threshold: *For a particular sensory modality, the size of the difference threshold relative to the standard stimulus is constant.* To return to our earlier example, the ratio of 10 grams to 300 grams is the same as the ratio of 20 grams to 600 grams, 1/30 in this case (the ratio that Weber actually obtained in his experiments). According to Weber's discovery, this means that the difference threshold for a 900-gram standard stimulus should be 30 grams, and it should be 40 grams for a 1,200-gram standard. What should the difference threshold be for a standard stimulus of 50 grams?

Fechner called relative constancy of the difference threshold **Weber's law.** This law is usually written as $\Delta I/I = K$, where I refers to the magnitude of the standard stimulus, ΔI is the difference threshold, and K is the symbol for constancy.

Weber's law, or the Weber fraction, as it is sometimes called, varies in size for different senses. For example, it is somewhat larger for brightness than it is for heaviness. A substantial amount of research has shown that Weber's law holds true for greater than 90 percent of the range of standard stimuli tested in a particular sensory modality. It fails to hold for very weak stimuli, such that the Weber fraction for very light standard stimuli is much larger than 1/30, which is what is found in the middle range.

> ### CONCEPT SUMMARY
>
> - **Psychophysical methods** attempt to determine **absolute** and **difference thresholds**

We now examine two approaches that have the goal of devising a ratio scale of an internal psychological dimension. The first approach was undertaken by Fechner; he relied on the results of classical psychophysical methods to provide the data for his psychological scale. The second approach we examine is a more modern one, devised by S. S. Stevens.

Fechner's Law.   According to Weber's law, the difference threshold bears a constant relation to the standard stimulus: $\Delta I/I = K$. Fechner assumed that Weber's law was correct, and with two additional assumptions developed his law of sensation measurement. Fechner first assumed that the absolute threshold indicates the point of zero sensation. Then, he assumed that the **just-noticeable difference (JND),** which is the internal sensation evoked by two stimuli that differ by one difference threshold, is the unit defining the intervals of an internal psychological scale. Because Weber's law was assumed to be accurate, Fechner believed that all JNDs produce equal increments in sensation, as shown in Figure 5–2. Each JND step on the psychological scale corresponds to the physical stimulus that is one difference threshold greater than the preceding stimulus. The first unit beyond the zero point corresponds to the physical stimulus that is one JND

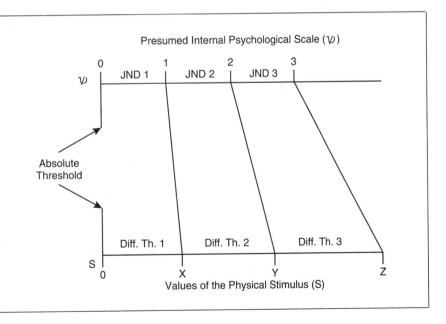

FIGURE 5–2
Fechner's law. Equal units on an internal psychological scale correspond to progressively greater units on an external physical scale (the difference thresholds): $\Psi = K \log (S)$.

Presumed Internal Psychological Scale (ψ)

Absolute Threshold

Diff. Th. 1   Diff. Th. 2   Diff. Th. 3

Values of the Physical Stimulus (S)

above the absolute threshold. The next point will be one JND above that, or two JNDs above the absolute threshold.

This process can be continued to build a psychological scale. Once this is done, there is a fixed mathematical relationship between the value of the physical scale corresponding to some point on the psychological scale and the physical value corresponding to the preceding point on the internal psychological scale. To find the physical-scale value that corresponds to a particular psychological value, we first take the physical value of the previous step on the external scale (for example, X in Figure 5–2) and multiply it by the Weber fraction. Then we add this product to our original value, so that $Y = X + X$ times the Weber fraction in Figure 5–2 (likewise, $Z = Y + Y$ times the Weber fraction). Summing in this fashion yields successive physical values that correspond to successive just-noticeable differences on the internal psychological scale. When this relationship is expanded and solved mathematically, we find that the psychological-scale value (ψ) is proportional to the logarithm of the physical-stimulus value. This equation (ψ = **K log stimulus**) is called **Fechner's law.**

According to Fechner's law, all JNDs produce equivalent increments in sensation; therefore, we should have a ratio scale (D'Amato, 1970). The sensation corresponding to six JNDs should be twice the sensation of three JNDs. However, two factors we discussed earlier should lead you to question whether Fechner devised a ratio scale of sensation. First, Fechner's zero point is arbitrary rather than absolute, because the absolute threshold is defined statistically as the average energy level that yields detection. Second, we know that Weber's law is only approximately true, which could result in psychological and physical units of varying sizes. There is an additional difficulty with Fechner's formulation. Fechner assumed that each JND was psychologically equal, but if you ask people about the magnitude of the sensory effects produced by stimuli of varying JNDs above threshold, there is poor correspondence between the two (D'Amato, 1970). Thus, Fechner's work is neither a ratio scale nor an interval scale. At best, it is an ordinal scale indicating that sensations are ordered in a particular way with regard to the physical stimuli that produce them.

Stevens' Power Law.   S. S. Stevens (1961) attempted to develop an internal scale of sensation more directly than did Fechner. Fechner used an **indirect scaling** method, in which the psychological scale was built up by putting successive JNDs in a row. The observers did not judge the magnitudes of the JNDs directly, so the psychological-scale values are derived from measures of discrimination; therefore, they are indirect. Stevens used several **direct scaling** techniques, in which the observer responded in psychological-scale units in the first place.

The primary direct scaling procedure used by Stevens was the method of **magnitude estimation,** which requires the observer to state a number that represents his or her sensation of the stimulus intensity. The first stimulus that the experimenter presents is arbitrarily assigned some convenient number, say, 100. Then other stimuli are assigned numbers, depending on how close the perceived intensity is to the first stimulus. For example, the experimenter could present a tone of moderate intensity and tell you it has a value of 100. Then a weaker tone might be presented. So you would give it a lower number, say, 87. These numbers reported by the observer represent perceived psychological values directly. When data are gathered in this way, the equation relating psychological value to physical value differs from the logarithmic relationship of Fechner's law. Instead, the equation obtained by Stevens (1961) is $\psi = K \text{ (Stimulus)}^n$, where n is an exponent. This equation is called **Stevens' law.**

If we assume that a stimulus of zero intensity always produces zero sensation, then we can accept Stevens' law as a ratio psychological scale. With a true zero, and with equal stimulus ratios producing equal sensation ratios (a power relation), we have satisfied the criteria for a ratio scale. If this is the case, then it seems reasonable to accept $\psi = K S^n$ as the way in which our internal sensations are related to the external world.

However, Stevens' work and conclusions have been criticized. There is debate as to what the observer is really reporting in the method of magnitude estimation. One controversy concerns whether observers report the intensity of sensation, as claimed by Stevens, or whether they instead report a learned association based on a correlation with a physical attribute linked to the stimulus—such that, for example, judgments of loudness reflect the experience that softer sounds are farther away from the subject (Warren, 1963).

A related problem has to do with the fact that different people use numbers differently. Some people, for example, always produce very large exponents in the equation of Stevens' law, and Stevens' law varies with the range of numbers used by the subjects (Marks, 1974).

A final problem with the magnitude estimation approach is related to operational definitions. Much research has shown that a particular sensory scale, such as brightness or pain, does not have just one psychophysical function that characterizes it. As Marks (1974) notes, you can accurately describe a power function for brightness only if you specify all of the other variables relevant to the perception of brightness—the color and duration of the light, the sensory adaptation of the observer, and so on. Varying these latter factors changes the value of the exponent in Stevens' law. We must operationally define the psychophysical function we obtain; otherwise, we would present a misleading view of the power function relating sensation to stimulus.

The preceding discussion of thresholds and psychophysical laws should convince you that the development of psychological measurement is difficult. Nevertheless, procedures such as the method of magnitude estimation have been valuable in psychology. The range of applicability of such procedures is very broad. For example, the method of magnitude estimation is not limited to developing psychological scales that have an obviously correlated physical dimension. Essay exams are often graded by magnitude estimates. Likewise, a substantial amount of research has examined the measurement of the severity of crimes and legal penalties by using magnitude estimation procedures (Sellin & Wolfgang, 1964; Stevens, 1966).

> **CONCEPT SUMMARY**
>
> - Fechner used an indirect method to determine the psychophysical relation between stimulus and sensation judgment, $\psi = K \log \text{stimulus}$
> - Stevens used the direct method of **magnitude estimation** and determined that the psychophysical relation between stimulus and sensation judgment was $\psi = K (\text{Stimulus})^n$

Psychometric Scaling

Cumulative (Guttman) Scales. In a **cumulative scale,** developed by Guttman (1944, 1950), the test results of a person with a higher rank than another person show that the higher-scoring individual scores just as high or higher than the other person on every item. Most psychologists call a cumulative scale a **Guttman scale.** The definition of a Guttman scale seems abstract but becomes more obvious when we consider a concrete example. Height could be developed into a good Guttman scale. A person might have to respond Yes or No to the following test items:

1. I am more than 54 inches tall.
2. I am more than 56 inches tall.
3. I am more than 58 inches tall.
4. I am more than 60 inches tall.
5. I am more than 62 inches tall.
6. I am more than 64 inches tall.
7. I am more than 66 inches tall.

If this were a cumulative scale that worked precisely according to Guttman's specifications, a person who responded positively to item number 4 will also have responded positively to numbers 1 through 3. Suppose that a person said Yes to item 5, then he or she would also say Yes to the first four items if the test were perfectly cumulative. On a perfect Guttman scale, a person who said Yes to item 6 will have said Yes to all the lower-numbered questions.

This hypothetical Guttman scale is not likely to replace any of the standard measures of length, but it does illustrate what comprises a cumulative scale. The example shows that in a perfect Guttman scale, the total score of a person should allow us to reproduce the responses of the individual exactly. If a person is a 3, then he or she responded Yes to items 1 through 3 and No to items 4 through 7. This reproducibility is highly likely in this example but much less likely when we consider more complex examples of Guttman scales.

Suppose you were interested in assessing the extent to which workers participate in union activities. You could simply ask people, "Do you participate—Yes or No," which would yield a nominal scale that does not provide much information concerning the construct of union participation. Kelloway and Barling (1993) used the Guttman cumulative scaling technique to try to get a more powerful measure of participation of workers in union activities. Previous work had not successfully measured union participation, which means that workers' satisfaction with union activity, whether they support the union, and related issues were not well understood. Although the earlier work on the issue had identified different ways in which the workers participated in union activities, a convenient way of scaling union participation was lacking. Kelloway and Barling examined the earlier information and believed that they could develop a cumulative scale reflecting degrees of involvement in union activities. They devised a seven-item scale, to which members of three different unions responded Yes or No. The lowest-scaled item was "I read union literature" and the highest was "I hold an office in the union." In all, over 1,200 union members completed the scale.

Some fictious results of using the scale devised by Kelloway and Barling are shown in Table 5–1. In the table we show how seven (hypothetical) workers responded to the scale, which is illustrated at the top of the table. Notice that all seven response categories are identified. Typically, a person's choice is converted into a number, so that each Yes is awarded a value of 1, and the total score is the total number of Yes responses.

In Table 5–1 the people are ordered according to their scale score. Jones is the highest and Barns is the lowest. Real results based on a large number of respondents would have several people with the same score, as Burns and Brown do in the example. Note that Smith and Brown do not have perfect cumulative answers. Both Smith and Brown have a Y response after an N, so the hypothetical results indicate a less than perfect scale.

Guttman evaluated the adequacy of his scales by the ratio of the numbers of appropriate responses to the total number of responses, which he called the **coefficient of reproducibility.** According to Guttman, .90 repre-

TABLE 5–1
Hypothetical Guttman scaling results for union participation. A Y stands for a Yes response, and N stands for No. In a perfect cumulative scale, Ns would not be intermixed with Ys, as is true for Smith and Brown.

Person	Level 1 Read Union Materials	Level 2 Meet with Union Reps	Level 3 Vote for Union Ideas	Level 4 Vote in Elections	Level 5 Attend Meetings	Level 6 Serve on Committees	Level 7 Hold Union Office
Jones	Y	Y	Y	Y	Y	Y	Y
White	Y	Y	Y	Y	Y	Y	N
Black	Y	Y	Y	Y	Y	N	N
Smith	Y	Y	N	Y	N	N	N
Brown	Y	N	Y	N	N	N	N
Burns	Y	Y	N	N	N	N	N
Barns	Y	N	N	N	N	N	N

sents the minimum value for an acceptable coefficient. In Table 5–1 the number of misplaced Y responses is 2, and the total number of responses is 49, so the coefficient of reproducibility is $47/49 = .96$, which is sufficiently high to indicate a good scale. In the research conducted by Kelloway and Barling, they report that the coefficients of reproducibility for their three samples were .92, .91, and .91. Thus according to the standard criterion, they demonstrated an adequate scale of union participation for people in three different unions.

Another example of Guttman scaling can be found in the work by Fleming, Leventhal, Glynn, and Ershler (1989), who examined drug use in middle-school children. The researchers wanted to determine the progression in substance use as it went from initial to regular use. Furthermore, they were interested in the cumulative relation among various substances. They found that cigarettes, marijuana, beer, liquor, and stimulants (or depressants) fell on a Guttman (cumulative) scale (in the order listed). Thus, substance abusers of middle-school age show a cumulative progression that fits a Guttman scale.

Most psychometricians view the results of cumulative scaling to be at the ratio level, because a person's score represents a count of the behaviors present, which could have a meaningful zero. A more conservative view notes that the score is based on a count of items that amount to a ranking of an individual. In Table 5–1, for example, Burns scored twice as high as Barns (2 versus 1). Can we legitimately view Burns's scores as representing twice as much union participation? It is not clear from the present example that this is the case. Nevertheless, the cumulative scaling technique is a popular one and has been used to scale a wide variety of constructs.

CONCEPT SUMMARY

- **Cumulative (Guttman) scale** is a psychometric scale in which a person with a higher rank than another is just as high or higher than that person on every item on the scale.
- **Coefficient of reproducibility** is a ratio of appropriate to total answers on a Guttman scale that should be at least .90.

Summated Rating (Likert) Scale. Because many constructs may not lend themselves to cumulative scaling, the **summated rating scale,** also called a **Likert scale** after its developer (Likert, 1932), appears more often in the technical literature. A summated rating scale provides a score for a psychometric property of a person that derives from how the person responds to several statements that clearly are favorable or unfavorable concerning the topic being measured. The respondent typically has five alternatives from which to select his or her answer to each statement: *strongly agree, agree, undecided, disagree,* and *strongly disagree.* Each response alternative is associated with a number, and then these ratings are summated for all the questions, which represents the respondent's score. For example, a *strongly disagree* choice receives a score of 5.

A concrete example will illustrate the development of a summated rating scale. Suppose we wanted to develop a scale of how people view their body image. We would gather several positive and negative statements concerning body image, have people respond to them, and have them sum their ratings. Consider these two questions (taken from an example used by Reckase, 1990), in which the standard response alternatives (*strongly agree, agree, undecided, disagree, strongly disagree*) are abbreviated (*SA, A, U, D, SD,* respectively). The usual instructions ask the respondent to indicate the answer that best describes her or his judgment about the statement. The first statement is positive and the second is negative with respect to attitudes about body image.

1. I have a well-proportioned body.
    SA   A   U   D   SD

2. I am noticeably oddly shaped.
    SA   A   U   D   SD

Numbers are assigned to the response categories, but they are reversed for the two questions. If the numbers assigned in question 1 were 5, 4, 3, 2, and 1 for the response categories SA, A, U, D, and SD, then they would be 1, 2, 3, 4, and 5 for question number 2. In this particular example, then, a high score would mean that the individual regarded his or her body image positively, and a low score would indicate the converse.

The Likert technique is a popular one, because it seems adaptable to measuring many constructs, especially those related to the respondent's attitudes. Desharnais, Godin, Joblin, and Valois (1990) wanted to determine how heart attack victims related their overall view of life toward their own health. They related two measures of their subjects' behavior, and both measures of the target behaviors were accomplished by Likert scales. The researchers assessed interviews from 158 patients who had recently had a heart attack. Initially they administered a test to determine whether the patients were optimists or pessimists. The degree of optimism or pessimism was measured by their score on the Life Orientation Test (Scheier & Carver, 1985). This test yields a summated rating based on items such as the following:

In uncertain times, I usually expect the best.

If something can go wrong, it will.

Optimists will strongly agree with the first statement and disagree with the second; "agreement" answers received high numbers, and "disagreement" ones were awarded low numbers. People were defined as optimists if they scored above the median score on the test (the median is the middle score); otherwise, people were classified as pessimists. Desharnais and his colleagues determined the health-related thoughts of their participants on a four-item Likert scale that they devised, which is illustrated in Table 5–2. Note that they had their participants respond on a seven-point scale rather than the five-point one, which is more typical.

Optimists scored lower than pessimists on the first three items, and they scored somewhat higher on the last one. Desharnais and his colleagues concluded that one's general view of the world (optimistic or pessimistic)

TABLE 5-2
The Likert (summated rating) scale devised by Desharnais and associates (1990) to assess health-related cognitions.

1. How likely do you think it is that you will have another heart attack during the coming year?

7	6	5	4	3	2	1
Very Likely	Likely	Somewhat Likely	Undecided	Somewhat Unlikely	Unlikely	Very Unlikely

2. How serious do you think a heart attack would be if you had one in the next year?

7	6	5	4	3	2	1
Very Serious	Serious	Somewhat Serious	Undecided	Somewhat Serious	Not Serious	Not at all Serious

3. How afraid are you of having another heart attack in the coming year?

7	6	5	4	3	2	1
Very Afraid	Afraid	Somewhat Afraid	Undecided	Somewhat Unafraid	Unafraid	Not at all Afraid

4. How likely do you think you can forestall another heart attack in the coming year?

7	6	5	4	3	2	1
Very Unlikely	Unlikely	Somewhat Unlikely	Undecided	Somewhat Likely	Likely	Very Likely

has an influence on how one views his or her health prospects. Furthermore, optimists are more likely than pessimists to believe that they can alter their health.

Items on a Likert scale are evaluated by seeing how they reflect the total score received by an individual. A statistical procedure called a **coefficient of correlation** is used to see whether the score on an individual item is positively related to the total score. When all the people who took the test are examined, a high score on a particular item should go with a high summated score; likewise, a low score on an item should go with a low total score. Such a direct relationship between the two sets of scores is called a *positive correlation* and is usually considerably less than perfect.

A positive correlation is a desired result when items are analyzed against the total score. What constitutes a bad result? One unwanted result would occur if the score on a specific item correlated negatively with the summated score. For example, if people scored low on the summated rating of the health scale, but they regularly said that they were very afraid that they were going to have another heart attack soon, there would be a negative coefficient of correlation between scores on that item and the total scores. This inverse relationship would likely lead the researcher to question the validity of the statement in question, because this negative relation reflects an attitude contrary to the attitude expressed by the total score. If the researcher discovered the inverse relationship as the scale was being constructed, then it is likely that the bad item would be reworded. If rewording did not remove the negative relationship between that item's score and the total, then it would be removed or replaced by another item. Other uses of the coefficient of correlation and how it is calculated are discussed in later chapters, because it can be very useful in understanding behavior.

The Likert procedure assigns a number to the ratings given to attitude statements or questions, and the scale score that a person receives is the sum of the ratings. The scale score assigned to a person is usually treated as coming from at least an interval scale. Sometimes, the scale score could be considered a ratio one if the numerical coding allows for zero values—such as having the scale illustrated in Table 5–2 to 0 to 6 instead of 1 to 7. A more cautious view is that the total score is made up of a number of ordinal scores (rankings), so that the difference between a 7 and 5 may not be the same as that between a 1 and a 3 on the health scale. Most Likert scales are derived from responses to several statements, which means that the lack of equal intervals on any one statement may be blurred across statements. The resulting summated rating might then be insensitive to problems associated with an individual statement, and it might be sensible to consider the scale scores as interval or ratio numbers.

CONCEPT SUMMARY

- **Summated rating (Likert) scale** is the sum of the ratings that people give to attitude statements. Typically people respond to positively and negatively oriented statements on five-point scales.
- **Coefficients of correlation** relate scores on an individual item to the summated score; there should be a positive relation between the two.

Self-Report Methods.   The two psychometric scales we have discussed represent **self-report methods,** because the psychological data come from a personal report by the respondent and not from observation methods, in which behavior is observed and measured more directly by the researcher. Thus, self-report methods yield data that usually cannot be corroborated immediately and directly by the observer. Not all psychometric scales are self-reports. Many scales, including intelligence tests and other assessment tests (for example, the Scholastic Aptitude Test), provide data that evaluate directly a person's characteristics. We examine the latter sorts of tests in subsequent chapters.

Self-report psychometric scales (and psychophysical ones, too) face a difficult problem. Consider the issue this way. Suppose you have devised a Likert scale to assess a person's depression. A respondent says on the test, "Yes, I agree that I cry regularly." How does the researcher know whether that answer reflects what the person actually does? Does the response represent a true reflection of the person's emotional state? Does the response reflect what the person does? Or, does the response simply correspond to what the respondent believes a typical person would say in answering such questions? Furthermore, answers to all questions may not have easy methods of verification, so how does the researcher determine the veracity of the total scale score? This very difficult problem poses the question of the validity or soundness of the measurement scale; namely, the problem of how we determine what we are measuring. This issue is addressed in the next section, as well as in other chapters.

RELIABILITY AND VALIDITY OF MEASUREMENT

The different types of scales permit us to make different conclusions. Thus, the validity of our conclusions depends, in part, on whether they are warranted by the type of measurement used. **Validity** refers to whether what we are doing is sound or meaningful. It is not meaningful, and therefore, invalid, to make ratio statements about characteristics measured at the ordinal level. *Validity* also refers to whether we have measured what we have intended to measure. We will consider several nuances of the concept of validity throughout the book, so be prepared to readdress this important concept.

A common form of validation is to check a measurement against some **criterion,** which is another measurement of behavior that serves as a standard for the measurement in question (see the Application section). In general terms, criterion validity involves relating one aspect of a person's behavior, such as intelligence, to another measure of his or her behavior, say success in school. If the relation is a strong one, then we can predict one behavior when we know the other, which is often called **predictive validity.** If an intelligence score is valid, then it should predict success in school.

Psychologists who desire a clear answer to a research question want the results and conclusions to be both valid and reliable. **Reliability** refers to the consistency of the measures of behavior. Reconsider the research on social loafing that was discussed in Chapter 2. Clear answers about the nature of social loafing would be impossible if measures of it were inconsistent. You might suppose that several attempts to measure the same thing would all yield the same numbers, unless of course someone had made an error. In fact, there is always some variability, or differences among scores, in a group of measures, even of the same thing. The amount of variability determines the reliability of the measuring instrument and procedure. Highly variable measures indicate low reliability, and vice versa. The measurement "error" to which psychologists and statisticians often refer is meant to imply not that someone made a mistake, but merely that certain unavoided factors caused unpredictable variability in the data. Psychologists try to reduce this variability, hence increasing the reliability of their measures, by taking their measures under the same conditions.

Psychologists often use sophisticated equipment to enhance the reliability of observations and measurements. In particular, the digital computer plays a major role in controlling experimental manipulations and recording dependent variables. For example, suppose you wish to examine how quickly people can respond to pictures that they see for a very short period of time. A properly programmed computer can precisely control the presentation time of the pictures, and it can consistently provide an accurate measure of the response times. One can, for example, program a computer to display a picture for just a few milliseconds (thousandths of a second). If the program sets the display time for ten milliseconds, then that display time will be precisely replicated each time a picture is shown. Also, response times can be measured with millisecond resolution, which is impossible to do with stop watches and difficult with many other kinds of apparatus. It is an understatement to say that the digital computer has markedly increased the reliability and precision of experimental control and measurement.

CONCEPT SUMMARY

- **Validity** refers to the soundness of a measurement and to whether we measure what we intend to measure.
- **Predictive validity** relates one measure of behavior to a criterion.
- **Reliability** refers to the consistency of the measures of behavior.

Test Reliability

The reliability of the results of tests and other descriptive measures of behavior is often checked by taking measures under the same conditions on successive occasions. If identical conditions could be ensured, then variability in measurement would have to be caused by a real change in the measured quantity. If your height is measured on two occasions, with the results 5'8" and 5'10", is this variability owing to error or to a real change in your height? The answer could be either, or both. But the more similar the conditions—shoes worn, posture—the less likely you would be to attribute the difference to error. Also, the closer the two measures were in time, the less likely you would be to attribute the difference to a real change in stature. You have some notion of how quickly stature can change, or of the stability of a person's true stature.

Intelligence and other psychological processes are more difficult to measure than stature, however. It is also more difficult to develop a notion of their stability. Do they vary at all, or do they remain fixed throughout life? If they change markedly, can they do so within a week, a month, a year, or ten years? If something changes, can we determine those factors that produce the change or are the changes the result of unreliable measurement? These are questions that psychologists would like to answer; the answers require measurement. But the alert reader will realize that we have now reasoned ourselves into a logical circle. Let us go around again, and try to get out.

Several measures of the same quantity will not, in general, exactly agree. This variability may be a result either of error or of a real change in the measured quantity. We cannot tell, without some additional assumptions, how much error there is in our measurement. Thus, how can we ask if a psychological process changes? A useful assumption—one that allows the logical circle to be broken—is that the measured quantity is stable over relatively short periods of time. (If a researcher measures your intelligence in the morning and then again in the afternoon under the same conditions, any change can be assumed to be caused by measurement error rather than a real change in intelligence.) With this assumption, a psychologist can estimate measurement error and attempt to improve and specify the reliability of the measuring instrument.

We will examine test reliability in the context of the concept of intelligence, which is not well defined theoretically and is difficult to measure. Some theorists postulate a number of separate mental abilities, perhaps more than a hundred (Guilford, 1967). Others believe that there is one primary mental ability and that although other more specific abilities may be isolated, they are less important. This primary ability has been described as "a capacity for abstract reasoning and problem solving" (Jensen, 1969, p. 19). To test for this ability, collections of problems or tasks are presented to individuals to solve, generally within a specified time period. The score that an individual achieves is then compared with scores obtained by others. Before placing much confidence in an individual's score, however, we need to know how reliable it is. Would the individual achieve about the same score if we were to test him or her again the next day, or a week later? Because we do not believe that the underlying ability changes appreciably over so short a time, we attribute a large change in scores to measurement error, indicating unreliability in our test. This procedure of giving the same test twice in succession over a short time interval is used to determine what is called the **test-retest reliability** of a measure. It is generally expressed as a coefficient of correlation between first and second scores obtained from a large sample of subjects. A high, positive correlation indicates high reliability.

A slightly different procedure can be employed to avoid problems such as specific practice effects. This technique involves giving alternate or **parallel forms** of the test on the two testing occasions. Again, if correlations between first and second scores are high, they indicate reliability of the tests. Also, the equivalence of the two forms of the test can be determined in this way.

A third procedure can be used to evaluate reliability with a single test presentation. This technique provides **split-half reliability;** it involves dividing the test items into two arbitrary groups and correlating the scores obtained in the two halves of the test. If these correlations are high, the test reliability is confirmed. In addition, the equivalence of the test items is established. The reliability and validity of the SAT are considered in the Application section.

CONCEPT SUMMARY

Test reliability is determined by the

- **test-retest** method
- **parallel forms** method
- **split-half** method

APPLICATION

THE RELIABILITY AND VALIDITY OF THE SAT

The College Board Scholastic Aptitude Test (SAT) is one of the most widely used and widely researched tests. Most of you have taken the SAT or a similar test. Is it a good test?

The SAT is a very reliable test. All forms of reliability have been examined, and on all counts the SAT does very well. Generally, reliability is measured by a correlation coefficient, which tells how two variables relate to each other. A perfectly reliable test, meaning that the two scores are identical at two different times or on alternative forms, would yield a coefficient of + 1.0. The usual finding is that the SAT gives reliability coefficients of + .9 or better. Thus, you need not be concerned about the reliability of the SAT.

What about the validity of the SAT? Validity is usually checked by examining the correlation between SAT scores and grades in the freshman year in college. This type of validity check, using grades as the criterion, is an example of predictive validity. The results here are good but not as dramatic as the reliability results. The typical validity coefficient is around + .35. This means that the SAT is a fair predictor of freshman grades. Usually, the high-school record is combined with SAT scores for predictive purposes, and this yields a much better prediction of freshman grades (a coefficient of better than + .6).

One area the SAT runs into trouble is in predicting the grades of students who score in the middle ranges (combined scores between 900 and 1200 on the verbal and quantitative components). Within this range other factors, such as motivation and emotional stability, seem to play a very important role in college success. Although the SAT is reliable and has fair validity, college success may be related to factors other than high SAT scores, especially the willingness to work hard and the desire to achieve.

SOURCE: Kaplan, R. M., & Saccuzzo, D. P. (1982). *Psychological testing: Principles, applications, and issues.* Monterey, CA: Brooks/Cole.

Statistical Reliability and Validity

Given a set of results, their reliability can be assessed statistically. The methods of inferential statistics (see appendix B) allow the **statistical reliability** of data to be assessed by showing how likely it is to obtain those results by chance. In an experiment, for example, inferential statistics are used to determine whether a difference obtained between conditions results from the operation of the independent variable or from chance factors. If the difference between conditions is great enough so that it would be expected to occur by chance in fewer than one case in twenty, then the researcher rejects the possibility that chance factors produced the result. Instead, the difference is accepted as evidence for a real or statistically significant effect of the independent variable. When the results of the Stroop experiment conducted in chapter 1 are analyzed statistically, we find that the differences are large enough to consider them reliable rather than owing to chance.

Sampling

Another statistical factor that influences the reliability of measures has to do with the number of observations that are made. When we take measures of behavior, we rarely investigate the entire **population** that we could study (for example, all college students). Rather, we usually select a **sample** to measure, such as volunteer psychology students in our college. Generally speaking, the greater the number of observations in our sample, the more confident we can be that the sample reflects the characteristics of the population. If a sample of persons is asked about preference for candidates in an upcoming election, we can be more confident that the survey results reflect the population of voters if the sample consists of 100,000 people than if it contains only 100.

Most statistical tests are sensitive to the size of the sample. That is, most tests are more likely to detect true effects of independent variables when the number of observations is large than when it is small. When a statistical test can detect effects, it is said to have **power.** The power of most statistical tests is increased by increasing the number of measures.

How a sample is determined also can affect the validity of the sample. Because only a sample of an entire population is usually studied in a research project, you need to try to obtain a sample that accurately represents the characteristics of the population. How can you be sure that sophomores taking introductory psychology at your institution are representative of all sophomores in colleges?

Sampling is discussed further in appendix B, and other aspects of representativeness are considered later. For now, we want to emphasize random sampling and its relation to sample size. **Random sampling** means that each member of a particular population has an equal chance of being selected for the sample. Unbiased random selection guarantees in the long run that the sample represents the population. This does not mean that a particular sample will be perfectly representative of the population, and hence a perfectly valid sample of the population; that cannot be guaranteed. What random selection does mean is that you can make a statistical or probabilistic guess that the sample is representative of the population. When a research procedure has features that do not limit conclusions to the procedural details itself, then we say that the research has **external validity.** Random sampling should allow us to have a sample that represents a larger population, which means that conclusions we draw may be externally valid. Let us see how this works.

You probably believe, intuitively, that large samples are more representative of the population than are small samples. You might expect, for example, that one unusual member of a small sample will distort your results more than if that deviant member was part of a larger sample. You can test this yourself by tossing coins. The more coins you toss (the larger your sample is of all coin tosses), the closer you get to seeing the ideal of 50 percent heads show up (Thompson and Buchanan, 1979).

The value of random selection is related to sample size in an interesting way. Kerlinger (1986) suggests that large sample sizes allow the effects of random selection to work. Very small samples are less likely to be representative of the population because even random selection can yield a limited or biased sample if the sample size is very small. An unusual member of a small random sample can have unfortunate effects even when that individual was selected at random. Thus, a large random sample is likely to yield a more externally valid representation of the population than is a small one. The effect of selecting by chance one unusual individual is diluted in large samples.

Random selection is an ideal that is rarely attained in psychology because it is extremely expensive and time consuming to try to sample from an entire population, such as all college sophomores. Because individuals differ in many ways, we can often assume that the population of possible scores in a research project can vary in a random way (Glenberg, 1988). If that is the case, then it is crucial that participants be assigned to experimental conditions on a random basis. In conducting an experiment on the effects of a brain operation on memory, it is necessary that the operation be the only difference between the operated and unoperated animals. Otherwise, random differences among the subjects could be confounded with the independent variable, and a clear answer to the research question might be unlikely. In this context, *confounding* refers to differences between groups that do not result from the independent variable. When an experiment has minimal confounding variables, then we say that it has **internal validity,** which allows us to make accurate conclusions about the effects of the independent variable on the dependent variable. Differences attributable to the characteristics of the subjects can be minimized by randomly assigning subjects to conditions. **Random assignment** means that any given subject has an unbiased chance of being in any condition of an experiment. When subjects are assigned randomly, the chances of individual differences confounding the outcome are minimized. Random assignment to conditions helps to increase the internal validity of the research procedure.

CONCEPT SUMMARY

- **Statistical reliability** determines whether results are owing to chance.
- **Random sampling** helps insure the external validity of a sample taken from a population.
- **Random assignment** to conditions helps insure the internal validity of an experiment.

Experimental Reliability

Statistical reliability is an important condition for taking seriously an experimental result, but many researchers prefer to see an experimenter also establish **experimental reliability.** If the experiment is repeated under essentially the same conditions, a replication, will the results be the same as they were before? An adage among researchers is that "one replication is worth a thousand *t* tests." (The *t* test is a well-known statistical test used to evaluate the statistical reliability between two conditions.) The gist of the adage is that many researchers are more convinced by replications of the experiment than by inferential statistics applied to the original outcome. Although an outcome may be deemed statistically reliable, the possibility remains that it could have occurred by chance (statistical reliability still allows a 5 percent error rate) or because of some unintentional confounding or error on the part of the experimenter. For example, perhaps smarter subjects happened to be assigned to one condition rather than to another. Although these possibilities might seem unlikely, they do sometimes occur. In some experiments, subjects are randomly assigned to conditions (see above), and then, prior to the main experiment, the various groups are given a pretest to determine whether the groups are actually equivalent (on the average) in ability. Occasionally, pretests of this sort turn up differences, before the independent variable has been introduced (see, for example, Tulving and Pearlstone, 1966). Because such problems can occur even in well-controlled research, researchers encourage replication of experiments, even when inferential statistics indicate that some effect is reliable.

CONCEPT SUMMARY

- **Experimental reliability** can be assessed by conducting replications of the experiment in question.

SUMMARY

1. Measurement is a systematic way of assigning numbers or names to objects and their attributes.

2. Measurement scales, such as the familiar scales for temperature and weight can assess four properties: difference, magnitude, equal intervals, and whether there is a true zero.

3. Measurement scales used in psychology differ in how much information they provide. Nominal scales simply measure differences. Ordinal scales measure differences and magnitude. Interval scales add equal intervals to the features of ordinal scales.

Ratio scales have all the properties of the other scales and a true zero point.

4. The scale of measurement determines the kinds of statistical treatment that the numbers can receive, and the scale of measurement also determines the kinds of conclusions that can be drawn from the results.

5. Intervening variables are often designated as theoretical constructs.

6. Theoretical constructs that have well-specified inputs and outputs often are measured psychophysically. On the other hand, theoretical constructs that must be assessed because of imprecise knowledge of inputs are usually scaled psychometrically.

7. Fechner, a founder of psychophysics, devised ways to measure absolute and difference thresholds.

8. According to Weber's law, the size of the difference threshold relative to the standard stimulus is a constant for a particular sensory modality ($\Delta I/I = K$).

9. Using an indirect scaling method by adding up just-noticeable differences, Fechner held that psychological judgments were related to the physical stimulus logarithmically ($\Psi = K \log$ stimulus). His law and methods result in an ordinal scale of sensory measurement.

10. Stevens used the method of magnitude estimation, which is a direct scaling method. His law of sensory measurement is a power one, $\Psi = K(\text{Stimulus})^n$, which is considered to result in a ratio scale.

11. A cumulative scale, which is often called a Guttman scale, is characterized by a scale in which a person with a higher rank than another person is just as high or higher than the other person on every item on the scale.

12. A cumulative scale is considered to be a good one if the coefficient of reproducibility, which is a ratio of appropriate to total answers, is at least .9.

13. A summated rating scale, also called a Likert scale, is the sum of the ratings that people give to attitude statements. Typically, people respond to positively and negatively oriented statements on five-point scales that go from *strongly disagree* to *strongly agree*.

14. Coefficients of correlation assess the relation between the score on an individual item and the summated score. Good items have scores that are positively related to the summated score.

15. The reliability of a measure refers to its consistency. Using standardized conditions is an important way to insure the reliability of measurement. Validity refers to whether measurements are sound or meaningful.

16. The reliability of test results can be shown by test-retest reliability, by split-half reliability, or by using parallel forms of the test.

17. Inferential statistics permit an assessment of statistical reliability by showing whether the results were owing to chance factors.

18. The larger the sample size from a population, the greater is the reliability and the power of the statistical tests.

19. Random samples help to increase the external validity of the sample.

20. Random assignment of subjects to conditions helps to increase the internal validity of an experiment.

21. Experimental reliability is assessed by conducting replications and is often preferred to statistical reliability.

■ KEY CONCEPTS

absolute threshold
coefficient of correlation
coefficient of reproducibility
criterion
cumulative scale
difference
difference threshold
direct scaling
equal intervals
experimental reliability
external validity
Fechner's law ($\Psi = K \log$ Stimulus)
Guttman scale
indirect scaling
internal validity
interval scale
just-noticeable difference (JND)
Likert scale
magnitude
magnitude estimation
measurement
nominal scale

ordinal scale
parallel forms
population
power
predictive validity
psychometric scaling
psychophysics
psychophysical scaling
random assignment
random sampling
ratio scale
reliability
sample
self-report methods
split-half reliability
statistical reliability
Stevens' law ($\Psi = K$(Stimulus)^n)
summated rating scale
test-retest reliability
theoretical constructs
true zero
validity
Weber's law ($\Delta I / I = K$)

■ EXERCISES

1. Discuss the differences between the various types of measurement scales. Indicate the scale properties of each.

2. [*Special Exercise*]. Consider each of the following measures and indicate the type of measurement scale that is involved: October 22, 1850; the number of alarm calls by a chickadee in one hour; third place in a beauty contest; having the fifth highest grades in a class of 29 people; and being a sophomore in college.

3. Outline a way of creating a Guttman scale of athletic ability for tennis.

4. Devise a way of using Likert techniques for assessing students' attitudes toward the presence of fraternities and sororities on campus.

5. Discuss why a test cannot be valid if it is not reliable.

6. Why is it likely that a confounding of subjects with levels of the independent variable make an experiment invalid?

■ SUGGESTED READINGS

Measurement theory is a complex topic. A good introduction can be found in:

McCall, R. B. (1990). *Fundamental statistics for the behavioral sciences* (5th ed.). San Diego: Harcourt Brace.
Numerous textbooks emphasize psychometrics. Any current textbook concerned with psychological testing will be helpful. The specifics of scaling can be found in Goldstein, G., & Herson, M. (Eds.). (1990). *Handbook of psychological assessment* (2nd ed.). New York: Pergamon.

Psychology in Action
Validity

The validity of self-report methods is usually much more difficult to determine than it is for observational scales. Both observational and self-report methods often have strong face validity, which simply means that the questions appear to be asking about the concept in question. At face value, then, we might think that a person who claims to cry frequently would be more unhappy than someone who denies that he or she cries frequently. The face validity of a test or its components may not be a good guide to its ability to measure behavior. For example, do you think a depressed person would sleep more or less than a nondepressed person? One possibility might be that someone suffering from depression would sleep constantly in order to escape from depressing thoughts. On the other hand, a depressed person might have difficulty in sleeping, because he or she is constantly thinking about unhappy things.

Which of these two reasonable expectations best describes a depressed person? More to the point of this chapter, what kind of questions should we ask on a self-report scale of depression? We are not going to tell you about the sleeping behavior of depressed people, because the issue here goes beyond the particulars of depression. This point is that face validity rarely captures the subtleties of a problem. Rather, a substantial amount of data will permit a sensible way of validating a particular construct. The typical course of scale development has a criterion in mind as well as a background of knowledge regarding the target concept. These two sources of information guide the development of the scale.

One way to understand this process is to examine the *Mental Measurements Yearbook*. This publication summarizes the characteristics of various kinds of psychometric instruments, including personality tests, intelligence scales, and aptitude tests. Information regarding a scale's reliability and validity are presented, and the typical review of a scale includes summaries of how the test was developed and standardized. You will find that perusing this book will be very informative. As an exercise for this chapter, you might try examining how the validity for several self-report scales has been determined. You might want to contrast those with the validity criteria that are used for psychometric scales that rely on more direct observations.

Observations are evaluated for

❏ Construct validity

❏ External validity

❏ Internal validity

Descriptive observations include

❏ Naturalistic observation

❏ Case studies

❏ Surveys

Descriptive observations

❏ Provide a database for controlled research

❏ Are often very flexible

❏ Examine the ecological function of behavior

Descriptive observations may suffer from

❏ Researcher bias

❏ Subject reactivity

❏ Internal invalidity

CHAPTER 6

OBSERVATION IN PSYCHOLOGICAL RESEARCH

In this chapter we examine observations in psychology. First, we consider the validity or truth of observations, which is evaluated according to whether they have construct validity, external validity, and internal validity. Then, we provide an overview of descriptive observations. Descriptive observations provide a valuable database and may lead to an understanding of the ecological function of a behavior.

Science is an intellectual enterprise that builds cumulatively. From a scientific perspective, we know more about the world today than people have known at any other time in history. On the other hand, literature, art, and most other humanities may be different today than they were in ancient Greece, but we probably cannot say that these disciplines are in better shape or more accurately represent the world.

One primary reason that science cumulates is that scientists strive for the most accurate observation possible of the world. As we have stated, science is self-correcting in that scientists develop theories and hypotheses that allow prediction about what should happen under specified conditions. These ideas are then tested by comparing the predictions to carefully collected observations. When the observations differ drastically from predictions, scientists modify or abandon their theoretical conceptions. Much of the scientific enterprise concerns empirical observation: the collection of data on some particular aspect of the world.

Observers are fallible. Seeing should not be believing—at least not always. Often our perceptions fool us, as we can see by the way we perceive the optical illusions in Figure 6–1. We have all seen magicians perform seemingly impossible feats before our eyes, when we knew that we were being tricked by natural means. Such tricks demonstrate that direct perceptions can be inaccurate if we are not careful, and sometimes even if we are.

Scientists, being human, are also subject to errors of observation. Essentially the research techniques employed by scientists—including logic, use of complicated apparatus, controlled conditions, and so on—are there to guard against errors of perception and to ensure that observations reflect the state of nature as accurately as possible. Even with our best methods and most careful techniques of observation, however, we can only approximate this ideal.

In this chapter we first consider the characteristics of sound (valid) observations and examine some of the difficulties associated with making them. Then we outline the major ways in which psychologists make observations.

VALID OBSERVATIONS

Psychological observations provide scientific understanding by describing behavior (**descriptive observations**), relating two or more behaviors (**relational observations**), and explaining the causes of behavior (**explanation**). When do we know that our descriptions, relationships, and explanations are good? Good observations of any kind are valid. **Validity** in this context refers to the truth of the observations. Because scientific truth changes as new observations are made (see Chapter 2), it is probably safest to assert that validity and its converse, invalidity, "refer to the best available approximation to the truth or falsity of propositions" (Cook & Campbell, 1979, p. 37). The validity of descriptions, relationships, and explanations is usually considered in three ways, which we examine in turn: construct validity, external validity, and internal validity.

FIGURE 6-1
Visual illusions. (a) the Müller-Lyer illusion. The vertical lines are the same length, but appear unequal due to the different directions of the fins in the two cases. (b) The illusion apparently distorts even an objective measuring device, the ruler. But close examination indicates that the ruler is not really distorted and that the lines are of equal length. (c) The rulers now appear bent, due to the influence of the circle. These illusions are maintained even though we ''know,'' as in (b), they cannot be so. Our observations can suffer distortions no matter how careful we are (examples taken from R. L. Gregory, 1970, pp. 80–81).

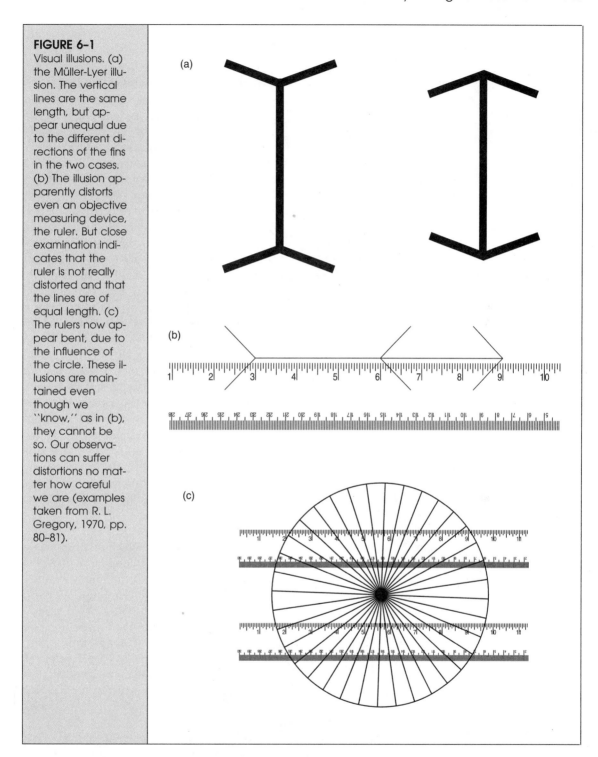

Construct Validity

In a particular research project, the degree to which the independent and dependent variables accurately reflect or measure what they are intended to measure is called **construct validity** (Cook & Campbell, 1979; Judd, Smith, & Kidder, 1991). Consider the Stroop experiment from Chapter 1. Are the three levels of the independent variable used in that experiment valid reflections of reading? Certainly, each task involves reading, so at least for this research project we might safely assume that these are valid ways to test aspects of reading. What about the dependent variable—the time to go through the lists—is it a valid measure of reading? Certainly, how smoothly and quickly one reads is a good indicant of reading. However, there are at least two ways in which our measure may be invalid. One source of invalidity is that some confounding variable could have influenced reading times rather than the independent variable.

Reading out loud may involve processes that do not occur when people read silently to themselves, which means that we may not be measuring "reading" as we usually consider it. This sort of confounding could result in very low construct validity, because we believe we are studying reading when we are really examining something else. The task imposed on the participants—reading aloud—resulted in confounding and, perhaps, low validity. Let us consider an example of another sort of confounding that was associated with the way in which the participants were tested.

Katz, Lautenschlager, Blackburn, and Harris (1990) have argued that the SAT test suffers from construct invalidity as a result of confounding. They found that people responded at better than chance levels (20%) on SAT reading questions in the absence of reading the passages. Because people did not have to read the passages to get correct answers, Katz and associates argued that the reading questions did not measure reading comprehension. Rather, these startling results seem to indicate either of two possibilities. The general knowledge and reasoning ability of the people could have allowed them to answer the questions correctly. Alternatively, information in the question allowed the people to determine the correct answer, because it was highly related to the information in the missing reading passage.

If Katz and associates are correct, then the usefulness of the reading comprehension portions of the SAT (and by extension similar multiple-choice reading tests) may be minimal. Recently, Freedle and Kostin (1994) claim to have evidence supporting the idea that the SAT reading tests measure comprehension. Through a series of analyses they, too, found evidence suggesting that the structure of the questions can influence the degree of correct answers. In addition, however, Freedle and Kostin showed that subjects do use information in the passages to answer the questions. More important, the passage information plays a stronger role in correct responding than do the questions themselves. Freedle and Katz cautioned that although their results seemed to show some construct validity for the SAT reading passages, additional work needs to be done to show precisely what is comprehended by the readers.

The Stroop test may have another confounding variable. If you had read the lists out loud as someone was timing you, you might have been somewhat nervous or apprehensive about being evaluated for your reading skill. This could have influenced your reading times in a number of different ways. Your apprehension may have led you to read faster and more accurately than usual so you would "look good." On the other hand, you might have been nervous and not performed as well as when you were not being timed by another person. Such reactivity by research participants is an important source of invalidity, and we discuss some ways to control it later in this chapter.

Another threat to construct validity is random error. You or your partner may have misread the timing device, leading to a recording error in one or more of the conditions. This source of invalidity might be important in the Stroop experiment because different modes of timing might have been used by different subjects. Thus, the dependent variable might not be a valid measure of reading time, and the experiment would have weak construct validity.

The above leads us to be suspicious about the construct validity of almost any variable that is manipulated and measured in psychological research. The reasons are shown in Figure 6–2. A variable could be composed of the construct of interest as well as confounding influences and error (Judd et al., 1991). The extent to which the other sources enter into observations determines the degree of construct validity. So, a prudent researcher tries to minimize construct invalidity by limiting the possibility of confounding and error.

We consider several ways of minimizing construct invalidity throughout the text, two of which are considered here. The first involves operational definitions. Recall that an operational definition is a recipe for specifying how a construct, such as reading, is produced and measured. The conditions that produce the concept are carefully specified, and the ways in which the concept is to be measured are defined. A concept such as reading, therefore, becomes tied to the independent variables that produce it and the dependent variables that measure it. In this fashion an operational definition is similar to the way in which good theoretical constructs are defined (see the discussions of intervening variables in Chapter 2 and theoretical constructs in Chapter 5).

FIGURE 6-2
The composition of a variable could include the construct of interest and two sources of invalidity: confounding variables and error (modified from Judd et al., 1991).

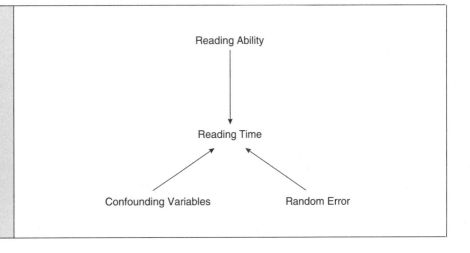

Although time was the dependent variable in the Stroop experiment, we need something besides an operational definition to ensure that the behavior is measured accurately. What we need is a protocol. A **protocol** is the specification of how the measurement is to be undertaken. Valid research adheres strictly to a protocol so that the behavior of all subjects is measured precisely, accurately, and the same under all levels of the independent variable.

Providing adequate operational definitions and following protocols do not guarantee construct validity, but they help to minimize invalidity, especially invalidity owing to random error.

CONCEPT SUMMARY

- **Construct validity** refers to the extent to which the variables accurately reflect or measure the behavior of interest.
- **Operational definitions** and **protocols** help minimize construct invalidity resulting from error.

External Validity

As we noted in Chapter 5, *external validity* refers to the extent to which one can generalize from the research setting and subject population to other settings and populations (Cook & Campbell, 1979). Observations with substantial external validity allow generalization to other situations and subject populations. Externally invalid observations are limited to the original research setting and population of subjects.

A researcher hopes that his or her observations represent a general psychological phenomenon. Thus, a prominent concern is **replication,** whether the observations can be replicated or repeated under different circumstances. In the Stroop experiment done in Chapter 1, we would not be interested in those observations if they were true only for college students. We can be confident in the generalizability of the results to other subject populations, because replications of the experiment show that the ordering of the three conditions is the same for adults, high-school students, and college students.

A more serious threat to external validity relates to the experimental setting. The tasks do not seem representative of the kinds of reading that most people do. However, as we noted in Chapter 2 and will detail later, the important criterion is not how realistic the tasks are but whether they represent an important psychological process. The general way to determine the generality is to conduct replications that vary the nature of the task and materials. A substantial variety of tasks have been used to induce the kind of conflict seen in our version of the Stroop experiment, which means that our observations have some external validity.

CONCEPT SUMMARY

- **External validity** refers to the extent to which the observations can be generalized to other settings and subject populations.
- **Replications** help assess the generality of the observations.

Internal Validity

We briefly mentioned internal validity in the previous chapter. **Internal validity** refers to whether one can make causal statements about the relationship between variables (Cook & Campbell, 1979). When observations are internally valid, the researcher can safely believe that one variable caused changes in another. If the observations are not internally valid, then the researcher is not able to make assertions about whether one variable caused another to change.

In principle, experimental observations permit causal statements. The experimenter varies the independent variable, which may cause changes in the dependent variable. Thus, we can say that a carefully conducted experiment is internally valid. In Chapter 1 we discussed the internal validity of the Stroop experiment when we introduced the topic of confounding. We noted that the validity of the experiment was suspect because the levels of the independent variable were confounded with the order in which they were experienced. This means that the results of that experiment may not be internally valid, because something other than the independent variable might have caused the observed changes in the dependent variable. Because scientists often strive to determine what causes what, the bulk of this text concerns how to make internally valid observations.

As a conclusion to this section on validity, we would like to stress what should be obvious from the discussion so far—making valid scientific observations is difficult. Each of the observation procedures that we discuss next can suffer form the three kinds of invalidity, so it is important to be wary of invalidity when conducting your own research and evaluating the research of others. Another source of error in making observations comes from the observer or scientist. The Application section considers some of the psychological factors that can undermine the validity of observations.

CONCEPT SUMMARY

- **Internal validity** concerns whether one can make causal statements about the relationship between variables.
- **Confounding** is a major threat to internal validity.

DIFFICULTIES OF OBSERVATION

Direct observation may seem a straightforward and simple process: we open our eyes, look hard, and see what is there. But the history of science is replete with examples of phenomena that have eventually turned out to be radically different from the way they were initially perceived. We consider two examples here, one from psychology and one from physics, to show that scientists must be continually vigilant for errors in their own observations.

Ivan P. Pavlov (1849–1936) was a Russian physiologist who won the Nobel Prize for medicine in 1904 for his work on how gastric juices operate during digestion. Pavlov also made important contributions to psychology by identifying and studying classical (or Pavlovian) conditioning. When Pavlov began studying learning in dogs, he and his coworkers discovered they had a problem that had not been apparent when they had previously been concerned only with the digestive system. The difficulty lay in how to describe the behaviors they were observing. Pavlov describes the problem of studying conditioned reflexes:

> But how is this to be studied? Taking the dog when he eats rapidly, snatches something in his mouth, chews for a long time, it seems clear that at such a time the animal strongly desires to eat, and so rushes to the food, seizes it, and falls to eating. He longs to eat . . . When he eats, you see the work of the muscles alone, striving in every way to seize the food in the mouth, to chew and to swallow it. From all this we can say that he derives pleasure from it. . . . Now when we proceeded to explain and analyze this, we readily adopted this trite point of view. We had to deal with the feelings, wishes, conceptions, etc., of our animal. The results were astounding, extraordinary; I and one of my colleagues came to irreconcilable opinions. We could not agree, could not prove to one another which was right. . . . After this we had to deliberate carefully. It seemed probable we were not on the right track. The more we thought about the matter, the greater grew our conviction that it was necessary to choose another exit. The first steps were very difficult, but along the way of persistent, intense, concentrated thinking I finally reached the firm ground of pure objectivity. We absolutely prohibited ourselves (in the laboratory there was an actual fine imposed) the use of such psychological expressions as the dog guessed, wanted, wished, etc. (Pavlov, reprinted 1963, pp. 263–264).

A second problem is relevant to observation in all types of research. This is the issue of how much our conceptual schemes determine and bias what we ''see.'' Pavlov's statement is eloquent testimony to the difficulty of establishing objective methods that would enable us all to see things in the same way. He had found it initially "astounding" and "extraordinary" that this difficulty existed and was surprised at the elaborate precautions needed to ensure objectivity. Philosophers of science have pointed out that our observations are always influenced by our conceptions of the world—if in no other way, at least by the particular observations we make (see, for example, Hanson, 1958, Chapter 2). "Pure objectivity," to use Pavlov's phrase, is quite elusive, if not impossible. Objective and repeatable observation in science is an ideal to be approximated, but we may never be completely confident that we have achieved it. Nevertheless, we must make every possible step toward this ideal, which is what much of the technical paraphernalia of science is designed to help us with.

The problem of observations being unduly influenced by expectations is not, however, automatically overcome by the use of sophisticated equipment, as is evident in an illustration cited by Hyman (1964, p. 38). In 1902, shortly after X rays were discovered, the eminent French physicist Blondlot reported the discovery of "N rays." Other French scientists quickly repeated and confirmed Blondlot's discovery; in 1904, no fewer than 77 publications appeared on the topic. However, the discovery became controversial when American, German, and Italian scientists failed to replicate Blondlot's findings.

The American physicist R. W. Wood, failing to find N rays in his own lab at Johns Hopkins University, visited Blondlot. Blondlot displayed a card to Wood with luminous circles painted on it. Then he turned down the room light, fixed N rays on the card, and pointed out to Wood that the circles increased in luminosity. When Wood said he could see no change, Blondlot argued that this must be because Wood's eyes were too insensitive. Next, Wood asked if he could perform some simple tests, to which Blondlot consented. In one case, Wood moved a lead screen repeatedly between the N rays and the cards, while Blondlot reported the corresponding changes in luminosity of the circles on the card. (The lead shield was to prevent passage of the N rays.) Blondlot was consistently in error, and often reported a change in luminosity when the screen had not been moved. This and other tests clearly indicated that there was no evidence for the existence of N rays, despite their "confirmation" by other French scientists.

After 1909, there were no further publications on N rays. The mistake was too much for Blondlot. He never recovered, and he died in disgrace some years later. We can see from this dramatic example that even with the sophisticated apparatus of physicists, errors of observation are possible and must be guarded against.

SOURCE: Hanson, N. R. (1958). *Patterns of discovery.* Cambridge: Cambridge University Press. Hyman R. (1964). *The nature of psychological inquiry.*
Englewood Cliffs, N.J.: Prentice-Hall. Pavlov, I. P. (1963). *Lectures on conditioned reflexes.* New York: International Publishers.

DESCRIPTIVE OBSERVATION METHODS

The most obvious ways of making observations in psychology have description of behavior as their major purpose. Descriptive observations enumerate what behaviors occur and in what quantity and frequency.

In this chapter we discuss three descriptive methods of gathering psychological data. One such method is **naturalistic observation,** which is the most obvious and, perhaps, the most venerable way of gathering data. Many people, such as bird-watchers, are amateur naturalists, but scientific naturalists, as we will see, are more systematic in their observations. For example, recent work has shown that when the risk of attack by predator hawks is imminent, chickadees give a much higher alarm call than when the risk posed by the predator is not so serious (Ficken, 1990).

An additional classic way of obtaining information is the **case study,** in which detailed information is gathered about a single individual. A recent case study revealed that when Ruth L., age 30, came to therapy, she was showering six or more times daily, washing her hands three times an hour, and completely cleaning her apartment twice daily (Leon, 1990).

Similar to the case study is the **survey,** in which detailed information is gathered from a number of individuals. Colasanto (1989) interviewed people in the San Francisco Bay Area the day following the earthquake that occurred on October 17, 1989. Thirty-seven percent of those people claimed to have been very frightened by the earthquake, and 15 percent of the Bay Area people were not frightened at all.

Another survey attempted to determine the sorts of memory problems suffered by elderly Americans (Lovelace and Twohig, 1990). Healthy, older adults with an average age of 68 claim that the most vexing memory problem they have is an inability to remember someone's name. However, most of these respondents report that memory difficulties have little effect on their daily functioning.

Descriptive research plays an important role in psychology. These procedures provide a major part of the database that can lead to subsequent more highly controlled research (Miller, 1977). Description of behavior is a necessary first step in understanding. A familiar example is Harlow's (1958) work on mother love in infant monkeys. Prior to his experiments, Harlow needed to know what behaviors baby monkeys exhibited; he also needed to know some of the things they seemed to like (their soft blankets) and dislike (the wire floor of the cage). With this background information, Harlow could attempt to explain the behavior via experimentation. Thus, we should not view description as somehow secondary or subordinate to experimentation because it lacks control. In the sense just mentioned, description is prior to experimentation. Now we examine the descriptive procedures in more detail.

Naturalistic Observations

One problem facing a person wishing to make naturalistic observations is determining what behaviors to observe. Human observers have a finite capacity to perceive and think about events. Although most of us can walk and chew gum at the same time, most of us cannot attend to and remember 20 different behaviors occurring over short periods of time. Thus, we must set a boundary on the range of behaviors that we plan to observe.

How do we delimit the range of behaviors to be studied? Part of the answer seems straightforward. If we are interested in human nonverbal communication, we observe it. However, this is not necessarily easy to do. In the first place, nonverbal communication is highly complex, which means that observers are faced with the same problem we started out trying to avoid. In the second place, examining nonverbal behavior presupposes that we already know some of the behaviors to describe. Obviously, we do not enter a research project devoid of all knowledge, which is especially the case when we are trying to test certain hypotheses. However, we do not begin description with all the answers. What usually happens is that we begin a series of studies, in which successive projects rely on previous data to refine and delimit the field of inquiry. Let us consider some examples to illustrate how naturalistic observations are conducted.

Ethology. Naturalistic research of interest to psychologists is perhaps most prevalent in the area of **ethology,** the study of naturally occurring behavior (often in the wild). Simply observing the behavior of animals or humans allows one to gain a global impression of the characteristics and range of behavior. However, one may soon desire more systematic observation. One way ethologists make more systematic observations is by identifying different categories of experience for the organism under study and then recording the number of times the organism engages in each behavior. These behaviors can be divided into large units such as mating, grooming, sleeping, fighting, eating, and so on, or into much smaller units. For example, an **ethogram** of the various behaviors involved in the courtship pattern of a fish, the orange chromide, is shown in Figure 6–3. An ethogram is a relatively complete inventory of the specific behaviors performed by one species of animal. By counting the number of times that any specific behavior occurs, ethologists can begin to get some idea of the significance of the behavior.

A complete ethogram may be the ideal to attain but is unlikely in practice. Identifying and classifying all the behaviors associated with chromide courtship would be cumbersome if the observer did not have particular hypotheses in mind. Timberlake and Silva (1994) have argued that observation categories should be designed to answer specific questions rather than to describe and classify behavior completely. They suggested further that observation categories should be unambiguous, so that the observer can easily judge that the behavior in question has occurred. If an observer is attempting a courtship ethogram, then he or she is likely to have to consider several aspects of the organisms' behavioral repertoire. Assigning behaviors to categories should be set up so that it can be done quickly and without much chance for error.

If two observers consistently categorized behavior in the same way, then the behavior categories probably are clear and unambiguous. Often, two or more observers categorize the behavior of the same organism, and then their results are compared to check on the degree of agreement.

FIGURE 6-3
Ethogram showing courtship pattern in orange chromide. An ethogram can be compiled for all behaviors of a species, or for only selected aspects of behavior. (From Drickamer, L. C., and Vesey, S. H. *Animal Behavior: Concepts, Processes, and Methods.* Boston: Willard Grant Press, 1982, p. 28).

a. *Charging:* An accelerted swim of one fish toward another.

b. *Tail Beating:* An emphatic beating of the tail toward another fish.

c. *Quivering:* A rapid, lateral, shivering movement that starts at the head and dies out as it passes posteriorly through the body.

d. *Nipping:* An O-shaped mouth action that cleans out the (presumptive) spawning site.

e. *Skimming:* The actual spawning movement whereby the fish places its ventral surface against the spawning site and meanders along it for a few seconds.

Interobserver reliability measures whether two or more observers yield similar results when they simultaneously observe the same behavior (Martin & Bateson, 1993). The degree of interobserver reliability can be measured in several ways, but it is typically measured by a coefficient of correlation (see Chapter 5). High agreement between two observers would be shown by a high positive coefficient of correlation. Correlations usually have a maximum value of $+1.00$, and high interobserver reliability occurs when the coefficient is greater than $+0.70$.

Ficken (1990) was able to isolate the types of alarm calls made by chickadees by an accurate ethogram of their calls. Obviously, however, Ficken had to be able to record and analyze the chickadees' vocal output. Obtaining accurate records of an animal's behavior in the wild is often difficult. It may be hard to observe an animal continuously in its natural habitat. Researchers cannot remain forever vigilant. The presence of human observers may make the measures reactive. These are only some of the greatest problems.

Applying similar techniques to human behavior is even more difficult, for people do not usually appreciate having their every action noted by curious scientists. Barker and his associates (for example, Barker and Wright, 1951; Barker, 1968) were pioneers in applying methods of naturalistic observation to humans in a number of settings. Let us examine some naturalistic observations of humans.

Flashing Eyebrows. The famous ethologist of human behavior Eibl-Eibesfeldt (for example, 1970, 1972) has done a substantial amount of field research on human facial expressions. He and his colleagues traveled around the world taking pictures of facial expressions in a variety of contexts. Careful examination of the expressions indicated that many are similar across cultures, and some are not. In the process of examining facial expressions associated with people greeting each other, Eibl-Eibesfeldt discovered that most humans give a brief eyebrow flash. He went on to examine this phenomenon in detail.

Generally, the eyebrow flash is a brief (one-sixth of a second) raising of the eyebrows, accompanied by a slight smile and a quick nod of the head. The eyebrow flash has been observed in people of many cultures, including Bushmen, Balinese, and Europeans. However, some cultures seem to differ in their uses of the eyebrow flash. The Japanese do not use the flash, because in Japan it is considered suggestive or indecent. Furthermore, Eibl-Eibesfeldt found that the flash occurred in other circumstances, such as in flirting and acknowledging a gift or service (that is, as a kind of thank you), in addition to greeting.

We can see from his work that previous observations suggested additional ones for Eibl-Eibesfeldt, and by delimiting his range of inquiry he was able to garner substantial information about a common human behavior.

Testing Neonates. Another example of refinement comes from studies of newborn humans (neonates). What do neonates do and what can we look for in their behavior? Most people think of neonates as being limited in their behavior. However, neonates can do more than eat, sleep, eliminate, and cry. All their senses are operative, and they possess a number of complex reflexes. Brazelton and his associates (for example, Lester and Brazelton, 1982) have spent many years refining a scale to assess the optimal performance of neonates in a variety of behaviors. Initially, the scale assessed reflexes (squeezing, blinking) and a few behaviors. Repeated observations of neonates from a variety of cultures and in a variety of situations led to changes, which, in turn, caused more changes. The resulting Brazelton Neonatal Behavioral Assessment Scale contains measurements of 16 reflexes and 26 behaviors. The reflexes are rated on a three-point scale (low, medium, and high), and the behavioral items, such as responses to a pinprick and hand-to-mouth activity, are rated on nine-point scales.

Earlier observations had suggested that the level of arousal was very important in respect to the appearance and magnitude of certain behaviors, so the current scale indicates when the neonate should be assessed on the various behaviors. For example, responses to a pinprick are assessed when the neonate is asleep or quiet, but not when the neonate is alert or crying. Hand-to-mouth behaviors can be assessed during any state.

Brazelton and his coworkers have been particularly concerned with individual and cultural differences in development, and they have conducted a substantial amount of more controlled research to examine these differences. The controlled research would not have been possible had they not made the exhaustive series of observations that led to the development of the assessment scale.

CONCEPT SUMMARY

- **Naturalistic observation** is refined by **ethograms** and by delimiting observation categories.
- **Interobserver reliability** assesses whether two or more observers can accurately categorize naturalistic observations.

The Case Study

Another venerable form of inquiry in psychology is the case study. Freud's psychoanalytic theory arose from his observations and reflections on individual cases. In general, a case study is the intensive investigation of a single case of some sort, whether of a neurotic patient, a spiritual medium, or a group awaiting the end of the world. An interesting case study of this last instance was provided by Festinger, Riecken, and Schachter (1956), who infiltrated a small group of persons who were indeed awaiting the end of the world. The members thought themselves to be in contact with beings from another planet, who had communicated to one member that the destruction of the earth was near. The group was expecting to be rescued by spacecraft before the catastrophe. Festinger and his colleagues were especially interested in the reactions of the group when (if?) the calamity did not occur. They observed that for many of the members of the group, belief in its delusional system actually increased rather than decreased after the predicted date of catastrophe had passed.

The case study is a type of naturalistic observation and is subject to all the disadvantages and the few advantages (to be discussed shortly) of that method. One chief disadvantage is that case studies usually do not allow firm inferences to be made about what causes what. Typically, all one can do is describe the course of events. Often, however, case studies provide implicit comparisons that allow the researcher to make some reasonable guesses as to what causes what. The case study of Ruth L., the compulsive cleaner mentioned earlier, revealed a very stern upbringing that involved an excessive emphasis on cleanliness and neatness. Because the severity of this emphasis on cleanliness was greater than that experienced by most people, the therapist concluded that it was a causal factor in her current compulsion to be neat and clean. This sort of conclusion needs to be tentative, however, because we do not know what kind of adult Ruth L. would have become had she had a more ordinary childhood.

A type of case study that best attempts to minimize the difficulties of making inferences is the **deviant-case analysis.** Here the researcher considers two cases that bear a number of similarities and yet differ in outcome. For example, one twin brother might become schizophrenic and the other not. The researcher attempts to pinpoint, through a careful comparison of the two cases, the factors that are responsible for the difference in outcome. Such comparisons usually cannot be made, because comparable cases that differ in only one factor are rare. Furthermore, any conclusions even from this method cannot really be considered firm or well established, because the researcher can never be certain that he or she has identified the critical causes in the differing outcomes.

These cautions notwithstanding, let us consider a case study reported by Butters and Cermak (1986) that illustrates how judicious use of the procedure can provide valuable information. The study is about P.Z., a world-famous scientist who suffered from severe memory loss (amnesia) in 1981 after long-term alcohol abuse. He had extreme difficulty both in remembering new information and in recollecting past events and people. The latter memory deficit was easy to determine, because two years prior to the onset of amnesia, P.Z. had written his autobiography. When he was queried about the names and events mentioned in his autobiography, he showed a drastic memory deficit. P.Z.'s memory for these events was compared with the retention of a similar-aged colleague (the comparison person for deviant-case analysis) who did not have a history of alcohol abuse. The comparison case did not show a memory deficit as serious as P.Z.'s, so Butters and Cermak reasoned that the long-term alcohol abuse was an important causal factor in P.Z.'s amnesia. Furthermore, P.Z.'s memory deficit for new information was very similar to that shown by other people with a history of alcohol abuse. This latter technique of comparing the case's behavior with that of others is essentially an experimental one, and this procedure is emphasized throughout this text.

CONCEPT SUMMARY

- **Case studies** suffer from an inability to determine what causes what.
- **Deviant-case analysis** compares two similar cases that differ in specific ways, which improves the inferential capabilities of case studies.

Survey Research

Case studies usually involve only a few subjects, and often these individuals are not at all representative of the population at large. P.Z., for example, was both a brilliant scientist and an amnesiac. Often researchers want to obtain information on a large random sample of people in a large geographic area (such as the Bay Area survey mentioned at the beginning of this section), even though the amount of information obtained from any one person is necessarily limited. This technique is little used in most areas of psychology, though it is familiar to most of you through its use in predicting elections and the like. With the precise sampling procedures now available, relatively few people can be queried, and the results will none-theless generalize well to the population at large.

Because the survey leads to results that are generally descriptive in nature, this method is not particularly popular with psychologists. Never-theless, clever use of the method may allow contributions to some areas of psychology. The work by Lovelace and Twohig (1990) that was summa-rized briefly at the outset of this section is a good example. The elderly subjects whom they surveyed reported that they relied very strongly on notes, lists, and other external memory aids to help them remember to do things. Further, the elderly respondents claimed not to rely on various memory "tricks" such as mnemonic devices. The results reported by Love-lace and Twohig agree with other survey data (Moscovitch, 1982), which show that compared with younger people, the elderly are much more likely to make lists and use date books and are less likely to resort to internal memory procedures, such as mnemonic devices. These results are provoc-ative, because they suggest that the elderly are somehow aware that they may have some memory limitations, which they try to minimize by relying on external memory aids. However, more controlled research is necessary before that conclusion can be confirmed.

A crucial issue in survey research relates to the sample that is sur-veyed. The researcher wants the sample to be representative of the popu-lation for whom the questions are designed. So, for example, a researcher interested in people's reactions to earthquakes would sample from a pop-ulation of people who had suffered from an earthquake. However, the problem still remains—does the sample surveyed present a reasonable pic-ture of the population?

In the previous chapter we noted that a large random sample is likely to be the surest way to have a representative sample. Unfortunately, large random samples are very expensive to conduct. Thus, other sampling pro-cedures are used to determine the makeup of the sample. A complete anal-ysis of sampling approaches can be found in Weisberg, Krosnick, and Bowen (1989), so here we will outline some of the general sampling tech-niques used by people conducting surveys.

Random samples are expensive, because each individual in the pop-ulation has an unbiased chance of being in the surveyed sample. If you wanted a random sample of all college students for a face-to-face interview, you might have to fly to Maine for one interview, then to Oregon for two, then to Indiana for several more, and so on. One way to simplify this prob-lem is to use a **stratified sample,** in which the population is divided into smaller units and random sampling is done from the smaller units. So, if 40 percent of the undergraduate students in the United States attend school in the northeast or in California, we would stratify the sample by region accordingly, to make sure that the proportion sampled from an area reflects the population distribution. Stratifying a sample is handy when two or more groups within a population are part of the sample. If we were par-ticularly interested in attitudes of male and female college students, for example, we might stratify on the basis of gender. This might yield more accurate results than sampling from all college students and then breaking down the sample into groups of interest. There are several variations of the stratification procedure, each with its own strengths and weaknesses (see Weisberg et al., 1989). We note here that probability sampling procedures such as the random and stratified techniques and the variants are often combined in large-scale surveys in which national issues are under investigation.

CONCEPT SUMMARY

- **Surveys** must have samples that are representative of the population in question.
- **stratified sampling** is a good alternative to random sampling.

ADVANTAGES OF DESCRIPTIVE OBSERVATIONS

As noted earlier, descriptive observation is extremely useful in the early stages of research, when one desires simply to gain some idea as to the breadth and range of the problem of interest (Miller, 1977). It does not, however, allow one to infer how factors may be related. In some cases, there is no way to employ more controlled methods of observation; therefore, only descriptive ones are available. If you want to know how penguins behave in their natural habitat, you simply have to observe them there. Still, for most psychological problems, descriptive observation is useful primarily in defining the problem area and raising interesting questions for more controlled study by other means, especially experimental ones. For example, the case study by Festinger and his colleagues of the group predicting the end of the earth helped lead to Festinger's (1957) cognitive dissonance theory of attitude change, which has been quite important in guiding social psychological research.

Descriptive techniques share features that make them very desirable scientific tools, especially when they are compared to controlled laboratory experimentation. Timberlake and Silva (1994) note that flexibility is a major asset of naturalistic observation. It can be inexpensive to do, because only minimal equipment and other facilities often are required, and it is often convenient and relatively easy to do it. When both of these possibilities are true, then a prudent researcher supplements controlled procedures, such as experiments and tests, with direct observation of behavior.

Another feature of all descriptive procedures is that they typically try to understand interesting, naturally occurring behaviors. Often, then, descriptive procedures may have an ethological and ecological slant to them (Timberlake & Silva, 1994; Todd & Perlmutter, 1980).

In the present context, **ecological function** refers to the role that various behaviors play in adapting to the environment—what function they seem to serve the organism. A good example of this approach in contrast to the standard experimental one can be seen in the work of Perlmutter and her associates (Perlmutter & Myers, 1979; Todd & Perlmutter, 1980). In controlled experimental settings, Perlmutter and Myers showed that the deliberate memory for lists of words is much worse for three-year-olds than for four-year-olds. However, the implicit memory of everyday events and actions that are studied naturalistically show much smaller advantages for the older children.

Let us examine the naturalistic work on memory, because it illustrates many of the important features of such research. Todd and Perlmutter observed children of various ages individually in two one-hour sessions. They carefully documented the spontaneous memory statements of the children, which were categorized according to their duration, frequency, and level of detail. Both the younger and older children recalled many novel events, such as a trip to the zoo, and many routine events, such as playing with particular toys. The major difference between the younger and older children lay in the ability of the older children to recall more events over longer retention intervals than the younger ones. Also, the older children tended to recall more aspects of their internal states, such as happiness or fear, than did the younger children. To check on these children's deliberate memory, Todd and Perlmutter noted that it took the younger children about five times as many repetitions as the older ones to memorize a two-sentence rhyme. The latter finding contrasts to the much smaller differences in spontaneous memory for events and activities, and agrees with controlled studies on memory for word lists.

Several other features of Perlmutter's work should be noted here. First, interobserver reliability was very high in classifying the memories into the categories noted above. Second, Perlmutter had the parents of the children corroborate the spontaneous memory claims. She found that the accuracy of both the younger and older children was very good according to the parent's determination. Obtaining corroborating evidence for the children's memories is very important and represents an important source of control that Perlmutter and associates added to naturalistic observation. Third, the research illustrates both the flexibility and ecological function often associated with naturalistic observation. The researchers had a great deal of latitude in observing the children—they could merely sit and talk nonchalantly to the children or they could ask the children questions if they were being comparatively silent. The ecological aspect of the research is apparent in the nature of the spontaneous memories that the children reported: visits to zoos, a doctor's appointment, and the like. Such events are markedly different than the sorts of things that are usually studied in experiments on memory, especially when the children are asked to deliberately learn and remember the material. Note that ecologically relevant experiments are possible, but naturalistic observation in particular, and descriptive research in general, allows ecological functions to be studied with ease. This means that descriptive observations often have high **ecological validity.**

CONCEPT SUMMARY

Advantages of descriptive observations include

- being an important source of basic knowledge
- flexibility
- ethological approach
- ecological validity

SOURCES OF ERROR IN DESCRIPTIVE RESEARCH

The primary problem unique to descriptive observation is that it does not readily allow us to assess relations among events. An investigator might note that grooming behavior in free-ranging monkeys occurs at certain times, following five different prior conditions (such as eating). If one is interested in finding out which antecedent conditions are necessary to produce grooming, descriptive observation cannot provide an answer, because these antecedent conditions cannot be manipulated. For this, one needs an experiment.

Descriptive observation may produce data that are deficient in other ways, too. Scientific data should be easy to reproduce by other people using standardized procedures, if these people doubt the observations or are interested in repeating them. Many descriptive methods, such as the case study, do not allow reproducibility; they are thus open to question by other investigators.

Another problem in descriptive approaches is maintaining as strictly as possible a descriptive rather than an interpretive level of observation— researcher bias. In the study of animals, the bias problem is often one of **anthropomorphizing,** or attributing human characteristics to animals. When you come home and your dog wags its tail and moves about excitedly, it seems perfectly natural to say that it is happy to see you. But this is anthropomorphizing, and if one were engaged in descriptive observation of the scene, it would be inappropriate. Instead, one should record the overt behaviors of the dog with the least possible attribution of underlying motives, such as happiness, sadness, or hunger.

Of course, the case studies of Freud are based entirely on just such interpretations of the facts. Besides being nonreproducible, such cases suffer from the possibility that if we are allowed to (a) select our data from case studies and answers people give to the questions we ask, and then (b) weave these "facts" into a previous conceptual system of our own devising, case studies could probably be used to "prove" any theory. This is not to detract from the creative flair and genius that are evident in Freud's system; he is, however, certainly open to criticism in terms of the evidence on which it is based.

Reactivity in Descriptive Research

In many areas of psychological research, we can view the reactions of the participants not only in terms of the project itself, but also in terms of everyday social interaction. Suppose you are responding to a survey that asks you to estimate the number of times a day you think about sex. Go ahead and make a guess. Now, suppose you are asked the same question in a personal interview. Would your answer in the interview be the same as the one given in the survey? You might be reluctant to say "I think about sex at least fifteen times a day." On the other hand, writing "15" in response to a question on an anonymous survey might not bother you at all. In general, ordinary social interaction may put demands on a research participant that changes the way he or she reacts.

Weber and Cook (1972) used the phrase **subject roles** to highlight the important social and psychological factors that occur in research and may influence the results. As used here, *role* refers to how the participants perceive the research setting and how they then react to it. Because the perceived role may determine how the subjects respond, unnatural responding, **reactivity,** could occur and confound the results. We will consider several examples of reactivity and some possible solutions.

The term **demand characteristics** was at one time the standard way to refer to subject reactivity. The phrase was coined by Orne (1962) to highlight the pressure put on people participating in research. Orne emphasized the obedience of the subject to the researcher's demands. We believe that reactivity is a more general term to describe the roles that subjects may adopt than is the phrase *demand characteristics.*

Naturalistic Observation. There are two general ways to guard against the participants' reactions ruining observations: (1) we can make unobtrusive observations, or (2) we can take unobtrusive measures (Webb, Campbell, Schwartz, and Sechrist, 1981).

First we will consider **unobtrusive observations.** Imagine that you are walking down a street in your hometown. Occasionally you greet a friend (perhaps with a handshake, perhaps with an eyebrow flash). As your walk continues, a man with a large camera approaches and proceeds to take moving pictures of you every time you greet one of your friends. How are you likely to react to this attention? Quite likely, your mode of greeting people would change dramatically. (Have you ever noticed how spectators behave at sporting events when they know the television camera is on them?) Eibl-Eibesfeldt guarded against participant reactivity in his research by using a camera with a special sideways lens. This lens permitted him to aim the camera 90 degrees from the subject; presumably, the subject would think that Eibl-Eibesfeldt was photographing something else. Thus, the subject would not react abnormally to the presence of the observer and his camera; instead, the subject would act naturally, which is what Eibl-Eibesfeldt intended. The special camera lens allowed the researcher to observe without intruding on the subject, which means that Eibl-Eibesfeldt used an unobtrusive observation technique.

In general, unobtrusive observations of subjects are likely to reveal more natural behavior than if the subjects are aware of being observed. In studying animals, researchers use unobtrusive observations whenever possible so that the behavior of interest will not be affected by the observer's presence.

Sometimes, however, either the subjects themselves, the terrain, or some other aspect of the project demands close contact. In these situations, **participant observation** often provides a solution. For example, Fossey (1972) spent a great amount of time observing the mountain gorilla. The mountain gorilla lives in central Africa, and its habitat is threatened by human beings who are moving into that area. The mountain gorilla's natural habitat is in the mountainous rain forest, which makes long-range unobtrusive spying out of the question. Fossey was particularly concerned with the free-ranging behavior of the gorillas, so she decided to become a participant observer. This was difficult, because the gorillas are not tame. She had to mimic the gorillas so that they would become accustomed to her presence. She mimicked aspects of the animal's behavior, such as eating, grooming, and making weird gorillalike vocalizations. As she said, "one feels like a fool thumping one's chest rhythmically or sitting about pretending to munch on a stalk of wild celery as though it were the most delectable morsel in the world. But the gorillas have responded favorably" (p. 211). It took several months for Fossey to gain the confidence of the gorillas, and she continued to live with and study the gorillas until her death in 1986. How would you like to act like a gorilla for ten or fifteen years?

Unobtrusive measures, in contrast to unobtrusive observations, are usually indirect observations of behavior. Unobtrusive measures are indirect because it is the result of behavior, not the behavior itself, that is being studied. Thus, instead of measuring behavior directly, we examine it after the fact by looking at what the behavior accomplished. Instead of observing a student's studying activities, we examine his or her transcript. Instead of living with the gorillas, we look at their effect on the environment. Obviously, unobtrusive measures are not suitable for all questions being investigated (an unobtrusive measure of an eyebrow flash might be difficult), but for some these measures are not merely good, they are the only ones that are feasible. Consider the question of graffiti in public restrooms. Who does it? What does the graffiti usually concern? A number of serious ethical questions (ethics are discussed in Chapter 3) would be raised if a researcher stood around in restrooms observing the patrons. However, the graffiti topics can be examined and can provide substantial information. Kinsey, Pomeroy, and Martin (1953) discovered that graffiti in men's restrooms was more erotic than graffiti in women's restrooms. Furthermore, they found more graffiti in men's rooms than in women's rooms.

Using unobtrusive measures is akin to a hunter following animal tracks or a police officer examining clues such as fingerprints. Tracks and clues are left behind and often allow us to infer things about the behavior that caused them. Recently, a popular psychological and anthropological unobtrusive measure has been to examine the garbage and other refuse that people discard. From the characteristics of the discarded objects, the observer attempts to understand some aspect of the behavior behind that refuse (for example, a discarded liquor bottle or love letter that has been thrown away could reveal information about behavior).

Case Studies. Case studies are individual histories, which means that much of the evidence in these studies is **retrospective** in nature. In other words, it comes from looking back into the past. Looking backward often causes problems. One difficulty is that the evidence may be inaccurate as a result of ordinary forgetting. We may not remember what our thoughts and actions were in nursery school because what has happened since then interferes with our memory of early events. Another difficulty with case studies is that participant reactivity may lead to **motivated forgetting.** Motivated forgetting refers to the active way in which humans reconstruct their past experiences. People may distort their memories to match their current beliefs. For instance, a politician who has changed views on a controversial issue such as the death penalty may recall the former stance as having been much more moderate than it really was. Similarly, people may inflate their memory for positive events. A powerful example of this type of positive distortion can be seen in the memory of John Dean during the Watergate scandal in the early 1970s. Appearing before a congressional committee, Dean described personal conversations between President Nixon and himself. In these descriptions, he generally overestimated his role in the conversation, and he tended to exaggerate any praise bestowed on him by the president (Neisser, 1981). We know that John Dean's recollections were distorted because audiotapes of these same conversations have since been compared with the congressional testimony. The example of John Dean illustrates that an effective method for dealing with motivated forgetting is to obtain corroborating evidence from other sources. Unfortunately, such evidence may be difficult to obtain, and if other people serve as additional sources, then their memories are subject to the same problems.

Surveys, Interviews, and Tests. To the extent that other forms of descriptive research rely on retrospective reports, they face the same reactivity problems (i.e., both ordinary and motivated forgetting) as case studies. However, many of the responses on tests and surveys are not retrospective, and we instead face problems resulting from **response style** or *response sets.* Different people may have habitual ways of answering questions. These habits may result from how they view themselves or from the expectations of the researcher and society (more on this later). In general, there are three kinds of response styles: yea-saying or **response acquiescence,** nay-saying or **response deviation,** and **social desirability.** College-bound high-school graduates tend to respond no to the question "Do you use marijuana daily?" Does this answer reflect the true behavior of these people, or does the answer reflect the habitual tendency to say no (response deviation)? Or the answer could be a socially desirable one, because marijuana is a controlled substance and many authorities frown upon its use. The high-school graduates not heading for college tended to answer yes to this question twice as often as the college-bound (Bachman and Johnston, 1979). Is this answer a true one, or does the answer simply indicate that these people are likely to acquiesce and say yes regardless of what the question is? Based on the answer to this one question, we cannot determine whether the answer is a true one or the result of a particular response style.

Edwards (1953, 1957) has developed an interesting solution to the response-style problem, at least for certain kinds of descriptive research. In particular, Edwards suggested the use of a **forced-choice test** in which participants must choose between two alternatives of equal social desirability in a personality test. On Edwards's test, called the Personal Preference Schedule, the respondent has to select one of two activities or indicate which of two thoughts or feelings better reflects the characteristics of the respondent. For example, the respondent might have to choose between playing tennis or water skiing. Although equal in social desirability, the two alternatives are hypothesized to be associated with different personality characteristics. Here, water skiing may be the more typical choice of extroverted individuals. The forced-choice technique decreases the influence of social desirability as well as eliminating the possibility of response acquiescence or response deviation.

Associated with the problem of response styles is one more difficult to cope with, the **volunteer problem.** Volunteer subjects differ in a number of ways from potential participants who do not volunteer (Rosnow and Rosenthal, 1970). Volunteers tend to be more intelligent, better educated, more cooperative, better adjusted, and in greater need of social approval than nonvolunteers. These characteristics of volunteers could strongly influence participant reaction. The volunteer problem might also limit the generalizbility of results in an experiment.

What the volunteer problem means in terms of your own research is that you have to be careful in sampling from the population of participants available to you. If your test or survey is boring and requires that the respondent go to extreme lengths to be cooperative (trudging through a blizzard at 11:00 P.M. to the psychology building), then the answers you get may be based on a biased sample of opinion (this is an example of selection bias; see Chapter 11). The problem is also serious, as Rosnow and Rosenthal point out, in opinion surveys that rely on volunteer mailings or phone-ins. What are we to make of the results of a magazine survey that relies on voluntary compliance of the readers? Or, how about the radio survey that solicits calls from its listeners? In both cases we do not know anything about the people who did not respond, nor do we know anything about the people who do not read that magazine or listen to that station. We can find out about the nonrespondents by expending a great deal of time and effort. Usually, this effort is not made.

There are three possible solutions to the nonrespondent problem, although none of these solutions is completely satisfactory. First, you can get a random sample of the entire population that is available to you. This means that every potential respondent has an equal chance of being questioned. Of course, this assumes that all subjects in the population will participate if questioned. Second, you could give the nonrespondents some kind of extra incentive to participate in your project. They could be offered money or be given detailed information about the research project. The extra inducements might bias the results of the research, however, by treating some subjects differently from others prior to participation in the project. Third, you could replicate your research with additional samples of subjects. Although your project may again be plagued with the same volunteer problem, this would be a good solution if the problems associated with volunteers and nonrespondents were not likely to recur in your replication.

CONCEPT SUMMARY

Descriptive observations may suffer from

- lack of reproducibility
- anthropomorphizing
- internal invalidity
- subject reactivity

SUMMARY

1. The validity of observations refers to their approximate truth or falsity.

2. Construct validity concerns the extent to which the dependent and independent variables reflect and measure the variables of interest.

3. External validity refers to whether the results of observations can be generalized to other research settings and populations.

4. Internal validity of observations deals with the possibility of determining whether one variable causes changes in another.

5. The descriptive methods of observation include naturalistic observations, case studies, and surveys.

6. Ethology is the study of naturally occurring behavior that is often systematized by an ethogram, which categorizes a number of different behaviors.

7. The accuracy of naturalistic observation is often determined by measures of interobserver reliability which is an assessment of how well two or more observers agree on how to assort behaviors.

8. Deviant-case analysis is a case-study procedure in which the researcher considers two cases that bear a number of similarities but differ in outcome.

9. Although random sampling is the best way to obtain a representative sample for a survey, stratified sampling, in which the population is divided into smaller units before random sampling, is usually undertaken because it is easier and less expensive than complete random sampling.

10. Descriptive research often lays down the empirical foundation for subsequent, more controlled research. Further, it tends to be more flexible than experimentation, and it can address important issues about the ecological function associated with particular behaviors.

11. Sources of error in descriptive research include anthropomorphizing and experimenter bias. Another difficulty relates to reactivity by the people or animals being observed. Human participants often adopt particular roles when they know they are being evaluated, which could undermine the research.

12. Unobtrusive measures and unobtrusive observations attempt to minimize reactivity by measuring the traces of behavior (unobtrusive measures) or by concealing the measurement process from the subjects (unobtrusive observations).

■ KEY CONCEPTS

anthropomorphizing
case study
construct validity
demand characteristics
descriptive observations
deviant-case analysis
ecological function
ecological validity
ethogram
ethology
explanation
forced-choice test
internal validity
interobserver reliability
motivated forgetting
naturalistic observation
participant observation

protocol
reactivity
relational observations
replication
response acquiescence
response styles
response deviation
retrospective
social desirability
stratified sample
subject roles
survey
unobtrusive measures
unobtrusive observations
validity
volunteer problem

■ EXERCISES

1. Define the three types of validity and relate them to the different classes of research methods.

2. Present some research hypotheses that cannot be studied in laboratory experiments. Indicate some alternative ways in which they could be studied.

3. [*Special Exercise.*] A researcher is interested in the extent of drug use among college students. She has the option of doing an anonymous survey, in which the students write down their answers, or a face-to-face survey, in which answers are given verbally. Each method has advantages and disadvantages—enumerate them.

■ **SUGGESTED READINGS**

An interesting article on the use and development of observational skills is Boice, R. (1983). Observational skills. *Psychological Bulletin, 93,* 3–29.

A detailed discussion of methodological problems and considerations in descriptive research can be found in the following two articles: Woolfolk, A. E. (1981). The eye of the beholder: Methodological considerations when observers assess nonverbal communication. *Journal of Nonverbal Behavior, 5,* 199–204; and Wildman, B. G., & Erickson, M. T. (1977). Methodological problems in behavioral observation. In J. D. Cone and R. P. Hawkins (Eds.), *Behavioral assessment.* New York: Brunner/Mazel.

Psychology in Action
A Memory Ethogram

Descriptive research usually relates to important and interesting problems. One problem that many students have is remembering to perform some action. This difficulty in *prospective memory* takes many forms in both school and nonschool activities: forgetting to prepare assignments, forgetting to hand in assignments, forgetting a parent's birthday, forgetting to go to the dentist, and so on. Research mentioned in this chapter done by Lovelace and Twohig (1990) and Moscovitch (1982) examined prospective forgetting and how it can be avoided.

For this exercise, you could either focus on your own prospective forgetting, or you could pool your observations with members of your class. In either case, the first step would be to develop the observation categories that you want to assess. That is, you need to develop a sort of ethogram of prospective forgetting so that you can either categorize your own lapses or survey the lapses of others. Your ethogram needs to have several dimensions, beginning with *what* is forgotten. Then you should include other aspects of the activity that seem relevant.

- Was the forgotten activity important or unimportant?
- Was it unusual or was it a routine activity?
- Was the forgotten event occurring with other important tasks, or was it isolated from typical activities?

These questions suggest observation categories in which to assign forgotten episodes. You might want to develop other categories, or you could, along with your classmates, decide on ways to extend the categories suggested by the above questions.

Another issue you might want to address in developing your ethogram has to do with the level of measurement that you want to have. The questions above suggest a dichotomous (two-valued) measure: important or unimportant, for example. Dichotomous measures like this assign an event to one of two categories, so they are measured at the nominal level. You might consider developing ordinal ways of assessing the forgotten episodes. A ten-point scale going from completely unimportant (a "1") to extremely important (a "10") would be a way to develop an ordinal measure of importance. You could, in fact, try to develop a Likert scale (see Chapter 5), which is often thought to have interval-level measurement properties.

Regardless of the approach that you take, you should note that carefully specifying the observation categories is essential for successful observation. Careful and accurate observation rests on the specification of the events to be measured.

Relational observations attempt to
- ❑ Determine the relationships between variables

Relational observations include
- ❑ Contingency table research
- ❑ Correlational research

Relational observations usually cannot
- ❑ Provide strong internal validity

Causation is best inferred from
- ❑ Experimental observations

CHAPTER 7

RELATIONAL RESEARCH

In this chapter we examine research that tries to assess the relationship between variables. Contingency tables examine how the frequency of observations change as a function of two nominal variables. Correlational research looks at both the magnitude and direction of relationships. At the end of this chapter we consider experimental observations from the standpoint of making causal statements about the effects of one variable on changes in another.

Scientists describe, relate, and experiment. In this chapter we focus on relational research. **Relational research** attempts to determine how two (usually) or more variables are related to each other. Typically, relational research does not involve manipulation of variables, as do experiments, so the data that are related are often called **ex post facto** data, which means *after the fact*. That is, the results that are related usually have occurred because of some naturally occurring events and are not the result of direct manipulation by an experimenter. The researcher categorizes or assesses the data and then probes for relationships.

CONTINGENCY TABLE RESEARCH

Much psychological research seeks to determine whether the outcome of one variable depends on the outcome of another (for example, Hurlburt, 1994). We will examine a particular research problem to illustrate one kind of relational research. Suppose that you want to determine the distribution of men and women in various major programs at your college. To examine this, you assess the frequencies with which women and men declare major programs and enter the outcome of your results in a contingency table. A **contingency table** is a tabular presentation of all combinations of categories of two variables, which allows the relationships between the two to be examined. An example of the development of a contingency table appears in Table 7–1.

Panel A of Table 7–1 shows the number of women majoring in various departments. More women are majoring in English than in any of the other departments listed. Economics has the fewest women majors. The number of men majors in the five departments appears in panel B. Note that more men major in history than in any other department. Psychology has the fewest men. Panel C illustrates the entire contingency table, and adds some important information—the relative frequency of men and women majors. The overall figures for men (59.3%) and women (40.7%) reflect the distribution of men and women in the entire student body. The relative frequencies for each cell in the table show the percentage of men and women in each major program. The contingency table illustrated in panel C is referred to as a 2×3 *contingency table*, because it has two rows and three columns. Contingency tables have to have at least two rows and at least two columns. The convention is to present the number of rows then the number of columns in the description. For this contingency table, one would describe it as "a two by three contingency table." A particular row-column combination is called a **cell**; for example, the cell entry indicating the percentage of women biology majors is 38.8%

The percentages in the table clearly indicate that there is a relationship between a person's sex and his or her choice of major at this particular college: History, Biology, and Economics have proportionately more men than women majors, and the reverse is true for Psychology and English. This kind of relationship indicates a lack of independence between sex and choice of major. If you wanted to statistically analyze the data in the table,

---

TABLE 7–1
Development of a contingency table indicating some of the major programs chosen by men and women at a small liberal arts college.

Panel A: The number of women majoring in five departments.

Major Program

History	Psychology	English	Biology	Economics
37	24	41	31	21

Panel B: The number of men majoring in five departments.

Major Program

History	Psychology	English	Biology	Economics
78	13	21	49	63

Panel C: A contingency table showing frequency and relative frequency in percentage of women and men majoring in five departments.

Major Program

Sex	History	Psychology	English	Biology	Economics	Total
Women	37	24	41	31	21	154
	32.2%	64.9%	66.1%	38.8%	25.0%	40.7%
Men	78	13	21	49	63	224
	67.8%	35.1%	33.9%	61.2%	75.0%	59.3%
Total	115	37	62	80	84	378
	100.0%	100.0%	100.0%	100.0%	100.0%	100.0%

---

you would probably use a χ^2 **test for independence,** which is a statistical test often used to determine whether the data in a contingency table are statistically significant. The data are statistically significant in this case (refer to Chapters 4 and 5, as well as appendix B for a discussion of statistical significance). This means that we can be reasonably sure that major selection is dependent on the sex of the student, the two variables are not independent of each other.

Now, let us examine an example of research using a contingency table analysis that has been published. In Chapter 3 we discussed the research of Plous (1991) who surveyed animal-rights activists as well as some nonactivists at a large animal-rights rally. The number of activists and nonactivists answering one of his survey questions is shown in Table 7–2. To help interpret this 2×3 contingency table, the percentages also appear. Note that the nonactivists were much less likely than the activists to believe that psychological research causes as much animal suffering as medical research. So, there is a relationship between being an activist and one's view of the harmfulness of certain kinds of research. The two variables are not independent of each other. According to Plous, this relationship may explain why animal-rights activists have tried to disrupt animal research in psychology.

Contingency table research is widely used to investigate the relationships between variables measured at the nominal level (activist/nonactivist

---

TABLE 7–2
A 2×3 contingency table adapted from data presented by Plous (1991).

	Which Kind of Research Causes More Animal Suffering?			
Group	Psychological	Medical	Equal	Total
Activists	64	56	281	401
	16.0%	14.0%	70.0%	100.0%
Nonactivists	8	20	25	53
	15.1%	37.7%	47.2%	100.0%
Total	72	76	306	454
	15.9%	16.7%	67.4%	100.0%

---

and type of research were the two nominal categories in the survey by Plous). The cell entries are usually frequencies (or relative frequencies), and almost always an individual can appear only in one cell. Thus, when people are repeatedly measured on a task, this type of research and the χ^2 analysis of it are inappropriate.

Subject reactivity can be a problem in contingency table research, especially when the participants have been interviewed or surveyed. Plous's work could have had reactivity, because he interviewed the participants in a face-to-face survey. However, not all contingency research need be obviously subject to reactivity. The data presented in Table 7–1 are completely ex post facto, so that the people who declared a particular major do not know that they have appeared in a particular cell of a contingency table. This at first may seem to be a big plus in favor of such research. However, you should be aware that the subjects' reactivity is unknown in this particular example. The real problem is that they could have chosen a particular major for reactive reasons ("Mom wants me to be an English major"). There is no simple way to determine that sort of reactivity if you collate the data from statistics prepared by someone who simply notes who majors in a particular program. So, what often occurs in ex post facto research is that there is subject reactivity of an unknown magnitude and an unknown source. When researchers assess rather than manipulate, they often stay in the dark with regard to such possible confounding as reactivity.

CONCEPT SUMMARY

- **Contingency table research** assesses the relationship between all combinations of categories of two variables.
- **A χ^2 test for independence** can be used to assess the statistical significance of contingency table data.

CORRELATIONAL RESEARCH

The second sort of relational research considered in this chapter is called **correlational research** and allows the researcher to determine simultaneously the degree and direction of a relationship with a single statistic. In previous chapters we have indicated how coefficients of correlation can be used to evaluate measurements and tests. Here we will discuss how correlations can be used directly as a research tool.

One example of the correlational approach to research concerns the relation between cigarette smoking and lung cancer. Researchers aimed to determine whether the two were related, and, if so, the direction—positive or negative—of that relation. Studies in the 1950s and the early 1960s consistently found a moderately high positive correlation between cigarette smoking and the incidence of lung cancer: the greater the number of cigarettes a person smoked, the more likely that person was to have lung cancer. Knowledge of this relation allows predictions to be made. Knowing how much a person smokes allows us to predict how likely that person is to contract lung cancer and vice versa. The prediction is not perfect, because not everyone who smokes gets lung cancer, and not everyone who gets lung cancer has smoked. Nevertheless, the predictions are good, and the Surgeon General's report in 1964 concluded on the basis of evidence that was mostly correlational in nature that smoking was dangerous to health. This evidence is sometimes difficult to interpret, and we will consider some of those difficulties after we examine the correlation coefficient itself.

The Correlation Coefficient

There are several different types of **correlation coefficients,** but almost all have in common the property that they can vary from -1.00 through 0.00 to $+1.00$. Commonly, they will not be one of these three figures, but something in between, such as $+.72$ or $-.39$. The *magnitude* of the correlation coefficient indicates the degree of relationship (larger numbers reflecting stronger relations), and the *sign* indicates the direction of the relation, positive or negative. Putting the appropriate sign in front of the correlation coefficient is necessary, because otherwise one cannot know which way the two variables are related, positively or negatively. It is common practice, though, to omit the plus sign before positive correlations, so that a correlation of .55 would be interpreted as $+.55$. It is a better practice always to include the sign. An example of a *positive* correlation is the relation between lung cancer and smoking. As one variable increases, so does the other (though not perfectly, that is, the correlation coefficient is less than $+ 1.00$). There is also a documented *negative* correlation between smoking and another variable, namely, grades in college. People who smoke a lot have tended to have lower grades than those who smoke less (Huff, 1954, p. 87).

There are actually several different types of correlation coefficients, and which is used depends on the characteristics of the variables being correlated. We shall consider one commonly used by psychologists:

Pearson's product-moment correlation coefficient, or **Pearson** *r*. Because this is only one of several, you should consult a statistics text to determine which is appropriate for your particular case.

Let us imagine that we are one of the many psychologists who devote their careers to the study of human memory. We hit upon a simple, intuitive idea concerning head size and memory: information from the outside world enters the head through the senses and is stored there. An analogy can be made between the head (where information is stored) and other physical vessels, such as boxes, where all kinds of things can be stored. On the basis of such analogical reasoning, which is common in science, we make the following prediction from our knowledge of the properties of physical containers: as head size of a person increases, so should the person's memory. More things can be stored in bigger boxes than in smaller, and similarly more information should be stored in larger heads than in smaller ones.

This "theory" proposes a positive correlation: as head size increases, so should memory. A random sample of the local population could be taken. The persons chosen could be measured on two dimensions: head size and the number of words they can recall from a list of 30, presented to them once, at the rate of one word every three seconds. Three hypothetical sets of results from 10 subjects are presented in Table 7–3. For each individual there are two measures, one of head size and the other of number of words recalled. Also, the two types of measures need not be similar in any way to be correlated. They do not have to be on the same scale. Just as one can correlate head size with number of words recalled, one could also correlate IQ with street-address number, or any two sets of numbers at all.

The mathematical assessment of correlation coefficients is discussed in Appendix A. If you are unfamiliar with this material, you might review box A–1, where the mathematical formula for *r* is presented. Pearson *r* is calculated for the data presented in column (a) of Table 7–3. Working

---

TABLE 7–3
Three hypothetical examples of data taken on head size and recall, representing (a) a positive correlation, (b) a low (near-zero) correlation, and (c) a negative correlation.

Subject	(a) Head size (cm.)	Recall (words)	Subject	(b) Head size (cm.)	Recall (words)	Subject	(c) Head size (cm.)	Recall (words)
1	50.8	17	1	50.8	23	1	50.8	12
2	63.5	21	2	63.5	12	2	63.5	9
3	45.7	16	3	45.7	13	3	45.7	13
4	25.4	11	4	25.4	21	4	25.4	23
5	29.2	9	5	29.2	9	5	29.2	21
6	49.5	15	6	49.5	14	6	49.5	16
7	38.1	13	7	38.1	16	7	38.1	14
8	30.5	12	8	30.5	15	8	30.5	17
9	35.6	14	9	35.6	11	9	35.6	15
10	58.4	23	10	58.4	16	10	58.4	11
	r = +.93			*r* = −.07			*r* = −.89	

through this example will help you better understand the basis of correlation coefficients. Researchers seldom use the mathematical formula to calculate *r* by hand. Most researchers now rely on calculators or computers to calculate correlation coefficients for them.

To give you a better idea of the graphical representation of correlations, called **scatter diagrams,** the data in the three panels of Table 7–3 are presented in the three panels of Figure 7–1, head size is plotted along the horizontal *X*-axis (the abscissa), and number of words recalled is plotted along the vertical *Y*-axis (the ordinate). The high positive correlation between head size and number of words recalled in the panel (a) in Table 7–3 is translated into a visual representation that tilts upward to the right, whereas the negative correlation in panel (c) is depicted as sloping downward to the right. Thus you can see how knowing a person's score on one variable helps predict (though not perfectly in these cases) the level of performance on the other. So knowing a person's head size in the hypothetical data in the (a) and (c) panels helps predict recall, and vice versa. This is the primary reason correlations are useful: they specify the strength of relations and allow predictions to be made. This last statement cannot be made about the data in panel (b), where there is essentially a zero correlation. The points are just scattered about, and there is no consistent relation, which is just what a low Pearson *r* reflects. Even in the cases where the size of the correlation is rather large, it will not be possible to predict perfectly an individual's score on one variable given his or her position on the other. Even with *r* = +.75 between head size and number of words recalled, it is still quite possible for a person with a large head size to recall few words, and vice versa. Unless the correlation is perfect (+1.00 or −1.00), prediction of one score when given the other will not be perfect, either.

What do you think the real correlation would be between head size and recall for a random sample of the population at large? Although we have not actually done such a study, we think it quite likely that it would be positive. Willerman, Schultz, Rutledge, and Bigler (1991) have conducted research on a related topic, the relation between brain size and intelligence or IQ. They found a correlation of +.51 between brain size and IQ in a

FIGURE 7–1
Graphical representation of the data in Table 7–3 showing the characteristic pattern of (a) a high positive correlation, (b) an essentially zero correlation, and (c) a strong negative correlation.

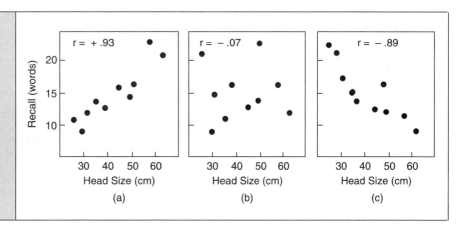

sample of 40 right-handed white introductory psychology students. Of course, the results from this study must be viewed as tentative pending confirming evidence from additional studies. What can we conclude from this and other correlational studies? How can correlation coefficients be interpreted? We turn to this issue next.

Interpreting Correlation Coefficients.   An important warning is always given in any discussion of correlation: The existence of even a sizable correlation implies nothing about the existence of a causal relationship between the two variables under consideration. *Correlation does not prove causation.* On the basis of a correlation alone, one cannot say whether factor *X* causes factor *Y*, factor *Y* causes factor *X*, or some underlying third factor causes both. Let us consider some examples. suppose we have found a correlation of + .70 between head size and recall of words in children. This is in general agreement with our theory that larger heads hold more information, but certainly there are other interpretations of this relationship. It could be argued that the high positive correlation between head size and recall is mediated or produced by some third variable underlying both, such as age. We know that people's heads grow as they age and that recall also improves with age. Therefore, age (or one of its correlates) might actually be responsible for the large positive correlation we have found between head size and number of words recalled. In other words, the internal validity of relational research is always suspect.

In correlational studies, we cannot conclude that any one factor produces or causes another, because there are likely to be a number of factors that vary simultaneously with those of interest. In an experiment, we attempt to avoid this problem by directly manipulating one factor while holding all the others constant. If we are successful in holding other factors constant, which is very difficult to do, then the influence of the manipulated factor on whatever we are measuring can be directly attributed to the factor of interest. Recall that when two factors (or more) are varied at the same time, so that we cannot know whether one factor, the other factor, or both operating together produce some effect, we say that the factors are confounded. Confounding is inherent in correlational research and leads to the interpretational difficulties with such research. In the example of the correlation between head size and recall, we cannot say that variations in head size produced or caused differences in recall, because head size was confounded with at least one other factor: age.

In other cases, the relation between two factors may seem to allow a causal interpretation, but again this is not strictly permitted. Some studies have shown a positive correlation between the number of handguns in a geographic area and the number of murders in that area. Proponents of gun control might use this evidence to support the contention that an increased number of guns leads to (causes, produces) more murders, but again this is not the only plausible interpretation. It may be that people in high-crime neighborhoods buy handguns to protect themselves, or that some third factor, such as socioeconomic class, actually mediates both. We can see, therefore, that no conclusion is justified simply on the basis of a moderate or even a high correlation.

Because correlations can be calculated between any two sets of scores, often even very high correlations are accidental and not linked to one another at all. There may be a very high correlation between the number of preachers and the number of pornographic movies produced each year since 1950, with both being on the increase. But it would take an unusual theory to relate these two in a causal manner.

A high degree of correlation is given greater weight in cases in which obvious competing explanations from confounding factors seem less plausible. Most of the early evidence linking cigarette smoking to lung cancer was correlational; yet the conclusion was drawn (over the protests of the cigarette manufacturers) in the 1964 Surgeon General's report that cigarettes were likely to lead to or cause cancer. This eventually led to warnings on cigarette packages and a ban on advertising cigarettes on television, among other things. The correlation was taken as indicative of a causative relationship, probably because competing hypotheses seemed implausible. It seems unlikely, for example, that having lung cancer causes one to smoke more cigarettes (to soothe the lungs?).

More plausible, perhaps, is the possibility that some underlying third variable (such as anxiety) produces the relationship. In fact, Eysenck and Eaves (1981) have argued that the correlation between lung cancer and smoking in humans is produced by personality differences. Certain personality types, according to Eysenck and Eaves, are more likely to smoke and also to get lung cancer. Thus they argue that the smoking-cancer correlation does not imply causation. We should mention, though, that the link between cigarette smoking and lung cancer has now been established by experimental studies with nonhuman animals, typically beagles. Most authorities disagree with the view of Eysenck and Eaves.

As another example of the pitfalls of the correlational approach, consider the negative relation mentioned previously between cigarette smoking and grades. More smoking has been related to poorer grades. But does smoking cause poorer grades? This seems unlikely, and certainly there are ready alternative interpretations. Students with poor grades may be more anxious and thus smoke more, or more sociable students may smoke more and study less, and so on. No firm conclusions on the causal direction of a relation between two variables can be established simply because the variables are correlated, even if the correlation is perfect. As is true for the descriptive methods, the correlational method is very useful for suggesting possible relations and directing further inquiry, but it is not useful for establishing direct causal relationships. The correlational method is superior to descriptive methods, because the degree of relation between two variables can be precisely stated and thus predictions can be made about the (approximate) value of one variable if the value of the other is known. Remember, the greater the correlation (nearer +1.00 or −1.00), the better the prediction.

Low Correlations: A Caution.   If high correlations cannot be interpreted as evidence for some sort of causal relation, one might think it should at least be possible to rule it out if the correlation is very low, approaching zero. If the correlation between head size and recall had been − .02, would this have ruled out our theory that greater head size leads to better recall? Or if the correlation between smoking and lung cancer had been +.08, should we have abandoned the idea that they are causally related? The answer: sometimes, under certain conditions. But other factors can cause low or zero correlations and may mask an actual relationship.

One common problem is that of **truncated range.** For a meaningful correlation coefficient to be calculated, there must be rather great differences among the scores in each of the variables of interest; there must be a certain amount of spread or variability in the numbers. If all the head sizes were the same in the panels of Table 7–3 and the recall scores varied, the correlation between the two would be zero. (You can work it out yourself using the equation for r in Appendix B.) If we looked only at the correlation between head size and recall in college students, it might be quite low, because the differences in head size and recall among college students might not be very great, compared with the population at large. This could happen even though there might be a positive (or negative) correlation between the two variables if head size were sampled over a wider range. The problem of restricted range can produce a low correlation, even when there is an actual correlation present between two variables.

You might think that everyone would recognize the problem of truncated range and avoid it, but it is often subtle. Consider the problem of trying to predict success in college from Scholastic Aptitude Test (SAT) scores at a college with very high admission standards. The scores on the verbal and quantitative subtests can range from 200 to 800, with average (mean) performance of just below 500. Imagine that mean scores at our hypothetical college are 700 on each subtest. The admissions officer at this college computes a correlation between combined SAT scores and freshman grades and finds it to be +.10, very small indeed. Her conclusion: SAT scores cannot be used to predict grades in college. The problem, however, is that the only scores considered are ones from a very restricted range, specifically very high ones. People with low scores are not admitted to the college. Obviously, the truncated-range problem is very likely to be a factor here, or in any research situation involving a limited sample of subjects with homogeneous characteristics. If the college had randomly admitted people, and if the correlation had then been determined between SAT scores and grades, it would probably have been much higher. Because psychologists often use homogeneous populations such as college students, the restricted-range problem must be carefully considered in interpreting correlations.

A final problem in interpreting low correlations is that one must be certain that the assumptions underlying the use of a particular correlation coefficient have been met. Otherwise, its use may well be inappropriate and lead to spuriously low estimates of relationship. These have not been discussed here, but it is imperative to check on these assumptions in a statistics book before employing Pearson r or any other correlation coefficient. For example, one assumption underlying Pearson r is that the relationship between the two variables is linear (can be described by a straight line) rather than curvilinear, as in the hypothetical (but plausible) relationship in Figure 7–2 between age and long-term memory. At very young ages, the line is flat; then it increases between ages 3 and 16, where it again levels off until

FIGURE 7–2
A hypothetical figure depicting a curvilinear relationship between long-term memory and age. Although memory is related to age in a systematic fashion and one could predict recall by knowing age, Pearson *r* would be quite low, because the relationship is not linear.

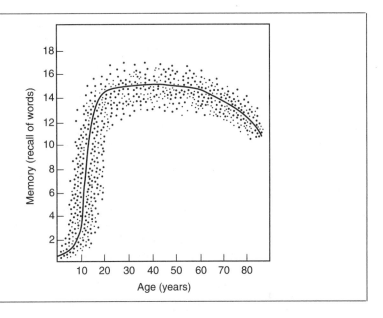

late middle age, where it drops slightly, until very old age, where it decreases at a greater rate (Howard & Wiggs, 1993). Thus one can predict recall of words from age fairly well, but Pearson *r* will be rather low, because the relationship between the two variables is not linear. This could, of course, always be checked by plotting a scatter diagram, as in Figure 7–2. Low correlations, then, may not reflect that a relationship is absent but only that the assumptions of the particular coefficient employed have not been met.

Reactivity in Correlational Research.   As mentioned in previous chapters, many of the subject reactivity problems found in descriptive research are also applicable to correlational research, because test results and survey data often provide the bases for correlations. In fact, demands on participants might be magnified in correlational research that involves two measures that are taken at the same time. Participants do not usually react passively to the inquiries of the researcher. Instead, they often try to figure out what is going on and respond according to their perceptions of the project and in ways that will make themselves look good to the researcher (Weber and Cook, 1972). For example, suppose you surveyed a college population about their sexual and religious attitudes. At the same time, you also asked them about their use of drugs. Most college students could figure out at least some of the purposes of the project, and as a consequence, their responses to the two sets of questions asked together might differ from their responses to either set asked alone.

Complex Correlational Procedures

Does watching violent TV programs cause aggressive behavior? Eron, Huesmann, Lefkowitz, and Walder (1972) measured children's preferences for violent programs and the children's aggressiveness as rated by their peers. For these third-graders, Eron and coworkers found a moderate positive correlation, $r = +.21$, indicating that children who were more aggressive tended to watch more violent TV (and less aggressive children tended to watch less violent programs). How are we to interpret this positive correlation? Can we say that watching violent programs causes aggressiveness? The answer is no. To see why this is the case, all we have to do is to turn our causal statement around and assert that being aggressive causes a preference for violent TV. We have no reasonable way to decide on the direction of causality, based on this one correlation coefficient. As we noted earlier, a valid causal statement cannot be made on the basis of a single correlation.

When we do not know the direction of causality (violent TV causes aggression versus aggressive traits cause a preference for violent programs), there is a strong possibility that some third, confounded variable is the cause of the obtained relation. Because the researchers have not controlled either the programs watched or the initial aggressiveness, they cannot rule out other variables, such as genetic differences in aggressiveness or differences in home life. Causal statements are difficult, if not impossible, to make on the basis of a single correlation coefficient.

The internal validity of correlational research may be enhanced by examining patterns of correlations. One technique is called the **cross-lagged-panel correlation procedure,** and Eron and coworkers used it in a 10-year follow-up study of the same children in the "thirteenth" grade. The results are summarized in Figure 7–3. The correlation between a preference for violent TV and aggression was essentially zero ($r = -.05$) in the thirteenth grade. Similarly, they found a negligible relation between preference for violent TV in the third and the thirteenth grade ($r = +.05$). They did obtain a moderate relation between aggressiveness in the two grades ($r = +.38$), indicating that it is a somewhat stable trait. Of more interest are the cross-lagged correlations (the ones along the diagonals of the figure) in assessing the direction of causation. Do aggressive people watch violent TV, or does watching violent TV produce aggressiveness? We can determine which of these two possibilities holds true by examining the diagonal correlations. Essentially no relation exists between aggressiveness in the third grade and watching violent TV in the thirteenth ($r = +.01$). However, a fairly substantial correlation exists between a preference for watching violent TV in the third grade and exhibiting aggressiveness in the thirteenth ($r = +.31$). In fact, the relation is even greater than the one between these two variables in the earlier study, when the subjects were third-graders. Thus the direction seems to be that watching violent TV programs in the third grade may produce aggressiveness later. The underlying assumption is that if one variable causes the other, the first (watching violent TV programs) should be more strongly related to the second (aggressiveness) later in time than when the second (effect) variable is measured at the same time as the first cause. In other words, causes should take some time to produce their effects (see Figure 7–3).

Using these cross-lagged-panel correlations and other complex analyses, Eron and colleagues concluded that watching violent TV programs

FIGURE 7–3
Correlations between a preference for violent television programs and aggression, as rated by peers for 211 males over a 10-year period. The important cross-lagged correlations are on the diagonals. (After Eron, Huesmann, Lefkowitz, and Walder, 1972. Copyright (1972) by the American Psychological Association. Reprinted by permission of the author.)

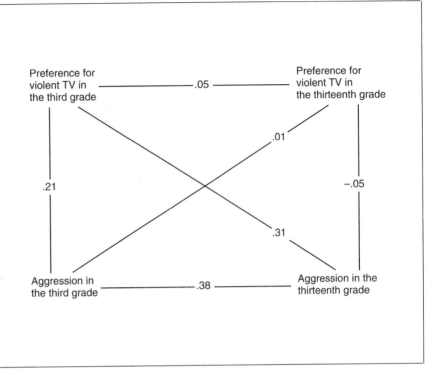

early in life probably causes, in part, aggressive behavior later in life. Recent research by Eron (1982) supports this conclusion (also see Huesmann et al., 1973). Of course, many other factors contribute to aggressiveness; this is just one example of how cross-lagged-panel correlations can aid in arriving at an explanation from correlational research. However, internal validity cannot be as strong as those that come from experiments, because the variables have not been manipulated by the researcher.

The general strategy of the cross-lagged procedure, then, is to obtain several correlations over time, and then, on the basis of the size and direction of the *rs*, determine what leads to what. The cross-lagged technique is fairly new to psychological research and has the obvious drawback that the research project may be very time consuming. Nevertheless, this method for determining causation from correlational research has been used in several problem areas, for example, to show that a large vocabulary enhances the ability to spell, rather than the other way around, and that air pollution is an important cause of death in large cities, rather than death being a cause of pollution (Cook and Campbell, 1979, Chapter 7).

As a general rule, remember that internal validity is always suspect in correlational research because of possible third-variable confounding. Cook and Campbell, as well as others (for example, Rogosa, 1980), have noted that many of the assumptions underlying complex correlational research are questionable. Thus, we have additional reasons to suspect causal statements made on the basis of correlational evidence.

CONCEPT SUMMARY

In correlational research **correlation coefficients** describe the strength and direction of relations, which permit prediction.

Correlations have suspect internal validity owing to

- the **third-variable problem**
- **truncated range**
- **unknown direction of causation**

Experimentation and Internal Validity

We have repeatedly cautioned you about incorrectly concluding that a correlation means causation. Causation is a controversial subject in science and philosophy, and we will now consider some of the issues. Owing to the influence of some philosophers of science, it has become unpopular among contemporary scientists to use the term *cause*, because the philosophical implications become frightfully complicated. Thinking too long about the cause of even a very simple event leads to an infinite regress of causes for that event. For this and other reasons, the term *cause* has dropped out of use in some circles (see Kerlinger, 1986, and the Application section on causation for further discussion).

In this book we muddle through, using the term *cause*, because its meaning is always limited; experiments lead to causal inferences because the independent variable is manipulated while all others are, in the ideal case, held constant. Whatever effect on the dependent variable that occurs in such cases has been caused by the factor that varied. Thus, we can say that when the Stroop experiment is conducted in such a way that confounding is minimized, changes in the levels of the independent variable caused changes in the dependent variable.

A more interesting point is that many factors that are experimentally varied are themselves quite complicated sets of independent events, any one of which could be the cause of an experimental effect. Time is a good example of such a variable. If we are interested in the effects of the length of time one studies a persuasive communication on the amount a person's attitude changes toward the communication, we vary the amount of time people spend studying the message. Suppose we find an increase in attitude change with increases in study time, when other factors are held constant. Can we say that time has caused an increase in attitude change? In a sense this is true, but in a more fundamental sense it is not. Presumably, it is some psychological process, acting over time, that causes the attitude change. It is something correlated with time, but not time itself, because time is not a causative agent. If we leave a bicycle outdoors in the rain and it rusts, we do not say that time caused the rust; chemical processes acting over time caused it.

Usually, a manipulated variable is actually composed of a number of complex and interacting parts, any one or set of which may actually cause some effect. For this reason, it is sometimes said that experiments are only controlled correlations, because the variable manipulated is actually

APPLICATION

Causation

If you generate a visual image of something you are trying to remember, you will retain it better than if you simply repeat the information over and over (Bower, 1972). The philosophical implications of *why* imagery enhances remembering can become extremely complicated. Thinking too long about the cause of even a very simple event can lead to an infinite regress of causes for that event. A regressive causal analysis of the effects of imagery might be as follows: Imagery causes better remembering than simple repetition. Why? Because imagery results in more associations than does repetition. Why? Because more protein molecules in the brain become active when imagery is used. Why? Because evolution determined the structure of the human brain. Why? Because . . .

In this book, we use the terms *cause* and *why* because their meanings here are always limited. Experiments can lead to causal inferences because one factor is varied while other factors are held constant, and we can say that the effect was caused by the factor that varied. In the typical psychology experiment, therefore, the immediate causes of an effect are determined. These immediate causes are called the **proximate causes** of an event and are to be distinguished from the **ultimate causes** (Mayr, 1982). Proximate causes derive from the immediate manipulations in an experiment (for example, instructions to the subjects to use imagery or repetition). Ultimate causes are those that are supposed to stop the infinite regress of ''why'' and ''because'' as outlined earlier. One kind of ultimate answer to our questions about imagery could be an appeal to evolution. Biologists argue that evolution is the ultimate cause behind all aspects of biology and, thereby, provides the physiological and genetic framework for ultimate causation in psychology (Mayr, 1982). According to such an analysis, imagery instructions would be the proximate cause of differences in retention, and evolutionary forces would be the ultimate cause for the effectiveness of those instructions. There are other possible ultimate causes (for example, a deity), and we could argue that something had to set evolution in motion (perhaps a ''big bang''). Because of these possibilities, the distinction between proximate causation and ultimate causation may not be clear or relevant. Therefore, many people prefer asking ''Under what conditions does imagery enhance memory?'' instead of ''Why does imagery enhance memory?'' Likewise, instead of saying ''Imagery causes better memory'' some people prefer to say ''Imagery may enhance (is an antecedent condition of, determines, or directly affects) memory.'' Because we generally will be talking about individual experiments, we will use the latter phrases interchangeably with *cause* and *why* where appropriate.

composed of a number of confounded parts. This is certainly an accurate characterization in at least some cases; even so we are far ahead of having a simple correlation, because we know the direction of effect. Take the example of how amount of time spent studying a persuasive communication affects attitude change. We could simply give the message to a number of people and let them read it for as long as they desired. We could time this for each person, and then see how much the person's attitude changed. If we found a positive correlation, we would not know whether the time people spent studying the passage caused more attitude change, or whether the more people decided to change their attitudes, the more they studied the passage to make sure they knew the facts. There are other possible reasons for the relationship, too. But in the experiment in which time is varied while other factors are held constant, we can say that more study time leads to (determines, produces, causes) more attitude change.

Experiments allow us to know the direction of the relation. This is their overwhelming advantage to correlations. They also inform us (which a correlation does not) that the causal factor is at least embedded in the independent variable, and not some third outside factor. It is in this sense that they tell us about causes and are internally valid, at least in principle.

CONCEPT SUMMARY

Experiments are internally valid because the causal variables are known and the direction of causation is known.

SUMMARY

1. Relational research attempts to show how two variables change together.

2. A contingency table is a form of research that looks at the frequencies of all combinations of categories of two variables.

3. The statistical reliability of a contingency table is often assessed by the χ^2 test for independence.

4. Usually, contingency tables assess the relationship between nominal variables.

5. Correlational research permits a determination of the strength and direction of relations among variables.

6. The internal validity of the correlational technique is suspect because of third-variable confounding, an unknown direction of causation, and sometimes by a truncated range of scores on one or more of the variables.

7. The cross-lagged-panel correlation procedure can increase the internal validity of the correlational technique by showing the direction of causation.

8. Experimentation allows causal statements in principle, which means that experiments can be internally valid.

■ KEY CONCEPTS

cell
contingency table
correlational research
correlation coefficient
cross-lagged-panel
    correlation procedure
ex post facto

Pearson's product-moment correlation coefficient (Pearson r)
proximate causes
relational research
scatter diagrams
truncated range
ultimate causes
χ^2 test for independence

■ EXERCISES

1. [*Special Exercise.*] A psychologist studied the remote memory of college graduates by seeing how many names of old television programs they could correctly recognize. The results indicated that there was no correlation between the subjects' intelligence-test scores and their ability to recognize the names of old programs ($r = +.07$). Assuming that the procedure of memory testing was valid and that the age of the subjects was not a problem, can you think of some problems in this research that would prevent you from making a valid conclusion about the small r?

2. An illustration of how Pearson r is calculated for the data in column (a) of table 7–3 is presented in box A–1 of Appendix A. Work through this example, and then calculate r values for the data in columns (b) and (c) of Table 7–3. Make sure that your r values are the same as those values given at the bottom of Table 7–3.

3. The table here shows some fictitious data from a college admissions office. For 10 students, we have the scores from the verbal portion of their Scholastic Aptitude Test (SAT) as well as their freshman grade point average (GPA). The GPA is on a four-point scale, where $F = 0$, $D = 1$, $C = 2$, $B = 3$, and $A = 4$ points. Calculate the correlation coefficient between these two sets of scores. What might you conclude?

Student	Verbal SAT	Freshman GPA
1	471	2.00
2	403	1.50
3	510	2.25
4	485	2.00
5	575	2.25
6	445	1.75
7	400	2.50
8	590	3.25
9	560	2.50
10	555	2.75

4. [*Special Exercise.*] There are a number of potential methodological problems associated with relational research. Some of them are discussed in this chapter. What are these methodological problems and how are they overcome?

■ SUGGESTED READINGS

An extensive discussion of correlational techniques and methods of observation can be found in Kerlinger, F. N. (1986). *Foundations of behavioral research* (3d ed.). New York: Holt.

An extensive discussion of research relating aggression to watching violent television can be found in Eron, L. D. (1982). Parent-child interaction, television violence, and aggression of children. *American Psychologist, 37,* 197–211.

Psychology in Action
Amount of Sleep and Tension Headaches

This project is a variation of a research procedure used by Hicks and Kilcourse (1983). These researchers were interested in the relationship between the number of hours of sleep subjects got and the frequency of tension or migraine headaches the subjects experienced. In a health survey, the researchers asked college students: **(1) Estimate the number of hours of sleep you usually get each night,** and **(2) Do you have tension or migraine headaches Often?_____ Sometimes?_____ Never? _____** . Hicks and Kilcourse found an inverse relationship between these two variables; that is, people with more headaches slept less than those with fewer headaches. The researchers' mode of categorizing the frequency of headaches and the amount of sleep naturally leads to a contingency table research design. The amount of sleep could be categorized as *inadequate* or *adequate.* Alternatively, you could categorize the amount of sleep along a ratio dimension (that is, the number of hours of sleep that are usually obtained).

An alternate way of conducting this research would be as a correlation design. To use a Person *r*, you would need to have two pairs of measures that are interval or ratio in nature. One way to do this would be as follows.

You can modify their second question by asking: "Estimate the number of tension or migraine headaches you have each month." Ask 20 or so of your college acquaintances the modified question and the one concerning the estimated number of hours of sleep. Survey enough people so that you do not have a truncated range on one of your variables. Then calculate the *r* between these two variables.

You can enhance the reliability of your results by combining your data with those of classmates. If you pool your data, make sure that you and the others doing the project are surveying different people. When your data are combined, you may wind up with a large number of subjects, so you will find that MINITAB or some other statistical package will be helpful in calculating *r*.

To anticipate a later Psychology in Action project (Chapter 11), you should collect some additional demographic data on your subjects, such as age, sex, and year in school.

Hicks, R. A., & Kilcourse, J. (1983). Habitual sleep duration and the incidence of headaches in college students. *Bulletin of the Psychonomic Society, 21,* 119.

BASICS OF EXPERIMENTATION

The researcher produces a comparison by letting one or more variables change while holding other variables constant

Independent Variables

❏ At least two levels of a variable are manipulated to provide a standard of comparison. Interactions may occur when there are two or more independent variables.

Dependent Variables

❏ Specific behaviors are measured in an experiment.

Control Variables

❏ In the ideal experiment, all other variables are held constant.

Experimental Group or Condition

❏ The treatment group or condition that receives the level of interest of the independent variable.

Control Group or Condition

❏ The group or condition that is untreated or receives a comparison (baseline) level of the independent variable.

Possible Sources of Error

❏ Subject reactivity

❏ External validity

CHAPTER 8

BASICS OF EXPERIMENTATION

A tightly designed, well-conducted experiment is the goal of psychologists who attempt to answer the question of why we act as we do. In this chapter we will consider the basic characteristics of a good experiment. The essential ingredient of an experiment is production of a comparison while holding other variables constant.

EXPERIMENTATION: AN EXAMPLE

Can you name

A famous theme park in the heart of Copenhagen

The world's largest single rock in Australia

The main law court in London

The actress who starred in *Yentl*

The actor who played the *Bionic Man*

The actor who played a Secret Service agent in *The Avengers*

You probably were able to answer some of these questions and were utterly unable to answer others. But there were perhaps some questions where you were not sure of the answer but where you felt you might know the answer. Indeed, the answer might be on the tip of your tongue. [Answers: Tivoli Gardens, Ayers Rock, Old Bailey, Barbara Streisand, Lee Majors, Patrick MacNee.]

The tip-of-the-tongue state has been much studied by experimental psychologists interested in human memory (Brown and McNeill, 1966). It occurs when you have partial knowledge of an answer and the feeling that you could recognize the answer if it were given to you. For example, Brown and McNeill discovered that when people said they were in tip-of-the-tongue states, they could correctly identify the first letter of the answer 57 percent of the time, even though the entire correct answer could not be produced.

What kind of information might help elicit correct answers from people in tip-of-the-tongue states? The answer to this question has important implications for understanding how we encode and store information in memory. Brennen, Baguley, Bright, and Bruce (1990) performed an experiment to discover if a visual picture aided recall in tip-of-the-tongue states. Their first experiment was very simple. They presented a list of fifty questions about television celebrities and noted when their experimental subjects, fifteen college undergraduates, reported they were in a tip-of-the-tongue state. On average, this happened 10.5 times per subject. Of course, some subjects had only a few tip-of-the-tongue states and some had many (the range was four to twenty-two incidences) but on average about 20 percent of the questions produced tip-of-the-tongue states. Once this state occurred, the experimenters either asked the question again or showed a picture of the face of the television personality. Results of this experiment are shown in Figure 8–1. Clearly, presenting faces did not help resolve tip-of-the-tongue states any better than merely repeating the question.

One experiment by itself seldom satisfies experimental psychologists, so Brennen et al. performed a second experiment both to expand their findings and to ensure that their initial results could be repeated. In this experiment they doubled the number of subjects to thirty. They also added a new condition where the person's initials were presented. So now there were three experimental conditions: (1) repeat the question, (2) present a picture, and (3) present letter initials. Results of this second experiment are shown in Figure 8–2.

These results tell us two important things: First, repeating the questions and presenting a picture were equally effective. This means that the results of the first experiment have been repeated. Second, presenting letter initials was much more effective in resolving tip-of-the-tongue states than either repeating the question or presenting a picture. This result implies that memory information is stored in such a way that only the spelling of a name, and not a visual image, can aid memory retrieval in tip-of-the-tongue states.

This conclusion illustrates how experiments let us find the causes of behavioral events. In the first experiment, similar results for repeating the question and presenting a picture did not allow us to distinguish between these two possible causes of aided memory retrieval. But in the second experiment, presenting letter initials did cause a memory improvement. How do experiments permit us to make such causal statements?

WHAT IS AN EXPERIMENT?

As discussed in Chapter 7, **experiments** are tests designed to arrive at a causal explanation (see Cook and Campbell, 1979). The conditions neces-

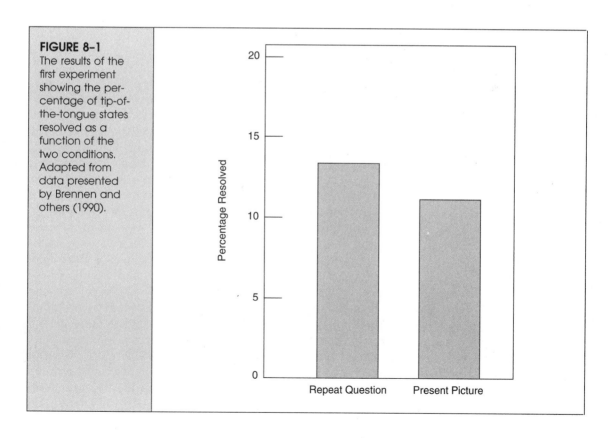

FIGURE 8–1
The results of the first experiment showing the percentage of tip-of-the-tongue states resolved as a function of the two conditions. Adapted from data presented by Brennen and others (1990).

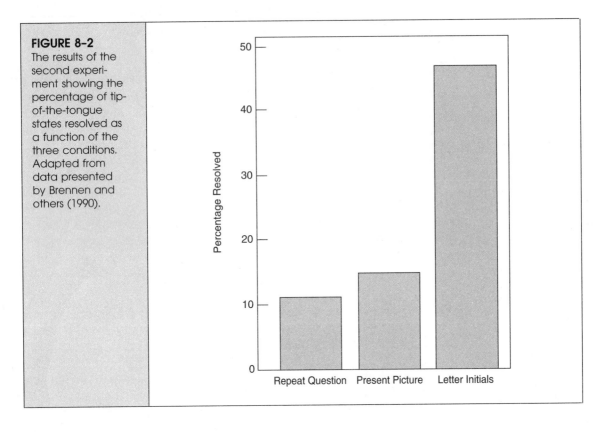

FIGURE 8-2
The results of the second experiment showing the percentage of tip-of-the-tongue states resolved as a function of the three conditions. Adapted from data presented by Brennen and others (1990).

sary for arriving at explanations were set forth in the nineteenth century by the philosopher John Stuart Mill (1843/1930). The conditions he outlined provide a good definition of an experiment.

Mill argued that causation can be inferred if some result, X, follows an event, A, if A and X vary together and if it can be shown that event A produces result X. For these conditions to be met, what Mill called the **joint method of agreement and difference** must be used. In the joint method, if A occurs then so will X, and if A does not occur, then neither will X.

Let us apply this reasoning to the experiment on tip-of-the-tongue states. Here the result X is a correct resolution of the tip-of-the-tongue state. The event A is presenting letter initials. Figure 8–2 showed that event A produced result X. Furthermore, if A is absent (for example, the question is repeated but no letter initials are presented) then result X is not produced. This is Mill's joint method of agreement and difference at work.

However, the situation even in this simple experiment is more complicated because event A does not always produce X and the absence of event A does not always fail to produce X. In Figure 8–2 presenting letter initials does not resolve 100 percent of the tip-of-the-tongue states. Similarly, merely repeating the question does resolve tip-of-the-tongue states a small percentage of the time, and this small percentage is greater than zero. Thus, in practice most experiments do not show causality all the time for every single trial in the experiment. Instead, most experimental psychologists are content if event A produces result X more than some other event B. (The question of how much more is answered by statistical analysis explained in Appendix B. For now, we ignore how much and only ask if there is any more X produced.)

So a more complete statement of causality is event A (presenting letter initials) produces more resolution of tip-of-the-tongue states (X) than event B (repeating the question) or event C (presenting a picture). At first, you might incorrectly conclude that event A causes X a great deal and event C causes only a little bit of X. But this would be wrong. Most experiments have within them a baseline condition that evaluates neutral events, such as the passage of time, that are not believed to have causal influence. For some event to exert causal influence on behavior, it must have a greater effect than the neutral baseline event. In this experiment, repeating the question is the neutral baseline event. Any small effect this might produce is not interesting by itself. Instead, this calibrates other events of potentially greater interest. For example, event C (presenting a picture) might be expected (from certain theories of memory) to produce a causal relationship with X. If the experimenters had omitted baseline event B (repeating the question) in Figure 8–1, they might have mistakenly concluded that event C caused X because more than zero percent of the tip-of-the-tongue states were resolved. But as Figure 8–1 showed, event B was as effective as event C. Therefore, we conclude that no causal relationship exists between event C and X. This lack of a causal relationship inspired the experimenters to perform yet another study (Figure 8–2) in which a causal relationship was obtained.

Experiments that fail to reveal any causal relationships are seldom published. Although the lack of a causal relationship where one might be expected due to theoretical reasons is important, it is even more important to show some causal relationship in an experiment. Failure to find any causal relationships could indicate a flaw in the experimental design (perhaps not enough subjects were tested, etc.). Thus, finding at least one causal relation in an experiment gives us some confidence that a failure to exhibit causality with some different event in the same experiment is more likely to be correct rather than to have happened because of some (unknown) deficiencies in the experiment itself.

The hallmark of an experiment is the production of a comparison by controlling the occurrence or nonoccurrence of a variable and observing the outcome. Boring (1954) noted that the concept of **control** in experimentation derives from the joint method of agreement and difference. One way we can view control is in terms of direct manipulation (A occurs or does not occur), which, according to the joint method of agreement and difference, leads to a basis for comparison (hence, the term *control group,* as explained later). Control also suggests that we can eliminate alternative explanations of our results. Usually control in experimentation is thought of in three ways: (1) there is a control condition for purposes of *comparison;* (2) the levels or values of the independent variable can be *produced;* and (3) the experimental setting can be controlled by holding certain aspects *constant* (for example, type of apparatus or method of measurement). These three types of control—comparison, production, and constancy—are crucial to the conduct of an experiment that will yield an explanation of why people and animals behave as they do. In fact, comparison, production, and constancy provide us with a definition of an experiment (see the Concept Summary).

CONCEPT SUMMARY

An experiment occurs when a particular *comparison* is *produced* while other aspects of the situation are held *constant*.

In summary, producing comparisons, as Brennen and colleagues did, can allow us to rule out the possibility of a mere correlation between variables. Correct use of Mill's procedure can lead to causal statements.

ADVANTAGES OF EXPERIMENTATION

Let us examine another research problem to illustrate the advantages of experimentation. One characteristic of modern life is that many of us are subjected to changes in atmospheric pressure during air travel. Furthermore, a substantial portion of the world's population lives at elevations between 2,000 and 10,000 feet. What this means is that many people are subjected to mild decompressions in barometric pressure. Are these decompressions hazardous, as are so many other things in the world today (such as pollution, pesticides, and food additives)? This question was the impetus for experiments conducted by Graessle, Ahbel, and Porges (1978). Early research indicated that greatly reduced barometric pressure (as occurs in altitudes greater than 10,000 feet) can retard both fetal and newborn development. Graessle and colleagues wanted to see whether lesser decompressions, more like those experienced during air travel, also affected the development of infants.

To study this problem, the researchers experimented with pregnant rats. The general procedure was to subject the rats to a series of mild decompressions similar to those experienced during air travel (around 6,000 feet), and then compare the growth and behavior of rats born to the mothers that experienced decompression with the growth and behavior of rats born to mothers kept at ground level (728 feet, in this instance).

Now for some particulars of their research. Pregnant rats were randomly divided into two groups: One group received seven daily decompressions for 20 days during pregnancy, and the second group of mothers was kept at ground level. Changes in pressure for the one group (up to a pressure equaling an altitude of 6,000 feet) lasted about 20 minutes. These changes in pressure were gradual, simulating the sorts of changes that occur during air travel. Following birth, all infant rats were weighed daily and received periodic testing of their ability to grasp a thin wire, turn over (the righting reflex), more on an inclined plane, and climb (pull themselves up a thin wall when suspended by their forepaws).

The *independent variable* (what was varied) was atmospheric pressure, and the *dependent variables* (the things observed and measured) included the weight of the babies and the various behaviors just described. In Brennen's experiments cuing condition was the independent variable, which had two levels in the first study and three levels in the second one. What was the dependent variable? At this point we need to mention a third class of variables, the *control variables,* which the experimenter holds constant. In the decompression experiment, control variables included similar housing and feeding conditions for all rats at all times, identical testing procedures, and the fact that the treated and untreated mothers were of the same strain of rats. Species, age, and persons to be identified were among the control variables in Brennen's work.

Ordinarily we call the group of subjects that receives the independent variable the **experimental group;** the designation for the untreated subjects is the **control group.** (Note that a control group is not the same as a control variable. The meaning of "control group" will become clear momentarily.) In the decompression experiment, the decompressed mother rats and their babies represent the experimental group. The mothers and infants that were kept at ground level as a comparison or baseline group make up the control group. These labels (experimental or control group) make sense in that the control group receives a different treatment, and an examination of this group's behavior serves to indicate changes that would occur in the absence of the independent variable. Thus, the control group *controls* for changes that may occur whether or not any particular variable is introduced into the situation. The experimental group, of course, defines the experiment for us. The experimental group is the one that receives the treatment of interest—decompression, in this case. (Note that we are using Mill's procedure to arrive at an explanation.) Graessle and colleagues found that rats given decompressions before birth began to climb at a later age than the control animals and that the prenatally decompressed rats gained weight more slowly than the controls.

The results of the decompression experiment are intriguing and may have important practical implications. If you were interested in this topic, you might have considered the possibility of doing this experiment with pregnant human beings. The ethics of that tactic would be questionable without knowing in advance the effects of mild decompressions. That is why we do many types of experiments, especially preliminary ones, on animals. An alternative approach to the decompression problem might be to do the research **ex post facto,** which means selecting our subjects after the fact. Thus, we could do a quasi-experiment (see Chapter 11). In quasi-experiments the levels of the independent variable are selected rather than manipulated directly by the experimenter. We would find infants whose mothers had flown on airplanes during pregnancy. Then we would compare their development with that of infants whose mothers had remained at ground level during pregnancy. Other than the tedious job of identifying the subjects in the first place (imagine trying to identify human subjects ex post facto for this study), the major drawback to the research done ex post facto is a loss of control. As we will discuss later, it is very difficult to hold potentially relevant variables constant after the fact. In particular, we would be hard put to find two groups of subjects whose only difference was that some had flown on planes prenatally and some had not.

We can conclude, therefore, that this animal study about the effects of mild decompression is more ethical, more economical, and better controlled than alternative research procedures. This experiment is not problem free, however. You might find it worthwhile to consider some of the difficulties associated with this experiment. One obvious problem concerns generalizing from rat development to human development.

CONCEPT SUMMARY

Experiment
A particular comparison is produced while other variables are held constant.

Experimental Group
Receives the important level of the independent variable.

Control Group
Serves as the untreated comparison group or receives a comparison level of the independent variable.

VARIABLES IN EXPERIMENTATION

Variables are what makes experiments run. Effective selection and manipulation of variables make the difference between a good experiment and a poor one. This section covers the three kinds of variables that must be carefully considered before starting an experiment: independent, dependent, and control variables. We conclude by discussing experiments that have more than one independent or dependent variable.

Independent Variables

Independent variables are manipulated by the experimenter. The brightness of a lamp, the loudness of a tone, the number of decompressions given to a rat are all independent variables, because the experimenter determines their amount. Independent variables are selected because an experimenter thinks they will cause changes in behavior. Increasing the intensity of a tone should increase the speed with which people respond to the tone. Increasing the number of decompressions given to a mother rat may change the rate of development of her babies. When a change in the level (amount) of an independent variable causes a change in behavior, we say that the behavior is under control of the independent variable. Failure of an independent variable to control behavior, often called a **null result**, can have more than one interpretation. First, the experimenter may have incorrectly guessed that the independent variable was important, and the null results may be correct. Most scientists will accept this interpretation only reluctantly, and thus the following alternative explanations of null results are common.

The experimenter may not have created a valid manipulation of the independent variable. Let us say you are conducting an experiment on second-grade children and your independent variable is the number of small treats (chocolates, peanuts, or whatever) the children get after each correct response in some task. Some children get only one, whereas others get two. You find no difference in behavior between the two groups. Perhaps if your independent variable had involved a greater range—that is, if it went from one piece of candy to ten pieces of candy—you would have obtained a difference. Your manipulation was not sufficient to reveal any effect of the independent variable. Or perhaps, unknown to you, the class had a birthday party just before the experiment started and your subjects' stomachs were filled with ice cream and birthday cake. In this case, maybe even ten pieces of candy would not have shown any effect. That is why, in studies of animal learning in which food is used as a reward, the animals are deprived of food before the experiment starts. Thus experimenters are careful to produce a strong manipulation of the independent variable. Failure to do so is a common cause of null results. Other common causes of null results are related to dependent and control variables, to which we now turn.

Dependent Variables

The **dependent variable** is observed and recorded by the experimenter. It depends on the behavior of the subject, which, in turn, is supposed to depend on the independent variable. The time it takes to press a switch, the speed of a worm crawling through a maze, the age when a rat climbs are all dependent variables, because they are observed and recorded by the experimenter.

One criterion for a good dependent variable is reliability (see Chapter 5 for a discussion of reliability in testing and measurement). When an experiment is repeated exactly—same subject, same levels of independent variable, and so on—the dependent variable should yield about the same score as it did previously. Unreliability can occur if there is some deficit in the way we measure the dependent variable. Let us say we want to measure the weight in grams of a candle before and after it has been lit for fifteen minutes. We use a scale that has a spring which moves a pointer. The spring contracts when it is cold and expands when it is hot. As long as our weight measurements are taken at constant temperatures, they will be reliable. But if temperature varies while objects are being weighed, the same object will yield different readings. Our dependent variable is then unreliable. Generally, we want our measuring devices to be consistent, just as it is crucial for the observer to be consistent (as in following a protocol, see Chapter 6).

Null results can often be caused by deficits in the dependent variable even if it is reliable. The most common cause is a restricted or limited range of the dependent variable so that it gets "stuck" at the top or bottom of its scale. Imagine you are teaching a rather uncoordinated friend how to bowl for the first time. You know from introductory psychology that reward improves performance, so you offer to buy your friend a beer every time he or she gets a strike. Your friend gets all gutter balls so you drink the beer yourself. Thus you can no longer offer a reward, which means that the unrewarded performance should decrease. But because it is impossible to do any worse than all gutter balls, you cannot observe any decrement. Your friend is already at the bottom of the scale. This is called a **floor effect.** The opposite problem, that of getting 100 percent correct, is called a **ceiling effect.** Ceiling and floor effects prevent the influence of an independent variable from being accurately reflected in a dependent variable (these effects are discussed in detail later).

A final source of null results is one associated with inferential statistics. The results of a statistical test (see Appendix B) may fail to reject the hypothesis that the experimental and control groups do not differ when, in fact, they do. This failure to reject the null hypothesis when it should be rejected is called a **type 2 error.** The likelihood of committing a type 2 error increases as we lower the level of statistical significance, but the likelihood can be decreased by increasing the power (sensitivity) of the experiment (see Appendix B).

Control Variables

A **control variable** is a potential independent variable that is held constant during an experiment. It does not vary, because it is controlled by the experimenter. For any one experiment, there are more desirable control variables than can ever be controlled in practice. In even a relatively simple experiment (for example, requiring people to memorize three-letter syllables), many variables should be controlled. Time of day (diurnal cycle) changes a person's efficiency, and ideally this should be controlled. Temperature could be important because your subject might fall asleep if the testing room were too warm. The time that has elapsed since a person's last meal might also affect memory performance. Intelligence is also related. The list could go on. An experimenter tries to control as many salient variables as possible, hoping that the effect of uncontrolled factors will be small relative to the effect of the independent variable. The smaller the size of the effect produced by the independent variable, the more important it is to carefully control other extraneous factors. Holding a variable constant is not the only way to remove extraneous variation. Design techniques, which we shall discuss in the next chapter, also control extraneous variables. However, holding a variable constant is the most direct experimental technique for controlling extraneous factors, and so we shall limit our definition of control variables to this technique. Null results often occur in an experiment because there is insufficient control of these other factors—that is, they have been left to vary unsystematically. This is especially true in studies outside of laboratories where the ability to hold control variables constant is greatly decreased. Remember, we call these unintended effects **confoundings,** because their influence confounds (or confuses) the proper interpretation of the results. An example of a confounded experiment is presented in the Application section.

Using Variables

In summary, a perfect experiment would have the dependent variable entirely controlled by the independent variable. In practice, this is not very

APPLICATION

CONFOUNDED EXPERIMENTS IN ADVERTISING

A major value of a tightly controlled experiment is that the results are unambiguous: You can be confident that the independent variable led to changes in the dependent variable. Your conclusion about the effectiveness of the independent variable depends on minimal effects of extraneous factors—confounding variables. An advertising campaign presented an incorrect conclusion because the intended independent variable (Pepsi versus Coke) was confounded with another variable.

In the advertisement, people were asked to choose between the two cola drinks. In one series Pepsi was in a cup labeled *S* and Coke in a cup marked *L*. Most people chose the drink in the *S* cup (Pepsi), so the conclusion was that cola drinkers prefer Pepsi. Is this a legitimate conclusion?

An experiment by Woolfolk, Castellan, and Brooks (1983) calls the advertising results into question. These authors reasoned that the labels on the cups may have had some influence on the choices made by the people in the advertisement. This supposition is based on the knowledge that labeling of various kinds can have a strong effect on consumer behavior. As a first step in their research, Woolfolk and her associates determined that college students like the letter *S* better than the letter *L*. Then the researchers had other students choose between the colas presented in cups labeled *L* and *S*. In this experiment, unlike in the advertisement, the letters were the only independent variable, because the type of cola in the cups was held constant. For half the subjects, both cups contained Pepsi; and for the other half, both cups contained Coke. Regardless of the type of cola in the cups, the students preferred cola *S* to cola *L* in 85 percent of the cases. Thus, it is possible that the conclusion in the advertisement was confounded by the preference for certain letters and did not result just from the preference for different colas. Let the viewer beware!

Woolfolk, M. E. Castellan, W., & Brooks, C. I. (1983). Pepsi versus Coke: Labels, not tastes, prevail. *Psychological Reports, 52,* 185–186.

likely. All experiments contain error, which can be defined as other (uncontrolled) influences that alter the dependent variable. The experimenter tries to cope with factors that influence the dependent variable in two ways.

First, factors can be studied as independent variables. In many cases, independent variables of minor interest are created to minimize error. For example, if an experiment is performed by several people, an independent variable called Experimenter may be created to account for variation in the dependent variable associated with different experimenters. If this were not done, such potential variation might show up as error in the experiment. Second, factors can be held constant as control variables. Other variation in the dependent variable, not produced by independent variables or not held constant by control variables, is error. Experimenters strive to minimize error.

CONCEPT SUMMARY

- *Independent* variable is *manipulated*
- *Dependent* variable is *observed*
- *Control* variable is held *constant*

Name the Variables

Because independent, dependent, and control variables are so important, we have included some examples here for you to check your understanding of these terms. For each situation, name the three kinds of variables. Answers are provided at the end of this section.

1. An automobile manufacturer wants to know how bright brake lights should be in order to minimize the time required for the driver of a following car to realize that the car in front is stopping. An experiment is conducted to answer this. Name the variables.

2. A pigeon is trained to peck a key if a green light is illuminated but not if a red light is on. Correct pecks get rewarded by access to grain. Name the variables.

3. A therapist tries to improve a patient's self-image. Every time the patient says something positive about himself or herself, the therapist rewards this by nodding, smiling, and being extra attentive. Name the variables.

4. A social psychologist does an experiment to discover if men or women give lower ratings of discomfort when they are one of six people crowded into a telephone booth. Name the variables.

Answers

1. Independent (manipulated) variable   Intensity (brightness) of brake light.

   Dependent (observed) variable   Time from onset of brake light until depression of brake pedal by following driver.

Control (constant) variables	Color of brake light, shape of brake pedal, force needed to depress brake pedal, external illumination, and so on.
2. Independent variable	Color of light (red or green).
Dependent variable	Number of key pecks.
Control variables	Hours of food deprivation, size of key, intensity of red and green lights, and so on.
3. Independent variable	Actually, this is not an experiment because there is only one level of the independent variable. To make this an experiment, we need another level (say, rewarding positive statements about the patient's mother-in-law). Then the independent variable would be kind of statement rewarded.
Dependent variable	Number (or frequency) of positive statements about self.
Control variables	None. This is a poor experiment.
4. Independent variable	Sex of the participant. Note: This is not a true independent variable, because the experimenter did not manipulate it. This is a quasi-experiment.
Dependent variable	Rating of discomfort.
Control variables	Size of telephone booth, number of persons (six) crowded into the booth, and so on.

More Than One Independent Variable

It is unusual in a psychology journal to find an experiment in which only one independent (manipulated) variable was used. The typical experiment manipulates from two to four independent variables simultaneously. There are several advantages to this procedure. First, conducting one experiment with, say, three independent variables is often more efficient than conducting three separate experiments. Second, experimental control is often better, because with a single experiment some control variables—for example, time of day, temperature, and humidity—are more likely to be held constant than would be the case with three separate experiments. Third, and most important, results generalized across several independent variables—that is, shown to be valid in several situations—are more valuable than data that have yet to be generalized. Fourth, just as it is important to establish generality of results across different types of experimental subjects and settings, we also need to discover whether some result is valid across levels of independent variables.

Let us say we wish to find out which of two rewards facilitates learning geometry by high-school students. The first reward is an outright cash payment for problems correctly solved, and the second is early dismissal from class—that is, each correct solution entitles the student to leave class five minutes early. Assume that the results of this hypothetical experiment showed early dismissal to be better. Before we make early dismissal a universal rule in high school, we should first establish its generality by comparing the two kinds of reward in other classes, such as history and biology. Here, subject matter of the class would be a second independent variable. It would be better to put these two variables into a single experiment than to conduct two successive experiments. This would avoid problems of control, such as one class being tested the week of the big football game (when no reward would improve learning) and the other class being tested the week after the game was won (when students felt better about learning).

When the effects produced by one independent variable are not the same across the levels of a second independent variable, we have an **interaction.** The search for interactions is a major reason for using more than one independent variable per experiment. This can be best demonstrated by example.

Piliavin, Piliavin, and Rodin (1975) were interested in discovering under what conditions a bystander would help someone in an emergency. The emergency was faked on a New York City subway car (the F train, appropriately enough). A white male carrying a cane stumbled and fell to the floor. Would other passengers aid this "victim"?

The experiment had two independent variables. In half of the trials, victims had an ugly red birthmark placed on their face with theatrical makeup. The presence or absence of this birthmark was the first independent variable. An observer wearing a white medical jacket (identifying him as a physician or a medical intern) was present in half the trials. The same observer was present without the white jacket for the other trials. So, the presence or absence of the supposed physician was the second independent variable. The combination of the two independent variables yields four conditions: (1) birthmark and intern; (2) birthmark and no intern; (3) no birthmark and intern; (4) no birthmark and no intern. The dependent variable was the percentage of trials in which passengers came to the aid of the victim by either touching the victim or asking him if he needed help.

Results of this experiment are shown in Figure 8–3, with each independent variable plotted alone. People were more willing to help victims who lacked an ugly birthmark. They were also more willing to help when no medical intern was present.

Figure 8–4 shows, however, that this interpretation of the results can be misleading. If, as Figure 8–3 implies, both independent variables have their own unique effect, the results should look like the two parallel lines plotted in Figure 8–5. Instead, the lines in Figure 8–4 are not parallel, which indicates an interaction between the two independent variables. The percentage of trials in which help was given depends on the levels of each independent variable. If the victim had no birthmark, then the presence or

FIGURE 8-3
Effects on helping of two independent variables. Each variable is plotted separately. (Data form Piliavin et al., 1975. Copyright 1975 by the American Psychological Association. Adapted by permission of the author.)

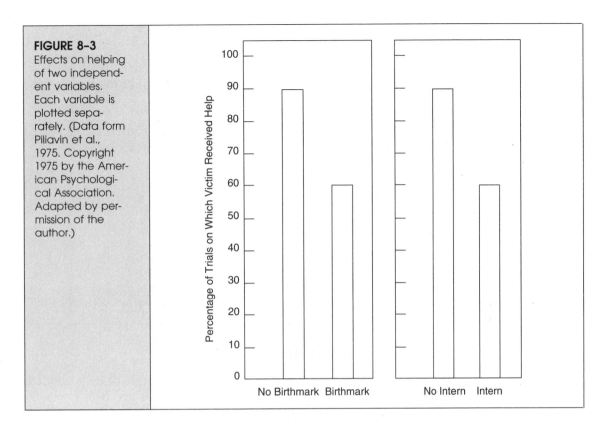

absence of an intern had little effect on helping. But when the victim had a birthmark, passengers were far less willing to help when an intern was present.

Now let us imagine that this experiment had been performed in two separate parts. In the first part, only the birthmark was varied. The experimenter would not have known that the presence of an intern would have reduced helping. In the second part, only the presence of the intern was varied. Results would have been quite different, depending on whether the victim had a birthmark. You can see that by doing the experiment in two parts, we would have lost a great deal of information.

Figure 8–4, which contains the actual results, shows an interaction. The effects of one independent variable depend on the level of the other independent variable. The least amount of help was given when the victim had a birthmark and the intern was present. Although Figure 8–4 should technically be drawn as a set of bar graphs, like Figure 8–3, it is instead drawn with lines to emphasize the interaction. In a line graph it is easy to visualize an interaction when lines are not parallel.

In summary, an interaction occurs when the effects of one independent variable are determined by the levels of other independent variables. When interactions are present, we do not discuss the effects of each independent variable separately. Because the effects of one variable depend on the levels of the other variables, we are forced to discuss interacting variables together. Interactions are an extremely important topic, so they will receive additional discussion in Chapter 10.

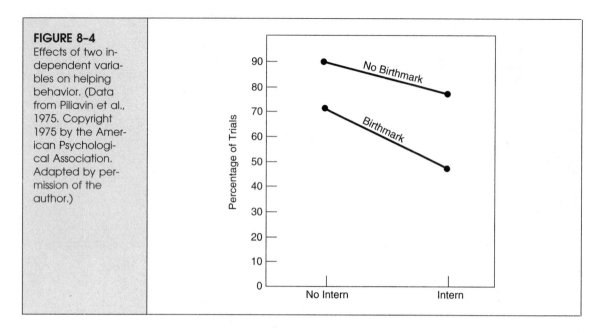

FIGURE 8-4
Effects of two independent variables on helping behavior. (Data from Piliavin et al., 1975. Copyright 1975 by the American Psychological Association. Adapted by permission of the author.)

More Than One Dependent Variable

The dependent (observed) variable is used as an index of behavior. The experimenter must decide which aspects of behavior are relevant to the experiment at hand. Some variables are traditional, but this does not mean they are the only, or even the best, index of behavior. Take, for example, the behavior of a rat pressing a bar or a pigeon pecking a key. The most common dependent variable is the number of presses or pecks observed. But the force with which a key is pecked can also lead to interesting findings (see Notterman and Mintz, 1965), as can the latency or time to respond.

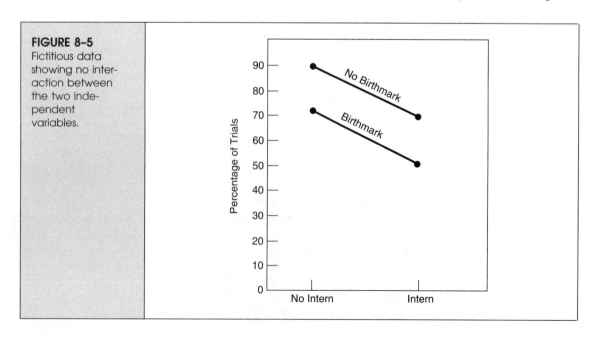

FIGURE 8-5
Fictitious data showing no interaction between the two independent variables.

Researchers can usually come up with several dependent variables that may be appropriate. Let us say we wish to study the legibility of the typeface that you are now reading. We cannot observe legibility, of course. What dependent variables might we observe? Here are some that have been used in the past: retention of meaningful information after reading text, time needed to read a fixed number of words, number of errors in recognizing single letters, speed in transcribing or retyping text, heart rate during reading, and muscular tension during reading. This list is far from complete.

Reasons of economy argue for obtaining as many dependent measures at the same time as is feasible. The truck driver workload experiment discussed in Chapter 2 (Figure 2–4) uses several dependent variables. Nevertheless, the typical experiment uses only one or at most two dependent variables simultaneously. This is unfortunate because, just as the generality of an experiment is expanded by having more than one independent variable, it is also expanded by having several dependent variables.

One reason for not using several measures is that the results may be hard to interpret. Sometimes it may not be possible to determine whether the dependent variables are measuring the same thing or different things. Another reason more dependent variables are not used is that it is statistically difficult to analyze several dependent variables at once. Modern computer techniques make the calculations feasible, but many experimental psychologists have not been well trained in these multivariate statistical procedures and thus hesitate to use them. Although separate analyses could be conducted for each dependent variable, this loses information in much the same way that separate analysis of independent variables ignores interactions. Because multivariate analysis is complex, we will not discuss it here. Nevertheless, you should be aware that it is often advantageous to use more than one dependent variable in an experiment.

CONCEPT SUMMARY

Variables in Experiments

Type	Operation	Example
• Independent variables	At least two levels of a variable are manipulated	Cue type; decompression
• Dependent variables	Particular behaviors are measured	Percentage resolved; infant growth and movement
• Control variables	Other variables are held constant	Strain of animals; general test environment

Multiple independent and dependent variables are important. An interaction occurs when the effects of one independent variable depend on the level of another independent variable.

POSSIBLE SOURCES OF EXPERIMENTAL ERROR

Reactivity in Experimentation

The problem of subject reactivity is not restricted to descriptive research. Research involving experimental procedures faces similar difficulties with reactivity. In fact, just telling someone that he or she is in a psychology experiment may cause reactivity problems. To illustrate, walk up to a stranger and say, "Please do me a favor by doing ten push-ups." Repeat your request to several others. Then, repeat the procedure, but this time say, "I'm doing a psychology experiment. Please do me a favor by doing ten push-ups." The odds are that you will get very little compliance from the first group of people and very few refusals from the second group. People sometimes will do things in the name of science and experimentation that they will not ordinarily do (Orne, 1962). In other words, experiments may not only examine behavior, they may produce it! Reactivity can be an important source of contamination in experimental data.

Orne (1962, 1969) noted that subjects entering an experiment have some general notions of what to expect and are usually trying to figure out the specific purpose of the experiment. They are likely to believe that reasonable care will be taken for their well-being and that whatever the experimenter asks them to do will serve a useful purpose. Because many psychological experiments would provide uninteresting results if the true purpose were known, elaborate deceptions are often used to mask the goal of the experiment. But, as Orne points out, these might sometimes be rather transparent. At any rate, the general problem exists as to how the subject's expectations affect or determine her or his behavior in an experiment. Orne notes:

> Insofar as the subject cares about the outcome, his perception of his role and of the hypothesis being tested will become a significant determinant of his behavior. The cues which govern his behavior—which communicate what is expected of him and what the experimenter hopes to find—can therefore be crucial variables. Some time ago I proposed that these cues be called "*demand characteristics* of an experiment." . . . They include the scuttlebutt about the experiment, its setting, implicit and explicit instructions, the person of the experimenter, subtle cues provides by him, and, of particular importance, the experimental procedure (Orne, 1969, p. 146, italics added).

Participant reaction may limit the generality of the results of an experiment because, if the results are produced by just the participants' perception of the experimental situation, they will not generalize to other situations. Frequently, when people know they are being observed, their behavior is greatly affected. One famous case of this is the **Hawthorne effect,** named after the Western Electric Company plant at which an experiment was conducted on factors affecting worker productivity (Homans, 1965). Six average women workers participated in a longitudinal study of factors affecting the rate at which they assembled telephone relays. First, the baseline rate of producing relays was measured. Then the women were placed in a special test room, and, after a period of adjustment to their new circumstances, they experienced a number of changes in their daily routine that were supposed to affect productivity. During one period of the study, rest pauses were inserted into their schedule, and later the frequency of pauses was increased. During another period, their method of payment was changed, the during yet another, a light lunch was provided, and so on. The experiment lasted for more than a year and the results were quite surprising. With few exceptions, no matter what changes were made—whether there were many or few rest periods, whether the workday was made longer or shorter, and so on—the women tended to produce more and more telephone relays. Although the reason for this change is difficult to determine (because a number of variables were confounded), the fact that the women knew they were in an experiment, felt the special attention, and wanted to cooperate are likely candidates. The workers knew that the experimenters expected the changes in the working conditions to affect them, so they did. The women kept working harder and harder. (For a different interpretation, see Parsons, 1974).

Because the changes in behavior apparently resulted from the fact that the workers were in an experiment and not because of the independent variables that were manipulated, we can say that the Hawthorne effect represents one kind of reactivity. Orne argues that to some extent experiments with humans always have this feature built in. The subject is an active participant interested in what is happening and is usually eager to help. Orne and his associates have done a great deal of research on demand characteristics in experimentation. Some of the most interesting studies deal with reactivity in hypnosis research.

Investigators have asked subjects under hypnosis to do all sorts of things, often with notable success. One apparently well-established finding is that subjects under hypnosis can be led to perform various antisocial and destructive acts, such as throwing acid in someone's face and handling venomous snakes (Rowland, 1939; Young, 1952). Orne and Evans (1965) suspected that this might have been owing more to the demand characteristics of the situation than to the effects of hypnosis. They asked subjects to perform a series of dangerous acts such as grasping a venomous snake, taking a coin from fuming acid, and throwing nitric acid in the experimenter's face. There were several treatment conditions: (1) subjects who were under deep hypnosis, (2) subjects who were told to simulate being hypnotized, (3) awake control subjects who were not asked to simulate hypnosis but who were pressed by the experimenter to comply with the requests, (4) awake control subjects who were not pressed to comply, and (5) people who were asked to perform the task without being made part of an experiment. The experimenter did not know which condition the subjects were in, so as to minimize bias. The results are summarized in Table 8–1. As would be expected, people not in the experimental setting refused to carry out the antisocial tasks, but as other investigators had reported, a high percentage of hypnotized subjects did carry out the tasks as instructed. However, *all* simulating control subjects also performed the tasks and even the nonsimulating controls, if pressed to comply, performed them to a large extent, which demonstrates the power of the experimental situation. Thus, hypnosis is not necessarily responsible for subjects performing the antisocial acts. Rather, reactivity to the experimental situation, including the set-

TABLE 8–1
Percentage of subjects who performed dangerous tasks in response to requests by the experimenter (adapted from Orne & Evans, 1965. Copyright 1965 by the American Psychological Association. Adapted by permission of the author.)

Subject Group	Grasp Venomous Snake	Take Coin from Acid	Throw Acid at Experimenter
Real hypnosis	83	83	83
Simulating hypnosis	100	100	100
Waking control—pressure to comply	50	83	83
Waking control—without pressure to comply	50	17	17
Nonexperimental	0	0	0

ting, the instructions, and the way subjects think they are supposed to behave while under hypnosis, is sufficient to produce the antisocial acts. Perhaps people can be induced to perform antisocial acts under deep hypnosis, but current studies do not offer reliable evidence to support this idea.

Weber and Cook (1972) described various social roles that could influence behavior in a laboratory setting. These roles are similar to the response styles we discussed. Subjects might adopt a **good-subject role** in accordance with the theory of demand characteristics put forth by Orne. A subject acting in a good-subject manner will do anything necessary to validate the experimental hypothesis. The **faithful-subject role** is one in which the participant attempts to be honest and faithful, even if he or she has some idea about the experimental hypothesis. The participant who exhibits a **negativistic-subject role** will attempt to sabotage or otherwise mess up the experiment (Masling, 1966, has called this the "screw you effect").

In an extensive review of the literature, Weber and Cook did not find much evidence that these roles played a significant part in the confounding of laboratory experiments. However, they did find some evidence for the importance of a fourth role—the **apprehensive-subject role** (also see Rosenberg, 1969). The apprehensive subject feels uncomfortable about being evaluated in an experiment, and because of this **evaluation apprehension** the participant tries to respond in a socially desirable way. Weber and Cook summarized a number of studies that point to evaluation apprehension as an important potential confounding in experiments. Unfortunately, predicting exactly what kinds of behaviors will be elicited by evaluation apprehension is very difficult. For example, Weber and Cook report that in conformity studies, subjects who have some idea about the purpose of the experiment tend to conform less than unaware subjects (because of apprehension, the aware subjects do not want to appear to be "sheep"). On the other hand, in learning studies in which better performance signifies a "better" subject, aware participants often perform better than unaware ones. Thus, it is hard to predict which changes in behavior may occur as a result of apprehension.

Countering the effects of reactivity in experimentation is often very difficult. Unobtrusive measures and observations may not work in a laboratory setting because most people know they are in an experiment. Consequently, many psychologists do their experiments in a natural setting. This **field research** is similar to naturalistic observation, except field experiments have a real or ex post facto independent variable. Going into the field, where people may be unaware that they are in an experiment, poses additional problems: Loss of control that is characteristic of laboratory experiments may exist, and unobtrusive measures may violate some of the ethical standards of research. Furthermore, as we will discuss in more detail later, field studies are not necessarily more externally valid than laboratory experiments. Dipboye and Flanagan (1979) found that field studies in industrial and organizational psychology generally involve a narrow range of subjects, settings, and dependent variables.

One way to insert unobtrusive measures into laboratory experiments is to use **deception.** Deception can push reactivity in a particular direction so that the subject will respond naturally to the true independent variable. In a famous example of deception by Milgram (1963), participants were led to believe that they were giving shocks to a "learner" in order to improve the rate of learning. In fact, the shock apparatus was fake and the learner just pretended to receive severe shocks. From the point of view of the participants, they willingly caused pain and suffering to another person. Many people regard this sort of deception as unethical (see Chapter 3).

Another way a researcher can try to control reactivity is to omit information about the experiment. For example, let us say that half of the participants in a memory experiment receive special instructions on how to learn and remember. The other half of the participants do not receive these instructions; this group serves as a baseline for "natural memorizing." The experimenter might not tell the participants in the control condition that other participants were treated differently. Despite its usefulness, omitting information about the experiment can present ethical problems, particularly when the information is relevant to an individual's decision about whether to participate in the experiment. For instance, participants in a study on anxiety may not be told that the experimental procedure is likely to make them feel uneasy and nervous. Alerting them of possible reactions might induce those very reactions; however, withholding this information is deceptive. Deception by omission may be warranted in some circumstances; however, when it is used, we must be careful to maintain the dignity of the person being studied.

When we withhold some pertinent information from the participant, we say we are running a *blind experiment.* A good example is a study by Carver, Coleman, and Glass (1976), who examined the suppression of fatigue by Type A and Type B men, which was mentioned in Chapter 1. Type A's are aggressive people who really strive to win in competitive situations, and they are supposed to be prone to coronary heart disease (Wright, 1988). Type B's are less aggressive and competitive, and they are less likely to have heart problems. Types A's and B's were put on an exercise treadmill to see how long they would exercise relative to their maximum capacity. Carver and associates also got subjective estimates of fatigue from the participants. During the course of the experiment, the researchers made every attempt to remove any hint of competition—both against the clock and against other people's performance on the treadmill. In fact, the subjects were told they would be removed from the treadmill after a predetermined time. In actuality, the time on the treadmill was determined by the participant, who indicated when he had had enough. Confronting the Type A's with evidence of competition might have enhanced their competitive drive, and the experimenters wanted the A's to become fatigued in the absence of any apparent competition. So, making the subject blind to the nature of the experiment seemed important. In this instance, the deception does not seem unethical. Carver and coworkers found that the Type A's worked longer on the treadmill than B's. Despite the extra effort, the A's reported less fatigue than the B's.

Another way to control reactivity is to conduct a **simulated experiment,** as Orne and Evans (1965) did in their hypnosis study. As mentioned earlier, they used people who simulated being hypnotized as well as people who were hypnotized. The logic here is straightforward. The demands of the situation are assumed to be the same for participants in both the experimental condition and the simulating control condition. If the experimental manipulation (hypnosis) is truly effective, then the behavior of the experimental group should differ reliably from that of the simulating group. Another approach to simulating an experiment is to tell simulating participants what the independent variable is and ask them what they would do in the experimental situation (Richman, Mitchell, and Reznick, 1979). If the results of the simulated experiment are highly similar to the results owing to the independent variable in the actual experiment, we can conclude that there are likely to be important reactivity factors contaminating the effects of the independent variable.

External Validity of the Research Procedure

Another area in which problems arise in the design of a research project concerns its relation to what is often termed the "real world." We might ask whether our research has anything to do with why people and animals think and act as they do. Have we selected an object of study that is representative? Is our research setting one that will yield a valid answer to our fundamental question? In sum, is our research externally valid?

We alluded to some of these issues in Chapters 2 and 4. Several problems associated with external validity must be dealt with before a project is begun. In this section, we will detail the problems of subject representativeness, variable representativeness, and setting representativeness. We will also present some ways in which these problems can be handled.

Subject Representativeness

Basic research in psychology draws a large number of its participants from two populations: white rats and college students. Rats and other animals are often used because the scientist can control the heredity and environment of animals more easily (and more ethically) than that of humans. Also rats and college students are readily available to most researchers. The justifications for using rats and college students are control, convenience, and ethics. The question remains: Are these organisms representative? Are data from these organisms pertinent to general statements about psychological processes? In other words, is there **subject representativeness**?

Limiting your observations to these populations may present some problems. A major difficulty is **reversibility** (Uttal, 1978). In mathematics, reversibility refers to an attempt to determine the problem or equation from a solution. Consider the answer 7. Can we figure out what led to 7? Not without more information. The answer 7 could have come from $4 + 3 = ?$, $377 - 370 = ?$, $\sqrt{49} = ?$, *How many days are in a week?*, or any of an infinite number of other possibilities. The answer 7 is not reversible. Thus, given the answer 7 twice, there is no way to know whether the 7s arose from the same equation or different equations. Reversibility poses a similar problem in research. Just because a particular behavior is observed both in a rat and in a human, it does not follow that the underlying processes (the mathematical equation) are the same in both instances. For example, if we damaged a rat brain in order to understand how the human brain works, we have to assume that the brain processes in both species are the same (have the same equation). Physiological psychologists assume that the solution (the rat's behavior) is unique to a particular equation (the rat's brain) and that the equation is the same for rats and humans. Thus, by reversing the solution (damaging the rat's brain to eliminate a particular behavior), we arrive at the problem (what aspect of the brain controlled that behavior). In other words, damaging the rat's brain should lead us to understand how its brain controlled particular behaviors, and because we assume equivalence between the brain of a rat and the brain of a human, we further our understanding of human brain functioning.

The difficulty, of course, is the assumption of equivalence between rats and humans. The problem remains even if one ignores physiology and tries to generalize across species at the purely behavioral level. There is still the assumption of equivalence in whatever mechanism is hypothesized to account for the behavior. Harlow summarized the dilemma this way: "Basically the problems of generalization of behavior between species are simple—one cannot generalize, but one must. If the competent do not wish to generalize, the incompetent will fill the field" (Harlow, Gluck, and Suomi, 1972, p. 716).

Despite the difficulties it poses, generalizing across species can lead to spectacular successes. In the nineteenth century, Mendel, a Czechoslovakian monk, determined the basics of genetics by studying garden peas. More recently, the discovery of neurotransmitters in the brain that function like opiate drugs was based on work concerned with neural transmission in the reproductive organs of rats. If we view the results of animal research as a model or analogy, then we recognize that our cross-species generalizations are always tentative. We may have to perform many tests on many species before we can make strong conclusions.

The difficulties we have just examined also pertain to research that uses college students as subjects. How representative are the results obtained from such studies? The answer to this question is vague; it depends on the purposes of the research and the boldness of the investigator. If we are concerned with processes that are likely to be shared by all humans, such as basic sensory processes or simple forms of learning and retention, we can be fairly sure that our data on college students will be representative of human beings in general.

A difficulty arises, however, when we are interested in complex psychological processes. Language, problem solving, and sophisticated memorizing strategies require that the subject possess characteristics that may not be common to everyone. We cannot limit our psychology to normal human adults living in Western cultures. Young children, Ibos living in Africa, and individuals with hearing impairments are likely to possess abilities different from those of the typical college student. Imagery may enhance memory in college students (Atkinson, 1975; Bower, 1972), but its success for young children has limits (Tversky and Teiffer, 1976), and cross-cultural differences in the use of imagery exist as well (Cole, Gay, Glick, and Sharp, 1971).

Because of the limits in generalizability from easily available populations, it is sometimes necessary to seek out participants from special populations. For instance, if we are interested in whether the incidence of depression found in young people is the same for elderly people, we must find a population of elderly individuals willing to participate in our study. Despite the convenience of the white rat and the college student, these populations alone cannot meet all research needs.

The moral here is that we should be careful in generalizing on the basis of a single sample of participants from a subset of the population at large. If we are too bold ("Imagery always aids memory, no matter who uses it."), we run the risk of being wrong. Again, if we view the college student as a model for psychological processes in the same way that we view the white rat as a model, we will recognize that some of our conclusions must be tentative. This is particularly true when basic research findings are used for applied purposes. The generalization should be tried out on the target population before a particular policy or practice is implemented. Time and effort would be wasted if, on the basis of Bower's (1972) work with college students, imagery training were instituted in a nursery school.

Variable Representativeness

We want our results to generalize across different subject populations. In the same way, we want our results to have **variable representativeness**— the ability to generalize across different experimental manipulations. For example, if a researcher were interested in whether background noise hurts reading comprehension, he or she might compare music to silence. If it were shown that noise and music both hurt comprehension relative to silence, the researcher would have an interesting finding; however, it would be premature to assume that the results would generalize for any kind of background noise. The results may have been unique to the kind of music chosen or to the particular volume at which the music was played. Likewise, the results may have been different if random environmental noises had been used instead of music. Further experimentation would be necessary to determine the generality of the effect of background noise. By using a wide range of independent variables to address a particular question, we can also get a better idea of how the variables we have chosen relate to the situation in the real world that we are trying to address.

Setting Representativeness

Perhaps the major issue associated with representativeness has to do with the setting. **Setting representativeness,** often called **ecological validity,** can be a serious problem in experimentation, where, by definition and through the imposition of control, the experimental setting is an artificial one. Neisser (1976, 1978, 1982), for example, questions the ecological validity of laboratory experiments, particularly those involving cognition and memory. He argues that psychologists have avoided studying natural memory in natural settings, which means that "the orthodox psychology of memory has very little to show for a hundred years of effort, perhaps because it has always avoided the interesting issues" (1982, p. 3). Neisser is correct in his concern for ecological validity, but, as we shall see, he is incorrect in his indictment.

When considering the problem of ecological validity, we need to distinguish between **realism** and **generalizability** (Berkowitz and Donnerstein, 1982). Realism refers to whether the experimental setting bears a resemblance to the real world. Do the experiments involving rats learning in Skinner boxes resemble any learning situation in the real world? The answer, of course, is probably not. However, the critical question has to do with the importance of this mundane realism. As was true of the problem of subject representativeness, our concern with ecological validity should be with its relation to psychological processes. If we can demonstrate that the processes exhibited by rats in artificial settings are similar to the processes occurring in the real world, then we can say that realism is not a crucial threat to external validity. Thus it follows that the ability of an experimental result to generalize to other situations is more important than its superficial resemblance to the real world. Various tests try to determine whether the processes observed in the laboratory are also the processes involved in settings representative to the real world. In Chapter 12 we will consider some other aspects of generalization, but for now we will examine some direct tests of generalizability.

The strategy used to test the generalizability of experimental results is to repeat the observations in a natural setting—a field study. Obviously, studying memory in a classroom or decision making in a courtroom is less controlled than the corresponding laboratory study. This is why laboratory experiments are conducted—to provide an internally valid causal statement about a psychological process. If we are going to try to generalize our results beyond the laboratory, we may need to conduct a less well controlled field experiment. Before considering such tests of generalization, we should note that field studies do not necessarily permit broad generalization. As pointed out earlier, Dipboye and Flanagan (1979) found that a narrow range of subjects, settings, and variables had been used in field studies done in industrial and organizational psychology. The tests should be varied and not just "natural."

Many applied psychologists have questioned the external validity of laboratory studies on decision making. A substantial amount of laboratory work has examined how people integrate many sources of information to arrive at a decision, and there are many sophisticated mathematical theories describing information integration (Anderson, 1981). Levin, Louviere, and Schepanski (1983) conducted a number of direct tests of the external validity of results from laboratory studies involving decision making, and they found excellent correspondence between the laboratory and the real world. They discovered that the choice of transportation to get to work, as well as choice of shopping location, are almost perfectly predicted by models derived from laboratory studies of decision making. They also report that several other behaviors in the real world coincide with results from strictly controlled experiments. These behaviors include gambling decisions, jury decisions, and occupational choices. Thus, laboratory studies of decision making may be contrived and artificial, but they also predict behavior in the real world.

What about Neisser's (1978) criticism of laboratory work in memory? Encouraged by Neisser's critique of memory, some memory researchers have abandoned their laboratories and have begun to conduct their research in real-world settings. Their experiments often lack the strict experimental control of laboratory research, but adherents to what is called the "Everyday Memory movement" argue that what they lack in control is more than made up by increased ecological validity. Banaji and Crowder (1989) responded strongly to Neisser's criticisms (and to the Everyday Memory movement in general), arguing that he ignored the distinction between realism and generalizability. Hence, Banaji and Crowder point out that results derived from laboratory experiments may or may not generalize to a variety of situations, but they also point out that results derived from everyday memory experiments, despite their surface realism, still may or may not generalize to other situations. Because surface realism does not guarantee an increase in generalizability, Banaji and Crowder question whether the loss of experimental control is worth the increased (surface) realism of the everyday memory experiments.

Banaji and Crowder's (1989) article has stirred up considerable controversy among memory researchers. In fact, a recent issue of *American Psychologist* (January 1991, Volume 46) includes nine articles (pp. 16–49) discussing the various aspects of this debate. In contrast to the stereotype of the cold, objective scientist, some of the authors exhibit a great deal of emotion in addressing this topic. We recommend that you read some of these articles. Although the debate is specifically addressed to the study of human memory, the issues raised regarding ecological validity are quite general, and the same arguments would apply to almost any area of psychology.

In summary, surface realism in an experimental setting does not guarantee ecological validity. In fact, an experiment can be ecologically valid with little or no surface realism. Nevertheless, some researchers argue that experiments with surface realism are more likely to lead to results with high generalizability, but this argument remains controversial. In any case, it is generalizability rather than surface realism that determines whether an experimental procedure is ecologically valid.

CONCEPT SUMMARY

Your choice of

- **subjects**
- **variables**
- **setting**

may all distort the underlying psychological processes. Generalization can be enhanced by using

- **different subjects**
- **different variables**
- **different settings**

SUMMARY

1. The joint method of agreement and difference permits causal explanation by showing that result X occurs when event A occurs, and that result X does not occur when event A does not occur.

2. An experiment can be defined as the production of a particular comparison while other aspects of the situation are held constant. Thus, comparison, production, and constancy are the hallmarks of control in experimentation.

3. Independent variables are those manipulated by the experimenter. It is important to select appropriate levels of the independent variable to avoid null results.

4. The dependent variable is the behavior observed and recorded by the experimenter. A reliable dependent variable is consistent. You need to guard against the possibility of ceiling and floor effects on your dependent variable by making sure that it does not have a restricted range of values.

5. A control variable is a potential independent variable that is held constant during an experiment. It is controlled to minimize confounding.

6. Using more than one independent variable is important in ensuring general results. When the effects produced by one independent variable are not the same across the levels of a second independent variable, we have an interaction.

7. Obtaining measures on more than one dependent variable can provide important information and increase the generality of the results of the experiment.

8. Reactivity often occurs in experiments. A famous example of reactivity is the Hawthorne effect, in which worker productivity improved throughout the course of an experiment, regardless of the experimental manipulations.

9. Invalid conclusions may be drawn from research if the subjects, variables, or settings distort the underlying psychological processes.

10. Because experiments are well controlled, and therefore artificial, the ecological validity of experiments if often questioned. The crucial problem is not realism, but whether the experimental results generalize to other settings, which they often do.

11. Many field studies (experiments done in natural settings) show that the results of laboratory studies do generalize to the real world.

■ KEY CONCEPTS

apprehensive-subject role
ceiling effect
confounding
control
control group
control variable
deception
dependent variable
ecological validity
evaluation apprehension
experiment
experimental group
ex post facto
faithful-subject role
field research
floor effect

generalizability
good-subject role
Hawthorne effect
independent variable
interaction
joint method of agreement and
    difference
negativistic-subject role
null results
realism
reversibility
setting representativeness
simulated experiment
subject representativeness
type 2 error
variable representativeness

■ EXERCISES

1. [*Special Exercise.*] An experimenter examined the effects of LSD on complex learning of rats. One group of rats was given a very small dose of LSD, so small a dose that it was unlikely to have any behavioral effects. A second group was given a large dose. Then, both groups ran through a complex maze several times. The dependent variable was the number of errors the rats made before obtaining the food reward at the end of the maze. The large-dose group made 4.5 times as many errors as the small-dose group, and the experimenter concluded that LSD can negatively affect complex learning. Comment on the levels of the independent variable that were used. What other dependent variables could be recorded? Comment on the conclusion by the experimenter.

2. Define what an experiment entails. Your definition should include mention of independent, dependent, and control variables.

3. Design an experiment to determine the effect of sex of the person to be identified on tip-of-the-tongue states. Specify the levels of your independent variable, describe your dependent variable, and note important control variables.

■ SUGGESTED READINGS

Numerous experiments on a variety of topics can be found in Elmes, D. G. (1978). *Readings in experimental psychology.* Chicago: Rand McNally.

Psychology in Action
Preference for Cola Drinks

A good follow-up to the findings of Woolfolk and associates (1983) that were discussed in the Application section would be to do the taste-test experiment appropriately. Perform the experiment with unmarked cups (or at least cups that do not have markings that are visible to your subjects). You will need some small paper cups and a supply of beverages (say, Pepsi and Coke, or perhaps Sprite and 7-Up). Allow each person to taste a small amount of each beverage and then indicate his or her preference. Make sure that your subjects do not know the brand names of your drinks (and, of course, make sure they do not see you pouring the drinks into the cups). A rating-scale procedure or a magnitude-estimation procedure (see Chapter 5) could be used as an alternative dependent variable. If you use one of these dependent variables, you will probably want to have your subjects make judgments about each drink separately along some dimension (say, a goodness-of-taste dimension).

One thing you should try to do in this experiment is to make sure that half your subjects taste Coke first, then Pepsi, and that the other half of your subjects taste the beverages in the reverse order. This reversal of order is called counterbalancing and is used to guard against the possibility that the order of tasting the drinks has an effect on the dependent variable. Counterbalancing is discussed in Chapter 9.

ADVANCED EXPERIMENTATION

EXPERIMENTAL DESIGN

Variables should be arranged to maximize internal validity

Between-Subjects Design

❑ In this simplest case, the experimental group receives the independent variable and the control group does not.

❑ To minimize the confounding of subject characteristics with group membership, randomly assign participants to conditions or match their characteristics between groups.

Within-Subjects Design

❑ Each participant receives all levels of the independent variable.

❑ To minimize confounding caused by carryover effects, the order of testing each level of the independent variable must be counterbalanced or randomized.

CHAPTER 9

EXPERIMENTAL DESIGN

A carefully designed experiment will permit valid conclusions to be drawn about the effects of the independent variable on the dependent variable. In this chapter, we consider how to design experiments with a between-subjects configuration, in which independent groups of subjects receive the different levels of the independent variable. We also consider a within-subjects configuration, in which all subjects receive all levels of the independent variable. A threat to validity for the between-subjects case has to do with the initial equality of the subjects in the different groups. In within-subjects experiments, the effects of one treatment may carry over to another, which could confound the effect of the independent variable.

INTERNAL VALIDITY IN EXPERIMENTS

In a properly conducted experiment, the situation is controlled so that changes in dependent variables result solely from changes in independent variables. In a good experiment, we can make valid causal statements about the results. A valid observation, as noted in Chapter 6, is one that is sound or genuine because it reveals a true effect. A properly designed experiment can have valid results, and experiments that lead to valid results are said to be **internally valid** (see Cook and Campbell, 1979). By means of control (such as the joint method of agreement and disagreement), the researcher rules out inadvertent confounding, and the results reflect the effects of the intended variables. As discussed in Chapter 8, Brennen et al. (1990) were able to assert that presenting letter initials was more effective in resolving tip-of-the-tongue states than presenting pictures. Their experiment was designed to maximize the effects of presenting pictures and to minimize the effects of extraneous variables, which means their work was internally valid.

Experiments are internally valid in principle. Internal validity does not occur automatically, but rather through a careful selection of variables and an adequate experimental design. Underwood has noted that there is one basic principle of research design: "design the experiment so that the effects of the independent variables can be evaluated unambiguously" (1957, p. 86). In this chapter, we will discuss features of experimental design that help provide internal validity. In particular, we will discuss advantages and disadvantages of two types of design: between subjects and within subjects. A **between-subjects design** is one in which independent groups of subjects receive the different levels of the independent variable. In a **within-subjects design,** all subjects receive all levels of the independent variable. To illustrate how experimental design is related to validity, we will first consider two situations in which design flaws could prevent valid causal statements.

Executive Monkeys

The topic of stress-induced ulcers, especially among high-powered executives, is a common one in the popular press. Early laboratory experiments by Brady (1958) and his colleagues (Brady, Porter, Conrad, and Mason, 1958) demonstrated the development of stress ulcers in "executive" monkeys. Brady initially tested monkeys to see whether they could learn to respond quickly by pressing a button to avoid electric shock. Monkeys that responded at a high rate during this test were allowed to be executives in a second phase of the experiment. In the second part of the experiment, an executive monkey and a "coworker" received strong electric shocks periodically over long periods of time (usually a four-hour session). This was considered to be a highly stressful work situation for the monkeys. The executive monkeys could press a button that would postpone the shock. In this avoidance task, the coworker of the executive received a shock every time the executive received one, but the coworker did not have any control over the occurrence of the shocks. The executive had control over the presentation of the shocks by being able to avoid them. If the executive did not press the button often enough, both he and his helpless coworker would get shocked. Brady found that the executives developed severe gastrointestinal ulcers and died, whereas the helpless coworkers did not develop any obvious disorders. This finding led Brady, along with many other psychologists, to conclude that the stress of management could produce ulcers under controlled conditions.

Brady's conclusion was considered to be a valid one for quite some time. But then a number of laboratory reports began to appear that seemed to indicate greater production of stress ulcers in helpless animals than in those who had control over electric shock (for example, Weiss, 1968). Were the earlier findings the result of poor design, or were the later results a fluke? Subsequent work by Weiss (1971) confirmed the fact that helpless animals were indeed more affected than those who had control, and his work suggested why the original studies about executive monkeys were flawed and, thereby, invalid. Weiss noted that Brady's executives responded at a high rate at the beginning of the experiment. Then Weiss demonstrated that animals which respond at high rates in a stressful avoidance task are likely to get ulcers, regardless of whether they are helpless or in control. Because the tendency to respond at high rates was confounded with the independent variable (helplessness or executive control) in Brady's work, some psychologists made the invalid conclusion that control under stressful situations leads to ulcers. The critical design flaw underlying the invalid conclusion was assignment of the highly responsive monkeys to the executive condition. Later we will consider some general rules for ensuring that the characteristics of the subjects do not have a confounding influence on the effects of the independent variable. Without such rules it would be difficult, if not impossible, to have an internally valid experiment.

Experiments with LSD

Lysergic acid diethylamide (LSD) is a hallucinogenic substance that was a popular and dangerous drug used to induce a "high" in the drug culture of the late 1960s and early 1970s. Because LSD was so popular and also seemed to produce some of the symptoms associated with schizophrenia, a severe mental disorder, psychologists tried to determine the effects of LSD on behavior in the controlled environment of the laboratory.

Laboratory research on the effects of LSD began in the early 1960s, and some of those studies provide useful lessons in designing internally valid experiments. We shall examine an early study by Jarrard (1963) that illustrates an experimental design in which each subject receives all levels of the independent variables (several different-sized doses of LSD, in this case). This type of design is called a within-subjects design and differs from the between-subjects design used by Weiss, in which different subjects received the various levels of the independent variable (the animals were either helpless or executives, but not both).

Jarrard wanted to determine the effects of several different does of LSD on well-established behavior. Initially, he trained rats to press a lever to obtain a food reward. When the behavior of the rats stabilized and they were performing well, Jarrard began testing the effects of LSD on the rate of lever pressing. His experiment involved six levels of the independent variable. The baseline or control amount of LSD was zero—the rats were injected with a saltwater solution that matched the salinity of their body fluids. The remaining five doses of LSD represented a proportion of each rat's body weight and were .05, .10, .20, .40, and .80 milligrams of LSD per kilogram of body weight. The general procedure involved placing the rats in the lever box immediately after injection for a two-hour test period. Several days separated each test of the injections.

At this point we need to consider several problems that could prevent Jarrard from having an internally valid experiment. Suppose Jarrard tested all his animals in the same order, going from the control dose to the largest dose. Such a design could lead to problems, because the susceptibility to LSD could change across successive administrations. The rats could become more tolerant of LSD (less affected by it), or they could become sensitized (more affected by it). In either case, tolerance or sensitization, the effects of later doses of LSD would be influenced by the rats' having received the earlier doses. This confounding effect also could occur if testing began with the largest dose and ended with the smallest.

Because Jarrard did not know whether LSD had long-term carryover effects such as tolerance and sensitization, he needed to find a way to administer doses so he could determine the effects of a particular dose independent of the other doses. He chose to counterbalance the order of doses across subjects. **Counterbalancing** refers to the systematic variation of the order of conditions in an experiment. The possible confounding effect of carryover from one dose to another was counterbalanced by having each dose appear equally often at each ordinal position in the test sequence. For example, one subject might have received the following sequence: control, .05, .40, .10, .80, .20. Another subject might have received .40, control, .10, .20, .05, .80. The remaining four rats would then receive different orders of treatments so that for all six rats, each dose was tested first, second, third, fourth, fifth, and sixth. This procedure should balance across doses any tolerance or sensitization that could occur as a result of repeated administration of LSD. On the average, each condition occurs at each ordinal position.

Jarrard found that the pressing of a lever for food was slightly enhanced by the two smallest doses of LSD and severely impaired by the two largest doses, compared with the effects of the saltwater injection (the control condition). These are internally valid results because they are not confounded by carryover effects caused by repeated testing of the independent variable. A major topic of this chapter is prevention of carryover effects in within-subjects designs.

EXPERIMENTAL DESIGN

The work of Weiss and Jarrard that we have just discussed illustrates the goal of good experimental design: to minimize extraneous or uncontrolled variation in order to increase the likelihood that an experiment will produce internally valid results. Here we will cover some common techniques used to improve the design of experiments. This discussion should provide you with an understanding of the aims of the psychologist designing a particular experiment.

The first design decision an experimenter must make is how to assign subjects to the various levels of independent variables. The two main possibilities are (1) to assign only some subjects to each level, as Weiss did, or (2) to assign each subject to every level, as Jarrard did. As mentioned earlier, the first possibility is called a between-subjects design and the second a within-subjects design. Let us reconsider Weiss's study from the standpoint of the two types of design and pretend that we are going to repeat his work. The two main conditions in that experiment were the executive condition, in which the animals had control over the shocks, and the helpless condition, in which the animals received shocks regardless of what they did. Let us assume that we have ten rats available for our study. A between-subjects design and a within-subjects design for the experiment are illustrated in Table 9–1. The between-subjects design calls for you to divide your subjects in half (into two groups of five rats each), with one group receiving the executive treatment and the other the helpless treatment. (The proper method for assigning subjects to each group will be discussed shortly.) The within-subjects design has all ten rats tested with both levels of the independent variable; that is, each rat is tested in the executive condition and in the helpless condition. (The proper method to determine the order in

---

TABLE 9–1

Between-Subjects and Within-Subjects Designs for Weiss's Experiment with Ten Rats as the Subjects (numbered 1 to 10)

BETWEEN-SUBJECTS DESIGN

	Independent Variable		
	Executive Group	Helpless Group	
Individual subjects	1	6	Half of the subjects
	2	7	are in the executive
	3	8	group and half are
	4	9	in the helpless group.
	5	10	

WITHIN-SUBJECTS DESIGN

	Independent Variable		
	Executive Condition	Helpless Condition	
Individual subjects	1	1	All subjects receive
	2	2	both the executive
	3	3	and the helpless
	4	4	treatments.
	5	5	
	•	•	
	•	•	
	•	•	
	10	10	

which each subject gets these two treatments will also be discussed later.) Before reading on, consider which design you would use and provide reasons. The factors involved in this sort of decision are considered below.

Between-Subjects Designs

The between-subjects design is conservative (safe) because there is no chance of one treatment contaminating the other—the same subject never receives both treatments. However, the between-subjects design must contend with the possibility that the subjects in the two groups are different enough to influence the effects of the treatments. Any between-subjects experiment has the potential for being confounded because of differences among the subjects in the two groups. For example, the results of Brady's experiment were confounded by putting the highly responsive animals in the executive condition.

Matching and Randomization.   In any between-subjects experiment, the researcher must somehow guarantee that as few differences as possible exist among the subjects in the various treatment groups. Clearly, if we took the five animals most susceptible to stomach ulcers and put them into the executive group, and we put the five least susceptible into the helpless condition, we might arrive at results that mask the true effects; we would have an internally *in*valid experiment. This is exactly what happened in the original executive-monkey experiment, because we now know that highly responsive animals are likely to ulcerate under stress. To prevent this kind of outcome, the experimenter tries to have groups that are equivalent at the beginning of the experiment.

One possible technique to use is called **matching,** in which important subject characteristics are matched in the various treatment conditions. In this experiment, one way to match subjects would be to administer a pretest to the animals to determine their response rates. Then subjects that had equal or very similar rates of response could be paired up. Unlike the procedure Brady used to assign subjects, this procedure calls for one member of each pair being randomly assigned to one group and the other member being assigned to the second group. One difficulty with matching is that an experimenter cannot match for everything. Indeed, the experimenter may not know what characteristics should be matched. Even though matched on some characteristics, the groups may differ on some other potentially relevant dimension. Thus, matching is done on the basis of the most likely confounding variables. Even so, matching on one variable could cause a mismatch on another.

In addition to the problems mentioned, another difficulty—**subject attrition**—can make matching an ineffective way to try to equate groups. Subject attrition means that one or more of the subjects in an experiment do not complete participation, or their behavior changes for reasons other than the independent variable. Attrition can occur for any number of reasons. For example, a subject might get sick and fail to continue. An animal subject might die or perform so poorly that the data are uninterpretable. A human subject in the experiment might refuse to continue to participate. In a long-term experiment, the subjects might mature, which means that their characteristics change during the course of the experiment. If we carefully match our subjects across conditions in order to equate our groups, then subject attrition in one group will make our groups unequal and our matching will have been in vain. This may be true even if just one subject is lost from a particular group.

If group characteristics are determined by an unbiased procedure (random assignment), attrition will have a less detrimental effect. However, attrition can still pose problems with both the reliability and the validity of our observations. If some form of attrition is likely, matching should not be used.

Randomization is a more common technique to ensure the formation of equivalent groups of subjects (see Chapter 5). One way to form two groups by randomization would be to assign arbitrary numbers to the subjects and then pull numbered slips of paper out of a hat or some other container. Similarly, when we are ready to assign a particular subject to a condition, we could throw a die, with even throws being assigned to one group and odd throws to the other. If we do not have any dice, a table of random numbers could be used to generate odd and even digits.

A table of random numbers is provided in Table C–7 in the Appendix. Random-number tables are very easy to use. To generate odd and even numbers, select a row of numbers in the table. Proceed across the row, noting whether each number is odd or even. If you reach the end of a row, simply select a different row of numbers and continue the procedure.

Each of these methods of randomization ignores the characteristics of the subjects and leads to a random, unbiased assignment to conditions. Randomization means that each subject has an equal and unbiased opportunity to be in any of the conditions of the experiment. Randomization is how Weiss improved the design of the executive-monkey experiment. However, randomization does not guarantee that groups will always be equal. By chance, more of the highly responsive animals might be assigned to one of the groups. The odds of this rare occurrence can be calculated by the methods of statistics. This is one reason experimental design and statistics are often treated as the same topic. However, experimental design has to do with the logic of arranging experiments, whereas statistics deal with calculating odds, probabilities, and other mathematical quantities. Although perfect matching may be preferable to randomization, in some cases we may not be sure about the basis of matching; when this happens, randomization is the preferred assignment procedure.

CONCEPT SUMMARY

BETWEEN-SUBJECTS DESIGN

Separate groups of subjects receive different levels of the independent variable. To control for individual differences

- randomly assign subjects to groups, or
- match subject characteristics in each group

Within-Subjects Designs

Many experimental psychologists prefer the within-subjects design to the between-subjects design. The within-subjects design is generally more efficient, because the performance of each subject is compared across the different experimental conditions. In our experiment, this means that any differences resulting from the executive and helpless treatments would not be caused by differences between the animals in the two conditions (as could be true of the between-subjects design), because all subjects receive all treatments. One implication of this feature is that fewer subjects are required.

As indicated in the earlier discussion of Jarrard's LSD experiment, the efficient within-subjects design brings with it the serious risk of **carryover effects** from one treatment to the next, which could result in an invalid experiment. That is, the effects of one treatment may carry over to another condition. Carryover effects are particularly serious if the conditions affect each other (or carry over) in different ways (e.g., the experimental condition affects the control differently than the control condition affects the experimental condition). Imagine that ten rats first underwent the helpless condition and then were placed in the executive condition in Brady's experiment with executive monkeys. As a result of their earlier experience with being helpless, the animals may react poorly to the executive condition, in which they now have control over the shocks. This would mask any true differences between the two levels of the independent variable. Any within-subjects experiment has the danger that experience in an early part of the experiment might change behavior in a later part of the experiment, because the effects of one treatment might carry over to the other treatment. This can be caused even by routine factors, such as practice or fatigue. How do we reduce this source of invalidity?

Randomization.   One way to minimize carryover among treatments is to randomly determine the order of their application. A random order can be established by using a table of random numbers or by writing the treatments on slips of paper and drawing them out of a hat. The logic is the same as that just described for assigning subjects to conditions in between-subjects designs. However, although randomization produces equivalent treatment orders in the long run, it is less likely to be suitable when there is only a small number of treatments. In most experiments, the number of subjects exceeds the number of treatments, so randomization is a good technique for assigning subjects to conditions but not for determining the order of treatments.

Counterbalancing.   As mentioned earlier, Jarrard used a technique called counterbalancing to balance the order of treatments across stages of his experiment. By balancing the effects of order of treatments across subjects, Jarrard was able to minimize carryover effects. In counterbalancing, each treatment occurs in each time period of the experiment. This means that every treatment has the same chance of being influenced by confounding variables. In other words, we *counter* the effects of potential confounding variables by *balancing* them over the periods when the treatments are administered.

Complete counterbalancing requires that all possible treatment orders are used. In the executive-monkey experiment this is easy, because there are only two orders of treatments: helpless then executive, executive then helpless. An example of such counterbalancing is presented in the Application section.

As the numbers of conditions increase, the numbers of possible orders get larger. Three treatments have 6 different orders, 4 treatments have 24 different orders, 5 conditions have 120 different orders, and so on. So, as the number of levels of the independent variable increases, complete counterbalancing soon becomes impractical. Instead, experimenters must settle for incomplete counterbalancing, in which each treatment occurs equally often in each portion of the experiment. In other words, condition A occurs first, second, and third equally often, as do conditions B and C. This arrangement is called a **Latin-square design**.

Table 9–2 shows a 4 × 4 Latin square, which contains four treatments (1, 2, 3, and 4). The columns of the square represent the sequence of these treatments, and the rows represent subjects being tested in the experiment. For example, subject 1 receives treatment 1 first, then treatment 2, followed by treatments 3 and 4. Other subjects receive these four treatments in a different sequence, or order, as we usually name this independent variable. Because a Latin square must always have equal numbers of rows and columns, the experimenter must use at least the same number of subjects as there are treatments. So Table 9–2 requires at least four subjects for the experiment. However, it is usually desirable to have more subjects than treatments for statistical reasons. This means that in practice the experimenter must obtain a number of subjects that is some multiple of the number of treatments in the Latin square. For the square shown in Table 9–2, an experimenter could use 8, 12, or 16 subjects, because these numbers can be divided by four leaving no remainder.

What sequence of treatments should be used for these additional subjects? The experimenter has two choices. First, the same Latin square can be used over and over again. For example, using the square from Table 9–2, subject 5 would receive the same order as subject 1, subject 6 the same as subject 2, subject 7 the same as subject 3, and subject 8 the same as subject 4. When this procedure is used, good statistical practice requires the experimenter to compute a test for square uniqueness. If this test turns out

TABLE 9–2
A Latin Square for Counterbalancing the Order of Four Treatments

		ORDER			
		1st	2nd	3rd	4th
	1	1	2	3	4
Subject	2	2	3	4	1
Number	3	3	4	1	2
	4	4	1	2	3

APPLICATION

Counterbalancing in the Wild

Saari and Latham (1982) wanted to determine the effect of payment schedule on the performance and attitudes of beaver trappers in southwestern Washington. The trappers worked for a forest-products company and were paid an hourly wage during the course of the following experiment.

After a baseline measure of trapping performance under the hourly payment scheme, two incentive conditions were introduced in a within-subjects design. When trappers were under a continuous reinforcement schedule, they received an additional dollar for each beaver that was trapped. When the trappers were under a variable ratio schedule of four, they received four dollars when they brought in a beaver, if they correctly predicted twice whether the roll of a die would yield an odd or an even number (by chance alone, the trapper could pick the correct solution one out of four times). Thus, in one condition there was always a one-dollar payment, whereas in the other the payment was on the average given once every four times. Counterbalancing of the order of treatments was accomplished in the following way. The trappers were randomly split into two groups, and then the groups alternated weekly stints under either the continuous or the variable payment schedule. The alternating schedule continued for the entire trapping season.

Saari and Latham found that the number of beavers trapped increased under both payment schedules, but the increase was much larger under the variable ratio schedule than under the continuous one. Furthermore, they found that the trappers preferred the ratio schedule to the continuous schedule.

These results are very similar to those found when rats or pigeons are put under variable ratio schedules of reinforcement. Generally, behavior is more persistent under variable schedules of reinforcement than under continuous ones.

SOURCE: Saari, L. M., & Latham, G. P. (1982). Employee reactions to continuous and variable ratio reinforcement schedules involving a monetary incentive. *Journal of Applied Psychology, 67,* 506–508.

to be statistically significant, it means that the partial counterbalancing of treatments was not successful and calls the results of the experiment into question. This is the danger of using a Latin square as opposed to complete counterbalancing. If the experimenter is unfortunate enough to select a particular Latin square that contains treatment sequences that somehow are related to effects of the treatments, the assumption that incomplete counterbalancing is sufficient fails. Fortunately, the statistical test for square uniqueness allows the experimenter to determine the success of this assumption. If the test is not significant, then the partial counterbalancing was successful, allowing the experimenter to avoid the expense of complete counterbalancing.

The second choice for testing additional subjects uses different Latin squares for each successive group of subjects. So, referring again to a 4 × 4 design, subjects 5 through 8 would get their own Latin square, which would have a different arrangement than Table 9–2. The advantage of this procedure is that as more Latin squares are used within an experiment, the chances of partial counterbalancing failing are decreased. So this is a reasonable choice when enough subjects are tested to allow using several different Latin squares. However, the disadvantage of this procedure is that it is not possible to calculate a statistic for square uniqueness. If the assumption of partial counterbalancing being adequate is wrong, the experimenter will never know because there is no appropriate statistical test.

Table 9–3 shows a special kind of Latin square in which each treatment precedes and follows every other treatment equally often. This is called a **balanced Latin square.** Although many experimenters believe it offers better opportunities for successful partial counterbalancing than do normal Latin squares, there is no statistical test to prove this. Even so, when it costs nothing extra to use a balanced Latin square, this should be done, because it cannot hurt the experiment and might help.

If the number of conditions in an experiment is even, the formula for obtaining the first row of a balanced Latin square is *1, 2, n, 3, n − 1, 4, n − 2,* and so on. Here *n =* the number of conditions. Therefore, as shown in Table 9–3, for an experiment with four conditions, the first row of a balanced Latin square would be 1, 2, 4, 3. The remaining rows of the square are obtained by simply adding 1 to each number in the corresponding column in the previous row, with the stipulation that if the resulting number is greater than *n,* then *n* should be subtracted.

If the number of conditions in an experiment is odd, then two squares are needed to have every condition following every other condition an equal number of times. The first square is obtained in exactly the same manner as described in the previous paragraph for an even number of treatment conditions. Thus, as illustrated in Table 9–4, for an experiment with five treatment conditions, the sequence for the first row would be

TABLE 9–3
Balanced Latin Square for an Even Number of Treatment Conditions

		ORDER			
		1st	2nd	3rd	4th
	1	1	2	4	3
Subject	2	2	3	1	4
Number	3	3	4	2	1
	4	4	1	3	2

TABLE 9–4
Balanced Latin Squares for an Odd Number of Treatment Conditions

		SQUARE 1 Order				
		1st	2nd	3rd	4th	5th
Subject Number	1	1	2	5	3	4
	2	2	3	1	4	5
	3	3	4	2	5	1
	4	4	5	3	1	2
	5	5	1	4	2	3

		SQUARE 2 Order				
		1st	2nd	3rd	4th	5th
Subject Number	6	4	3	5	2	1
	7	5	4	1	3	2
	8	1	5	2	4	3
	9	2	1	3	5	4
	10	3	2	4	1	5

1, 2, 5, 3, 4. The remaining rows are obtained as described above. The second square is simply a reversal of the sequences of the first square. Thus, the sequence of the first row of the second square in a five-condition experiment would be *4, 3, 5, 2, 1.*

Counterbalancing is useful not only for assigning treatment orders, but also for determining the order of testing when there is more than one dependent variable. The primary concern is to balance any potential carryover effects for any given subject. To illustrate, let us reconsider the decompression study described in Chapter 8. In that study, baby rats received several tests so that the experimenter could determine whether prenatal decompression had affected them. Suppose there is reason to believe that the infant rats' performance on one test, such as climbing, could influence their behavior on another test, such as grasping. So, even though the different measures are not independent variables in the usual sense, the order in which they are administered may affect what is measured. One test might make the infant rats tired or could, conceivably, enhance their muscle tone. If we have two measures, *A* and *B,* we can completely counterbalance the order of assessment across subjects so that the average effect might be balanced.

In conclusion, complete counterbalancing is the safest technique for within-subjects experimental designs. When the number of treatments is small, complete counterbalancing is always preferred to Latin squares. However, with larger numbers of treatments, complete counterbalancing is often not practical. Then the experimenter must assume the risk of using partial or incomplete counterbalancing with a Latin square. A statistical test for square uniqueness (beyond the scope of this textbook, but see Kirk, 1982, or other advanced statistics texts) is available to determine if incomplete counterbalancing was successful. If it was not successful, the experiment must be repeated using a different Latin square or perhaps avoiding a within-subjects design entirely. Although Latin squares and within-subjects designs are very efficient, they are not appropriate for all experiments.

CONCEPT SUMMARY

WITHIN-SUBJECTS DESIGN

All subjects receive all levels of the independent variable. To try to minimize carryover effects

- randomize the order of treatments, or
- counterbalance the order of treatments

CONTROL CONDITIONS

Most experiments contain some *control group* (between-subjects design) or **control condition** (within-subjects design). In its simplest form, the control group is the group that does not receive the levels of interest of the independent variable. It is misleading to say that the control group does not receive the independent variable, because independent variables must by definition have at least two levels, one of which may be the control level. For example, say we are interested in analyzing the effect of noise on studying. Using a between-subjects design, we would expose one group of subjects to loud noise for half an hour while they were studying; this is the level of interest of the independent variable. A control group would study the same material for half an hour, but in a quiet setting. Then we would test both groups on the material. Any difference in test performance between the two groups would be attributed to the effect of noise.

In the experiment just described, the control group did not receive any treatment (no noise was introduced). This is not always the case. As you will recall from Chapter 8, we described a study on decompression in which the control condition was ground-level pressure at 728 feet. Another control condition could have been sea level (zero altitude). In another part of the country, 1,000 feet might have been the appropriate control altitude. The important characteristic of a control condition is that it provides a **baseline** against which some variable of the experiment can be compared. Sometimes the best baseline is no particular treatment, but many times the best baseline requires some activity. This problem occurs sometimes in memory research.

Let us say that a group of subjects is required to learn two different lists of words (Table 9–5); the experimenter is interested in how learning one list interferes with learning the other. The experimental group (receiving the level of interest of the independent variable) first learns list A, then

TABLE 9–5
Examples of Experimental and Control Groups for List Learning

	First Period	Second Period	Third Period
Experimental group	Learn list A	Learn list B	Test list A
Control group	Learn list A	Do arithmetic	Test list A

learns list B, and then is tested again on list A. The experimenter would like to show that learning list B interferes with remembering list A. But before any conclusion of this sort can be reached, a comparison control condition is required. Merely comparing the results of the final test of list A with the results of the first test is insufficient, because subjects might do less well on the second list-A test simply because they are tired, or do better because of extra practice. If a control condition with no treatment were used, a control group would learn list A, then would sit around for the time it takes the experimental group to learn list B, and then would be tested again on list A. But this would be a poor control condition because subjects might practice or rehearse list A while they are sitting around. Practicing would improve their final performance on the last list-A test and incorrectly make the experimental group look as if learning list B interfered with learning list A more than it really did. A proper baseline condition would occupy the control group during the time the experimental group was learning list B. Perhaps these subjects would be instructed to do arithmetic or some other busywork that would prevent rehearsal. An example of such an experimental design is shown in Table 9–5. Another example is the baseline condition used by Jarrard in the LSD study. He used a placebo injection of saline instead of no injection at all. The reason for this injection baseline is that the injection itself could have disrupted the behavior of the rats. Without this comparison, there may have been an inappropriate assessment of the effects of LSD.

Sometimes the control condition is contained implicitly within the experiment. Suppose we want to study learning in rats, and our independent variable is the number of food pellets (one or five) we give the rats when they make the correct response. No experimenter would bother to include a control group or condition with zero pellets, because no learning could occur under this odd circumstance. The control condition is implicit, in that five pellets can be compared with one, and vice versa. The experimenter might well be as interested in the effects of a single pellet as in five, so we probably would not explicitly call the one-pellet level a control condition. But it does provide a baseline for comparison—and so, for that matter, does the five-pellet condition, because the one-pellet results can be compared with it.

Mixed Designs

Experiments need not be exclusively of within-subjects design or between-subjects design. It is often convenient and prudent to have some independent variables treated as between-subjects and others as within-subjects in the same experiment (assuming the experiment has more than one independent variable, of course). If one variable seems likely to cause transfer or carryover effects (for example, administering a drug), it can be made a between-subjects variable while the rest of the variables are within-subjects. This compromise design is not as efficient as a pure within-subjects design, but it often is safer. Mixed designs are described in more detail in the next chapter.

CHOOSING AN EXPERIMENTAL DESIGN

We have noted that the between-subjects design precludes carryover effects from one treatment to another, and that the within-subjects design does not confound subjects with conditions. Furthermore, we have suggested that the within-subjects design is usually more efficient than the between-subjects design, so obtaining repeated observations from the same subjects may be preferable to using independent groups. In this section, we will consider some rules of thumb for selecting an experimental design, regardless of the particular research topic. At the end of this section, there are several experimental problems for which you are to choose a design.

Carryover Effects

If your independent variable is likely to have a permanent effect on the subject and would prevent subsequent unconfounded testing, then a between-subjects design should be used. What sorts of independent variables would operate in this way? Independent variables that permanently alter the state or development of the subject would certainly have carryover effects. These might include effects of prenatal compression, prenatal nutrition, nearly all kinds of physiological damage (brain lesions, some drugs, toxic chemicals, and so on), most time-dependent variables (the effect of persuasion on later consumer behavior or the effects of a particular reading technique on second-grade achievement), and any other variable whose effects are likely to be irreversible. Most subject variables (sex, age, ethnic group, and so on) require a between-subjects design, but these variables are not true independent variables. The special problems associated with research involving subject variables is examined in Chapter 11.

If you are interested in changes of behavior over time, such as improvements in learning, changes of strategy in a particular task, or optimal performance on a task, then you will want to use some variant of a within-subjects design. You will need to either expose your subjects to repeated measures (for example, you might place rats in a maze twice each day for a month) or give each subject several treatments over time. In effect, you are looking for a carryover effect, which is really what a great deal of learning research is all about.

Individual Differences

You might think it trivial of us to say that people differ from each other. However, **individual differences** among subjects are not a trivial problem when it comes to designing a good experiment. If your subject pool contains individuals who are markedly different from each other or if you expect that large individual differences in behavior are likely to show up in your experiment, you may be better off using a within-subjects design rather than a between-subjects design. The within-subjects design automatically takes care of differences among your subjects. As long as you counterbalance appropriately (and carryover effects are not a problem), you can control for these individual differences in a within-subjects design.

A case in point is testing the effectiveness of drugs. Drug manufacturers know that people and animals differ in their sensitivity to drugs, which is one of the reasons Jarrard used a within-subjects design to test the effects of LSD. Once the drug is marketed, many different types of people will be taking the drugs. Therefore, it is imperative that many different types of people be tested and that several drugs be tested on the same person. Within-subjects administration of several levels of a drug compared with a placebo will also control for individual differences that may appear on the behavioral or attitudinal task used to assess drug effects. For example, a within-subjects design is important when studying the effects of a drug on pain tolerance, because we know ahead of time that there are tremendous individual differences in reaction to pain in the absence of any externally administered substance.

Obviously, if a drug is likely to have long-term effects, a between-subjects design must be used. Another reason that many clinical tests of drug effectiveness use between-subjects designs is that subjects with certain diseases are selected. The experimental group of subjects is given the drug, and a control group with the same disease is given a placebo or another drug. If one of the drugs is effective, then for humanitarian reasons all patients in the study receive it after the experimental comparison is completed.

Many research problems pose a particular dilemma: You must balance carryover effects against the possible contaminating effects of large individual differences. There is no easy solution to this problem. Sometimes the easiest way is to do the study one way (for example, within-subjects) and then do it the other way (between-subjects). Although such a tactic may seem inefficient, in the long run it will add to the generality of the results.

Design Problems

For each of the following problems, decide on a within- or between-subjects design. If you think the situation warrants it, set up your experiment with both types of design. For practice, you should indicate the independent, dependent, and control variables. If you choose a within-subjects design, specify the counterbalancing procedures, and if you use a between-subjects design, indicate how subjects will be assigned to conditions. Regardless of your design, indicate your reasons for selecting either the within- or the between-subjects configuration.

1. A researcher wants to see which is easier to learn: hard-to-pronounce syllables (such as WMH, JBT, SJK) or easy-to-pronounce syllables (such as LEJ, NAM, HEK). Two lists, containing either 20 pronounceable syllables or 20 hard-to-pronounce syllables, will be prepared. Each element in a list will be shown for two seconds. At the end of the series, the subjects will try to write down the syllables from memory. Specify the design configurations, counterbalancing or subject assignment scheme, reasons for your design selection, and the variables.

2. A cleanser manufacturer is interested in the effects of package color on the sales of Scrubbo super cleanser. Cartons of Scrubbo that are identical except for the background color of the label (maroon, pink, or aqua) will be prepared. Sales will be monitored for the next four months. Specify the design configurations, counterbalancing or subject assignment scheme, reasons for your design selection, and the variables.

3. A child psychologist wants to determine the effects of cloth versus paper diapers on toilet training. Day-old infants will be used to begin the project. The age at which diapers are no longer needed (to the nearest week) will be determined. Specify the design configurations, counterbalancing or subject assignment scheme, reasons for your design selection, and the variables.

4. A researcher wants to determine whether rats learn a complex maze more quickly when practice is spaced (spread out in time) rather than massed. The effects of massing practice trials (one trial every ten seconds) will be compared with the effects of distributing practice trials (one every ten minutes). The number of trials the rats need to learn the maze perfectly will be counted. Specify the design configurations, counterbalancing or subject assignment scheme, reasons for your design selection, and the variables.

5. The Burpo beer company is test marketing flavored light beers. It wants to see whether consumers prefer strawberry-, licorice-, or avocado-flavored Burpo. Several bottles of each flavor will be made. Consumers will fill out a questionnaire on how much they like the flavor, body and aroma of the various flavors. Specify the design configurations, counterbalancing or subject assignment scheme, reasons for your design selection, and the variables.

CONCEPT SUMMARY

Summary of Control Techniques for Between- and Within-Subjects Designs

To Control for	Between-Subjects Design	Within-Subjects Design
Individual differences (sex, age, I.Q.)	Randomized assignment—unbiased assignment of subjects to groups	Individual differences automatically controlled
	Matched assignment—Hold variable constant across groups (e.g., test only females)	
	Equate variables across groups (e.g., use equal numbers of right-handed and left-handed subjects)	
Situational differences (time of day the data are collected, room temperature)	Randomize the effects of these variables	Same as between-subjects
	Hold constant or equate these variables	
Carryover effects (order of testing, assignment of materials)	Usually carryover effects do not occur; if they do, use same techniques as in within-subjects	Randomized order Complete counterbalancing Incomplete counter-balancing (Latin-square designs)

SUMMARY

1. Experiments with well-chosen variables and clean designs permit accurate conclusions to be drawn from the results. Such experiments are said to have internal validity.

2. In a between-subjects design, different subjects are assigned to the different levels of the independent variable.

3. In a within-subjects design, each subject receives all levels of the independent variable.

4. With a between-subjects design, there is no chance for the effects of one treatment to contaminate the effects of another. However, the differences between the people in the different groups may confound the effects of the independent variable.

5. The within-subjects design is more efficient than the between-subjects design, and we do not have to be concerned about differences between subjects contaminating the results. However, we do have to worry about the carryover of one treatment to another.

6. To ensure that the individual differences between subjects in various groups are not confounding a between-subjects experiment, we should assign the subject to conditions on a random basis. Alternatively, the subjects' characteristics can be matched across groups.

7. By varying the order of presenting the treatments, we can minimize the carryover effects in the within-subjects design. The order can be randomized or completely counterbalanced. When there is a large number of treatments or levels of the independent variable, we can achieve incomplete counterbalancing by using a balanced Latin square.

8. A control group or control condition provides a baseline against which some variable of an experiment can be compared.

9. If the independent variable is likely to have a permanent effect on the subject and would prevent subsequent unconfounded testing, then a between-subjects design should be used.

10. If large individual differences in thought or behavior are likely to occur, a within-subjects design may be preferable to a between-subjects design.

■ KEY CONCEPTS

balanced Latin square
baseline
between-subjects design
carryover effects
control condition
counterbalancing
individual differences

internal validity
Latin-square design
matching
randomization
subject attrition
within-subjects design

■ EXERCISES

1. [*Special Exercise.*] What is wrong with the following experimental design? To study how the creation of mental images affects retention,

an experimenter used a within-subjects design. A long list of unrelated words was presented to the subjects, with each word being presented one at a time. Half the words were printed in black ink and the other half in red ink. The subjects were told to create a vivid mental image of the red words and to simply say the black words over and over to themselves until the next word was shown. After all the words were presented, the subjects had to write down as many of the words as they could, in any order they wished.

2. [*Special Exercise.*] Find the problem in this between-subjects experiment. An experimenter wanted to determine how a monetary payment affected attitude change. The first 22 subjects to appear at the laboratory were offered 15 dollars if they agreed to publicly endorse an unpopular candidate. The next 22 subjects to appear at the laboratory were offered one dollar if they agreed to endorse the same candidate. The percentage of people who agreed to the request in each group was the dependent variable.

■ SUGGESTED READINGS

A complete discussion of the advantages and disadvantages of between- and within-subjects designs can be found in Kerlinger, F. N. (1986). *Foundations of behavioral research*. New York: Holt, Rinehart & Winston.

For a discussion of subtle biases that can occur with the use of within-subjects designs, see the following article: Poulton, E. C. (1982). Influential companions: Effects of one strategy on another in the within-subjects designs of cognitive psychology. *Psychological Bulletin, 91*, 673–690.

An interesting historical perspective of the use of control conditions in the design of experiments can be found in Boring, E. (1954). The nature and history of experimental control. *American Journal of Psychology, 67*, 573–589.

Psychology in Action
The Stroop Effect

An interesting within-subjects experiment is a follow-up to the one in which you participated in Chapter 1. That experiment used a within-subjects design, and the three conditions were reading digits, naming the number of pluses, and naming the number of digits, where the name of the digits was incongruent with the number of digits (for example, you read "3 3," and you were to say "2"). Your follow-up could include a fourth condition in which the name of a digit and its quantity were congruent (for example, 4 4 4 4). You could use the three series from the original experiment and devise your own congruent fourth series. There are 32 items in a series, and the numbers (or quantities) 1 through 4 are counterbalanced in the sequence via a Latin square. You will need a stopwatch or clock to determine the time it takes to read through each series.

To design this experiment appropriately, set up a counterbalancing scheme to determine the order in which a subject receives each condition. A balanced Latin squares is the best way to do this, so that across subjects each condition occurs first, second, third, and fourth equally often, and each treatment precedes and follows every other treatment equally often (see Table 9–3).

Additional information on reading and naming can be found in Chapter 12 under the heading "Stroop Effect." This effect is named after a scientist named Stroop who first used conflicting reading and naming stimuli to study these processes (Stroop, 1935). In its use of conflicting and congruent quantities of digits, your follow-up experiment is similar to one done by Windes (1968), who used a between-subjects design. Your experiment is also similar to one done by Hintzman and associates (1972), who, using a within-subjects design, printed names of colors in congruent or incongruent ink colors, and then asked the subjects to name the ink color.

You might want to combine your results with those of your classmates. Each member of the class could test four subjects. Each set of four subjects would complete a single balanced Latin square used to determine the order of conditions. Your interest should focus on the differences among the three naming conditions: neutral (+ +), incongruent (3 3), and congruent (2 2). If your results follow those of Hintzman and coworkers, you should find that the congruent is faster than the neutral, which serves as the control condition, and the incongruent is slower than the neutral.

Hintzman, D. L., Carre, F. A., Eskridge, V. L., Owens, A. M., Shaff, S. S., & Sparks, M. E. (1972). "Stroop" effect: Input or output phenomenon? *Journal of Experimental Psychology, 95,* 458–459.

Windes, J. D. (1968). Reaction time for numerical coding and naming of numerals. *Journal of Experimental Psychology, 78,* 318–322.

COMPLEX EXPERIMENTATION

Interactions between independent variables

Between-Subjects Experiments

Description	*Features*	*Problems*
2 × 2 factorial design: 2 independent variables, each with 2 levels yielding 4 independent groups	2 main effects and an interaction of the 2 variables	Confounding of subjects with groups

Within-Subjects Experiments

Description	*Features*	*Problems*
2 × 2 within factorial design (treatments × treatments × subjects); each subject receives each level of each independent variable (4 treatments in a 2 × 2)	More efficient than between designs; each subject is its own control; main effects and interactions can be determined	Confounding via carryover effects must be minimized—counterbalance or randomize; use several observations in each condition to increase reliability

Mixed Designs

Description	*Features*	*Problems*
A combination of independent variables manipulated both between and within subjects	Has virtues of the above; very good for looking at interaction of practice (trials) with another independent variable	All controls above must be considered, but carryover is usually a variable, so its effects are measured

CHAPTER **10**

COMPLEX EXPERIMENTATION

This chapter discusses the design and interpretation of experiments that have more than one independent variable. Such multifactor experiments emphasize the interaction between independent variables. Multifactor experiments can be viewed as extensions of one-variable experiments. Some designs vary the independent variables between subjects and others vary them within subjects. It is also possible to have a mixture of a between-subjects and within-subjects manipulation of the independent variables. We will consider all three of these possibilities here.

FACTORIAL DESIGNS

Why perform complex experiments? Later we will see that increased control in quasi-experiments comes about by including both subject variables and true (externally manipulated) independent variables in the study. However, increased control is not the primary reason for conducting laboratory experiments with more than one independent variable. Rather, the major reason has to do with the complexity of thought and behavior. Limiting experimental analysis to a one-at-a-time variable manipulation cannot mirror the numerous, intertwined forces that influence people outside the laboratory. Therefore, multifactor experiments are likely to have better ecological validity than single-factor experiments. The topic of ecological validity—whether an experiment has external as opposed to internal validity—was discussed earlier. We can increase the generality of our results by doing experiments that attempt to match the complexity of forces that combine to influence our thought and behavior. In addition, complex causal statements can be made, which should increase internal validity.

Does this mean that what we have said before about analysis is invalid? No. In any research problem, the basic factors need to be determined before we can make more complex observations. In much the same way that naturalistic observation and correlational studies often precede basic experimentation, simple experiments often provide the groundwork for more complex ones. Scientific maturity occurs gradually. The database grows slowly, and the theories gradually develop. We begin with description and prediction, and we end with explanation. Explanation itself goes through a developmental process—from simple experiments to complex ones.

A 2 × 2 Experiment in Social Psychology: The Sleeper Effect

An extremely common finding in memory research is that information fades over time. When new information is presented, you can easily remember it immediately. But as time passes, your ability to recall this information decreases. However, there is an interesting finding in social psychology in which the passage of time improves the effect of a persuasive message. This interesting quirk is called the **sleeper effect.** Imagine that you have just watched a television commercial for a new food product: Low-fat diet pizza. You can indicate how persuasive this message was by rating how likely you are to run to your local grocery store and purchase this new food. Let us pretend that, on a scale of one to ten, your rating was five. If you are asked to rate this food again at a later time, and you give a rating that is higher than five, you have just demonstrated the sleeper effect: The impact of the persuasive message has increased over time.

To obtain the sleeper effect, the persuasive message must be accompanied by a **discounting cue.** This is a message that causes you to distrust the accuracy or credibility of a persuasive message. For example, imagine that you have just read a one-page rave review of a new sports car manufactured by General Motors. If you were then told that the review came from the pages of *Car and Driver* magazine, your reaction would be different than if you were told that the review was written by the General Motors press department. *Car and Driver* would be a confirming cue that improves your belief in the message, whereas the General Motors press department would be regarded as a biased source of information. The sleeper effect is most likely to be obtained when the cue—a discounting cue—casts a doubt on the source of the message.

Although many explanations of the sleeper effect have been offered, those that focus on the role of memory have been the most popular (Pratkanis, Greenwald, Leippe, & Baumgardner, 1988). One such explanation is called the dissociation hypothesis. At the time of presentation, the persuasive message and the discounting cue are strongly attached. Thus, they tend to cancel one another out, and little opinion change occurs. After time has passed, the link between the message and the cue gets weaker. In particular, while the message is remembered, the discounting cue is forgotten. The discounting cue is not retrieved because the link between message and cue has weakened over time. This causes a net positive change in opinion, resulting in the sleeper effect.

To explain the logic behind a 2 × 2 experimental design, we shall consider a portion of recent results on the sleeper effect reported by Pratkanis and coworkers (1988). In a **2 × 2 factorial design,** there are two independent variables, each with two levels, or values. The word *factorial* indicates that all possible combinations of all levels of each independent variable are examined. Thus as shown in Figure 10–1(a) a 2 × 2 factorial design contains four combinations of conditions: {1A}, {1B}, {2A}, {2B}. In the Pratkanis experiment, two independent variables were (1) whether the discounting cue was presented before or after the persuasive message, and (2) the length of the delay (either 0 or 6 weeks) between the message and the opinion rating. Thus, there were four combinations of interest: {before-

FIGURE 10–1
(a) The four treatment combinations in a 2 × 2 factorial design, in which separate groups of subjects receive each combination. (b) The 2 × 2 factorial design of the experiment by Pratkanis and coworkers (1988).

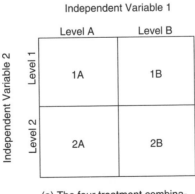

(a) The four treatment combinations in a 2 x 2 factorial design, in which separate groups of subjects receive each combination.

(b) The 2 x 2 factorial design of the experiment by Pratkanis and coworkers (1988).

none}, {after-none}, {before-6 weeks}, {after-6 weeks}. The design of the experiment is shown in Figure 10–1(b).

Figure 10–2 shows the effects of cue presentation on the opinion rating. The line is almost flat, indicating little effect. On the basis of Figure 10–2, we would conclude that cue presentation does not alter the sleeper effect. The effect of a single independent variable in a factorial experiment is called a **main effect.** Figure 10–2 shows that the main effect of cue presentation is almost zero because there is almost no difference between the ratings for level A (before) and for level B (after) for cue presentation.

Now look at Figure 10–3, which shows the effects of delay on the opinion rating. Here there is a main effect. The rating is higher, indicating greater persuasion, at the six-week delay. This result is, of course, the sleeper effect. However, based only on Figures 10–2 and 10–3, which show only main effects, we would conclude that the sleeper effect and effects of cue presentation are unrelated. Although the experiment reveals a sleeper effect, it appears that the effect has nothing to do with whether the discounting cue comes before or after the persuasive message.

FIGURE 10–2
Effects of cue presentation on the sleeper effect. Adapted from Pratkanis and co-workers (1988). (Copyright 1988 by the American Psychological Association. Reprinted by permission of the author.)

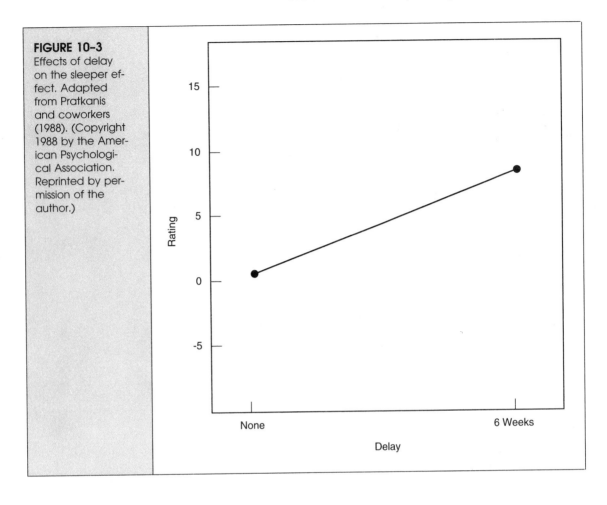

FIGURE 10-3
Effects of delay on the sleeper effect. Adapted from Pratkanis and coworkers (1988). (Copyright 1988 by the American Psychological Association. Reprinted by permission of the author.)

However, this conclusion is wrong. Figure 10–4 shows results for all four combinations in the 2 × 2 factorial design. The interpretation of results here is quite different. When the cue comes before the message, there is no sleeper effect. When the cue comes after the message, there is a large sleeper effect. So, contrary to the wrong conclusion drawn from Figure 10–2 and 10–3, the timing of the discounting cue is absolutely crucial. An accurate interpretation of these results requires knowledge of all four combinations of independent variables. This outcome is called an **interaction.** An interaction occurs when the effects of one independent variable depend on the level of another independent variable. In Figure 10–4 the effects of delay depend on the presentation of the discounting cue. Thus, there is an interaction between delay and presentation.

According to Pratkanis and colleagues, the results of Figure 10–4 cast doubt on the dissociation explanation of the sleeper effect because the dissociation explanation predicts a sleeper effect regardless of when the cue is presented. A better explanation is called *differential decay.* It states that the impact of the cue decays more rapidly than that of the message (Pratkanis et al., 1988). Presenting the cue before the message eliminates the sleeper

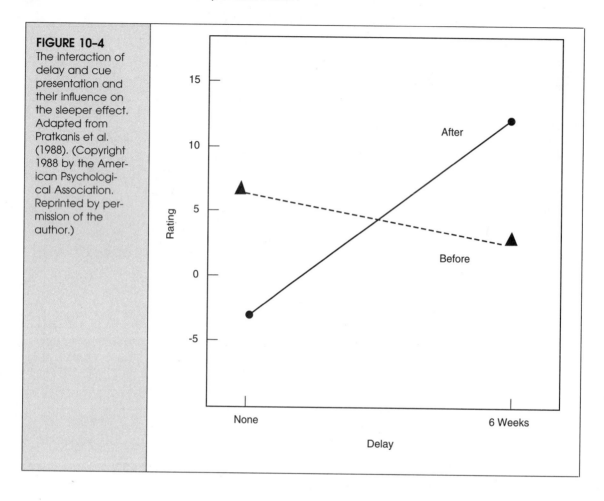

FIGURE 10-4
The interaction of delay and cue presentation and their influence on the sleeper effect. Adapted from Pratkanis et al. (1988). (Copyright 1988 by the American Psychological Association. Reprinted by permission of the author.)

effect by weakening the persuasive impact of the message. However, as is the case with most critical experiments, a firm believer in the dissociation explanation might also adopt this latter explanation and argue that postulating a second factor—persuasive impact to explain the lack of a sleeper effect—applies equally to the dissociation hypothesis. Although Pratkanis and coworkers offer other arguments for differential decay, especially those that relate the sleeper effect to other findings in memory research, it is clear that more research is required to pin down this interesting quirk. Recent work has also related the sleeper effect to familiarity and to stimulus characteristics. Begg, Anas, and Farinacci (1992) argued that influences of both familiarity (which is not under intentional control of subjects) and recollection (which can be controlled) are relevant to the sleeper effect. Riccio, Ackil, and Burch-Vernon (1992) relate the sleeper effect to the concept of stimulus generalization, a concept that goes back to early work on classical conditioning: as a stimulus is changed from the original conditioned stimulus, its ability to evoke a response decreases systematically. In the words of Pratkanis and colleagues: "Long live the sleeper effect."

CONCEPT SUMMARY

INTERACTIONS

In multifactor experiments, an interaction occurs when the effects of one independent variable depend on the level of other independent variables.

Patterns of Interaction

Main effects are statistically independent of interaction effects. This means that knowing the amount and direction of main effects provides no information about possible interaction effects. In this section we discuss three sets of artificial data that all have identical main effects. However, the patterns of interaction are quite different.

Figure 10–5 shows that the main effect of independent variable 1 is 20 units and the main effect of independent variable 2 is 60 units. These main effects hold for all the examples in this section.

Figure 10–6 shows a 2 × 2 factorial combination with no interaction between independent variables 1 and 2. Once a value has been selected for one particular cell of the 2 × 2 matrix, all of the other cell values are determined by the main effects. Let us take cell A1 to illustrate this point. It has an arbitrary value of 20 units. To find the value for cell B1, we add the main effect of independent variable 1: 20 + 20 = 40, the value for cell B1. To find the value for cell A2, we add the main effect of independent variable 2: 20 + 60 = 80. We now have three of the four cells filled in. There are two possible ways to calculate the value for cell B2. First, one could add the main effect of independent variable 1 to cell A2: 20 (main effect) + 80 (value in cell A2) = 100. Second, we could add the main effect of independent variable 2 to cell B1: 60 (main effect) + 40 (value in cell 1) = 100. We get the same result (100) either way. Thus, results are additive, and additivity is another term that means no interaction has occurred between independent variables.

These results are plotted in Figure 10–7. In Figure 10–7(a), independent variable 2 is plotted on the x-axis, and two different lines are drawn for the two levels of independent variable 1. In Figure 10–7(b), independent variable 1 has been plotted on the x-axis. Both ways of drawing Figure 10–7 are correct. In both graphs, the two lines are parallel. This is a clear visual

FIGURE 10–5
Main effects.

Independent Variable 1			Independent Variable 2		
A	B	B – A	1	2	2 – 1
50	70	20	30	90	60

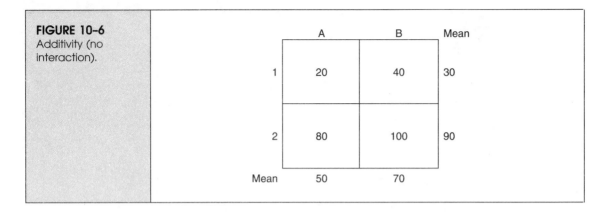

FIGURE 10-6
Additivity (no interaction).

indication of additivity. When there is no interaction between two variables, they appear as parallel lines when graphed.

Figure 10–8 contains a 2 × 2 matrix with an interaction between independent variables 1 and 2. If we tried to construct the cell values by adding the main effects as we did in Figure 10–6, the answer we would get would be wrong. (Try this for yourself.) When an interaction is plotted (Figure 10–9), lines do not appear parallel. Although Figure 10–7 and 10–9 represent identical main effects, the two graphs look quite different.

Figure 10–10 represents a very important kind of interaction, called a **crossover interaction.** When it is plotted (Figure 10–11), the two lines actually cross over one another. Crossover interactions are the most convincing form of interaction because they cannot be explained by problems in measuring and scaling the dependent variable (see Chapter 5 for mathematical properties of different kinds of measurement scales). Again, Figure 10–10 has exactly the same main effects as Figures 10–8 and 10–6. But Figure 10–11 looks quite different from Figure 10–9 and 10–7.

The moral of this section should be very clear. Patterns of interaction must be carefully considered before one tries to interpret any main effects in an experiment that has more than one independent variable.

FIGURE 10-7
Additivity.

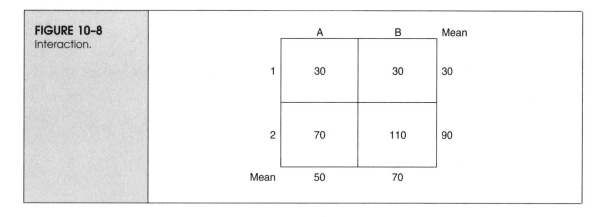

FIGURE 10-8
Interaction.

Control in Between-Subjects Factorial Designs

In a between-subjects design, each combination of independent variables is administered to a separate group of subjects. We want to make sure that the characteristics of the subjects are not confounded with group membership. In the ideal case, we would randomly select our subjects and then randomly assign them to our conditions. We are usually unable to have total random selection of our subjects because we do not have the procedures available to select, in an unbiased fashion, from *all* rats or *all* college students. It is therefore essential that we assign our subjects to conditions in a way that minimizes the possibility of confounding subject traits with our manipulations. When there are many groups in a factorial design, unbiased assignment is crucial. (Recall that Chapter 9 outlines ways to randomly assign subjects.)

Another way to make unbiased assignments of subjects to groups is to use a balanced Latin square to determine group membership. The way to use this counterbalancing technique for subject assignment in a 2 × 2 design is as follows: Label the four groups (for example A, B, C, and D) and then make a balanced square for those symbols. Use the order of conditions in the rows of the resulting Latin square to determine assignment. The first subject to appear in the laboratory is assigned to condition A, the

FIGURE 10-9
Interaction.

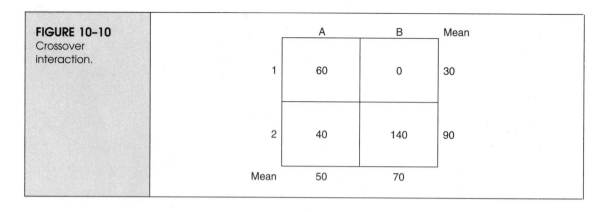

FIGURE 10-10
Crossover
interaction.

second to B, the third to D, and the fourth to C. Then use the next row to assign the next four subjects, and so on until all subjects are tested. You may have to construct many squares or use the same square repeatedly if you have more subjects than cells in your square. The purpose of this procedure is the same as random assignment to conditions: to make sure there is little relation between the subject's characteristics and assignment to a particular group. One advantage of the Latin-square technique is that in a large experiment that takes a long time to conduct, the order in which the treatments are conducted is known well in advance and also balanced across time. Thus, any historical factors that might be confounded here are balanced across groups.

In general, randomization, counterbalancing, and other control techniques help prevent potential confounding variables from interacting with the independent variables. In your design, you should try to reduce the possibility of such unwanted interactions. There are no hard-and-fast rules for choosing a control technique. The ones used are often chosen pragmatically. The particular control procedure you use is up to you: Make sure that you minimize confoundings and that you use controls that are easy to implement.

We limited the discussion of between-subjects designs to what is often called a **random-groups design,** which refers to unbiased assignment of subjects to conditions. An alternative method of assignment is matching

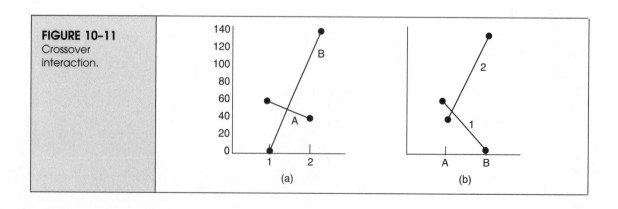

FIGURE 10-11
Crossover
interaction.

(see Chapter 9). In a **matched-groups design,** the experimenter tries to reduce the variability of observations between groups resulting from subject differences by matching the subjects on other variables. Thus, in the sleeper-effect experiment we just described, subjects could be matched on the basis of IQ before randomly assigning them to conditions. (Each subgroup of matched subjects is randomly assigned to the groups.) In our earlier discussions, we pointed out the difficulty of matching on relevant variables. Some subject variables, such as sex and age, can be matched across groups, or they can serve as quasi-independent variables. If matching is going to be difficult, you might want to use a complex within-subjects design, which we will discuss next.

CONCEPT SUMMARY

FACTORIAL DESIGNS

All possible combinations of each level of each independent variable are examined. For example, a 3 × 3 case having independent variable A with levels A1, A2, and A3 and independent variable B with levels B1, B2, and B3 yields nine groups:

- A1B1
- A1B2
- A1B3
- A2B1
- A2B2
- A2B3
- A3B1
- A3B2
- A3B3

COMPLEX WITHIN-SUBJECTS DESIGNS

The within-subjects design is often used instead of a between-subjects design, because within-subjects manipulation is more economical (requires fewer subjects) and automatically controls for individual differences. Of course, if permanent carryover effects are likely, a within-subjects design may be inappropriate.

Using a within-subjects design can result in a substantial reduction in the number of subjects needed for testing. However, the reduced number of subjects may require that you increase the number of observations per subject in each condition to ensure that your data are reliable. We should obtain numerous samples of a subject's behavior (just as is done in small-n experiments: see Chapter 11). By doing so, we reduce the likelihood that some extraneous factor has influenced the results. For instance, in many learning, memory, perception, and reaction-time experiments, events occur rapidly, placing great demands on the subject. If the subject coughs or blinks at an inappropriate time, we may incorrectly underestimate performance on that trial.

Thus, whereas in a between-subjects design we test a large number of subjects, in a within-subjects design we obtain several observations on a small number of subjects. Even with numerous observations per subject, the within-subjects design is usually more efficient than the between-subjects one.

A Complex Within-Subjects Experiment

Do you like to solve puzzles? Many people do. One kind of popular puzzle is the anagram, which consists of a word in which the letters have been rearranged. The solver tries to recreate the word from the anagram. Psychologists have examined many of the factors involved in anagram solution, because these puzzles seem to represent a relatively simple sort of problem-solving task. (Many psychologists probably study anagram solution because they like to solve them themselves.) One important variable in anagram solution is the frequency of the solution word. The higher the frequency of the word in written English, the easier people can solve an anagram of the word (Mayzner and Tresselt, 1966). One hypothesis suggests that the effects of solution-word frequency occur because people generate words as they are attempting to solve anagrams, and they are more likely to generate high-frequency words than low-frequency ones.

Dewing and Hetherington (1974) noted that the imagery of a word is associated with ease of learning and remembering. They predicted that if high noun imagery (a word such as *chair*) leads to greater availability than does low noun imagery (a word such as *truth*), then anagrams whose solution words have high imagery should be easier to solve than those whose solution words have low imagery. It should be easier to solve *AHICR* than URTTH. The researchers also wanted to determine the effects of hints on the ease with which subjects solved the anagrams. They presented a structural hint (the first and last letter of the solution word), a semantic hint (the title of the category to which the solution word belonged), or no hint. They hypothesized that if availability is important, the structural hint would help more when there were low-imagery solution words than when there were high ones because the structural hint would delimit the number of possible solutions. However, if the subjects did not generate low-frequency words as solutions to the anagram, then semantic clues would not help them solve low-imagery anagrams. Therefore, Dewing and Hetherington examined the effects of two independent variables on anagram solution: the imagery value of the solution word (high versus low) and the type of hint (none, structural, or semantic).

If this were a between-subjects experiment, we would call this a 2 × 3 factorial design. However, Dewing and Hetherington used a within-subjects design in which all levels of each independent variable were experienced by all subjects, and thus we have what is usually called a **treatments × treatments × subjects design.** This designation derives from the type of statistical analysis associated with the design (see Appendix B). Because in this experiment all combinations of variables were tested (as in a between-subjects design), within-subjects factorial is a good shorthand label. In this experiment, there were six conditions (2 × 3), representing all combinations of the levels of each independent variable: Anagrams with low-imagery solution words were solved with three different hints, and anagrams with high-imagery solutions words were solved with the same three types of hint. Dewing and Hetherington chose to use a within-subjects design rather than a between-subjects one because individuals differ markedly in their ability to solve anagrams. By using a within-subjects design, the researchers were assured that each subject served as his or her own comparison across conditions, which eliminated individual differences as a confounding factor in the experiment.

Before considering the results of this experiment, let us examine some additional details of the procedure. Every subject had to solve two anagrams under each of the six (2 × 3) conditions. The high- and low-imagery words were chosen carefully: They were all five-letter nouns, they were all of about the same frequency of occurrence in written English, and different anagrams were developed for each word and administered to different subgroups of subjects. The time taken to solve each anagram was the dependent variable.

The results of the experiment by Dewing and Hetherington are shown in Figure 10–12. As is true of a multifactor between-subjects design, you need to examine the results for both main effects and interactions. When there are two independent variables, you need to look for two main effects and one interaction. Note in Figure 10–12 that much faster solution times

FIGURE 10–12
Anagram solution times in seconds as a function of the imagery of the solution word for the three hint conditions. (Copyright 1974 by the American Psychological Association.)

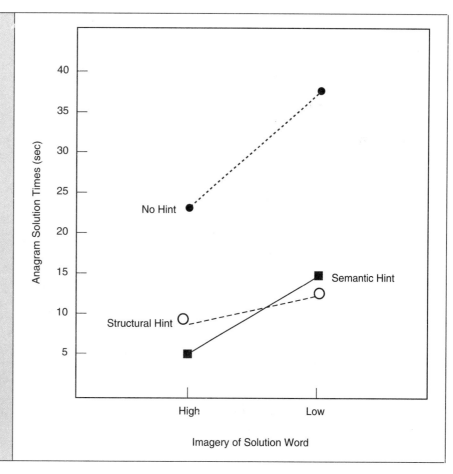

occurred for the high-imagery solution words than for the low-imagery ones. Note also the striking effects of the hints: Performance was much slower when no hint was given. The lines of the functions are not parallel, so you should expect an interaction. The effects of the hints depended on the imagery value of the solution word. For the high-imagery words, the semantic clue aided solution more than the structural hint did, but for the low-imagery words, the opposite was the case. Statistical analyses by Dewing and Hetherington confirmed that both main effects were reliable, and there was a statistically significant interaction.

The role of imagery in a practical setting is discussed in the following Application section.

Control in Complex Within-Subjects Designs

When a complex within-subjects design is used, you need to be concerned about carryover effects just as you do when only one independent variable is varied within subjects. Furthermore, you need to guard against many kinds of confounding that can occur in any multifactor experiment.

How did Dewing and Hetherington avoid the possibility of carryover effects from one treatment to another? They needed to be sure that having solved one type of anagram with a specific hint (say, a high-imagery solution word with a structural hint) did not influence the ability to solve another type of anagram with a different clue. Another potential carryover they had to consider was practice, because each subject had two tries on each type of anagram, and the subjects might have gotten better at solving anagrams during the course of the experiment. Dewing and Hetherington minimized carryover effects by having a different random order of the twelve anagrams for each subject. Presumably, the cards on which the anagrams and hints were written were shuffled before testing began. Thus, each condition had an unbiased chance of being tested in any of the twelve test orders, and each condition had an unbiased chance of being preceded and followed by every other condition. Because there are 72 subjects, Dewing and Hetherington had 72 random orders of presenting the twelve conditions, and it is unlikely that any inadvertent carryover occurred to confound the results.

The use of a random order should guard against both types of carryover (effects from condition-to-condition, and practice effects). However, Dewing and Hetherington did not have to worry much about differential practice effects, because earlier research had shown that practice effects are minimal unless the subjects receive several weeks of practice. Nevertheless, it would have been dangerous for them to have confounded conditions with order of testing. A small amount of confounding could occur, and there is no reason to tempt fate.

Two alternative procedures for controlling carryover in the anagram experiment are **block randomization** and counterbalancing (see Chapter 9). The major difference between block randomization and complete randomization is that the order of treatments is randomized twice in the block-randomization technique. Each of the six conditions appears once in a

APPLICATION

IMPROVING THE LEARNING OF FOREIGN-LANGUAGE VOCABULARY

Many laboratory experiments indicate that imagery and the type of rehearsal can improve retention. Do these kinds of results also occur in more practical situations?

Atkinson (1975) indicates that certain kinds of rehearsal techniques can dramatically improve the learning and retention of foreign-language vocabulary. One procedure that has been successful is called the keyword method. We will outline how this method is appropriate for learning Russian vocabulary, although it has worked in the learning of other languages as well. The keyword method splits vocabulary learning into two parts. In the first part, the subject associates a spoken foreign word with the keyword. This is easily done because the keyword sounds very much like the foreign word. In the second part, the subject tries to form a mental image of the keyword and the English translation interacting in some way. So, first the foreign word is connected to the keyword and then the keyword is connected to the English translation.

In Russian, the word *dym* (as spelled in our alphabet) sounds similar to the English word *dim* and means smoke. If we use the English word *dim* as the keyword, *dim* and *dym* are first linked together. Then we might form a mental image of a dim picture that has been clouded by smoke. In Atkinson's experiments, subjects hear the foreign words and are given the keyword and the English translation. The subjects provide their own mental image linking the keyword to the translation.

Learning is much faster with the keyword technique than without it—control subjects take about one-third longer to learn the same number of translations as do similar subjects who use keywords. Tests of retention up to about six weeks later indicate that the subjects using keywords recall about 65 percent more than the controls. Use of memory techniques in many situations can lead to superior retention.

SOURCE: Atkinson, R. C. (1975). Mnemotechnics and second-language learning. *American Psychologist, 30,* 821–828.

random order in the first six trials, and then each treatment is tested again in a random order in the second block of six trials. One advantage of block randomization over complete randomization is that the blocking procedure guarantees that every condition will be tested before a particular condition is tested again. Across test trials, therefore, block randomization is less likely than complete randomization to confound test order and condition. Typically, block randomization is determined for each subject, just as a different random order was determined for each subject by Dewing and Hetherington.

Counterbalancing could minimize carryover effects as well. One way to counterbalance would be to generate 6×6 balanced Latin squares for the six treatments and assign two rows to each subject to determine the order of presenting the conditions. An advantage of this procedure over randomization (either blocked or complete) is that balanced Latin squares ensure that each treatment precedes and follows every other treatment equally often. A disadvantage might be that the researchers would have to test subjects in multiples of six to be sure that all sequences in the Latin squares were administered.

Some additional aspects of the design used by Dewing and Hetherington are noteworthy. Because the high-imagery and low-imagery solution words came from different semantic categories, Dewing and Hetherington wanted to be sure that the semantic hints they used were not better for one class of solution word than the other. Prior to conducting the anagram experiment, they conducted pilot work (see Chapter 1) in which they had ten other subjects rate the degree of association (on a five-point scale) between each solution word and its semantic clue. The raters, who did not know the purpose of the anagram experiment, determined that the degree of association between semantic hints and solution words was about the same for the high- and low-imagery words. Alternatively, Dewing and Hetherington could have attempted to find high- and low-imagery words that belonged to the same semantic categories so that the same semantic clue could be given to each. This would have been difficult, because it is hard to conceive of a low-imagery piece of furniture to pair with the high-imagery word *chair*. Other matches for high- and low-imagery words are also unlikely.

Another variable that could have been controlled but was not is the spelling of the solution words. The high- and low-imagery solution words had different first and last letters, and this may be an important confounding. However, finding words with the same first and last letters that differed only in imagery would be difficult. One thing Dewing and Hetherington did to account for different spellings was to consider the frequency with which successive letter pairs in the solution word occurred in the English language. This is known as bigram frequency. Earlier research had noted that the bigram frequency of the solution word interacted with the bigram frequency of the anagram. Solution times were fastest for anagrams whose bigram frequency matched the bigram frequency of the solution word. This was true for both high and low bigram frequencies. In Dewing and Hetherington's experiment, solution-word bigram frequency was similar for the high- and low-imagery words, and, as noted previously, the experimenters used three different anagrams for each solution word.

Finally, we should note that Dewing and Hetherington completely counterbalanced clue conditions across the three anagrams generated for a particular word. In other words, the three sets of anagrams were combined factorially with the three hint conditions. In the nine lists of anagrams generated by this 3 × 3 combination, each of the treatment conditions was assigned to each anagram. This procedure probably was effective in eliminating a confounding of materials with conditions, which means that a particular anagram could not account for the differential effect of the hints.

CONCEPT SUMMARY

COMPLEX WITHIN-SUBJECTS DESIGNS

Every subject receives all combinations of each level of the independent variables. For example, Dewing and Hetherington's (1974) experiment had the following conditions: an independent variable for solution-word imagery (high imagery or low imagery) and an independent variable for type of hint (semantic, structural, or none). A factorial combination of the 2 × 3 conditions yields high, semantic; high, structural; high, none; low, semantic; low, structural; and low, none.

MIXED DESIGNS

There are advantages and disadvantages to both pure within-subject designs and pure between-subject designs. Many experimenters used **mixed designs** to get the best of both worlds while minimizing possible disadvantages. A mixed design has one or more between-subject independent variables and also one or more within-subject independent variables.

To illustrate a mixed design, we will consider an experiment dealing with driving a car. Driving can be studied in a real car on the road or in a driving simulator in a laboratory. There are obvious safety advantages to using a simulator for this research. But simulators are not as realistic as cars on a highway. Is driving behavior different in a car versus in a simulator?

To answer this question Blaauw (1982) compared two groups of drivers who were tested in a real car and in a driving simulator. Experienced drivers were 24 males who had their licenses for at least three years and who had driven at least 30,000 kilometers. Inexperienced drivers had either just completed a driver-training course or just received their license. Because the same driver cannot be both experienced and inexperienced, this independent variable must be a between-subject variable. Between-subject variables are often used to test different subject populations, such as experienced versus inexperienced drivers, young versus older drivers, and so

FIGURE 10–13
Vehicle lateral position for experienced and inexperienced drivers. (data from Blaauw, 1982.)

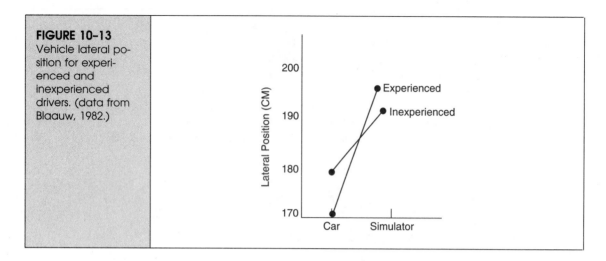

on. All drivers were tested in the car and in the simulator. Thus, this is a within-subject independent variable used to increase the efficiency of the experimental design. This entire experiment illustrates a mixed design, because there is one between-subject independent variable and one within-subject independent variable.

Figure 10–13 shows a small part of the experimental results. The dependent variable is vehicle lateral position defined as the distance between driver and the right-lane marker. (Many other dependent variables not discussed here were also used in the study.) For both experienced and inexperienced drivers, lateral position was greater in the simulator than in the car. Greater driver experience did not affect lateral position in the simulator. Blaauw concluded that the simulator lacked absolute validity as a car substitute for lateral control performance. Because the simulator did not move, many of the kinesthetic cues present in a real car could not be duplicated in the simulator. This caused drivers to behave differently in the car and in the simulator. However, other results, not summarized here, showed that the simulator was valid for certain other aspects of driving performance. For the full story, you should examine Blaauw (1982).

SUMMARY

1. Multifactor experiments have more than one independent variable, and these variables may have more than two levels.

2. When more than two independent variables are varied, we have a factorial design in which all possible combinations of the levels of the independent variables are examined. In a 2 × 2 factorial design, there are four combinations of levels of independent variables.

3. The primary reason for using multifactor designs is to look for interactions. An interaction is when the effects of one independent variable depend on the level of other independent variables.

4. When there are two independent variables, there are two main effects (one associated with each variable), and there can be an interaction.

5. Treatments × treatments × subjects is the designation usually given to factorial designs in which the variables are manipulated within subjects.

6. The control procedures used in multifactor experiments can be complicated, but they are similar in principle to the procedures (randomization, counterbalancing, and so on) used in experiments that have just one independent variable.

7. In a mixed design, one or more variables are varied between subjects and one or more variables are varied within subjects.

■ **KEY CONCEPTS**

block randomization
crossover interaction
discounting cue
interaction
main effects
matched-groups design

mixed designs
random-groups design
sleeper effect
treatments × treatments
   × subjects design
2 × 2 factorial design

■ **EXERCISES**

1. Discuss the advantages of using complex within-subjects designs as opposed to complex between-subjects designs.

2. [*Special Exercise.*] A researcher varied the size (large or small) of the food reinforcement that was given to rats in a straight-alley maze. The time it took the rats to run down the alley was the dependent variable, and the mean time in seconds for each block of ten trials was as follows:

	BLOCK 1	BLOCK 2	BLOCK 3	BLOCK 4
Large reward	38	30	20	15
Small reward	52	32	16	12

The experimenter concluded that because the overall time was slower in the small-reward group, large rewards lead to more rapid learning. What other conclusions can be drawn from the data in the table? Draw a figure showing these results.

3. [*Special Exercise.*] An experimenter is interested in studying the effects of practice on retention. If a within-subjects design is used and the independent variables are types of rehearsal (rote and elaborative)

and number of presentations (1, 2, 3, and 4), indicate how the words to be remembered could be counterbalanced over the four different numbers of presentations. What are some additional confoundings that must be eliminated?

■ SUGGESTED READINGS

Several complex experiments are reprinted in Elmes, D. G. (1978), *Readings in experimental psychology*. Chicago: Rand McNally. See especially articles 14 and 25.

Psychology in Action
Distraction and Difficulty in Letter Detection

Detection of various kinds of targets (for example, planes on a radar screen) usually deteriorates when the observer is distracted or is under stress of some sort (Broadbent, 1971). The purpose of this experiment is to see whether distraction interacts with the difficulty of the detection task.

The subject's task will be to read through a newspaper article at a rapid rate, crossing out certain letters as he or she is reading. Half of the detection periods will occur in a quiet setting and the other half will take place where moderately loud music is playing. Thus you will need a newspaper and a radio (or some other source of music).

The difficulty of the task will be determined by the particular letters that the subjects are to cross out. Half the time the subjects should cancel out all the u's they can find, and on the rest of the trials they should cancel out all the fs. The letter f was chosen because people generally make a substantial number of errors when they try to detect f (Read, 1983). This occurs because the letter f is often pronounced as a v (as in the word *of*), and people usually do not cancel out those fs. The letter u was chosen because it occurs with about the same frequency as the letter f, and only occasionally is it pronounced in an unusual fashion (as a w in words beginning with a q, which means you might want to select newspaper passages that do not contain the letter q).

You should probably use a within-subjects design in this experiment, so you will have to figure out some sort of counterbalancing scheme (see Chapter 9) for the four conditions: detecting the letter u in a quiet setting, detecting the letter f in a quiet setting, detecting the letter u with music playing, and detecting the letter f with music playing.

Subjects should be tested in each condition once. Allow each subject to read for 30 seconds. After testing, you can calculate the error rate by dividing the number of correct detections (f or u) by the total number of fs or u's in the passage. (Be sure that you detect all the fs when you are scoring the data.) You should combine your results with those of other students to increase the stability of your data.

Look for an interaction in your results. Usually, the most difficult detection task is the one most affected by the distraction.

Broadbent, D. E. (1971). *Decision and stress.* New York: Academic Press. Read J. D. (1983). Detection of Fs in a single statement: The role of phonetic recoding. *Memory & Cognition, 11*, 390–399.

SMALL-*N* EXPERIMENTATION

Numerous observations on small numbers of subjects

Operant-Conditioning Designs

- ❑ Reversal design (ABA)
- ❑ Multiple-baseline design

Clinical Psychology

- ❑ Multiple personality disorder

QUASI-EXPERIMENTATION

Increasing internal validity when the variables are selected, not manipulated

Sources of Invalidity in Quasi-experiments

history   maturation   selection bias

mortality   delayed effects   regression artifacts

How does one make valid causal statements in Case Studies?

Case Studies?

- ❑ Use *deviant-case analysis* (a nonequivalent control group); examine several dependent variables

Interrupted Time Series?

- ❑ Use *nonequivalent control group*; study several dependent variables; search for additional natural treatments

Subject-Variable Research?

- ❑ Use *matching* on potentially relevant characteristics; beware of regression artifacts

Developmental Research (Age)?

- ❑ Use *cross-sequential design* to minimize generation and time-of-test confoundings; include *true independent variable* and look for interactions

CHAPTER 11

ALTERNATE EXPERIMENTAL DESIGNS

In this chapter we examine alternatives to the typical experiment in which an experimenter manipulates an independent variable and tests a large number of subjects. First, we consider experimental designs using a small number of subjects, which require special control procedures. Then, we examine situations that are almost ordinary experiments—quasi-experiments, which always have suspect internal validity.

SMALL-*N* EXPERIMENTATION

In the simplest case, an experiment involves the production of a comparison between experimental and control conditions. Both between- and within-subjects designs usually include a large number of subjects, although the number is often less in the within-subjects case. Large numbers of subjects are required so that an unusual participant does not skew the results. Such designs are called **large-*n* designs** and have become the norm in psychological research; powerful statistical techniques (see Appendix B) allow the researcher to determine whether differences between the conditions are worth worrying about. An alternative approach to such designs is the **small-*n* design,** in which a very few subjects are intensely analyzed.

Operant-Conditioning Designs

Two areas within experimental psychology have resisted the use of large-*n* designs. One is psychophysics (see Chapter 5). A researcher doing psychophysical research worries less about individual differences among subjects than do researchers in other areas, such as memory, because the behaviors that are measured in psychophysics are less complex and greater control over conditions usually is possible than in memory research. The emphasis on experimental control is the hallmark of the second research area that uses small-*n* designs—the experimental analysis of behavior in terms of operant conditioning. Skinner (1963) urged using small-*n* designs in operant research, because he wanted to emphasize the importance of experimental control over behavior and deemphasize the importance of statistical analysis. Skinner believed that statistical analysis often becomes an end in itself, rather than a tool to help the researcher make decisions about the experimental results. The logic of small-*n* design in operant-conditioning research has been detailed in Sidman's (1960) book, *Tactics of Scientific Research.* The experimental control usually achieved in traditional research with large numbers of subjects and statistical inference is strived for in small-*n* research by very carefully controlling the experimental setting and by taking numerous and continuous measures of the dependent variable. Small-*n* methodology is especially appropriate to the clinical application of operant techniques to modify behavior. Typically, a therapist deals with a single client at a time, which is the limiting case of a small-*n* design. Although a therapist may treat more than one patient at a time with similar methods, the numbers are very small relative to those seen in most large-*n* research. We examine small-*n* design in the context of behavior problems in children and then in a variant of case study research.

Consider the following scenario: Concerned parents seek psychological help for their child because she has temper tantrums several times a day. These tantrums are noisy with a lot of yelling and crying, and they are violent—she often kicks things and bangs her head on the floor. When the therapist, who is a specialist in behavior modification using operant-conditioning techniques, first sees the child, what conclusions is he or she to draw? What causes this behavior? What can the therapist do to remove it and return the child to a more normal existence?

A behavior therapist would seek to discover what in the learning history of the child has produced such troublesome behavior. The focus would be on the contingencies of reinforcement that produce and maintain the child's crying, kicking, and head banging. The proposed therapy would be designed to change the contingencies of reinforcement, so that the child is rewarded for appropriate and not maladaptive behavior. An interpretation of the plight of our fictional child might go something like the following.

One potent source of reinforcement for children is parental attention, and young children will go to great lengths to attract their parents' attention. Once, when the child was feeling alone and neglected, she began to whine and cry. The parents attended to her and thus reinforced the behavior. The next time the child felt lonely, she again tried the crying gambit—and was again reinforced. Before long, the child found that she had to cry more loudly for attention, because her parents were both becoming used to it and trying to ignore it in hopes that she would stop. Every time the child increased the extremity of the behavior, the parents would once again start paying attention, at least for a while. So, the problem behavior increased in intensity and frequency, which resulted in the parents seeking the help of the therapist. The parents unwittingly shaped the child's behavior by reinforcing increases in extreme behavior. Just as a pigeon can be trained to walk around in figure eights by first being rewarded for making movements that approximate a figure eight, so can a child be reinforced for head banging and temper tantrums by being rewarded for successive steps along the way.

The therapist's interpretation of the child's behavior is that it has been sustained by an unfortunate set of reinforcement contingencies. Therapy involves changing the contingencies, so that positive behavior is rewarded and negative behavior is not. The therapist's job, in large part, is to help the parents become effective behavior therapists themselves. The parents should start paying attention to the child when she is behaving normally. If the tantrums persist, they should try to reinforce her for lessening their intensity. If the child throws a violent tantrum to which the parents must pay attention, they should wait for a momentary lull before attending, which would reward lessening the intensity and gradually shape the tantrums to be less severe. Best of all would be to ignore the tantrums completely, if possible, which should extinguish them, because they are no longer followed by reinforcement.

The *AB* Design.   Before examining solid small-*n* designs, we take a look at a common but invalid way to evaluate the effectiveness of a therapy. Research concerning the effectiveness of a therapy should be incorporated into the treatment whenever possible. This seems a fairly simple matter: measure the frequency of the behavior that needs to be changed, then institute the therapy and see if the behavior changes. We can call this an **AB design,** where *A* represents the baseline condition before therapy, and *B* represents the condition after therapy (the independent variable) is introduced. This design is used in much medical, educational, and other applied research, where a therapy or training procedure is instituted to determine its effects on the problem of interest. However, the *AB* design (Campbell and Stanley, 1966) is poor and should be avoided. It is an inadequate design because changes occurring during treatment in the *B* phase may be caused by other factors that are confounded with the factor of interest. The treatment might produce the change in behavior, but so could other sources that the researcher is not aware of or has failed to control. We cannot conclusively establish that change was caused by the therapy because of a lack of control comparisons. A confounding variable might have produced the change in the absence of an independent variable. Remember, confounding occurs when other variables are inadvertently varied with the primary factor of interest, in the case of the little girl, the therapy. It is crucial to control carefully the potential confounding variables, so that the primary one is producing the effect. This cannot be done in the *AB* design, because the therapist-researcher may not even be aware of the other variables.

A standard solution to the problem involves a large-*n* design. We have two groups to which subjects have been randomly assigned. One, the experimental, receives the treatment; the other, the control, does not. If the experimental condition improves with the therapy and the control does not, we may conclude that the treatment and not some extraneous factor produces the result. In the case of therapy on an individual, such as the case of the tantrum-throwing girl, there usually is no potential control group and only one subject in the experimental "group." Because a large-*n* design depends on having a substantial number of subjects in the experimental and control conditions, it is inappropriate for use in evaluating many therapeutic situations.

The *ABA* or Reversal Design.   As an alternative to the *AB* design, which is flawed, the experimenter may reverse the conditions after the *B* phase to yield an **ABA design,** which is also called a **reversal design.** The second *A* phase in the *ABA* design serves to rule out the possibility that some confounding factor influenced the behavior observed in the *B* phase. Returning the conditions of the experiment to their original baseline level, with the independent variable no longer applied, allows the experimenter to determine whether behavior returns to baseline level during the second *A* phase. If it does, then the researcher can conclude that it was the independent variable that effected change during the *B* phase. This generalization would not apply if a confounding variable happened to be perfectly correlated with the independent variable. Such a situation is unlikely.

In our example of the child throwing tantrums, the therapist would instruct the parents to get baseline measures on the number of crying episodes, tantrums, and head banging when they reacted just as they normally would. Then the therapist would instruct them to alter their behavior by rewarding the child with attention when the child engaged in good behavior and by trying to extinguish the tantrums and other behavior by ignoring them altogether. If this produced a change in the frequency of the tantrums over a period of several weeks, then the therapist might ask the parents to reinstitute their old pattern of behavior to ensure that it was their attention to the child at inappropriate moments that was really controlling the child's behavior and not something else. (If the therapist were not interested in research, of course, he or she might just leave well enough alone after the successful *B* phase.) If the original treatment produced no effect on the dependent variable, the frequency of tantrums, it would be necessary to try something else. The techniques of behavior modification based on operant analysis have met with great success in the treatment of certain sorts of psychological problems. Here, we consider an example.

Hart and coworkers (1964) investigated the excessive crying of a four-year-old nursery-school pupil, Bill, who otherwise seemed quite healthy and normal. The crying often came in response to mild frustrations that other children dealt with in more effective ways. Rather than attribute his crying to internal variables, such as fear, lack of confidence, or regression to behavior of an earlier age, the investigators looked to the social learning environment to see what reinforcement contingencies might be producing such behavior. They decided, with reasoning similar to that already discussed in the case of our hypothetical little girl, that adult attention was the reinforcer for Bill's crying behavior. Hart and colleagues set about testing this supposition with an *ABA* (actually *ABAB*) design.

First, it was necessary to gain a good measure of the dependent variable, crying. The teacher carried a pocket counter and depressed the lever every time there was a crying episode. "A crying episode was defined as a cry (a) loud enough to be heard at least 50 feet away and (b) of 5 seconds or more duration." At the end of each nursery school day, the total number of crying episodes was recorded. We could, perhaps, quibble some with this operational definition of a crying episode (did the teacher go 50 feet away each time to listen?), but let us assume it is valid and reliable.

During the initial baseline of phase *A*, Bill was treated as he normally had been, with attention being given by the teacher to his crying. During the 10 days of the first baseline period, the number of crying episodes was between 5 and 10 a day, as shown in the left-most panel of Figure 11–1, where the frequency of crying episodes on the ordinate is plotted against

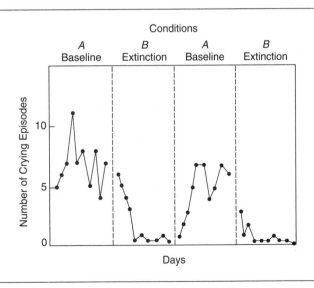

FIGURE 11–1
The number of crying episodes exhibited by Bill, a nursery-school student, during the four phases of an *ABAB* design initiated to control his problem crying. (From Wolf and Risley, 1969, p. 316).

days on the abscissa. For the next 10 days (the first B phase), the teacher attempted to extinguish the crying episodes by ignoring them, while rewarding Bill with attention every time he responded to minor calamities (such as falls or pushes) in a more appropriate way. As can be seen in Figure 11–1, the number of crying episodes dropped precipitously, so that there were between 0 and 2 during the last six days of the first B phase. This completes the AB phase of the design; once again, we cannot be certain that the reinforcement contingencies were responsible for Bill's improved behavior. Perhaps he was getting along better with his classmates, or his parents were treating him better at home. Either of these things (or others) could have improved his disposition.

To gain better evidence that it was actually the reinforcement contingencies that changed Bill's behavior, the investigators returned to the baseline: Bill was again reinforced for crying. At first, he was rewarded with attention for approximations to crying (whimpering and sulking); after crying had been established again, it was maintained with attention to each crying episode. As the third panel in Figure 11–1 shows, it took only four days to reestablish crying. This led to the conclusion that the reinforcement contingencies and not any number of other factors were responsible for the termination of crying in the first B phase. Finally, because this was a therapeutic situation, the investigators instituted a second B phase similar to the first, in which Bill's crying was once again extinguished.

In this investigation, no inferential statistics were employed to justify the conclusions drawn. Rather, with good control of the independent variable and repeated measures on the dependent variable, the differences between conditions in this experiment were striking enough to decrease the need for inferential statistics. Use of ABA small-n designs can allow powerful experimental inferences.

Extensions of the Reversal Design.   As in the standard within-subjects experiments, small-n experiments often include carryover effects that prohibit using the reversal design. If the treatment introduced in the B phase has long-term effects on the dependent variable, then reversal is impractical. Furthermore, the experimenter may want to obtain several samples of the subjects' behavior under the same independent variable or under several independent variables. There are a number of ways to solve these problems, but we will consider just two.

Rose (1978) used what could be called an $ACABCBCB$ design, where A phases refer to baseline conditions, and B and C phases include different independent variables. Rose was interested in the effects of artificial food coloring on hyperactivity in children. Two hyperactive eight-year-old girls were subjects. They had been on a strict diet, the K-P diet (Feingold, 1975), which does not allow foods containing artificial flavors and colors and foods containing natural salicylates (many fruits and meats). On the basis of uncontrolled case studies (AB designs), Feingold reported that the K-P diet reduced hyperactivity.

Rose's A phase was the behavior of the two girls under the ordinary K-P diet. The B phase was another type of baseline. It involved the introduction of an oatmeal cookie that contained no artificial coloring. The C phase included the independent variable of interest: oatmeal cookies containing an artificial yellow dye. This artificial color was chosen because it is commonly used in the manufacture of foods, and it had the additional benefit that it did not change the taste or appearance of the cookies. (When asked to sort the cookies on the basis of color, judges were unable to do so systematically with regard to the presence of the dye.) The subjects, their parents, and the observers were blind to when the children ate the dye-laced cookie. Various aspects of the two girls' behavior were recorded during school by several different observers. One dependent variable that Rose measured was the percentage of time that the girls were out of their seats during school. Rose found that the girls were most active during the *C* phases, when they had ingested a cookie with artificial coloring in it. Rose also noticed that there was no placebo effect. That is, the percentage of time out of their seats was essentially the same during the *A* phases (no cookie) and the *B* phases, in which the girls ate cookies without artificial coloring. So, Rose concluded that artificial colors can lead to hyperactivity in some children.

Multiple-Baseline Design. Rose's extension of the reversal design allows an experimenter to examine the effects of more than two levels of the independent variable. However, the extension does not permit experiments involving independent variables that are likely to have strong carryover effects. The **multiple-baseline design,** illustrated in Figure 11–2, is suitable for situations in which the behavior of interest may not reverse to baseline levels (that is, when there are permanent carryover effects).

Two features of the multiple-baseline design are noteworthy. First, notice that different behaviors (or different subjects) have baseline periods of different lengths prior to the introduction of the independent variable. The baseline periods are to the left of the vertical lines, and the treatment periods, in which the independent variable has been introduced, are to the right of the vertical lines. Using such a design in the case of Bill (described earlier) might involve a continual baseline monitoring of some other unwanted behavior (say, picking fights) when the extinction period for crying

FIGURE 11–2
An outline of the multiple-baseline design. Different people (between-subjects) or different behaviors (within-subjects) have baseline periods of different lengths. The vertical lines indicate when the independent variable (the treatment) was introduced.

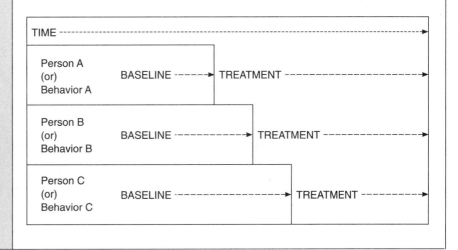

was introduced. Then after several days perhaps, the extinction procedure could be applied to the fighting behavior. The design and results of this hypothetical experiment are shown in Figure 11–3. Notice that, in general, one behavior is allowed to occur under baseline conditions while the other behavior is being treated. If the untreated behavior holds steady prior to the introduction of the independent variable and then changes afterward, the assumption is that it is the independent variable that alters the behavior and not some other change taking place over time. However, if the target behaviors are not independent—that is, if the treatment of one influences the occurrence of the other (Bill's fighting decreases when crying is extinguished)—then the changes in behavior can not be attributed to the independent variable. This problem leads us to the second important feature of the multiple-baseline design illustrated in Figure 11–2.

The multiple-baseline design can be used as a small-*n* equivalent of the between-subjects design. As shown in Figure 11–2, instead of several behaviors being monitored as in a within-subjects design, different people can be monitored for different periods prior to the introduction of the independent variable. This type of multiple-baseline design, as is true of the ordinary between-subjects design, should be appropriate for situations in which the independent variable will have strong carryover effects. The between-subjects multiple-baseline procedure is also appropriate for cases where target behaviors are likely to be influenced by each other, such as could have occurred in our hypothetical experiment concerning Bill.

An experiment by Schreibman, O'Neill, and Koegel (1983) nicely illustrates the between-subjects form of the multiple-baseline design. Schreib-

FIGURE 11–3
Hypothetical results of a multiple-baseline experiment on Bill. Two behaviors, crying and fighting, are extinguished after different baseline periods.

FIGURE 11-4
The normal sib-
lings' use of cor-
rect behavior-
modification pro-
cedures, and the
autistic children's
appropriate re-
sponses. The base-
line period is to
the left of the ver-
tical line for each
pair of children.
The pluses and
bull's-eyes show
behavior in a gen-
eralization setting
(From Schreibman
et al., 1983, in
*Journal of Applied
Behavior Analysis,*
vol. 16, p. 135.
Copyright 1983 by
the Society for the
Experimental
Analysis of Behav-
ior, Inc. Reprinted
by permission of
the publisher and
the author.)

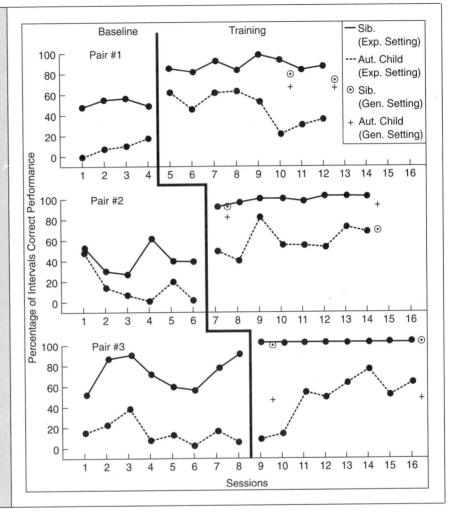

man and her coworkers were interested in teaching behavior-modification
procedures to the normal siblings of autistic children so that they could
become effective teachers of their autistic siblings. Autism is a behavior
disorder of unknown origin. It is characterized by impoverished social behavior, minimal language use, and self-stimulation of various kinds. For
each of three pairs of siblings—one normal (mean age was 10 years) and
one autistic (mean age was 7 years)—several target behaviors, such as
counting, identification of letters, and learning about money, were chosen
for the normal sibling to teach the autistic sibling. Because the normal siblings had to learn correct behavior-modification techniques, such as reinforcement for appropriate responding, the experimenters first recorded
baseline measures of the normal siblings' use of correct behavior-
modification techniques and the correct performance of the target behaviors
by the autistic children. The baseline data for each pair of children are
shown to the left of the vertical lines in Figure 11–4. Learning behavior-
modification techniques is likely to influence a wide variety of behaviors

of both the teacher and the pupil (the normal and autistic, respectively), so a multiple-baseline design across pairs of children was used. Changes in the behavior of normal and autistic children after the normal siblings were trained to use behavior-modification procedures are shown to the right of the vertical lines in Figure 11–4. Note that correct performance by both children in each pair increased after the beginning of training. Schreibman, O'Neill, and Koegel concluded that the training, and not some other confounding factor (such as changes resulting from being observed), altered the behavior.

Another interesting feature in Figure 11–4 is the data points represented by plus signs and bull's-eyes. These symbols show the children's behavior in a setting that was entirely different from the training room, one in which the children did not know they were being monitored by the experimenters. Behaviors in this generalization setting was very similar to the behavior in the training room, so the treatment program was effective in making general changes in the children's behavior.

The operant-conditioning research designs described above are representative of the powerful research techniques developed by Skinner and his followers. Careful control has provided an enormously valuable database for psychology. Furthermore, as we have seen, the procedures have been used in applied settings with substantial success. The small-n procedures of operant analysis are important tools for psychologists who wish to understand thought and behavior.

CONCEPT SUMMARY

SMALL-N DESIGNS IN OPERANT-CONDITIONING RESEARCH

Reversal Design (*ABA* or *ABAB*)
Interspersed between baseline periods (*A*) are independent-variable phases (*B*). If the behavior reverses to baseline levels, we assume that the independent variable caused the changes that occurred during the *B* periods.

Extensions of the Reversal Design
More than one independent variable is used, and there are numerous baseline periods.

Multiple-Baseline Design
Several behaviors (within-subjects) or several people (between-subjects) receive baseline periods of varying length, after which the independent variable is introduced.

Clinical Psychology

Multiple Personality Disorder. Someone suffering from multiple personality disorder has several distinct personalities, each of which claims to have no direct awareness of the others. Furthermore, each personality cannot remember events that occur to the other personalities, although it can remember events that happened to it. Thus, memory dysfunction is a crucial part of the multiple personality syndrome.

Nissen and her colleagues (Nissen et al., 1988) were able to study a patient with multiple personality disorder. Their research strategy focused on a variety of memory tests that would allow them to determine to what extent one personality had access to the knowledge of other personalities. Because this research is based on a single subject ($n = 1$), it is an example of the case study, which always is classified as a small-n experiment, even though a survey of patients with multiple personality disorder found a mean of 13 different personalities per patient (Putnam et al., 1986).

The patient they studied was a 45-year-old right-handed Caucasian woman who had been divorced five times. She has shown 22 different personalities ranging in age from 5 to 45 years. Three personalities are male, and three are left-handed. Testing focused on eight personalities.

The general experimental procedure was to present information to one personality, and after a retention interval of 5 to 10 minutes, have the patient's psychiatrist request a change of personality. The new personality would be given a task that ordinarily would be sensitive to the prior information.

Results showed that there were some tasks in which one personality was influenced by knowledge presented to another personality and other tasks in which it was not. Simple and clear tasks did show influence. For example, one such task used four-alternative forced-choice recognition. Alice was shown 54 photographs from old high-school yearbooks and asked to rate them (i.e., sad, happy, or neutral). Bonnie was then shown a different set of 54 photographs and also asked to rate them. Bonnie then received the four-alternative forced-choice recognition test in which four faces were presented and Bonnie had to indicate or guess which face seemed most familiar. When the alternatives included one face previously shown to Bonnie, she selected that face 52 percent of the time. When the alternatives included a face that Alice, but not Bonnie, had seen before, Bonnie selected that face 42 percent of the time. This is higher than the 25 percent that would be expected by chance if Bonnie had been uninfluenced by what Alice saw. When the alternatives included one face that Alice had seen and also one that Bonnie had seen, Bonnie selected the face she had seen 33 percent of the time. On the remaining trails, given that Bonnie did not select the face she had seen, she selected the face that Alice had seen 63 percent of the time, again indicating her selection had been influenced by what Alice saw.

A more ambiguous task, repetition priming of stem completion, did not show such influence. Alice saw words and judged how pleasant each one was. Bonnie then received a list of 24 words and judged how pleasant each one was. Bonnie then received a list of 48 three-letter word stems and had to complete them. Each stem had 10 possible correct answers. Half of the word stems could be completed to make a word Alice had seen. Bonnie did not exceed the level of chance (10 percent) in creating such words. Thus there was no influence from words seen by Alice. When this procedure was repeated for Bonnie five days later, there was an influence from words that had been previously presented to Bonnie. So this ruled out the possibility that Bonnie by herself would not show the repetition effect. The authors interpreted this finding to imply that ambiguous stimuli are more likely to have personality-specific interpretations and so would not show influence from one personality to another.

This is an interesting study because it combined two different methodologies in psychology that are seldom used together. The case study is most often used in clinical psychology, whereas studies of memory most often involve many subjects. This experiment reminds us that it is possible to be creative by combining different techniques within a single experiment.

CONCEPT SUMMARY

SMALL-*N* DESIGNS IN CLINICAL PSYCHOLOGY

Multiple Personality Disorder
The case study is a small-*n* design often used in clinical psychology.

QUASI-EXPERIMENTATION

Internal Validity in Quasi-Experiments

Quasi-experiments refer to experimental situations in which the experimenter does not directly manipulate variables as in a typical laboratory experiment. In a quasi-experiment, some or all of the variables are selected, which means that they are not under direct control of the experimenter. Either the effects of natural "treatments" (such as disasters) are observed, or particular subject variables (such as age, sex, weight) are of interest. In either case, we must be wary of internal validity, because the experimenter does not manipulate the variables. In other words, the joint method of agreement and difference is not under direct control. Quasi-experiments have the advantage of being intrinsically interesting, and they also allow researchers to examine variables that would be unethical to manipulate directly. We consider the pitfalls of quasi-experiments and how to minimize those problems.

Natural Treatments.   Ex post facto analyses of the effects of some naturally occurring event, such as a disaster or a change in school curricula, are usually interesting and important but are often difficult to interpret in a causal fashion. Most quasi-experiments involving naturally occurring treatments have a structure that is similar to some of the small-*n* experiments (*ABA*) discussed earlier. We might, for example, have records of third-grade achievement before and after (the *A* phases) the introduction of a new method for teaching reading (the *B* phase). Note carefully: This example does not represent a true reversal design, because there is not a removal of the treatment to allow a return to the original baseline. In fact, most quasi-experiments of the general form **observation-treatment-observation** cannot be true reversal designs for two reasons: (1) the treatment is not under the experimenter's control; and (2) most natural treatments, such as curriculum revision, are likely to have long-term carryover effects. We must be concerned not only with carryover effects, but also with the changes in the subjects themselves. If we examine the effects of a new reading program on third-grade achievement, one thing that is confounded with the introduction of our treatment is a change in the age of our subjects. Although age itself does not cause anything, many important changes correlate with age: more experience in school, better test taking, improved linguistic skills, better social adjustment, biological maturation, and the like. These changes, which are called **maturation,** nearly always can confound the results of research concerned with natural treatments. Furthermore in a classroom setting, numerous outside influences could affect the results. Because the researcher does not have direct control over the setting, the subjects are not insulated from numerous possible distractions as they are in a true experiment. This source of confounding is called **history** by Cook and Campbell (1979).

Thus, two particular threats to internal validity with naturally occurring treatments are the history of the subject and any changes in the subject that occur over time. Either or both of these factors could vary directly, inversely, or not at all with the intended treatment. In addition, the effects of history and change could interact in several different ways. Ways to minimize these difficulties (for example, matching) generally involve more active participation on the part of the experimenter. One thing that could be done in ex post facto analysis of the effects of reading techniques is to find a control-group third-grade class that did not have this new technique imposed on it, which would result in a quasi-experimental design similar to the one shown in Table 11–1. This looks like an ordinary experimental design, but remember—we have no direct control over the situation, and, as we shall soon see, by adding a matched control group we have incurred additional threats to internal validity. This type of design is sometimes called a **nonequivalent control group** design because random assignment to conditions is not used, and matching is attempted after the fact. Because

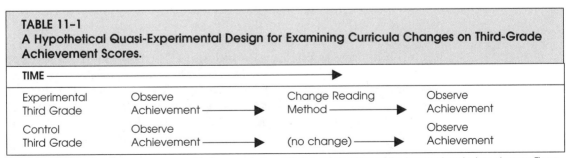

TABLE 11–1
A Hypothetical Quasi-Experimental Design for Examining Curricula Changes on Third-Grade Achievement Scores.

TIME ⟶

| Experimental Third Grade | Observe Achievement ⟶ | Change Reading Method ⟶ | Observe Achievement |
| Control Third Grade | Observe Achievement ⟶ | (no change) ⟶ | Observe Achievement |

Note: The third-grade classes are assumed to be very similar, differing only in terms of the imposed curriculum change. There was not random assignment to the two groups, and usually the control group is determined ex post facto. Thus, this design includes a nonequivalent control group.

the subjects are not randomly assigned to groups, we have the possible problem of **selection bias.** As discussed in Chapters 5 and 9, random assignment to conditions generally equates the subject characteristics in the various conditions of the experiment. With natural treatments, on the other hand, we select our subjects, not assign them, and we have no guarantee that our selection will be as unbiased as randomization in a true experiment.

We will now consider two quasi-experimental designs that appear in the psychological literature: the one-shot case study and the interrupted-time-series design.

One-Shot Case Studies.   We can view the **one-shot case study** in the following way: We have a long-term treatment on an individual and after the fact we obtain some measurements of that individual's thought and action. If we use the same notation that we used for the reversal design, we can call this an *AB* design (where *A* is the history and *B* is the current behavior). Treatments occur and then we observe their effects. Note that the treatments do not allow baseline observations. Viewing the one-shot case study as an *AB* design immediately points to the threat to internal validity: There is no baseline or control condition.

If a small-*n* design cannot be used, then deviant-case analysis is one way to obtain a control group in case-study research. In deviant-case analysis (see Chapter 6), we take an individual as similar as possible to our case except for a crucial missing treatment (a drunkard for a father, a disabling illness, and so forth) and determine how the individuals are different from each other. The similar individual is a nonequivalent control, not a true control. Reconsider the case of P.Z. that was discussed in Chapter 6. P.Z. was an elderly, world-famous scientist who suffered from a severe memory loss. P.Z. had a history of alcohol abuse (Butters & Cermak, 1986). Deviant-case analysis was used to determine whether the memory deficit could be attributed to the alcohol abuse. A similar-aged colleague of P.Z. was tested for the retention of facts and names that should have been familiar to him and to P.Z. The colleague is the companion person for the deviant-case analysis. Whereas P.Z. showed a severe retention loss, the colleague did not. Because the comparison case had not abused alcohol, Butters and Cermak concluded that alcohol was the causal factor in the memory loss.

In this deviant-case analysis, the quasi-independent variable—alcohol abuse—was selected, not manipulated. Further, the comparison case is a nonequivalent control, because the case also was selected and not randomly assigned to the "control" condition. These threats to internal validity make it difficult to come to firm causal conclusions. The best that the researcher can hope for is to probe for suspected causal factors as carefully as possible. The comparison case permits the tentative conclusion that simply being old or being a scientist do not by themselves result in severe memory deficits. Additional comparisons showed that P.Z.'s inability to remember new information was similar to that exhibited by other alcoholics (also a nonequivalent control group). Alcohol abuse is the prime suspect remaining.

In a sense, therefore, interpreting a case history is similar to doing detective work. The typical case study involves a large number of dependent variables. Thus, the researcher who wishes to make causal statements on the basis of a case study has to look for important clues and then interpret the meaning of those clues in the context of all the other observations. Be careful how you interpret this discussion. As a laboratory research design, the one-shot case study with only one or two dependent variables would be sloppy and internally invalid. It is simply a terrible experimental design. However in the typical case study, in which a great deal of information is available, causal "detective" work is often more reasonable and more likely to lead to internally valid conclusions. The researcher gains control by increasing the number and complexity of the observations. Remember too that case studies often involve retrospective reports, which means that the life-history "facts" may be forgotten or distorted. A cautious investigator might tentatively accept the reports as internally valid.

Case studies are a major source of descriptive data for clinical psychology. As we have just seen, deriving causal conclusions from them is very difficult. Can case studies be used for prediction? This issue is addressed in the Application section.

Interrupted-Time-Series Design.   The **interrupted-time-series design** is often encountered in quasi-experimental research, and it represents the logical extension of the general observation-treatment-observation design (see Table 11–1). In the simplest time-series design, we have a single experimental group for which we have multiple observations before and after a naturally occurring treatment. Instead of examining just one or two third-grade classes, we could observe third-grade classes over several years. Or we could follow the achievement of the pupils across their entire school career. We need to know when the time series is interrupted by some treatment. Then we compare observations before and after the treatment to see whether it had any effect. Suppose we had records of public-school achievement for a city that added fluoride to its water one year. We would plot achievement against time and look for changes in achievement subsequent to fluoridation.

Such a hypothetical time-series analysis is shown in Figure 11–5 (page 286). What we look for in a time-series analysis are changes following interruption by the treatment. Note the rather dramatic increase in achievement following the introduction of fluoride. Can we assert that fluoride causes better achievement? No—for the same reason that we have difficulty interpreting a single correlation coefficient. Possibly, fluoride had an indirect effect, which means that some confounding factor is the principal cause. Perhaps fluoride reduced absenteeism resulting from dental appointments, and it was the reduced absences that permitted higher achievement. The possibility of such indirect effects makes it difficult for researchers to arrive at internally valid conclusions.

In our example, we could examine the absence rate before and after the introduction of fluoride. This could be done by plotting absence rate as well as achievement over time. Or we could try to find a control group that was similar to our experimental group but was untreated with fluoride. Finding a satisfactory control group might be difficult (imagine trying to find a town that differed from yours on only one dimension). Furthermore, such a control group would be nonequivalent and would leave us open to

PREDICTING BEHAVIOR FROM CASE STUDIES

Case studies provide substantial information about an individual, and clinical psychologists often rely on them to determine the causes of current behavior. However, such an endeavor may be difficult, and valid causal statements from case studies may be impossible. Are case studies good for predicting future behavior? You know that prediction on the basis of correlations can be successful. Can the information from a case study be used in the same way?

Given that you are a psychology major taking a college-level course in research methods, can we predict that you will be a research psychologist? Based just on your case, our prediction is likely to be inaccurate. If we examine the case histories of some psychologists, it is easy for us to see that prediction can be poor.

John B. Watson (1878–1958), founder of the school of behaviorism in psychology and pioneer in the field of learning, was a philosophy major as an undergraduate. After he was forced out of academic psychology because of an adulterous affair with a graduate student, he became an executive in a large advertising agency.

Probably none of his classmates or teachers would have predicted that B. F. Skinner would become an influential and famous

the problems of matching. Of course, our control group would have to have an absence rate similar to that of the experimental group, but it would still be nonequivalent because random assignment was not used.

Although a no-treatment control is often desirable, there are other things to look for in a time-series analysis that may be helpful (back to the detective's clues). We can use several dependent variables, such as absenteeism and the number of extracurricular activities, but we also can examine other treatments in much the same way that a case study is combed for additional hints. Time series often involve a long time period, so the researcher has to rely on the availability of complete and accurate records. In our example, we would need to have detailed records of every student, the administration, and the faculty in order to make internally valid statements. Without these records, we could not rule out plausible alternative explanations.

Even with the records, there may be difficulties. The innumerable other changes that can take place mean that confounding is always a threat to internal validity. Over a 30-year period, performance in school could change for several reasons, and these natural treatments could operate in-psychologist. Skinner was an English major as an undergraduate, and after graduation he spent some time leading a bohemian life as an aspiring writer of fiction.

As a more contemporary example, consider Gordon H. Bower, the distinguished investigator of learning and memory. Bower, who wanted to be a psychiatrist, attended college on a baseball scholarship. He had received offers of professional baseball contracts, but a fortunate experience in an experimental psychology course and a desire to avoid the military draft led him to choose experimental psychology over baseball.

Each of these vignettes indicates that accurate predictions from case studies can be difficult. This difficulty is very obvious in the field of criminal law, where it is often necessary to predict whether convicted felons will continue their criminal behavior or be law-abiding citizens following their release. There is considerable controversy in psychology and psychiatry concerning attempts to predict the future actions of a dangerous criminal, such as a murderer or a rapist. Accurate predictions about rapists and murderers are crucial, but difficult. Usually only a weak probabilistic statement can be made: "The chances are that this criminal will not rape again." Most people do not consider this a strong enough prediction. To generate more accurate predictions, we need more detailed information than a simple case study can provide. At the very least, a substantial number of correlations among various kinds of behavior patterns must be made before reasonable predictions are possible. An important area of research awaits you.

dependently or they could interact. Teachers and administrators change, curriculum changes, and economic changes occur, which could all lead to internal invalidity. A major source of confounding in a long-term time series is what is called **mortality.** Pupils graduate and move away, or they may die. Such changes in the group of subjects would lead to a special form of selection bias (Cook and Campbell, 1979), because the same subjects would not be studied before and after the introduction of the treatment.

The difficulties of the interrupted-time-series design are magnified when the effect of the treatment is delayed or masked by other variables (Cook and Campbell, 1979). The effects of fluoride are unlikely to be immediate. Fluoride reduces dental problems, such as cavities. If absenteeism changes because of a reduction in cavities, then we might have additional interpretive problems. Cavities take time to develop, and fluoride does not eliminate cavities once they have taken hold. Thus, the effects of fluoride might be delayed, and we would not be in a position to interpret what caused the changes in achievement. Furthermore, the effects of fluoride could be masked by the intrusion of some variable that counteracts its effects, such as a bubble-gum factory moving to town.

FIGURE 11–5
A hypothetical example of a time-series analysis of the effects of fluoride on school achievement scores.

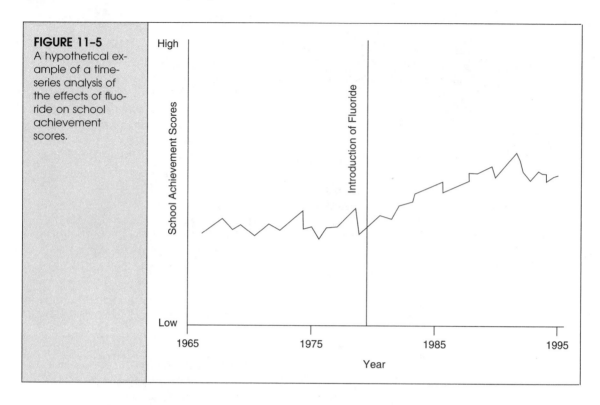

These cautions notwithstanding, the interrupted-time-series design is very useful, especially in applied research. A good example of a time-series analysis is a study by McSweeny (1978) who showed that the introduction of a small fee for directory assistance (the "Information" operator) dramatically reduced the number of directory-assistance calls. Because most such calls were for numbers and addresses that were published, the telephone company wanted to eliminate these nonessential calls to keep the lines open for essential assistance. The number of daily calls in Cincinnati dropped by about 70,000 following the introduction of the 20-cent fee, showing that the strategy was an effective one.

Phillips used time-series analyses to investigate some of the psychological reasons leading to death. In an extensive and interesting series of papers, Phillips examined some of the causes of natural death (1972), the precipitants of suicide (1977, 1978), and the causes of homicides (1983). His general strategy involves determining the number of deaths before and after a particular event. Thus, death rate is the dependent variable, and the quasi-independent variable is the event that interrupts the time span over which Phillips makes his observations. Let us examine how he used an interrupted-time-series analysis to investigate the effects of mass-media violence on homicide rates in the United States.

Phillips began his study of the effects of media violence on homicides by carefully examining the literature on television violence and aggression (see the discussion in Chapter 7 about the work by Eron and associates). From this literature, he concluded that aggression was most likely to occur following a story in which violence appeared to be (1) justified, (2) exciting,

(3) real, and (4) rewarded. A natural violent event that fits these characteristics is a heavyweight-boxing match. Using an interrupted-time-series analysis, Phillips determined the number of homicides that occurred before and after boxing matches that received wide media presentation over the period 1973–1978.

Phillips found a remarkable 12.4 percent increase in homicide rates following the publicized boxing matches. He also found that this increase could not be attributed to extraneous variables such as the season of the year or the day of the week. If there is a causal relationship here, how did Phillips determine the aspects of prize fighting that lead to increase in homicides? Phillips became a detective. First, he determined that boxing matches do not simply precipitate a homicide that would have occurred in the absence of the match. He arrived at this conclusion by showing that the number of homicides did not go down before boxing matches, which they would have to do if the homicide rate is roughly constant over time and is merely pushed into reality by the match. Second, Phillips ruled out the possibility that the homicide rate increased because boxing matches are associated with gambling. He found that other major sporting events usually associated with gambling, such as the Super Bowl and the World Series, do not lead to an increase in the homicide rate.

Phillips concluded that the relationship between boxing and homicide rate is probably a result of modeling; that is, social learning processes that induce people to model or imitate others seem to account for the increase in homicides following the major prize fights. Phillips's reasoning went like this: If imitation or modeling is important, then the victims of homicides should be similar to the victim in the boxing match. This means that if a young white male loses a boxing match, for example, then the murders of young white males should increase, but the murders of young black males should not. Phillips found substantial evidence to support his modeling idea: The increase in homicide rate following a boxing match mostly includes murders of people who are very similar to the losers of the match.

CONCEPT SUMMARY

INCREASING INTERNAL VALIDITY

In case studies, use

- deviant-case analysis
- nonequivalent control
- multiple dependent variables

In interrupted-time-series studies, use

- nonequivalent control
- multiple dependent variables

(Beware of confounding caused by lack of control)

Phillips's use of the interrupted-time-series analysis has been a valuable way to determine the effects of media violence on homicide rate. His use of detective work in trying to arrive at a causal analysis of his findings is a good lesson in probing for answers and rejecting alternative explanations.

Designs Employing Subject Variables

Much research in psychology is concerned with differences in the way various groups of people behave. A **subject variable** is some measurable characteristic of people. Examples are numerous and include intelligence (IQ), weight, anxiety, sex, age, need for achievement, attractiveness, race, ability to recall dreams, as well as many types of pathological conditions (schizophrenia, alcoholism, brain damage, and so on). Subject variables are often used in psychological research, but their use demands special consideration because investigation or selection of them is made after the fact. Thus, because the subject variables are not manipulated directly, designs using subject variables represent one more type of quasi-experimental research.

In experiments, an investigator has control over manipulation of the independent variable; it can be manipulated while all else is held constant. If we are interested in the effect of pornographic movies on physiological arousal and later sexual excitement, we can take two statistically equivalent groups of people (or the same people at different times), show them a movie with pornographic scenes included or omitted (while we hold other variables constant), and measure their responses. We can then be confident (but never certain) that the difference between the movies produced any observed differential effect in arousal. The case is very different with subject variables, though. An experimenter cannot manipulate a subject variable while holding other factors constant; he or she can only select subjects who already have the characteristic to some degree, and then compare them on the behavior of interest. If the subjects in the different groups (say, high, medium, and low IQ) differ on the behavior, we cannot conclude that the subject-variable difference produced or is responsible for the difference in behavior. The reason is that other factors may vary with the subject variable and thus be confounded with it. So if high-IQ subjects perform some task better than low-IQ subjects, we cannot say that IQ produced or caused the difference, because the different groups of subjects are likely to vary on other relevant dimensions such as motivation, education, and the like. When subject variables are investigated, we cannot safely attribute differences in behavior to them, as we can with true experimental variables. Such designs, then, essentially produce correlations between variables, and we should be wary of the same types of confounding that occur in correlational research. We can say that the variables are related, but we cannot say that one variable produced or caused the effect in the other variable.

This is a very important point, so let us consider an example. Suppose an investigator is interested in the intellectual functioning of people suffering from schizophrenia. People diagnosed as belonging to this group are given numerous tests meant to measure various mental abilities. The researcher also gives these tests to another group of people, so-called normals, as a control measure. He or she discovers that schizophrenics do especially poorly (relative to normals) in tests involving semantic aspects of language, such as understanding the meaning of words or comprehending prose passages. The investigator concludes that the schizophrenics perform these tests more poorly *because* they are schizophrenics and that their inability to use language well in communication is a likely contributing cause of schizophrenia.

Studies like this are common in some areas of psychology. Conclusions similar to those just mentioned are often drawn, but they are completely unjustifiable. Both conclusions are based on correlations, and other factors could well be the critical ones. Schizophrenics may do more poorly than normals for any number of reasons. They may not be as intelligent, as motivated, as educated, or as wise at taking tests. Possibly, the fact that they have been institutionalized for a long time with resulting poverty of social and intellectual intercourse accounts for the differences. We cannot conclude that the reason the two groups differ on verbal tests is schizophrenia or its absence in the two groups. Even if we could, it would certainly not imply the other conclusion, that language problems are involved in causing schizophrenia. Again, all we would have is a correlation between these two variables, with no idea of whether or how the two are causally related.

Use of subject variables is very common in all psychological research, but it is absolutely crucial in areas such as clinical and developmental psychology, so the problems with making inferences from such research should be carefully considered. A primary variable in developmental psychology is age, a subject variable, which means that much research in this field is correlational in nature. In general, the problem of individual differences among subjects in psychology is often ignored, though there are often appeals to consider the problem as crucial (for example, Underwood, 1975). Let us look at some ways to make more sound inferences from experiments that use subject variables.

Matching. The basic problem in the investigation of subject variables, and in other quasi-experimental research, is that whatever differences are observed in behavior may be caused by other confounded variables. One way to try to avoid this problem is by **matching** subjects on the other relevant variables. In the comparison of schizophrenics and normals we noted that the two groups were also likely to differ on other characteristics, such as IQ, education, motivation, institutionalization, medication, and perhaps even age. Rather than simply comparing the schizophrenics with normals, we might try to compare them with another group more closely matched on these other dimensions so that the main difference between the groups is in the presence or absence of schizophrenia. For example, we might use a group of neurotics who, on the average, are similar to the schizophrenics in terms of age, IQ, length of time institutionalized, sex, and some measure of motivation. When the two groups have been matched on all these characteristics, then we can more confidently attribute any difference in performance between them to the factor of interest, namely, schizophrenia. By matching, we attempt to introduce the crucial characteristic of experimentation—being able to hold extraneous factors constant to avoid confoundings—into what is essentially a correlational observation. Our goal is to be able to infer that the variable of interest (schizophrenia) produced the observed effect.

There are several rather serious problems associated with matching. For one thing, matching often requires a great deal of effort because some of the relevant variables may be difficult to measure. Even when we go to the trouble of taking the needed additional measures, we may still be unable to match the groups, especially if few subjects are involved before matching is attempted (for example, research on an unusual type of brain damage or other medical disorder). Even when matching is successful, it often greatly reduces the size of the sample on which the observations are made. Thus, we then are less confident that our observations are reliable (stable and repeatable).

Matching is often difficult because crucial differences among subjects may have subtle effects. In addition, the effects of one difference may interact with another. Thus, *interactions* among matched variables may confound the results. To illustrate these difficulties, let us reconsider some of the work done by Brazelton and associates on neonatal behavior mentioned in Chapter 6 (Lester and Brazelton, 1982).

Brazelton's primary interest is in cultural differences in neonatal behavior as measured by the Brazelton Neonatal Behavioral Assessment Scale. The general strategy is to compare neonates from various cultures and ethnic groups with neonates from the United States. In these quasi-experiments, culture or ethnic group, which is a subject variable, is the quasi-independent variable. Attempts are usually made to match the neonates from different cultures along various dimensions such as birth weight, birth length, and obstetrical risk (including whether the mother received medication during birth, whether the baby was premature, and so on). Lester and Brazelton show that there is a synergistic relationship among these factors. **Synergism** in a medical context means that the combined effects of two or more variables are not additive—the combined effect is greater than the sum of the individual components—which means that the variables interact. The way in which neonatal characteristics and obstetrical risk interact is as follows. Studies have shown that the behavior (as measured by the Brazelton scale) of slightly underweight infants is more strongly influenced (negatively) by small amounts of medication taken by the mother than is the behavior of neonates who are closer to the average in weight. So it is very difficult to match subjects appropriately because low birth weight interacts with medication, which has effects on the behavior of the children. Even though the neonates are carefully selected, the synergistic relation between the matched variables can influence the results. This is an especially difficult problem in Brazelton's work, because much of his research has examined neonates from impoverished cultures, where birth weight is low and obstetrical risk is very high. Generally, you should remember that matched variables are rarely under direct control, which means that the possibility of confounding is always present.

Another problem with matching involves the introduction of the dreaded **regression artifact.** Under certain conditions in many types of measurements a statistical phenomenon known as **regression to the mean** occurs. The mean of a group of scores is what most people think of as the average—the total of all observations divided by the number of observations. For example, mean intelligence in a sample of 60 people is the sum of all their intelligence-test scores divided by 60 (see Appendix A). Generally, if people who received extreme scores (that is, very high or very low) on some characteristic are retested, their second scores will be closer to the mean of the entire group than were their original scores.

Extreme scores are likely owing to measurement error. If the error is random and normally distributed (see Appendix A), then subsequent measures will have smaller errors—they will be less extreme. Consider an example. We give 200 people a standard test of mathematical reasoning for which there are two equivalent forms, or two versions of the test that are equivalent. The average (mean) score on the test is 60 of 100 possible points. We take the 15 people who score highest and the 15 who score lowest. The means of these groups are 95 and 30, respectively. Then we test them again on the other form of the test. We might find that the means of the two groups are 87 and 35. On the second test, the scores of the two extreme groups regressed toward the mean; the high-scoring group scored more poorly, whereas the low-scoring group had somewhat better scores. This sequence of events is illustrated in Figure 11–6. In the high-scoring group, some people whose true scores are somewhat lower than the scores they received were simply lucky on the first test and scored higher than they should have. When retested, these subjects tended to score lower, nearer their true score. The situation is reversed for the low-scoring group.

This regression toward the mean is always observed when there is a less-than-perfect correlation between the two measures. The more extreme the selection of scores, the greater the regression toward the mean. It also occurs in all types of measurement situations. If abnormally tall or short parents have a child, its adult height will probably be closer to the population mean than to the height of the parents. As with most statistical phenomena, regression to the mean is true of groups of observations and is probabilistic (that is, it may not occur every time). For example, in the second test of mathematical reasoning, a few individual subjects may score higher or lower than before, but the group tendency will be toward the mean. In any event, if we had selected subjects on the basis of their rea-

FIGURE 11-6
Hypothetical changes in IQ scores resulting from regression to the mean. The high-scoring and low-scoring subgroups regressed toward the mean of the entire group when they were retested.

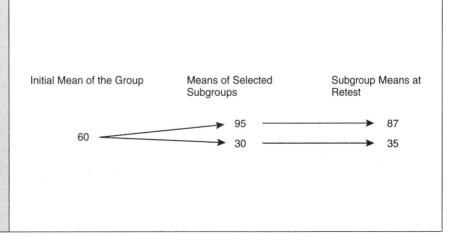

Initial Mean of the Group   Means of Selected Subgroups   Subgroup Means at Retest

60   95   87

30   35

soning scores and then matched them in two groups, subsequent differences may have been caused by some treatment or may have been the result of regression to the mean. If we do not have the true scores, and if we do not use random assignment, then regression to the mean may be a confounding factor leading to changes in behavior.

Ex post facto research and quasi-experiments with subject variables are conducted often to evaluate educational programs, so those who practice such research need to be aware of the many thorny problems associated with it. Without matching, an investigator may not be able to say much about the results. Matching helps alleviate the problem of confoundings in some cases, but then the possibility of regression artifacts arises. And many researchers seem unaware of this problem.

When matching is a practical possibility, and when regression artifacts are evaluated, we can be somewhat more confident of conclusions from our results. But we still have only a correlation, albeit a very carefully controlled one. Matching is useful, but it is not a cure-all. In our example involving schizophrenics, if the schizophrenics perform worse than the new matched control group of neurotics, can we then conclude that schizophrenia *produces* inferiority in language usage? No, we cannot. There could be something else, some other difference between the two groups. We can never be sure that we matched on the relevant variables. Perhaps neurotics are superior in their use of language!

CONCEPT SUMMARY

MATCHING
Be alert for

- synergism
- regression artifacts

Age as a Variable.   One subject variable, age, deserves its own discussion for two reasons. In the first place, developmental psychology is a popular and important part of scientific psychology. In the second place, age as a variable poses very difficult confoundings that have generated some interesting and powerful research designs.

Suppose we are interested in determining the effects of age on the ability to use two types of learning strategies. One type of strategy might improve recall (Tversky and Teiffer, 1976), because when our subjects use this strategy correctly they will be able to associate one thing with another. In remembering the names of simple objects (for example, *knife, tree,* and *cat*), subjects recall one object which helps them recall another object (for example, recalling *cat* reminds them of *tree,* because cats climb trees and trees make them think of *knife,* because they carve their initials in a tree with a knife). We will call this the recall strategy. The other strategy might help your subjects recognize things (as in a multiple-choice test). In this recognize strategy, subjects look for minute differences among objects so that they can later specify which of several similar objects was actually shown to them.

We decide to see how children of different ages utilize these two strategies. How are we going to design our project? The most straightforward (and most likely) design is the **cross-sectional method.** Using this method, we would select children of different ages (for example, age 5, 8, and 12) and then randomly assign half of each age group to one of the strategy conditions. Or we could use the more time-consuming **longitudinal method.** Hence, we would test a subject when he or she was 5, then at 8, and then again at age 12. In the cross-sectional method, we figuratively cut through the age dimension, and in the longitudinal method we follow a particular individual along the age dimension. These two developmental methods are quite often used in studies in which age is a variable, yet they both contain serious confoundings that could make the internal validity of the research highly suspect.

What are some of these serious confoundings? Before we can discuss them, we need to discuss age itself. Age is a subject variable, so it cannot be considered a true independent variable. Age is a dimension; in particular, it is a time dimension along which we can study behavior. Some developmental psychologists have suggested that we consider age as a dependent variable because it is a variable that varies with other subject characteristics from birth to death (Wohwill, 1970).

In any event, we cannot directly vary age, so we must be wary of any concomitant variables associated with it. Different research designs have different confoundings. In the cross-sectional method, age is confounded with the generation of birth. Not only is one of the authors of this textbook 22 years older than his son, he and his son also differ in terms of the generations in which they were born, and generation itself is a complex variable. In this sense the generation gap is real—someone born in 1942 is not just 22 years older than someone born in 1964. The older person was born into a different world populated by different people who had different attitudes and education than the counterparts (what the developmental psychologists call cohorts) of the younger person.

When we use the longitudinal method, we follow a particular individual who will maintain the same cohorts. With this method, therefore, we do not have to worry about the generation/age confounding. However, the longitudinal method confounds age with time of treatment or testing. If you test the memory of a child at age 5 and then at age 12, not only is the person seven years older on the second test, but the world has changed in the interim. Using the longitudinal method, we might find that college students' attitudes about energy conservation in 1991 have changed since the subjects were 5 years old in 1977. Is the change in attitude owing to a change in age or to a change in the world?

Figure 11–7 shows some research designs that can be used when age is a variable. The **time-lag design** (the design indicated along the diagonal) aims at determining the effects of time of testing while holding age constant (only 19-year-olds are tested in this example). As is true of the cross-sectional design, the time-lag design confounds cohorts of the subjects with the target variable.

Schaie (1977) has outlined many sophisticated designs to overcome the confoundings we have just described. One of these designs is illustrated in Figure 11–7. The **cross-sequential design,** indicated by the central box, involves testing two or more age groups at two or more time periods. This design includes features of the other three designs we have mentioned. Subjects of different ages are tested at the same time as in the cross-sectional method; an individual is tested successively as in the longitudinal method; and different subjects of the same age are tested at different times as in the time-lag design. In the cross-sequential design, therefore, the researcher can determine the effects of most of the potential confoundings. Consider just one example from Figure 11–7—the 20-year-old who was born in 1975. The effects of age are tested both longitudinally and sectionally (a 20-year-old is compared with subjects of different ages in 1995 and that 20-year-old is tested again in 1996). If the effects of age are the same in both of these comparisons, then we can rule out cohorts and time of testing as important confoundings.

The cross-sequential design is cumbersome. Many subjects have to be tested over a period of time, which may make a research project impractical. Therefore, this design is not used as often as it probably should be. Most developmental researchers use the more manageable cross-sectional design.

A typical cross-sectional experiment has age as a quasi-independent variable as well as another true independent variable. In the Tversky and Teiffer (1976) study outlined earlier, three age groups were tested on their ability to use the recall strategy and the recognize strategy. The recall strategy improved retention at all ages (5, 8, and 12), but the recognize strategy proved beneficial only to the oldest children. Such results are an example of an **interaction** (see Chapter 8), which means that the effects of one variable are dependent on the level of the other variable—the effects of type of strategy depended on the age of the subjects.

The tactic of using age and a true independent variable in developmental research means that the researcher expects an interaction. Whatever variables are confounded with age (in the Tversky and Teiffer study, age was confounded with grade in school in addition to the usual confoundings associated with a cross-sectional design) might be differentially affected by a true independent variable. The clever psychologist tries to pinpoint what components of age determine thought and behavior, and the search for particular interactions may help. The purpose of both the cross-sequential

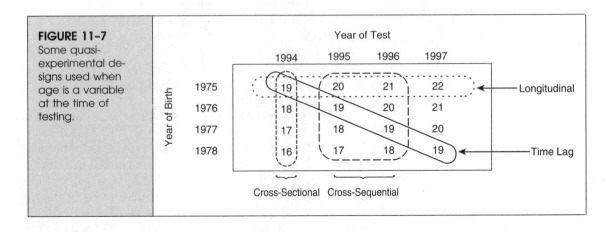

FIGURE 11–7
Some quasi-experimental designs used when age is a variable at the time of testing.

design and the search for interactions is to enhance the internal validity of developmental research. Age is a complex variable, and we must simplify it in order to have a valid analysis.

A final way that the internal validity of research with subject variables can be enhanced is to use construct validity as a mode of converging operation (see Chapter 12). Instead of searching for interactions to try to tease apart the true effects of a subject variable from those effects owing to variables that are correlated with it, we could coordinate the results with a particular theory. Highly refined theories of personality and child development use this technique. For example, Piaget developed a comprehensive theory of child development that makes particular predictions about the kinds of behavior exhibited by children at different stages of cognitive development (Piaget and Inhelder, 1969). Although these stages are partially associated with chronological age, they are presumed to be a function of maturation and experience. Thus, the stage of development, as shown in certain kinds of behaviors, and not age, is viewed as the causal factor. Piaget's theory specifies how and when these stages will occur, so that age-related behavioral differences should fit into the network of the theory. When the predicted changes do occur (that is, when they agree with Piaget's theory), we say that there is construct validity for the theory. The theory permits one to rule out the effects of a correlated variable (age in this case) and converge on an explanation of why certain behaviors are observed.

CONCEPT SUMMARY

THREATS TO INTERNAL VALIDITY IN QUASI-EXPERIMENTAL RESEARCH WITH SOME SOLUTIONS

Research Procedure	Threat to Internal Validity	Ways to Enhance Internal Validity
Case studies	Source of causation; baseline "condition" maturation; history; selection bias	Deviant-case analysis (a nonequivalent control); detective work
Interrupted time series	Changes in subjects and environment; delayed effects	Nonequivalent control group; detective work
Subject variables	Dimensions on which to match; regression artifacts	Matching; include true independent variable and seek interactions
Age as a variable	Confoundings with time of testing, generation of birth	Cross-sequential design; include a true independent variable and seek an interaction; converging operations

SUMMARY

1. The use of small-n designs usually assumes that valid conclusions can be reached by making large numbers of observations on a few subjects in a carefully controlled situation.

2. The reversal design (ABA design) is a common within-subjects design that involves independent-variable periods (B phases) interspersed among baseline periods (A phases).

3. One extension of the reversal design involves numerous baseline periods and more than two levels of the independent variable.

4. The multiple-baseline design involves assessing different behaviors (within-subjects) or different people (between-subjects) for baseline periods of different length prior to introducing the independent variable.

5. The multiple-baseline design is useful when the independent variable has strong carryover effects or when the behaviors to be altered are not independent of each other.

6. The case study is a common small-n design used in clinical psychology.

7. In research that is internally valid, straightforward statements can be made about cause and effect. In quasi-experimental research, in which there is no direct control over the independent variables (they are examined after the fact), causal statements may not be possible because of confoundings.

8. Quasi-experiments have one or more ex post facto components: either naturally occurring variables or subject variables (or both).

9. When there are natural treatments, problems such as history, maturation, selection bias, and nonequivalent control groups may confound the results.

10. One-shot case studies and the interrupted-time-series design are two quasi-experimental procedures with low internal validity. The researcher must be a good detective to determine the causal agents in these procedures, because mortality and delayed effects are threats to internal validity.

11. Likewise, the researcher needs to be a good detective when he or she tries to handle subject variables by matching subjects on the basis of particular characteristics. Just what characteristics are to be matched often poses a difficult problem, and those characteristics may regress toward the mean in many instances, and interactions among the matched variables may occur.

12. Age as a subject variable provides many real threats to internal validity because it is confounded with numerous other factors.

13. Using the cross-sequential design and looking for interactions of age with true independent variables are two ways to enhance the internal validity of developmental research.

■ KEY CONCEPTS

ABA design	nonequivalent control group
AB design	observation-treatment-observation
cross-sectional method	one-shot case study
cross-sequential design	quasi-experiment
history	regression artifact
interaction	regression to the mean
interrupted-time-series design	reversal design
large-*n* design	selection bias
longitudinal method	small-*n* design
matching	subject variable
maturation	synergism
mortality	time-lag design
multiple-baseline design	

■ EXERCISES

1. Discuss the logic underlying the use of the reversal design and extensions of it. How do these relate to Mill's joint method of agreement and difference?

2. [*Special Exercise.*] A considerable amount of evidence indicates there is an inverse relationship between birth order and intelligence (Zajonc and Marcus, 1975). Birth order refers to the order in which children enter the family unit (first born, second born, and so on). Intelligence tends to be lower for later-born children than for the earlier ones. List as many factors as you can that might be confounded with birth order. How might you determine which of these factors is important in influencing intelligence? In other words, how do we enhance internal validity when birth order is the variable? What quasi-experiments can be done?

3. The *Journal of Applied Psychology* often reports studies that used an interrupted-time-series design. Examine several recent issues and note, in particular, any control conditions that are included.

■ SUGGESTED READINGS

You will find that the following book discusses both the design of small-*n* experiments and the application of behavior-modification techniques to your own problems: Williams, R. D., & Long, J. D. (1979). *Toward a self-managed life style* (2nd ed.). Boston: Houghton-Miflin.

An interesting source of clinical case studies is the work of Oliver Sacks. One of his most intriguing books is: Sacks, O. (1985). *The man who mistook his wife for a hat and other clinical tales.* New York: Summit.

Donald T. Campbell has written a great deal about quasi-experimental research. The best place to begin is with the first book listed here. More detail is presented in the second one. Campbell, D. T., & Stanley, J. C. (1963). *Experimental and quasi-experimental designs for research.* Chicago: Rand McNally. Cook, T. D. and Campbell, D. T. (1979). *Quasi-experimentation: Design and analysis issues for field settings.* Chicago: Rand McNally.

Can You Put Yourself on a Better Schedule of Reinforcement?

All of us have habits we would like to break, and other habits we would like to develop. Smoking, drinking, nail-biting, watching too much television, and not studying enough are some of the bad habits that college students often say they would like to alter. Failure to control these behaviors is often blamed on laziness or a defective personality. However, a behavioral analysis of such problems suggests a simple alternative to these interpretations: bad habits are being reinforced, and to change them we must alter the schedule of reinforcement by which we live. If all these bad habits are learned, then they can be altered by learning, too. The general aim is to alter the reinforcements in our lives so that they occur after desirable behavior and not after undesirable behavior.

Suppose you are in danger of flunking out of school because you study too little and, being addicted to the movies, you attend them too often. You know you have a problem, but you are in a rut and you do not know how to get out. What can you do to modify your behavior?

The first step is to set a goal for yourself. It is not enough to say that you want to study more; you must have a concrete, measurable goal. Say you decide to study six hours a day outside of class. Your second step would be to institute some means of carefully monitoring your study behavior. How much do you already study, on the average? You should carry a notebook and record every studying episode as it occurs each day, and then total these episodes at the end of the day. You can also get a weekly average. Say you discover at the end of a week that you are averaging 59 minutes of studying per day; obviously you are a long way from your target of six hours a day.

The next step is to set yourself a realistic goal in your first attempt. It might be too much of a shock to your system to go directly from one to six hours of studying per day; worse, you might give up early on, deciding it is impossible. So let us assume that you plan to increase your studying to two hours a day at first. But how? You should analyze the situation and see what activities prevent you from studying. The main deterrent is your going to the movies, but surely other activities also intrude. You might set up an activity schedule to monitor your behavior, as shown in the table on page 301.

You should then try to change your environment so that it is more conducive to study. Try to avoid those friends who might encourage you to go to the movies. Do not avoid them entirely, of course, but plan to spend more time at the place where you study. Analyze your study area—are there many distractions? (These might include roommates, magazines, radios, and televisions.) If there are many distractions, abandon your room as a place of study and find a quiet hideaway where only you and your books will be present. Studies have shown that if you can associate a particular place exclusively with study behavior and then force yourself to go to this place, you can increase studying dramatically. Finally—and this is one of the most important steps—you must figure out a reward for yourself for successfully studying the allotted amount of time. For example, you could promise yourself that if you have studied two hours each day during the first week, you can go to the movies with your friends. Thus one of the main reinforcers in your life—going to the movies—is made contingent on other behavior. In essence, you are reinforcing yourself for studying.

During the next week, try studying three hours a day, continuing to carefully monitor your time and study habits. In each successive week, increase your amount of study per day, until you reach your goal in a few weeks. Technically, you are *shaping* study behavior in yourself by reinforcing successive approximations to the target behavior, just as animals are taught complicated tricks by being reinforced for gradual approximations to them. If you can keep the reinforcement contingencies in place, you will have dramatically changed your behavior.

The case we have used here may not apply directly to your situation, but in all likelihood you have habits you would like to break or change. You can do so by applying the rules specified here: Set a concrete target goal and by reinforcing yourself for each step taken, gradually alter your behavior to approximate that goal. R. D. Williams and J. D. Long have written a book, *Toward a Self-Managed Life Style*, that explores the possibility of changing many areas of our lives by effectively reinforcing positive behavior and not rewarding negative behavior. Besides methods for improving study habits, they discuss behavioral self-management programs for losing weight, increasing exercise, managing time, controlling smoking and drinking, and becoming more assertive.

Time	Monday	Tuesday	Wednesday	Thursday	Friday	Saturday	Sunday
7:00							
8:00							
9:00							
10:00							
11:00							
12:00							
1:00							
2:00							
3:00							
4:00							
5:00							
6:00							
7:00							
8:00							
9:00							
10:00							
11:00							

FINISHING PSYCHOLOGICAL RESEARCH

INTERPRETING THE RESULTS OF RESEARCH

How to assess whether the research is both reliable and valid

Questions to Answer

❏ *Is there a scale-attenuation problem?* Are there ceiling or floor effects?

❏ *Is a regression artifact present?* Do the data provide a "true" measure of the behavior?

❏ *Are the experimental results reliable?* Has the experiment been replicated directly? Have conceptual or systematic replications been undertaken?

❏ *Have the results and concepts been validated by converging operations?* Do the results of several converging observations eliminate alternative explanations of the results?

CHAPTER 12

INTERPRETING THE RESULTS OF RESEARCH

After you have collected and analyzed your data, you are in a position to interpret them. This chapter will help you understand some of the pitfalls that impede correct interpretation of your data. We will consider problems associated with the interpretation of both specific results and results from a connected series of studies. Your data, even if collected and statistically analyzed correctly, may be difficult to interpret if performance is extremely good or extremely bad (the scale-attenuation problem). Often, your subject's true score or performance differs from the data you have collected, which means that a regression artifact has occurred. Have you obtained reliable results—would you find the same effect if the research were replicated? Are your data valid—do several results converge on an understanding of a concept? Solutions to these problems are suggested.

INTERPRETING SPECIFIC RESULTS

The Problem of Scale Attenuation

The first topic we consider here is important but is often overlooked in psychological research. The general problem is how to interpret performance on some dependent variable in an experiment when performance exceeds the limitations of the measurement scale. When performance is at the upper limit of the scale, we say we have a **ceiling effect.** An example of a ceiling effect might be a math test which is so easy that nearly everyone in the class gets all of the problems correct. When performance is at the bottom of the scale, we say we have a **floor effect.** An example of a floor effect might be another math test which is so difficult that no one in the class gets any of the problems correct. Collectively, ceiling and floor effects are known as **scale-attenuation effects.**

To best illustrate scale-attenuation effects, we will use an example of a physical rather than a psychological scale. The advantage of a physical scale is that its accuracy can be objectively determined. We will therefore look at how ceiling effects can make the measurement of a physical characteristic, namely weight, problematic. We will then show how scale attenuation can hinder the interpretation of psychological measures.

Suppose two obese men decided to make a bet as to who can lose the greatest amount of weight in a certain amount of time. One man looked much heavier than the other, but neither was sure what he actually weighed, because they both made a point of avoiding scales. The scale they decided to use for the bet was a common bathroom scale that runs from 0 to 300 pounds. On the day they were to begin their weight-loss programs, each man weighed himself while the other watched and, to their great surprise, both men weighed in at exactly the same value, 300 pounds. So despite their different sizes, the men decided that they were beginning their bet at equal weights.

The problem here is one of ceiling effects in the scale of measurement. The weight range of the bathroom scale did not go high enough to record the actual weight of these men. Suppose that one really weighed 300 and the other 350, if their weights had been measured on a scale that had a greater range. After six months on the weight-loss program, let us further suppose, each man actually lost 100 pounds. They reweighed themselves at this point and discovered that one now weighed 200 pounds and the other 250. Because they thought they had both started at the same weight (300), they reached the erroneous conclusion that the person who presently weighed 200 had won the bet (see Figure 12–1).

Unfortunately, scale-attenuation effects in research may not be as obvious as the ceiling effect in our contrived example. However, scale attenuation can lead to highly erroneous conclusions, so it is important that you know what to look for in your own research and in the work of others. You should not only be wary of the scale used to measure behavior, but also consider the task imposed on the subjects participating in the project. For example, suppose you devised a memory experiment that involved

FIGURE 12-1
The left panel (a) illustrates the situation as the obese men believed it to be—they started at the same weight and one lost twice as much as the other. The right panel (b) reveals the actual case, with the ceiling effect in the scale of measurement removed. In fact, both men lost 100 pounds. Scale attenuation (ceiling and floor effects) can hide actual differences that may exist between conditions in an experiment.

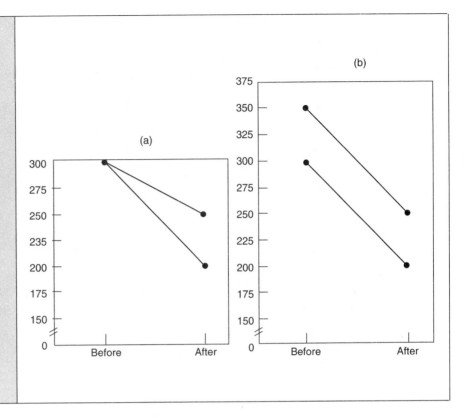

recalling phone numbers. The people in your experiment had to study a typical seven-digit phone number for one minute and then had to dial that number on a telephone. You would probably discover that all of your subjects did fine; in fact, they all remembered the numbers perfectly. What does that tell you? If a task is too easy (or too difficult), differences in behavior will not appear. Whenever you examine research results, you should ask yourself: Are the limits on performance I observe legitimate ones, or are they imposed by the measurement scale or the task used to assess behavior?

The Eyes Have It: Scarborough's Experiment.   Let us consider the results of an experiment that contains a scale-attenuation problem. Scarborough (1972) was interested in the question of modality differences in retention. Do we remember information better if it comes through our eyes or through our ears? Is information better remembered if it is presented to both the ears and the eyes simultaneously than it if is presented to only one or the other? These questions have both theoretical and practical importance. When you look up a phone number and need to remember it while you cross the room to the telephone, is it sufficient to simply read the number silently to yourself as you usually do, or would it be better for you to also read the number aloud so that information enters both your ears and your eyes?

In Scarborough's experiment, all subjects received 36 consonant trigrams (for example, *JBT*) presented for .7 second. There were three groups of six subjects; the method by which the trigrams were presented differed for each group. One group saw the trigrams (visual-only condition); another group heard the trigrams (auditory only); and a third group both saw and heard the trigrams (visual plus auditory). Three between-subjects conditions (visual only, auditory only, visual plus auditory) were combined with six within-subjects conditions (retention intervals of 0, 3, 6, 9, 12, or 18 seconds) in the experiment. The retention interval is the delay between trigram presentation and attempted recall.

The results of Scarborough's experiment are reproduced in Figure 12–2, where the percentage of times a trigram was correctly reported is plotted as a function of retention interval. It is apparent from this figure (and Scarborough's statistics offer support) that subjects who received only visual presentation of the trigrams generally recalled them a greater percentage of the time than subjects who received only auditory presentation. Furthermore, receiving the information in both modalities simultaneously did not produce any better recall than receiving the information only visually; the percentage correct at each retention interval is roughly the same for visual-only and visual-plus-auditory subjects. So far so good. But what else can we conclude from Figure 12–2? Can we conclude anything about the rates of forgetting information that is presented auditorily and visually? Is the rate of forgetting the same or different in the two cases? Did you ask yourself about the source of limitation on performance?

FIGURE 12-2
The probability of correctly recalling a stimulus trigram as a function of the three presentation conditions and the duration of the counting task. Notice that (a) visual presentation is generally superior to auditory presentation, and (b) simultaneous auditory and visual presentation is no better than visual-only presentation. (Scarborough, 1972. Copyright 1972 by the American Psychological Association. Reprinted by permission of the author.)

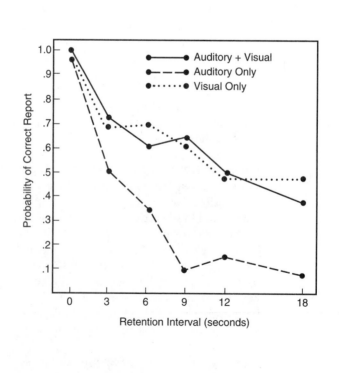

Scarborough was quite careful on this score. Although the auditory-only and visual-only functions appear to diverge increasingly as the retention interval becomes longer, Scarborough did not draw the conclusion that the rate of forgetting is greater for information presented through the ears than through the eyes. However, consider what Massaro (1975) has to say about this experiment:

> The figure shows that the curves intercept the Y ordinate at roughly the same point and diverge significantly. The intercept value at zero sec. provides a measure of the original perception and storage of the stimuli, since it measures how much information the subject has immediately after the presentation of the stimuli, when no forgetting has taken place. The rate of forgetting can be determined from the slopes of the forgetting functions. According to this analysis, Figure [12–2] shows that the items presented auditorily are forgotten much faster than the items presented visually. (pp. 530–531)

Unfortunately, this conclusion must be called into question. We have the same problem the obese men had: Our scale at the ceiling is not sensitive enough. Performance at the zero-second retention interval is very nearly perfect in all conditions. When performance is perfect, it is impossible to tell whether there are any real differences among conditions because of scale attenuation, in this case a ceiling effect. If the scale of the dependent measure were really long enough, it might show differences between auditory and visual presentation even at the zero-second retention interval. So Massaro's conclusion that the rate of forgetting is greater for auditory than for visual presentation cannot be accepted on the basis of the argument we just quoted, because the assumption of equivalent performance at the zero-second retention interval may not be correct. There is no better way for us to know the rate of forgetting in the two conditions than there is for the obese men to know the rate of weight loss in judging who won their bet. In neither case can we assume equivalent initial scores before the measurement of loss begins.

Possible Solution.   How can we avoid misinterpretation after the data are collected? (We might have considered using an additional dependent variable, such as time to respond, but the experiment had been completed. Response, or more commonly, reaction time, might have spread out the scale by showing faster times for better-learned trigrams.)

One way to avoid this problem in Scarborough's experiment is to ignore the data points at the zero-second retention interval and ask whether the rate of forgetting is greater between three and eighteen seconds for auditory than for visual presentation. We can do this by computing an interaction between presentation and retention interval over the range of 3 to 18 seconds. However, by simply inspecting Figure 12–2, we get some idea as to whether the auditory-only and visual-only points are diverging increasingly. We see that they are diverging increasingly between 3 and 9 seconds, but after that the difference between them remains constant. However, this lack of an increasingly larger difference over the last three points may be caused by a floor effect in the auditory-only condition because performance is so poor, especially on the last point (only 7 or 8 percent correct). We must be very careful in interpreting data when ceiling or floor effects exist. A prudent investigator would hesitate to draw any conclusion from the data in Figure 12–2 about rates of forgetting, which is just what Scarborough did. But we should also note that over the retention intervals where there are neither ceiling nor floor effects (3, 6, and 9 seconds), forgetting seems to be greater with auditory than with visual presentation.

Unfortunately, there are no hard-and-fast rules for avoiding scale-attenuation problems. Researchers usually try to design their experiments to avoid extremes in performance, and they often test small groups of pilot subjects (see Chapter 1 for a discussion of pilot work). If these subjects perform near the ceiling or floor of the scale, then revision of the experimental task often will be necessary. For example, if performance in a memory experiment is too good (remember the hypothetical telephone-number experiment described at the beginning of the chapter), the amount of material being given can be increased so as to lower performance. Similarly, if the task is so hard that people barely remember anything, the task can be made easier by reducing the amount of material, presenting it more slowly, and so on. The careful investigator will usually make the effort to test pilot subjects before launching into an experiment that may turn out later to have been flawed by ceiling or floor effects. As noted in Chapter 1, the testing of pilot subjects also permits the researcher to learn about other problems in the design or procedure of the experiment.

CONCEPT SUMMARY

BEWARE OF CEILING AND FLOOR EFFECTS

Conduct pilot work to determine scale sensitivity and task difficulty.

Regression Artifacts

A serious problem in many areas of research is known as statistical **regression to the mean,** or the **regression artifact.** The word *artifact* in this context refers to an unwanted effect that occurs during an investigation (thus, it is a synonym for confounding factor), and *regression* means to go back to the mean or true score (this problem was outlined in Chapter 11—now we will consider it in detail).

You can best appreciate this unwanted phenomenon by allowing yourself to become a victim of it. Try the following exercise, proceeding through the steps as given:

1. Roll six dice on a table in front of you.

2. Place the three dice showing the lowest numbers on the left, and the three dice showing the highest numbers on the right. In case of ties, randomly assign the dice to the two groups.

3. Compute and record the mean number-per-die for each group of three dice.

4. Raise both hands over your head and loudly proclaim, "Improve, in the name of science."

5. Roll the three low-scoring dice and compute a new mean number-per-die for the low group.

6. Roll the three high-scoring dice and compute a new mean number-per-die for the high group.

7. Compare the pre- and posttreatment scores for both groups of dice. Combine your data with that of your classmates, if possible.

On the average, this experiment will produce an increase in the performance of the low group and a decrease in the performance of the high group. You might be tempted to conclude that invoking the name of science has a beneficial effect on underachieving dice, but that overachieving dice require more individual attention to maintain their outstanding performance. Such conclusions, however, fail to consider the effects of regression to the mean. This regression artifact reflects the tendency of many types of measures to yield values close to their mean. You know that the role of a fair die can yield values from 1 to 6, but that the average value from many rolls will be about 3.5. The likelihood of the average of three dice being close to 3.5 is higher than the likelihood of this average being close to 1 or 6. Thus, when you select three dice that give you a low average and then you roll them again, they will tend to yield a higher average value (a value closer to the mean of 3.5). In the same way, the three dice in the high group should yield a lower value when rolled again.

What does all this have to do with psychological research? By now you are well aware of the fact that accurate measurement lies at the heart of assessing the effects of a variable. Whenever there is a measurement error, such as the regression artifact, there is also the possibility of wrongly concluding that some sort of change has occurred or has failed to occur. Although this statement may appear less than profound to you, a number of psychological studies have been faulted for failing to take adequate account of its truth.

Quasi-experimental designs (see Chapter 11), like the dice exercise, are particularly susceptible to bias because of the regression artifact. In such studies, you will remember, subjects are not assigned to treatment and control groups on a random basis, but on the basis of some factor or factors not under experimental control, such as IQ scores or SAT scores. Whenever subjects are assigned to groups because of particularly high or particularly low test scores, regression artifacts are a danger. In a group chosen for low values on some measure, regression to the mean might inflate the apparent effect of some treatment (e.g., "Improve, in the name of science.") Conversely, when a group is chosen for high values on some measure, the effects of a treatment might be masked by the group's tendency to score closer to the mean (and hence lower) on a second test.

The reason regression to the mean often occurs is that all psychological measures are subject to a certain amount of unreliability, or measurement error. Without measurement error, no regression artifact is possible. For instance, if you were to measure the height of each of your classmates to the nearest foot and then measure the shortest and tallest of them again, you would be unlikely to observe any regression to the mean because such gross physical measurements are nearly perfect. With any measure that is not perfectly reliable, however, the group of subjects obtaining the highest scores contains not only those who really belong in the highest category, but also others who are placed in this category owing to chance errors of measurement. On a retest, the chance measurement errors that inflated some of the scores are unlikely to be as large; therefore, the observed score will not be as high. The regression artifact does not imply that the true score of the subject has changed. Regression to the mean merely implies that the initial measurement contained error. To illustrate this point more clearly, an example of regression to the mean with a physical scale might be useful. Imagine that you measured the weight of each of your classmates on an unreliable bathroom scale: On any given weighing, it could err by as much as 25 pounds in either direction. As a consequence, some people of average weight were recorded as being very heavy, others as being very light. If you were to weigh everyone again on the same scale, it is unlikely that the average people who weighed in at the extreme ends of the scale would get the same erroneous readings a second time. The second weighing of the high and low weight people would therefore show regression to the mean; however, no one would claim that there was any actual change in weight.

Regression in Compensatory Education.   The importance of regression artifacts in quasi-experimental studies of education has been the subject of much debate. One influential study of the effects of the Head Start program of the 1960s (Cicirelli & Granger, 1969) received particular attention. In this study, called the Westinghouse-Ohio study, children completing their Head Start experience were randomly selected for evaluation. A control population of children from the same area who had been eligible for the program but had not attended was then defined. Control children were selected at random to be matched with experimental children on the basis of sex, racial or ethnic group membership, and kindergarten attendance. After the final selection of experimental and control subjects was made, additional measures of socioeconomic status, demographic status, and attitude were compiled and compared in the two groups. Differences were reported to be slight. Measures of experimental (Head Start) and control (no Head Start) children's academic achievement and potential were then computed and compared. The general conclusion from this large study was that Head Start was not effective in removing the effects of poverty and social disadvantage.

Other psychologists (Campbell and Erlebacher, 1970a) were quick to criticize this study on several grounds. First, they pointed out that the results of the study were undoubtedly caused partially by regression artifacts. Worse, the magnitude of the artifacts could not be estimated, casting doubt over the entire set of findings.

What is the basic problem? Can you see why the matching of subjects may not have been effective? Cicirelli and Granger laudably tried to match the sample of disadvantaged children who had been in the Head Start program with others from the same area who had not been in the program. Differences that show up later between the two groups should result from the program. Right? Not necessarily. That conclusion is correct only if the two samples came from the same underlying population distributions, which is unlikely.

What is more likely is that the two populations differed, with the disadvantaged treatment (Head Start) children coming from a population that was poorer in ability than the control (no Head Start) children. The treatment children were usually preselected to be from a disadvantaged background: That is why they were included in the program. The control subjects, on the other hand, who were not in the program, were likely to be from a different population that was greater in ability (a nonequivalent control group). The basic problem was that subjects were not randomly assigned to conditions, so the researchers tried to match control subjects with experimental subjects. To match samples from these different populations, the experimenters had to select children *above* the population mean for the disadvantaged treatment group and *below* the population mean for the control group. But when this was done, the regression artifact was introduced. When each group was retested, the subjects' performance tended to regress to the mean of the group; in other words, the disadvantaged group tended to perform worse on the retest and the control group tended to perform better.

Regression to the mean can occur in the absence of any treatment being given and despite matching. Because in the Head Start study we already expected a difference between groups (favoring the control), regression to the mean makes it difficult to evaluate the outcome of the study. Cicirelli and Granger found no difference between the groups. Given that the treatment (Head Start) group was probably worse to begin with, does this mean the group actually improved because of Head Start?

It is impossible to answer this question, because in the Westinghouse-Ohio evaluation of Head Start the direction or magnitude of regression artifacts could not be assessed. In the preceding paragraph, we made reasonable assumptions concerning regression artifacts in this type of study. Strictly speaking, however, we cannot conclude that Head Start had no effect. In fact, we cannot draw any conclusion on the basis of that study, because we do not know how regression artifacts affected the results.

In general, then, regression artifacts of a difficult-to-estimate magnitude are highly probable in this type of study, a fact acknowledged by most researchers. Why, then, would such studies be conducted, particularly when important political, economic, and social decisions will be based on their results? This question was raised both by Campbell and Erlebacher (1970a, b) and by Cicirelli and his supporters (Cicirelli, 1970; Evans and Schiller, 1970). Their answers were quite different, and they represent the type of issue that frequently confronts scientists but which science can never resolve. Campbell and Erlebacher (1970a) proposed that bad information was worse than no information at all; that if properly controlled experiments could not be performed, then no data should be gathered. On the other side of the issue, Evans and Schiller replied, "This position fails to understand that every program *will* be evaluated by the most arbitrary, anecdotal, partisan, and subjective means" (p. 220). Campbell and Erle-bacher concurred but stated that "we judge it fundamentally misleading to lend the prestige of science to any report in a situation where no scientific evaluation is possible" (1970b, p. 224). As a final solution, they proposed that a commission "composed of experts who are not yet partisans in this controversy" be convened to decide the matter.

Possible Solutions. We may not be able to decide this issue on strictly rational grounds, but we can all agree that a research study should be conducted according to the best scientific procedures available. After the fact, of course, we are not able to interpret the results of a quasi-experimental study in which there are substantial and unknown regression artifacts. The question becomes: How could the Westinghouse-Ohio study have been properly conducted? The best way would have been to randomly assign participants to either the no-treatment or treatment conditions. There is no substitute for random assignment in eliminating confounding factors (that is, there is no substitute for doing a true experiment). However, it seems unfair to give half the children who seek the help of a remedial program no training whatsoever. Of course, there is no guarantee at the outset that the program will be beneficial to them; that is what the study is designed to discover. The same issue arises in medical research when a control group with a disease is given a placebo rather than a treatment drug. The argument could be made in both cases that in the long run more people will be aided by careful research into the effectiveness of treatments than may be harmed because treatment is withheld. Unfortunately, the issue is not quite that simple. In the case of medical research, for example, preliminary testing of an antiencephalitis drug showed that 72 percent of the patients receiving the drug survived the disease and led normal lives, but only 30 percent of the control group, which received placebos, survived (Katz, 1979). Is such a toll necessary for effective research design in drug development? Again, the issue is difficult to resolve solely on rational or scientific grounds.

There are other solutions to the regression problem (in the Westinghouse-Ohio study) besides random assignment. One is to randomly assign all the children to different groups and put them in different programs to pit the effectiveness of the programs against one another. The difficulty here is that we do not have a no-treatment baseline, and if the programs turn out to be equally effective, we would not know whether any of them were better than no program at all.

CONCEPT SUMMARY

- **Regression artifacts** mask true behavior in quasi-experiments and matching studies.
- Use random assignment to treatments whenever possible.

INTERPRETING PATTERNS OF RESEARCH

The problems of scale attenuation and regression artifacts focus on the results of a particular piece of research. The topics we want to examine now are concerned with interpreting patterns of research. No single observation can stand alone for long. When we are confronted with the results of psychological research, we must always ask whether they are reliable and valid. In Chapters 5 and 6 we discussed the reliability and validity of data. Here we will expand on some of that discussion so you can grasp the importance of determining whether a particular result displays regularity and whether a particular result displays regularity and whether a particular datum fits with other, related observations.

Reliability and Replication

Suppose we have been hired to assess presidential preferences in the United States. Our job is to find out who the people seem to prefer for president in the upcoming election. After we develop a survey, we take a random sample of the people in the United States. What sorts of things will make us confident of our results? First, we can be more confident that the results accurately reflect the attitudes of the population if our sample consists of 100,000 people rather than only 100. Second, we should expect a second random sample to yield a similar result (assuming that one of the major candidates has not committed a gross moral or legal transgression during the time between the two surveys). Large numbers of observations and a repeatable result are two key factors to ensure reliability. We should always try to maximize the number of observations and devise our research in a way that allows us to determine whether our results are consistent over time.

Test Reliability.   In Chapter 6, we discussed the ways in which **test reliability** is assessed. Remember that a reliable test is one that yields consistent results. If a test is inconsistent because it is poorly designed (and not because of changes in the person taking the test), we will be unable to determine whether the test is measuring what it is supposed to measure. Thus, an unreliable test is also one that is invalid. The same is true of experiments, which we will discuss next.

Experimental Reliability: Replication.   The basic issue regarding reliability of experimental results is simply this: If an experiment were repeated, would the results be the same as those found the first time? Obviously, repeatability is a crucial topic in psychological research, for an experimental outcome may be worthless if we cannot have reasonable certainty that the results are reliable. Because we usually are unable to conduct the same study twice using the same subjects (with the possible exception of some small-n work), we usually repeat an experiment with a different sample of subjects. If the results of the two experiments are similar, we can be confident that we have demonstrated reliability.

Many psychologists find **experimental reliability** more convincing than statistical reliability, because a statistically reliable finding in a single experiment may be the result of a set of accidental circumstances that favor one condition over another. We emphasize that the results of any particular experiment are to be viewed against the background of others on the same issue. If a phenomenon is not repeatable, we are likely to find out rather quickly. **Replication,** a synonym for *copy* or *reproduction,* is the term usually used to describe experimental reliability. We will now consider an example of replication in the context of a series of famous experiments conducted by Luchins (1942).

Luchins's Einstellung (Set) Experiments. Abraham S. Luchins (1942) was interested in the following: "Several problems, all solvable by one somewhat complex procedure, are presented in succession. If afterwards a similar task is given which can be solved by a more direct and simpler method, will the individual be blinded to this more direct possibility?" Subjects may develop a particular approach to a class of similar problems. After the problems are changed so that this set (as in mind set) is no longer the most efficient method of solution, will people hang on to the set, or will they recognize the more direct method? The German word for *set* is **Einstellung;** our everyday problem solving frequently involves an Einstellung: We try our habitual ways of attacking a particular problem even though we may have more efficient procedures readily available to us.

Luchins usually used the water-jar problem in his experiments. People were given two or three jars of water of varying capacity and were supposed to figure out how to obtain a required amount of water by performing arithmetic operations on the volumes the jars would hold. For example, if jar A holds 6 gallons, jar B holds 15 gallons, and jar C holds 2 gallons, how can you obtain exactly 7 gallons? In this example, you could fill jar B (15), then fill jars A (6) and C (2) from the contents of B, leaving 7 gallons in B. The basic 11 problems appear in Table 12–1. To become familiar with

---

TABLE 12-1
The Water-jar Problems Luchins used in his Einstellung Experiments

PROBLEM	GIVEN THE FOLLOWING EMPTY JARS AS MEASURES			OBTAIN THE REQUIRED AMOUNT OF WATER
	A	B	C	
1	29	3		20
2	21	127	3	100
3	14	163	25	99
4	18	43	10	5
5	9	42	6	21
6	20	59	4	31
7	23	49	3	20
8	15	39	3	18
9	28	76	3	25
10	18	48	4	22
11	14	36	8	6

the Einstellung effect, solve all 11 problems in order before you continue reading.

In Luchins's first study, the first problem served as an illustration of the task. The appropriate solution is to take the larger jar (29) and subtract the smaller jar (3) three times to get the desired amount (20). Subjects next solved problems 2 through 6, which may be considered set-establishing problems because they all are most easily solved by the same method of solution. In each case, the solution is to take the largest jar (always the middle one), subtract the first jar once, and finally subtract the last jar twice. If we label the jars A, B, and C from left to right, then the set the subjects developed for problems 2 through 6 can be represented as $B - A - 2C$.

Besides the experimental or Einstellung group, there were two others. One group, a control of sorts, began with problems 7 and 8 so that the experimenter could see how the group would solve them with no induced set solution. Another group was treated in the same manner as the Einstellung group, except that before problem 7 each subject wrote "Don't be blind" on the response sheet. Luchins had the subjects write this phrase so that they would be cautious and not be foolish when they solved subsequent problems. Thus, the primary dependent variable was the number of subjects using the Einstellung solution ($B - A - 2C$) on problems 7 and 8, even though problems 7 and 8 had much more efficient and direct solutions ($A - C$ for 7 and $A + C$ for 8). The results were that none of the control subjects used the inefficient solution in solving problems 7 and 8, 81 percent of the Einstellung subjects used the inefficient solution on 7 and 8, and the "Don't be blind" warning reduced the use of the Einstellung solution to about 55 percent. Furthermore, after doing problem 9, which cannot be solved via the set-inducing method, 63 percent of the Einstellung subjects continued with the old solution on problems 10 and 11, whereas only 30 percent of the "Don't be blind" subjects reverted to the set solution.

How reliable are the results from this experiment? Luchins's work was published before the use of statistical tests was common in psychological research, so statistical tests to establish reliability were not performed. However, such tests were largely unnecessary in this case, because Luchins provided us with evidence that his results could be replicated in other experiments. Many experiments are included in the original report, and the results are in general agreement with the Einstellung results just outlined. Altogether, Luchins tested more than 9,000 subjects in his original studies. As noted previously, experimental reliability or replication is an exceptionally convincing way to demonstrate the reliability of a phenomenon—the Einstellung effect is a reliable one.

There are three types of replications: direct, systematic, and conceptual. **Direct replication** is simply repeating an experiment as closely as possible with as few changes as possible in the method. Luchins replicated his original experiment several times with only slight changes in the subject population tested; such experiments constitute cases of direct replication.

In a **systematic replication,** all sorts of factors are changed that the investigator considers irrelevant to the phenomenon of interest. If the phenomenon is not illusory, it will survive these changes. So, for example, in a systematic replication of Luchins's experiments, we might vary the nature of the problems so that the set involves a different rule (or several different rules), vary the instructions, vary the type of subjects used, and so on. The Einstellung effect should be robust across all of these manipulations. If it is not, then we have found that variables previously thought to be irrelevant are actually important, and this is crucial knowledge.

In a **conceptual replication,** we attempt to replicate a phenomenon or concept in an entirely different way. In the language of Chapter 6, we simply use a different operational definition of the concept. Luchins examined other tasks besides the water-jar problem to establish the Einstellung phenomenon in diverse situations. He used series of geometry problems, words hidden in letters, and paper mazes. Although the operational definitions of a problem and of a solution changed from experiment to experiment, in each case, subjects solved several problems that had a unique solution before they came to the critical problems that could be solved either by the Einstellung solution or by a much more simple and direct solution. Just as in the water-jar experiments, subjects usually used the old, circuitous solution and ignored the more efficient solution. These experiments constitute conceptual replications of the concept of Einstellung. Although Luchins's classic experiment is more than a half-century old, it is still being replicated in modern times (Schooler, Ohlsson, and Brooks, 1993) and still is cited in current literature (Duncan and Praetorius, 1992).

You should note the following carefully: The problem of reliability of results is interwoven with the problem of generality and validity. As we progress from direct to systematic to conceptual replication, we show not only reliability, but also increasing validity. Are we studying something that ties in with or is related to our knowledge of other psychological phenomena in a reasonable way? A conceptual replication is closely related to converging operations, which are procedures that validate a hypothetical construct used to explain behavior by eliminating alternative explanations.

CONCEPT SUMMARY

To ensure experimental reliability, conduct

- **direct replications,** in which as little as possible is changed
- **systematic replications,** in which many things are varied to determine which variables are truly relevant
- **conceptual replications,** in which the same question is asked using different variables in order to demonstrate generality

---

Converging Operations

Suppose that Luchins had conducted just the one experiment outlined in Table 12–1. What sorts of conclusions could he have drawn from his results (assume, too, that he directly replicated the study so that he knew his results were reliable)? Can he legitimately conclude that Einstellung caused the results? Without additional independent evidence, he could have said

APPLICATION
A FAILURE TO REPLICATE

A variety of behavior-modification techniques (see Chapter 11) have been very successful in treating certain kinds of psychological disorders, including phobias and anxiety, among others. However, these techniques have been spectacularly unsuccessful in treating smoking and overeating behaviors. Current estimates indicate that only 10 to 20 percent of the people treated for smoking or obesity maintain the benefits of behavior therapy (Schachter, 1982). In other words, about 80 to 90 percent of the smokers return to smoking after the therapy, and about the same percentage of obese people gain weight after therapy.

Why is there such a dramatic failure to replicate the success seen with other disorders? The standard interpretation is that smoking and overeating are addictions, which means that these habits are more difficult to break than other unfortunate habits, such as snake phobias. Recently, Schachter has argued that this interpretation is misleading. Schachter interviewed a substantial number of people in two areas of New York state. These people, who represented a broad cross-section of the population, were asked a number of health-related questions. What Schachter found was surprising. The success rate for smokers who had tried to quit was nearly 64 percent, and the average length of time they had refrained from smoking was about seven years. The corresponding figures for the obese people who had tried to lose weight were 63 percent and more than eleven years of successful weight reduction. These results are markedly different from the low success rates observed for smokers and overeaters after they had completed formal therapy. Why?

There are at least two reasons Schachter found higher success rates. First, people in the general population are likely to have tried to quit smoking or lose weight several times; in contrast, the therapy results generally refer to one stint in therapy. Thus, the repeated attempts at self-therapy may have increased the number of successful outcomes. Second, those who seek professional help might do so because they have been very unsuccessful in treating themselves. For whatever reason, those who undergo therapy may have a particularly tenacious problem, which would bias against successful results.

Schachter offers his findings as encouragement to those who have tried to lose weight or quit smoking and have failed. "If a first you don't succeed, try, try again."

Schachter, S. (1982). Don't sell habit-breakers short. *Psychology Today, 16,* 27–33.

that the results were owing to a "water-jar effect" or "$B - A - 2C$ effect" rather than an Einstellung effect. This is because each of these concepts was part of the one experiment, and each is a reasonable cause of the results. By doing systematic and conceptual replications, Luchins ruled out the alternative hypotheses of effects limited to particular variables and made the concept of Einstellung a reasonable explanation of the rigidity seen in many problem-solving situations.

In other words, the results of experiments that had different rules and different problems converged on the Einstellung hypothesis by systematically eliminating alternative hypotheses. **Converging operations,** then, are a set of two or more operations that eliminate alternative concepts that might explain a set of experimental results. The importance of converging operations in psychological research was initially emphasized in a landmark paper by Garner, Hake, and Eriksen (1956). They noted that converging operations are necessary to validate operationally defined concepts (see Chapter 1) as well as experimental results. When an abstract concept, Einstellung, for example, is limited to one operational definition, the meaning of the concept is effectively limited to a description of the operations involved. When the concept can be operationally defined in several different ways, however, it can have meaning beyond its operations. Thus, Einstellung refers to a blindness to an easy solution to a problem as a result of prior experience with similar problems having more difficult solutions. The meaning of the term transcends its operational definitions and has construct validity (see Chapter 6). Because converging operations are crucial to an understanding of psychological research and psychological theorizing, we will consider two more examples of converging operations at work.

Stroop Effect: Input or Output?   Before the discussion continues, we want you to try a simple experiment. All you need are some index cards, colored markers, and a watch with a second hand or, even better, a stopwatch. Take 16 index cards and, using your markers, write the name of the color in its color—that is, with green marker write "green," and so on. If you have eight markers, repeat each color twice. If you only have four markers, repeat each color four times. Take another 16 index cards and write color names that do not correspond to the ink—that is, with a green marker write "red," and so on. Your stimuli are now complete. Pick one of your two decks, and for each card, name the color of the ink. Time how long it takes you to go through all 16 cards. Do the same for the other deck. Did you go faster using the deck that had compatible color names and inks?

You probably found that you responded more slowly when ink colors and color names were mismatched than when they were compatible. Furthermore, you probably noticed that you made mistakes, stuttered, and hesitated when the color names and inks were in the incompatible condition. A variation of this frustrating experiment was first done by Stroop (1935); the **Stroop effect** refers to the increase in time required to name the ink color when the ink and color names do not match. This is the same kind of experiment in which you participated in chapter 1, where the mismatch was between the quantity of the digits and the names of those digits.

The Stroop effect is a highly reliable one; the question is, what causes the Stroop effect? One possibility is that it results from the input or perceptual aspects of the task. Stroop and others found that reading is usually faster than naming; therefore, the perceptual argument is that reading color words inhibits the perception of the ink color. An alternative hypothesis is that output (the subject's responses) is affected, not perception. The output notion goes like this: After the subject has perceived both the ink color and the color word, there is response competition when two different color names are elicited—one by the ink and another by the word. On the basis of Stroop's original work, we have no way of deciding between these two hypotheses. Which is important: the perceptual system or the response system?

A simple but clever experiment was conducted by Egeth, Blecker, and Kamlet (1969) to answer this question by using converging operations. Three important conditions from one of their studies are shown in Figure 12–3. The control or baseline condition is shown at the top of the figure (neutral condition). Subjects saw two colored patches with a neutral symbol (XXXX) embedded in them. These patches were either the same color or different colors. An important factor in this study is that instead of responding with color names, the subjects responded SAME when the color of the two patches matched and DIFFERENT when the colors of the two patches were different.

The crucial conditions of the experiment are illustrated in the next rows of Figure 12–3. As in the baseline condition, the subject responded SAME or DIFFERENT on the basis of the colors of the two patches. In the perceptual inhibition condition, color names appeared in the colored patches, and on a given trial the same color name appeared in both boxes. Both colored patches could be the same and match the color name (a SAME trial), or the colored patches could be different, with only one patch matching the names (a DIFFERENT trial). Response competition arises when several responses struggle to be executed (Kantowitz, 1974; St. James, 1990). For example, at a stoplight a red signal calls for a driver to step on the brake with her foot. A green light calls for stepping on the accelerator pedal. If only one signal lamp occurs, there is no response competition. But if the traffic light is defective so that both red and green signals are illuminated, there will be response competition between brake and accelerator pedals because prior learning has strengthened the connections between (1) red traffic lights and brake pedals, and (2) green traffic lights and accelerator pedals.

In the perceptual inhibition condition there is no prior learning to connect color names and the responses SAME or DIFFERENT. Thus, there should be no response competition in this condition. Should responding in this condition be slower than the neutral condition, this result could not be explained by response competition. Therefore, any Stroop effect obtained in the perceptual inhibition condition must result from perceptual inhibition rather than response competition. However, the results obtained by Egeth and his associates were that response times were equal for the perceptual inhibition condition and for the neutral (control) condition. This means that no Stroop effect was obtained. The perceptual similarity between the colors of the patches and the color names failed to produce any Stroop effect. Although this outcome suggests that perceptual factors are not an important cause of Stroop interference, converging operations are needed to bolster this conclusion.

FIGURE 12-3

An outline of some of the conditions in the work by Egeth, Blecker, and Kamlet (1969). In all three conditions, subjects responded SAME when there was agreement among the stimuli and DIFFERENT when there was a mismatch. Subjects saw two colored patches on each trial and responded on the basis of the colors. The neutral condition served as a control by having neutral symbols (XXXX) embedded in colored patches. Color names were in the patches in the perceptual inhibition condition—the color names should inhibit the perception of the colors. SAME or DIFFERENT appeared in the patches in the response competition condition—reading the response SAME in different colored patches should inhibit the correct response of DIFFERENT. The Stroop effect occurred in the response competition condition but not in the perceptual inhibition condition.

	Response	Symbols in Colors		Color of Patches
Neutral Condition	Same	XXXX	XXXX	Both patches red
	Different	XXXX	XXXX	One patch red, one blue
Perceptual Inhibition Condition	Same	RED	RED	Both patches red
	Different	RED	RED	One patch red, one blue
Response Competition Condition	Same	SAME	SAME	Both patches red
	Different	SAME	SAME	One patch red, one blue

So far so good. We seem to have eliminated one alternative as an explanation of the Stroop effect Now for a converging operation that will bring back the Stoop effect and identify the processes involved. To accomplish this, Egeth and coworkers used the condition outlined at the bottom of Figure 12–3. In the response competition condition, the subjects once again responded SAME and DIFFERENT. However, in this condition the words SAME or DIFFERENT rather than neutral symbols or color names appeared in the colored patches. The experimenters reasoned that if response competition is important, then mismatches between SAME or DIFFERENT and the stimulus information should result in slower responding than in the neutral condition. In other words, if conflict among responses causes the Stroop effect, then responding should be slower in the response competition condition than in the neutral condition. This is exactly what they found. The Stroop effect returned: Now the responses SAME and DIFFERENT took longer when they conflicted with the response in the stimulus. Recall that the identical response words did not produce a Stroop effect in the perceptual inhibition condition. Thus, the converging operations removed the perceptual process as an explanation for the results, leaving us to conclude that a response process accounts for the Stroop effect. Other studies on the Stroop phenomenon also lead to the conclusion that response competition is an important contributing factor to Stroop interference (see MacLeod, 1991, for a recent review and McClelland, Cohen, and Dunbar, 1990, for a modern theoretical account of the Stroop effect).

Personal Space.   The concept of **personal space** implies that people are surrounded by invisible bubbles designed to protect them from a wide variety of social encroachments. How do psychologists know that such a bubble exists? It cannot be sensed directly by vision, smell, touch, and the other senses, so the concept must be evaluated indirectly. The next two experiments demonstrate that there is a personal-space bubble; they use two different kinds of spatial invasion and yield similar results.

Ironically, the personal-space bubble that helps a person maintain privacy is best studied by invasions that violate the privacy it affords. A simple experiment conducted by Kinzel (1970) shows one operation that defines personal space. Kinzel was interested in the personal-space bubbles surrounding violent and nonviolent prisoners. Thus one independent variable—more precisely, a subject variable (see Chapter 11), because it was not manipulated—was classification of prisoners as violent (having inflicted physical injury on another person) or nonviolent. Each prisoner stood in the center of an empty room 20 feet wide and 20 feet long. The experimenter than approached from one of eight directions (the second independent variable) until the prisoner said "Stop" because the experimenter was too close. The dependent variable was the distance between prisoner and experimenter when the prisoner said "Stop." If there is no personal-space bubble, the experimenter should be able to walk right up to the prisoner (distance = 0 feet). Control variables were the room and the experimenter, which were the same throughout the experiment. Results of this experiment are shown in Figure 12–4. It is clear that violent prisoners have larger personal-space bubbles than do nonviolent prisoners.

This experiment may not have entirely convinced you that personal-space bubbles exist. In Kinzel's experiment, the personal-space bubble was operationally defined as the point at which the subject said "Stop." A concept based on only one experiment is just a restatement of that particular experimental finding. You may think that there is something strange about a person walking right up to another person without saying anything. Certainly if this happened to you on the street you would think it unusual, to say the least. The next experiment avoids this potential difficulty.

To avoid actively invading someone's personal-space bubble, Barefoot, Hoople, and McClay (1972) gave subjects the opportunity to invade the experimenter's bubble. The experimenter sat near a water fountain and pretended to read a book. Anyone getting a drink of water had to invade the experimenter's personal space. The independent variable was the distance between the experimenter and the water fountain. This could be either 1 foot, 5 feet, or 10 feet. This last distance is large enough so that it exceeds the bounds of the experimenter's personal space and thus is a control con-

FIGURE 12-4
Looking down on the personal-space bubble of violent and nonviolent prisoners. (After Kinzel, *The American Journal of Psychiatry,* vol. 127, pp. 59–64, 1970. Copyright 1970 by the American Psychiatric Association. Reprinted by permission.)

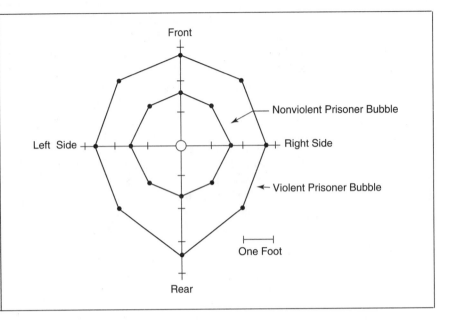

dition. A confederate kept track of the number of persons passing by the fountain in each of the three experimental conditions. The dependent variable was the percentage of passersby who drank from the fountain. When the experimenter was 1 foot away, only 10 percent drank; 5 feet away, 18 percent drank. Finally, at a distance of 10 feet, 22 percent drank from the fountain. More recently, Ruback and Snow (1993) found that territorial behavior at water fountains was also influenced by race, with white and black subjects reacting differently to intrusions.

Using a very different operational definition of personal space, these results agree with those of the active-invasion paradigm used by Kinzel. The single concept of a personal-space bubble explains findings of both experiments. Hence, the experiments provide converging operations supporting the personal-space concept.

The examples of converging operations we have just detailed are actually rather simple because only a small number of experiments or conditions were needed to provide validity and generality. In actual practice, many concepts and phenomena require considerable amount of independent evidence before they can be considered valid.

Concepts defined in terms of converging operations are not static. They are modified as we gather additional evidence relevant to the concept. For example, there may be tasks involving incompatible stimuli and responses that place exceptional demands on our perceptual system. Thus, some kinds of Stroop phenomena could result from both input and output effects. In a similar fashion, future research may show that the size of the personal-space bubble differs in active and passive situations: Your bubble may be larger when someone invades it than when you enter the personal space of another person. Because our knowledge is never complete, the meaning of a concept is always open to revision. As we interpret the results of our research, we should therefore keep in mind that our interpretation and conclusions are always tentative: Our words on any issue are unlikely to be the last (see Chapter 2).

CONCEPT SUMMARY

CONVERGING OPERATIONS

- Provide **validity** for concepts and hypotheses.
- Eliminate **alternative explanations** by two or more operations.

SUMMARY

1. Several pitfalls may make it difficult for experimenters to interpret the results of their research.

2. Some of these pitfalls pose problems in particular research projects, and others make it difficult to interpret patterns of research. Scale attenuation and regression artifacts can lead to the misinterpretation of the results of a specific project; replications (reliability) and converging operations (validity) are important for interpreting patterns of research.

3. Scale attenuation refers to an inability to observe differences in thought and behavior because performance is either too good (a ceiling effect) or too poor (a floor effect).

4. The scale must be spread out or the task modified in order to handle the attenuation problem.

5. Regression to the mean is likely to occur whenever subjects are selected on the basis of high or low scores on some dependent measure. The regression artifact refers to the tendency of subjects with extreme scores on a first test to have scores closer to the mean on a second test.

6. Random assignment is the best way to guard against regression artifacts.

7. An experiment that can be replicated is a reliable one, as is a test whose results are consistent.

8. The three types of replications are: direct, systematic, and conceptual.

9. Converging operations are several independent procedures that support the meaning of an abstract concept.

10. The need for converging operations demands that scientific research on a problem be varied and extensive.

■ KEY CONCEPTS

ceiling effects	regression artifact
conceptual replication	regression to the mean
converging operations	replication
direct replication	scale-attenuation effects
Einstellung	Stroop effect
experimental reliability	systematic replication
floor effects	test reliability
personal space	

■ EXERCISES

1. [*Special Exercise.*] Here is another design problem for you. Reread the description of Luchins's experiment outlined in Table 12–1. There seem to be several problems with that study; see whether you can pinpoint two or three of them. As a hint, consider the following questions: Did Luchins use an appropriate control group? If not, what should be the control condition? Are there points in the study that require counterbalancing? What additional dependent variables might have been informative?

2. Examine figures and tables in several recent journal articles. See whether you can discover any ceiling or floor effects. If you find any—and it may take a while—read the article to determine whether the investigator was aware of the scale-attenuation problem. Can the problem be rectified?

3. Pinpointing regression artifacts may be difficult. However, in an attempt to discover a regression problem, you might find it worthwhile to examine several assessment studies that use subject variables. If you find evidence for a regression artifact, try to determine why the study was published. Remember our discussion of medical research and the difficulty of random assignment. Try these two journals: *Journal of Educational Psychology* and *Journal of Applied Psychology.*

4. Try to find an example of each type of replication in recent journals. You may not find any examples of direct replication, and yet Barber (1976) has asserted that direct replications are crucial to the advancement of psychology. Why do direct replications seldom appear in the literature?

5. More often than not, good examples of converging operations can be found in a single journal article. Papers by Paivio, Mayer, and Thios and D'Agostino, listed in the suggested readings, offer evidence of converging operations at work. You might take a look at these articles.

■ SUGGESTED READINGS

The following three articles illustrate both reliability and converging operations. Read them carefully. They are also available in the book *Readings in experimental psychology* by Elmes (Chicago: Rand McNally, 1978): Mayer, R. E. (1977). Problem-solving performance with task overload: Effects of self-pacing and trait anxiety. *Bulletin of the Psychonomic Society, 9,* 283–286; Paivio, A. (1975). Perceptual comparisons through the mind's eye. *Memory and Cognition, 3,* 635–647; Thios, S. J., & D'Agostino, P. R. (1976). Effects of repetition as a function of study-phase retrieval. *Journal of Verbal Learning and Verbal Behavior, 15,* 529–536.

Psychology in Action
Studying Mental Blocks

- *Folk* is pronounced *foke*, with the *l* being silent. *Polk* is pronounced *poke*, again with the *l* being silent.
- How is the name of the white of an egg pronounced?

If you just pronounced *yolk* in answering the question, this section is for you. *Yolk* is an erroneous answer; the white part of an egg is the *albumen*. The *yolk*, as you probably know, is the yellow part. The sentences prior to the question featured words that rhyme with *yolk* and therefore primed you for the word *yolk*. When you were asked the question about eggs, *yolk* readily came to you as the answer. If you had not been primed with the two sentences, you probably would not have responded *yolk*. The recent experience of reading the sentences blocked you from giving the correct answer.

Here are two more examples, although you may be more wary now:

- Pronounce the word produced by the letters *T-O-P-S*. What does a car do at a green light? Say *tin* out loud ten times. What is an aluminum can made of?

Although you may have answered these questions correctly, if you try them on a friend we think you will find them effective in producing the erroneous answers *stop* and *tin*. You should probably ask the questions aloud, rather than tell your friend to read them.

Such blocks in memory retrieval may play a part in limiting creative thinking (Roediger and Neely, 1982). When people try to solve a problem and fail, they often say that their minds are "in a rut." Usually they mean that when they attempt to solve the problem they are blocked from retrieving a new solution by repeatedly thinking of all the erroneous solutions that previously have been tried. This is the same as the Einstellung effect shown by Luchins's subjects.

You can study the same effect by having some friends read through the priming sentences before the target ones. Compare their behavior with others who do not read the priming sentences. You should consider having the latter group read (or hear) some nonpriming sentences in order to control for the amount of mental work you have your subjects do.

If you are interested in additional ways of studying mental blocks, the following references may be of interest.

Fingerman, P., & Levine, M. (1974). Nonlearning: The completeness of the blindness. *Journal of Experimental Psychology, 102,* 720–721.

Roediger, H. L., & Neely, J. H. (1982). Retrieval blocks in episodic and semantic memory. *Canadian Journal of Psychology, 36,* 213–242.

WRITING RESEARCH REPORTS

What to Include in the . . .

❏ **Abstract:** What you did to whom and what you found

❏ **Introduction:** Why you are doing this research; the hypothesis you are testing

❏ **Method:** A description of all variables; enough detail so that someone else can repeat your project

❏ **Results:** Tables and/or figures that summarize your results, point the reader to the most pertinent data

❏ **Discussion:** State how your results relate to the hypotheses tested; include relevant inferences and conclusions

❏ **References:** All references cited in your paper belong here

CHAPTER 13

PRESENTING RESEARCH RESULTS

Presentation of results is an important step in research. This chapter guides you through the process of writing research reports, explains the process of submitting articles for publication, and offers advice for giving oral presentations to explain your research.

How to Write a Research Report

You have now learned how to formulate an idea for an experiment, review the literature, design a procedure, collect your data, and analyze your results. If your project was carefully done and you obtained interesting data, you are now obligated to publicize your results. We believe that to maintain the self-correcting nature of science, it is important to publish good data. However, this does not mean that journals should be cluttered with information derived from every undergraduate project. If your research is promising, you will receive encouragement from your instructor. Regardless of whether you will try to publish the results of your experiment, it is likely that your course requires a written report of your results.

In the following section, we will review the format of a typical report and discuss some of the stylistic considerations that make up a comprehensible paper. If you follow our suggestions for reading articles (see chapter 4), you will probably have a pretty good idea about the format of a research report, and you will probably have a good feel for technical writing style. Some aspects of technical writing are not too obvious, so we will discuss them here. What we present are general guidelines. If you need additional information, examine R. J. Sternberg's (1993) book, *The Psychologist's Companion* and (1992) article, "How to Win Acceptances by Psychology Journals: 21 Tips for Better Writing," and D. J. Bem's (1987) chapter, "Writing the Empirical Journal Article." The 1994 revision of the *Publication Manual of the American Psychological Association* (fourth edition) will also help, because it is the official arbiter of style for almost all of the journals in psychology and education. The sample article in chapter 4 is also a useful source of information.

Format

The outline of a typical report in Figure 13–1 emphasizes the sequence and format of pages you will have to put together in your APA-style manuscript. This version of the article is known as the **copy manuscript** and is assembled in a particular manner to facilitate the editorial and publication process. A run-through of that sequence will give you an idea of what you are supposed to include.

Your cover page contains the **title** of your project, your name, your affiliation (your institution or place of business), and your **running head.** The running head is the heading that will appear at the top of the published article, and it is typed in capital letters near the top of the cover page of the copy manuscript. This **short title,** which appears at the top of each page of the copy manuscript, consists of the first few words of the title and is used to identify the manuscript during the editorial process only. The short title and running head should not be confused. You should double-space the lines on the cover page and every other page of the copy manuscript.

The next page, page 2, contains the heading "Abstract," and the **abstract** itself. Do not indent the first line of the abstract. On this page and

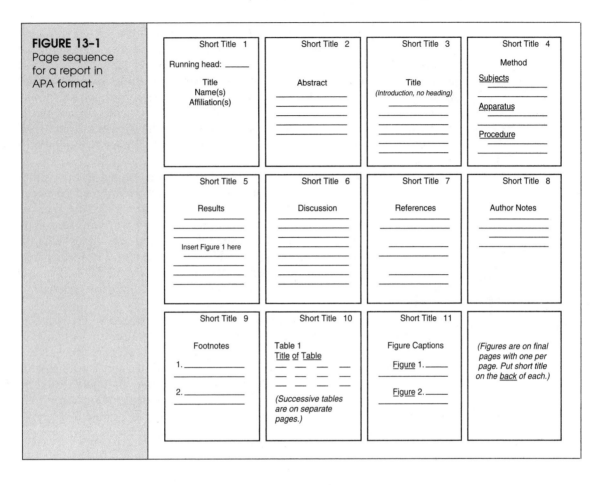

FIGURE 13–1
Page sequence for a report in APA format.

on all subsequent ones (except the figures), you should have an abbreviated title and the page number in the top right-hand corner of the page.

At the top of page 3 is the full title, followed by the **introduction.** Ordinarily, you do not have a heading for the introduction. After your introduction is finished, the **method** section begins. Generally, for a write-up of one experiment, you will type the word "Method" in the center of a line to begin the section. You should begin the method section immediately after the introduction; a page break is not used here. Note the format shown for the headings on page 4 in Figure 13–1. The side headings, such as "Subjects," "Apparatus," and "Procedure," help guide the reader by breaking down the method section into three subsections.

The **results** section immediately follows the method. Do not include **figures** and **tables** in the body of this section; they come at the end of the report. In the copy manuscript, indicate their approximate location as shown on page 5 of Figure 13–1. Next comes the **discussion,** which ends the major textual portion of your report.

The **references** begin on a separate page. The format for presenting references is complex, and you should use care in preparing them. The article in Chapter 4 contains many of the different styles of references that you will have to document. Look them over carefully, and if you have any questions, ask your instructor. You might also study the APA *Publication Manual* and recent journal articles. Any author notes and footnotes appear on separate pages after the references. For most college laboratory reports, footnotes are not necessary. When you prepare something for publication, you may acknowledge financial aid and intellectual support, which should appear on the author-note page. General acknowledgments are not numbered. Other, perhaps peripheral, information should appear as numbered footnotes on a separate footnote page, but such footnotes are generally discouraged.

Following the footnotes are your data tables mentioned in the results section. Each table should be on a separate page and numbered consecutively, according to its appearance in the results section. Make the titles of your tables short but communicative. **Figure captions** are numbered consecutively and appear on a separate page following the data tables. Finally, you have your figures, each on a separate piece of paper. Put your name (or the short title) and the number of the figure on the back. Tables and figures are separated from the text, one per page, to facilitate the typesetting process.

As mentioned before, copy manuscripts are organized in this fashion to accommodate the publisher. However, you should note that there is a special section in the APA *Publication Manual* about the accepted format for student papers submitted for a course requirement but not for publication. For example, in student papers, tables and figures may be interspersed in the text. You should check with your professor or department regarding the preferred format for class projects. However, we recommend learning the APA publication format, because it provides good practice for preparing your future publications.

Sample Manuscript

A sample manuscript appears on the following pages. You should note the sequence of pages, where typing begins on a new page, and what information is provided in each section. The only aspect missing from this manuscript that may appear in one of yours is a separate footnote page. Note carefully how the references are cited in the reference section.

The following paper is copyright 1987 by the American Psychological Association. Reprinted by permission of the author and publisher.

Comish, S. E. (1987). Recognition of facial stimuli following an intervening task involving the Identi-kit. *Journal of Applied Psychology, 72,* 488–491.

Recognition of Facial Stimuli   1

Running head: RECOGNITION OF FACIAL STIMULI

Recognition of Facial Stimuli Following an Intervening

Task Involving the Identi-kit

Sara Elizabeth Comish

University of Alberta

Abstract

The Identi-kit is a tool for constructing a facial composite. The types of errors made on a recognition task, following an intervening task involving the Identi-kit, were examined in this study. One hundred and eight introductory psychology students viewed a target composite-face and made an Identi-kit reconstruction. Subsequently, they were required to identify the original composite-face from a lineup of six composite-faces. Subjects who made an Identi-kit reconstruction were prone to make more errors on the recognition task than participants in a control condition, $p < .01$. False alarms were promoted when the subjects saw a lineup containing foils modified to resemble the subjects' own reconstruction errors, $p < .05$. This finding suggests that memory for facial stimuli can be influenced by viewing misleading information.

Recognition of Facial Stimuli   3

Recognition of Facial Stimuli Following an Intervening

Task Involving the Identi-kit

There is a commonly held belief that memory for faces is
immune to interference; this belief is expressed by the oft heard
statement, "I never forget a face." Support for the role of
interference in facial memory, however, can be found in
experimental studies. Deffenbacher, Carr, and Leu (1981) found
that individual's memory for photographs of faces was highly
susceptible to retroactive interference, unlike their memory for
nouns and objects, which was relatively immune to the
interference. Loftus and Greene (1980) examined the extent to
which facial memory was influenced by reading misleading
descriptions of a previously shown target face. In a later
recognition task with the target face absent, the majority of
subjects who had read the misleading information picked a face
with the misleading information. This finding raises the issue
of whether facial memory can be altered by viewing misleading
information.

A useful tool for studying this issue is the Identi-kit, a
technique that consists of transparencies of line drawings of
different facial features that can be superimposed on each other
to make a composite-face. A similar system is the Photofit,
which consists of actual photographs of features instead of line

drawings. Studies that have used composite techniques to examine interference in memory for faces have yielded conflicting results. Mauldin and Laughery (1981) found that use of the Identi-kit to construct a target face improved recognition of the same target face in a later recognition task. On the other hand, Davies, Ellis, and Shepherd (1978) found different results. They found a trend in the opposite direction, which indicated that making a Photofit reconstruction could interfere with later recognition of a target face (although this difference failed to attain statistical significance). In both of these studies, subjects viewed a target face and then made a composite reconstruction. The recognition tasks that were used to assess memory involved photograph lineups that were not altered to resemble subjects' composite reconstruction.

It is reasonable to assume, however, that the source of any interference from Identi-kit reconstruction may result from viewing one's own errors in Identi-kit reconstruction as a holistic face and that maximum interference can be expected when the distractors used during the recognition task are similar to the individual's errors in Identi-kit reconstruction. The purpose of this study was to determine the effect of an intervening task involving misleading information on later recognition. In order to test this, subjects in two conditions made Identi-kit reconstructions of a target composite-face. The third condition was a control condition in which subjects did not

Recognition of Facial Stimuli   5

make an Identi-kit reconstruction. For the subsequent

recognition task, subjects saw a lineup consisting of the

original target composite-face and five foils. The subjects were

yoked on the recognition task to allow for the determination of

whether interference was a result of making Identi-kit

reconstructions per se or if it occurred only when the distractor

foils resembled the participants' own Identi-kit reconstruction

errors.

Method

Subjects

One hundred and eight introductory psychology students

participated in partial fulfillment of a course requirement.

Thirty-six subjects were randomly assigned to each of the three

conditions.

Materials

The Identi-kit, available from Smith and Wesson, Inc., is a

box containing transparencies of facial features. It is

accompanied by the Identi-kit Handbook, which is a pictorial

index of the features available in the kit.

Design and Procedure

A three-group design was employed. In the Identi-kit/own-

errors condition, subjects made an Identi-kit reconstruction of a

target composite-face and, in a later recognition task,

encountered foils modified to resemble the subjects' own Identi-

kit reconstruction errors. Subjects in the Identi-kit/other-

errors conditions also made an Identi-kit reconstruction but were
yoked to a subject in the Identi-kit/own-errors condition so that
the foils in the recognition task were those of a subject in the
Identi-kit/own-errors condition. In the control/other-errors
condition, subjects saw the target composite-face but did not
make an Identi-kit reconstruction. They were also yoked so that
the foils in the recognition task were those of a subject in the
Identi-kit/own-errors condition.

Initially, all subjects viewed one of two target composite-
faces -- photocopies of an Identi-kit reconstruction of either a
man or a woman -- for 10 s until it was removed. Subjects in the
Identi-kit/own-errors condition and the Identi-kit/other-errors
condition then made an Identi-kit reconstruction that involved an
initial choice of facial features from the Identi-kit Handbook.
A composite face was made using these features and shown to the
subjects, who were allowed to change any of the features. On
average, the reconstruction process took 13 min. Following this,
subjects performed a filler task in which they were given 7 min
to rate two photograph faces on trait dimensions. In order to
ensure that the time that elapsed between the initial exposure to
the target composition-face and the recognition task was the same
for subjects in all conditions, the subjects in the
control/other-errors condition spent 20 min rating the two
photograph faces.

Finally, the subjects performed the recognition task, in which they were asked to select the original composite-face from a lineup consisting of the original target composite-face and five distractors. This task was not a forced choice and subjects were allowed to indicate that the target composite-face was not present in the lineup. In the Identi-kit/own-errors condition, each distractor foil was the same as the original target composite-face except that one error from the individual's Identi-kit reconstruction was substituted for one feature of each distractor. Thus, the first distractor was the same as the target except for the hair, the second distractor was the same as the target except for the nose, the third differed on the lips, the fourth differed on the eyes, and the fifth differed on the eyebrows (see Figure 1 for an example of a typical lineup). These distractor foils were photocopied and placed in a lineup, counterbalanced to vary the order of the target and the foils. Using this technique the target appeared in each position six times in each condition, with the positions of the foils randomly determined. Subjects in the Identi-kit/other-errors condition and control/other-errors conditions saw the same lineup in the recognition task as the subject in the Identi-kit/own-errors condition to whom they were yoked.

Insert Figure 1 about here

The data from an additional four participants in the Identi-kit/own-errors condition and from an additional three subjects in the Identi-kit yoked condition were not included in the analyses because one or more features in the Identi-kit reconstruction was identical to the original target composite-face. When the correct feature was selected for the Identi-kit reconstruction, it was not possible to modify the lineup distractor foils in the manner described previously. These subjects were replaced.

The dependent variable was scored a <u>hit</u>, a <u>miss</u>, or a <u>false alarm</u>. A hit was a correct recognition of the original target composite-face; a miss was an incorrect "not present" decision; and a false alarm was an incorrect selection of a distractor foil. In addition, subjects' satisfaction with their reconstruction and the subjects' certainty with regard to their recognition were obtained on scales from <u>not</u> <u>at</u> <u>all</u> <u>satisfied</u> (1) to <u>totally</u> <u>satisfied</u> (7) and from <u>not</u> <u>at</u> <u>all</u> <u>certain</u> (1) to <u>totally</u> <u>certain</u> (7), respectively.

Results

All data were collapsed over the two target composite-faces and converted to percentages, which are presented by condition in Table 1. A one-way analysis of variance (ANOVA) across the three conditions was performed on the number of overall errors. A significant difference was found for the overall number of recognition errors, $\underline{F}(2, 105) = 4.86$, $\underline{p} < .01$. A Newman-Keuls

Recognition of Facial Stimuli   9

comparison revealed that the control/other-errors condition
produced significantly fewer errors than either of the Identi-kit
reconstruction conditions.   The estimated ω^2 was .065.

Insert Table 1 about here

A further one-way ANOVA was performed on the number of false
alarms. A significant difference was found among the conditions,
F(2, 105) = 4.46, p < .05. A Newman-Keuls comparison revealed
that the Identi-kit/own-errors condition differed significantly
from the other two conditions, demonstrating that when the foils
resembled subjects' Identi-kit errors, subjects were more prone
to incorrectly identify the modified foils. In this case, the
estimated ω^2 was .059.

Although an ANOVA on the number of overall errors and on
both of the types of errors is redundant -- because the two types
of errors sum to give the number of overall errors -- the effect
of Identi-kit use on the different types of errors is of
particular interest in this study. Therefore, an additional
ANOVA was performed on the number of "not present" responses
(misses). There was a significant difference among the
conditions, F(2,105) = 3.75, p < .05, and the Newman-Keuls
comparison revealed that the subjects in the Identi-kit/other
errors condition made significantly more "not present" responses

than subjects in either the Identi-kit/own-errors condition or the control/other-errors condition. The estimated ω^2 was .047.

An ANOVA was performed on subjects' confidence ratings, and there were no significant differences among the conditions, $\underline{F}(2,105) = 1.46$, ns. Wells and Lindsay (1985) have suggested that confidence ratings of "choosers only" (i.e., those subjects that make a recognition choice rather than those that indicate that the target composite-face was not present) should be analyzed separately to determine whether confidence ratings have predictive use. No significant differences were found among the conditions when a one-way ANOVA was performed on the confidence ratings of "choosers only." $\underline{F}(2,89) = 0.422$, ns. The low accuracy-confidence correlation, however, is consistent with previous eyewitness studies (see Wells & Murray, 1984).

A point-biserial correlation between confidence and accuracy was performed for "choosers only" by condition and was not significant, highest $\underline{r} = -.221$. Further, it was not significant when performed on the data of all subjects, highest $\underline{r} = -.24$. A point-biserial correlation between subjects' satisfaction with their Identi-kit reconstruction and accuracy of recognition was also not significant for all subjects ratings nor was it significant when the analysis was performed on "choosers only," highest $\underline{r} = -.27$.

Recognition of Facial Stimuli   11

Discussion

The use of the Identi-kit itself promotes overall errors on the recognition task. The lineup foils in this study were modified by only one feature to resemble the Identi-kit reconstructions. This was sufficient, however, to bias people in favor of foils that resembled their own Identi-kit reconstructions. When the lineup foils resemble people's own Identi-kit reconstructions, the errors that are promoted are false alarms to composite-faces that resemble their Identi-kit reconstructions. Errors are promoted even when the composite-faces in the lineup are not similar to the subject's original Identi-kit reconstruction.   In these cases, the predominant errors are misses, that is, failures to correctly identify the original target composite-face by saying that it is not present. Therefore, it appears that people who make an Identi-kit reconstruction are biased away from the original target composite-face.

The findings in this study appear to conflict with the results obtained by Davies et al. (1978) and Mauldin and Laughery (1981). The differences between the present study and the experiments of Davies et al. and Mauldin and Laughery are, however, numerous. Their null results, for example, may be due to a failure to allow the subject to make a "not present" response. Alternatively, the high similarity between distractors and target achieved in the present study, compared with the others, might account for the different results. Most important, no study prior to this has used Identi-kit reconstruction errors to build distractor composite-faces in which the target is embedded. This contingency between Identi-kit reconstructions and the recognition task in the Identi-kit/own-errors condition allowed for an optimal test of the potential interference effects of the Identi-kit task on subsequent recognition.

What is the source of the recognition errors? It is possible that the Identi-kit task creates interference because it involves viewing the misleading errors incorporated into a complete face. A person making a recognition decision may be easily confused between the original memory and the memory of the Identi-kit reconstruction. This is particularly likely to occur when a composite-face similar to a person's own Identi-kit reconstruction is present in the lineup.

The distribution of facial features in the foils that subjects had falsely identified was also examined. In general, people seem to make more recognition errors when features of less importance, such as eyebrows or lips, were altered. This is consistent with previous studies (see Ellis, 1984, for a review). Recognition errors involving the more important features, hair and eyes, were primarily made only when the altered features resembled the Identi-kit reconstruction. This suggests that more

Recognition of Facial Stimuli   13

confusions occur for less important features and for important features that resemble Identi-kit reconstructions.

Although the Identi-kit task was shown to interfere with recognition in this study, there are a number of caveats to consider in generalizing these findings to police lineups. First, it is not known how representative Identi-kit composite-faces are of photographs of real individuals, let alone the extent to which Identi-kit encoding operations compare with the encoding of live faces. Thus, performance on an Identi-kit lineup task may not be indicative of performance on a real lineup task. Second, the lineups used in this experiment consisted of highly similar composite-faces, faces much more similar than a typical police lineup. In the first condition, the foils were altered so that one feature was precisely the same as the subjects' Identi-kit reconstruction -- an occurrence that is highly unlikely in a typical police lineup. Third, the target stimuli in this study were limited to only two Identi-kit composites that may not be representative of other faces. Fourth, the reconstructions from which the lineups were created shared no features with the target composite. Finally, the subjects in this study may have had poorer memories for the target than aroused witnesses to a crime and thus made poorer reconstructions. For these reasons, it is necessary to be

Recognition of Facial Stimuli   14

cautious in extrapolating from these results to police lineups.

Recognition of Facial Stimuli   15

References

Davies, G. M., Ellis, H. D., & Shepherd, J. W. (1978). Face identification: The influence of delay upon accuracy of Photofit construction. Journal of Police Science and Administration, 6, 35-42.

Deffenbacher, K. A., Carr, T. H., & Leu, J. R. (1981). Memory for words, pictures and faces: Retroactive interference, forgetting and reminiscence. Journal of Experimental Psychology: Human Learning and Memory, 7, 299-305.

Ellis, H. D. (1984). Practical aspects of face memory. In G. L. Wells & E. F. Loftus (Eds.), Eyewitness testimony: Psychological perspectives (pp. 12-37). New York: Cambridge University Press.

Loftus, E., & Greene, E. (1980). Warning: Even memory for faces may be contagious. Law and Human Behavior, 4, 323-334.

Mauldin, M., & Laughery, K. (1981). Composite production effects on subsequent facial identification. Journal of Applied Psychology, 66, 351-357.

Wells, G. L., & Lindsay, R. C. L. (1985). Methodological notes on the accuracy-confidence relation in eyewitness identifications. Journal of Applied Psychology, 70, 413-419.

Recognition of Facial Stimuli   16

Wells, G. L., & Murray, D. M. (1984). Eyewitness confidence. In G. L. Wells & E. F. Loftus (Eds.), <u>Eyewitness testimony: Psychological perspectives</u> (pp. 155-170). New York: Cambridge University Press.

Recognition of Facial Stimuli   17

Author Note

Portions of this article were presented at the meeting of the Canadian Psychological Association held in Toronto, Canada, June 1986.

I am indebted to Gary Wells for the thoughtful help and guidance he provided during the course of this research. In addition, I am grateful to John Pullyblank, John Turtle, and Brendan Rule for their comments on an earlier version of this article; to Constable Bates of the Royal Canadian Mounted Police for his time and comments; and to two anonymous reviewers for their extremely helpful and meticulous comments.

Correspondence concerning this article should be addressed to Sara Elizabeth Comish, who is now at the Department of Psychology, University of Victoria, P. O. Box 1700, Victoria, British Columbia, Canada, V8W 2Y2.

Table 1

Performance on the Recognition Task: Data Converted Into

Percentages by Condition

	Condition		
Performance	Identi-kit (own errors)	Identi-kit (yoked)	Control (yoked)
Total errors	86.11_a	77.78_a	56.56_b
Misses	8.33_a	27.78_b	8.33_a
False alarms	77.78_a	50.00_b	47.22_b
Correct (hits)	13.89	22.22	44.44

Note.   Percentages that do not share a common subscript differ at $p < .05$.

Recognition of Facial Stimuli   19

Figure Caption

<u>Figure 1</u>. The original target face, a typical Identi-kit

reconstruction, and the subsequent lineup. (Foils are identical

to the original target face, except for the indicated facial

feature obtained from the reconstruction.)

Target Face

Reconstruction

Foil - Hair

Foil - Nose

Foil - Lips

Foil - Eyes

Target Face

Foil - Eyebrows

Style

Now that you have some idea of format, let us consider style. After suffering through some obscurely written article, you will no doubt recognize the advantage of clear, unambiguous writing. The **APA format** helps standardize the order and general content. However, making sure that the reader understands what you are saying is up to you. We have read many research reports prepared for our classes, and we have found the biggest problem is transition, or flow, from one section to the next. Many students write as though they were composing a surprise-ending short story, even though their report should be as straightforward as possible.

Your title should be short (10 to 15 words) and concise. Usually the title states the independent variables and dependent variables of the study.

Your abstract should include your variables (independent, dependent, and important control variables), number and type of subjects, major results, and important conclusions. Students often include too much detail in the abstract; remember, you only have a few words (fewer than 960 characters), so state only the most essential aspects of the project so that a potential reader will have a general, but clear, idea of what was done and what was found. The body of your report should expand on the abstract. (This is why most abstracts are written last, even though the report might be clearer if the abstract were written first, as the outline for the main part of the work.)

In the introduction, you should state why you are interested in a particular issue, what other investigators have found, and what variables you will be examining. You should begin by stating a broad perspective on the issue, then quickly narrow down to the specific question that interests you. You should lead the reader through the *relevant* research, always keeping in mind that you are setting up your own research question. Thus, avoid discussion of tangential issues. Toward the end of the introduction, give the reader an overview of your experiment, specifying your hypotheses explicitly and outlining any predictions derived from theories you have discussed. By the end of the introduction, the reader should see your experiment as filling an important gap in our knowledge.

In the method section, state how you examined the variables you described at the end of the introduction. Here, it is important to be clear and complete. By the time you write the method section, you are quite familiar with the details and complexities of your experiment. This familiarity makes it difficult to realize that the reader of your report is learning of these details for the first time. As you write, try to tell the reader everything he or she would need to know in order to be able to repeat your experiment, but do not include any extraneous variables. Often people divide their method section into three subsections: subjects, materials, (or, apparatus) and procedure. The subjects section specifies the number of subjects participating in the study, the population from which they were drawn (e.g., the introductory psychology class at your university), and their incentive for participating (e.g., course credit). If any subjects were discarded for any reason, that should be mentioned in this section. The **materials** (or, apparatus) section should describe all relevant aspects of the materials used in the experiment. The next section, the procedure section, often begins with a description of the experimental design, then states the instructions given to subjects (if they are human), and generally leads the reader through the various phases of the experiment.

In the results section, state what happened when you examined the variables. Clarity is important here. Avoid simply listing your statistical analyses with minimal comment. Instead, state each finding in plain English first, then support it with statistics. Your results section should end with a summary of the purpose and results of your experiment.

In your discussion, state what the effects of the variables mean for the issue at hand. The biggest danger in this section of the paper is lack of organization. Before you begin writing, you should know the points you want to make. Make them concise and easy to understand. The discussion should follow up the issues pointed out in the introduction. Also, as in the introduction, avoid straying onto tangents. When the reader has completed your report, he or she should be able to state the main conclusions in a sentence or two. Be careful, however, in the conclusions you draw; avoid grandiose statements. Science advances in small steps; your experiment need not be earthshaking to be scientifically important.

Finally, the body of your report should represent a tight package, not a disjointed essay containing sections that seem independent of each other. You have to tell your readers what you were trying to do more than once. Do not be afraid to be somewhat redundant by having each section build on the previous one. If you repeat the purpose of your research often enough, every reader will have gotten something from your report by the time he or she gets to the reference list. Table 13–1 summarizes the information that should be included in each section of your report.

TABLE 13–1
A Summary of the Information in Each Section of a Research Report

SECTION	INFORMATION
Title	Experiments State independent and dependent variables—"The effects of X on Y." Other studies: State the relationships examined—"The relation between X and Y."
Abstract	In less than 960 characters, state what was done to whom and summarize the most important results.
Introduction	State what you plan to do and why (you may have to review results from related research). Predicted results may be appropriate.
Method	Present enough information to allow someone else to repeat your study exactly the way you did it. For clarity use subheadings (*Subjects, Apparatus,* etc.) and make sure that dependent, independent subject, and control variables are specified.
Results	Summarize important results in tables or figures. Direct the reader to data that seem most relevant to the purpose of the research.
Discussion	State how the results relate to the hypotheses or predictions stated in the introduction. Inferences and theoretical statements are appropriate.
References	In APA format, list only those references that were cited in your report.

The APA *Publication Manual* outlines writing style considerations as follows: Orderly expression of ideas, smoothness of expression, economy of expression, precision and clarity, and they offer strategies to improve one's writing style. These guidelines warrant some discussion, so we now consider aspects of writing style.

Scientific writing demands clarity, so each word has to be chosen carefully. Consider these sentences that regularly appear in undergraduate research reports: "I ran the subjects individually." "The white albino rat was introduced to the Skinner box." Actually, none of the subjects in the study from which the first sentence was pulled did any running during the course of the project. What the author meant to say was, "I tested the subjects individually." From reading about rats introduced to Skinner boxes, you might conclude that the researcher had very clever rats. The rat did not shake hands with a box; all that happened was that the rat was put into the operant-conditioning chambers. Furthermore, "white albino" is redundant. All albino rats are white. The lesson here is that in scientific writing, you must be careful to choose the correct word or phrase and avoid ambiguity. Also, be cautious when using pronouns such as *which, this, that, these,* and *those.* Many students find it irresistible to begin a paragraph with one of these pronouns, and more often than not the referent for the pronoun is not easy to determine. You can usually avoid any ambiguity by including the referent of the pronoun each time it is used.

After you have decided on your words and phrases, put them together carefully. A common problem among some writers is to shift verb tenses abruptly. In general, use the past tense in the review of other studies in your introduction (Smith *found*) and in your method (the subjects *were*). When you are describing and discussing your data, the present tense is usually appropriate (The data *show* that . . ., which *means* that).

Make sure that collective and plural nouns agree with their verbs and pronouns. Plural words that end in *a* are troublesome, such as *data, criteria,* and *phenomena.* Each of these nouns is plural, so they require plural verbs and pronouns. "These data *are*" is correct, but "this phenomena *is*" is not correct. The singular forms for these nouns are: *datum, criterion,* and *phenomenon* (this phenomenon *is*).

Many scientific writers overuse the passive voice in their reports. Consider this statement: "It is thought that forgetting is caused by interference." Although this sentence is fairly concise (and it is precise), it is also stuffy and less direct than "We think that interference causes forgetting," which is really what was meant. Be careful about using either the active or the passive voice too much. If you overuse the passive voice, your report sounds stuffy. If you overuse the active voice, you may take interest away from what you did and place too much emphasis on yourself (I think, I did, and so on). If you want to emphasize what was done and not who did it and why, use the passive construction. On the other hand, if you think that the agent of the activity is also important, or if the reason for the action is important, use the active voice.

The careful writer avoids language that is sexist. The APA recommends that the use of *he* (and *his* and *him*) as a generic pronoun be avoided by changing to a plural construction or by using *he and she.* Generally, the writer should strive for accurate, unbiased communication. The *APA Publication Manual* contains a section devoted to the reduction of language bias.

Scientific writing requires the use of consistent terminology; if you assign labels to things (e.g., labeling subject groups: Informed and Uninformed), use these labels throughout the paper. You may have been taught in English classes to try to vary descriptions of repetitive things to avoid boring the reader. However, in scientific writing, changing terminology only adds confusion. It is important that the reader know that when you introduce a new term, it refers to a concept different from ones previously discussed.

Writing a cogent, well-organized research article is a skill that requires considerable effort and practice. More is involved than simply allocating information to the correct sections. There are many fine points of style, usage, and exposition that distinguish lucid, well-written articles from obscure and tortuous ones. While writing your report, you should make frequent use of standard references for points of style and grammar. In addition, consult the APA *Publication Manual* regarding aspects of technical writing that are particularly relevant to psychology journal articles, including the organization and content of each section, the economy and precision in the expression of ideas, the presentation of data and statistics, and so forth. We highly recommend the aforementioned book by Sternberg (1993), a recent article by Sternberg (1992), and a chapter by Bem (1987) for excellent advice and specific examples of good and poor style, phrasing, and organization in psychology articles. Finally, and perhaps most importantly, you should allocate time for revising and rewriting your manuscript, with the aforementioned stylistic comments in mind. No one can write a publishable manuscript on the first try; revision is a crucial part of the writing process.

How to Publish an Article

Assume that your article has been written, proofread, and corrected, and the last page has just emerged from your printer. Now what? Although it is unlikely that your first student effort will produce an article of professional quality, you may nevertheless find it interesting to discover what happens when a professional psychologist submits an article to a journal.

The first step is to send copies of the manuscript (the technical term for an unpublished work) to a small number of trusted associates who can check it over to make sure that it has no obvious or elementary flaws and that it is written clearly. Once the comments come back, the indicated corrections are made and, with some trepidation, the author commits the manuscript to the mail, addressed to the editor of the most appropriate journal. After this, it is necessary to exhibit great patience for the next few months. The review process is slow. (The editor who receives the manuscript typically is extremely busy juggling many responsibilities—teaching, conducting his or her own research, supervising undergraduate and graduate students, and so on. Two or three weeks after submitting the article, the author receives a form letter thanking him or her for interest in the journal and acknowledging receipt of the manuscript. The manuscript gets a number (such as 94–145), and if an associate editor has been assigned to handle it, the author is instructed to direct all future correspondence to that editor.

The editor sends copies of the manuscript to two or three reviewers. Some journals allow the author to have anonymous reviewing, where the author's identity is concealed. This is for those who do not believe in the impartiality of reviewers. The reviewer, who may also review for several other journals, may take a day or two to carefully read and evaluate a manuscript. Then a summary statement is sent to the editor. When the reviewers are in agreement, the editor's decision is easy. Should the reviewers disagree, the editor must carefully read the manuscript and sometimes may request a third opinion. Finally, an editorial decision is reached and the author receives a letter stating either (1) why the manuscript cannot be published, (2) what kind of revisions are needed to make the manuscript acceptable, or (3) that the journal will publish the article. Because rejection rates for manuscripts are quite high in most journals (above 70 percent), editors spend a great deal of time devising tactful letters of rejection.

Whether or not the article was accepted, the comments of the reviewers are most valuable. The best psychologists in the area have provided, free of charge, their careful opinions about the research. Of course, reviewers can also make mistakes. Any author who disagrees with a review has the privilege of writing to the editor. Although this action will usually not result in the article being accepted, it is important that rejected authors have the right to appeal or protest. Anyway, there are always other journals.

If the article was accepted for publication, the author is still not yet finished. Some revision of the manuscript may be required. The copyright for the article is signed over to the publisher. Some months later, the author receives galley or page proofs from the publisher. These must be carefully checked to ensure that the words and tables set in type by the printer match those in the original manuscript. After making corrections, the author returns the article to the publisher. Several months later, the article finally appears in the journal. The entire process, from submission of the manuscript until final publication, takes a year or more. Authors do not get paid for articles in journals, but on the other hand, neither do they get charged for the privilege of appearing in print. Having a research report published in a journal makes the results available to any interested scientist. Moreover, it makes the results available to researchers many years in the future.

HOW TO GIVE AN ORAL PRESENTATION

Another avenue for sharing results is psychological conventions. Although most research is eventually submitted to a scientific journal, conventions are often the first place that research is reported. Psychologists gather in groups of varying size to present the results of their most recent research. Some of these conventions are very specific in the type of research reported (e.g., neuropsychological research only), whereas others are much more general, including all areas of psychology. These conferences allow scientists to meet and discuss recent and ongoing research—work that has not yet been published. The results of student research are sometimes presented at such conferences. After conducting a research project, if you think it is worth sharing with the scientific community, you might ask your professor about appropriate conventions in your area. If your professor agrees that the work is good enough to present at such a convention, he or she will explain to you how to submit your research.

Oral presentations are also important in many other settings—in class presentations, in informal research groups, or to your psychology class or Psi Chi group. The tips below should help you with these other sorts of talks, too.

Content

If your paper is accepted, you will probably be given approximately 15 minutes in which to present your research and about 2 to 3 minutes at the end to answer questions. In general, your talk will differ from a written report in that you will be able to present only a portion of what you would write. Therefore, you should not get bogged down in detail, whether it be related research, procedural details, statistics, or secondary findings. You will only have time to present the basic problem and why it is interesting, your method of attacking the problem, and what you found.

Your talk should begin like a brief introduction of a written report: state the question and why it is interesting. Knowing when to define terms and when to assume that your audience already knows the technical terms you will use can be a tricky issue. However, because your audience will likely be somewhat diverse, a good rule is to define any terms that are not generally known by all psychologists. You should briefly review the research in the literature that is most directly related to your experiment, state your research question as well as any hypothesis you had.

After setting up the question, give a description of how you tried to answer it. Define your independent and dependent variables. Give enough detail here to be understandable, but be careful not to get bogged down in procedural detail. You should then present your results. Present the data in the clearest way possible; usually this means using figures or tables containing means or other descriptive data. As in written reports, do not simply describe the statistical tests performed and their significance levels. Instead, tell your audience in general terms what your results were (e.g., people performed better in the visual condition than in the auditory condition) and then back your statement with a significance test, or just say the results are statistically significant by appropriate tests.

You should wrap up the talk with a reminder of your original hypothesis and whether (or not) it was upheld. You should then state the conclusions that you draw from your research. If you plan to continue research in this area, you might briefly describe the next questions your research will be addressing.

Style

We have several stylistic suggestions for presenting your results. First, although it is probably advisable to memorize the first and last sentences of your talk, you should not read the talk. Instead, make a brief outline of the points you wish to make and speak from the outline. This approach may seem difficult at first, but with practice, you can learn to speak from an outline. This method will allow you to make eye contact with the audience and will make your talk more interesting and easier to follow.

Whenever possible, it is advisable to use visual aids, such as overheads or slides. These help your audience follow your logic in the introduction and method sections, and they are crucial in presenting results. One popular approach is to have an overhead containing a brief outline of the introduction, one with an outline of your experimental method, a figure or table with your results, an overhead with a written summary of your results, and finally one with your conclusions. Be careful not to clutter your visual aids with too much detail, and make sure that the font is big enough that people in the back of the room will be able to see your overheads or slides clearly.

Finally, practice your talk! Practice by yourself until you feel comfortable speaking from an outline and you get the talk to last the correct amount of time. Some people find that speaking in front of a mirror helps them to notice distracting gestures that they should try to avoid. A tape recorder can be used to help you notice extraneous sounds ("ums" and "uhs"), which should be avoided. Taping yourself will also allow you to notice other unwanted habits, such as excessive use of run-on sentences. After you feel comfortable with your talk, ask your friends to listen and provide constructive criticism. Finally, you might ask your professor to listen to your talk; he or she will likely have many suggestions for making the talk more effective. Further advice on giving research talks can be found in Darley and Zanna's (1987) chapter.

The oral presentation of research is an important method used by scientists to present their research to interested parties. Due in part to the lags of at least one year between submission of a manuscript to a journal and actual publication of the paper, research presented at conferences is almost always more recent than that found in the journals. Thus, it is beneficial for scientists to attend conference presentations. It is also in the best interest of scientists to present their own research at conferences because this forum allows them to receive immediate feedback on their research from experts who share their interests. Thus, the ability to give effective oral presentations is a central part of the career of a research psychologist.

SUMMARY

1. The APA format provides a framework for writing a report. Reports should be written in a clear, unambiguous style.

2. After an article has been written and reviewed by colleagues, it can be submitted to a journal for publication. The publication process can sometimes take one year.

3. Oral presentations of research can be presented at conventions. Research presented at these conventions is almost always more recent than that found in journals.

4. For psychological science to progress, reports must be presented and published, and knowledgeable consumers must critically evaluate them.

■ KEY CONCEPTS

abstract

APA format

copy manuscript

discussion

figure captions

figures

introduction

materials

method

references

results

running head

short title

tables

title

STATISTICAL APPENDIXES

DESCRIPTIVE STATISTICS

Organizing and summarizing

Useful Computational Formulae
Measures of Central Tendency *Measures of Dispersion*

Mode

The most frequent score

Median

The middle score

Mean

$$\bar{X} = \Sigma X / n$$

Variance

$$s^2 = \frac{\Sigma X^2}{n} - \overline{X^2}$$

Standard Deviation

$$s = \sqrt{\frac{\Sigma X^2}{n} - \overline{X^2}}$$

Facts about the Normal Distribution

❑ Of all scores, 68 percent are within ± 1 standard deviation of the mean.

❑ Of all scores, nearly 96 percent are within ± 2 standard deviations of the mean.

❑ Of all scores, 99.74 percent are within ± 3 standard deviations of the mean.

❑ Standard scores (z scores) are differences between individual scores and the mean expressed in units of standard deviations.

Explanation of Symbols

❑ X and Y are individual scores (data).

❑ n is the number of observations or subjects.

❑ Σ refers to the act of adding (or summing).

❑ X^2 is each score squared.

❑ ΣX^2 refers to adding up the scores after each has been squared.

❑ $(\Sigma X)^2$ means the square of the sum of the raw scores.

DESCRIPTIVE STATISTICS

DESCRIPTIVE STATISTICS: TELLING IT LIKE IT IS

We have conducted research in order to collect data about a psychological topic. What are we going to do with the numbers? First, we need to systematize and organize them. We do not have to look at the whole array of numbers produced by subjects in the different conditions of an experiment. Instead, we can look at a briefer version. Descriptive statistics provide the summarizing and systematizing function. The two main types of descriptive statistics are *measures of central tendency* and *measures of dispersion* (variability).

Let us consider a hypothetical experiment. A drug company has sponsored a test of the effects of LSD on the behavior of rats, so we decide to see how the drug affects the rats' running speed. Forty food-deprived rats have been trained to run a straight-alley maze for a food reward. We randomly assign them to two groups. To one group we administer LSD by injection and observe the effect on the speed with which the rats run the alley for food thirty minutes after the injection. The other group is tested in a similar manner thirty minutes after receiving an injection of an inert substance. The following are the running times (in seconds) for the twenty control subjects: 13, 11, 14, 18, 12, 14, 10, 13, 13, 16, 15, 9, 12, 20, 11, 13, 12, 17, 15, and 14. The running times for the subjects receiving the LSD injections are 17, 15, 16, 20, 14, 19, 14, 13, 18, 18, 26, 17, 19, 13, 16, 22, 18, 16, 18, and 9. Now that we have the running times, what do we do with them? We might want some sort of graphical representation of the numbers. One type of graph is the **histogram** shown in the two panels of Figure A–1, where the running speeds in seconds appear along the abscissa (*x*-axis), and the frequency with which each occurred in the two conditions is displayed along the ordinate (*y*-axis). Running times for the control subjects

FIGURE A-1
Histograms representing scores for twenty subjects in the control and experimental conditions of the hypothetical LSD experiment.

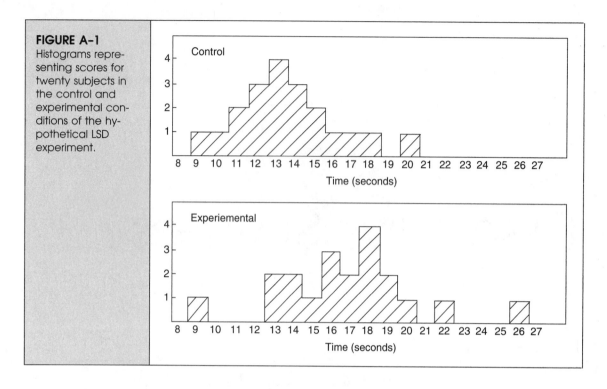

are given in the top histogram, and those for the experimental subjects are shown in the bottom one. Another way to represent the same information is a **frequency polygon.** Its construction is equivalent to that of the histogram; you can visualize this type of graph by connecting the midpoints of the bars in the histogram. (Examples of *frequency polygons* appear in Figure A–2.) In both conditions in Figure A–1, the greatest number of scores occurs in the middle and the scores tend to decrease in frequency as running times become smaller or larger. Both the histogram and frequency polygon are types of **frequency distributions.** They help systematize the data, but there are more efficient summary descriptions.

Central Tendency

The most common summary description of data is a measure of central tendency, which indicates the center of the distribution of scores. By far the most common measure of central tendency in psychological research is the **mean.** The mean $(\bar{X})$ is the sum of all the scores (ΣX) divided by the number of scores (n), or $\bar{X} = \Sigma X / n$. It is what most people think of as the average of a set of numbers, although the term *average* technically applies to any measure of central tendency. The sums of the running times for the experimental and control conditions in our hypothetical experiment were 338 and 272 seconds, respectively. Because there were twenty observations in each condition, the means are 16.9 seconds for the experimental condition and 13.6 for the control group.

The mean is by far the most useful measure of central tendency and almost all inferential statistics, which we come to later, are based on it.

Therefore, this statistic is used whenever possible. However, two other measures of central tendency are sometimes employed. The second most common measure is the **median.** It is the score above which half of the distribution lies and below which the other half lies. The median, then, is the midpoint of the distribution. When there is an odd number of scores in the distribution, such as 27, the median is the 14th score from the bottom or top, because that score divides the distribution into two groups of thirteen scores. When the number of scores (n) is an even number, the median is the arithmetic mean of the two middle scores, if the scores are not tied. So the median of the scores 66, 70, 72, 76, 80, and 96 is (72 + 76)/2, or 74. When the two middle scores are tied, as in the distribution of scores from the hypothetical LSD experiment, the convention is to designate the median as the appropriate proportion of the distance between the limits of the particular score, where the limits are a half score above and below the tied score. Consider the distributions of scores from our experiment. If we arrange the twenty control running times from lowest to highest, we discover that the eighth, ninth, tenth, and eleventh scores are all 13. Under such conditions, the tenth score is considered the median and it lies three quarters of the distance between the limits of 12.5 and 13.5. So the median would be 12.5 + .75, or 13.25, for the control subjects. By the same reasoning (and you should try it yourself), we find that the median for the experimental subjects is 17.

Why is the median used? The primary reason is that it has the desirable property of being insensitive to extreme scores. In the distribution of scores of 66, 70, 72, 76, 80, and 96, the median of the distribution would remain exactly the same if the lowest score were 1 rather than 66 or the highest score were 1,223 rather than 96. The mean, on the other hand, would differ widely with these other scores. Often this benefit can be extremely useful in summarizing data. In our LSD experiment, suppose that one of the rats given LSD had stopped halfway down the alley to examine a particularly interesting feature of the runway before continuing on its way to the goal box, and its time to complete the runway was 45 minutes or 2,700 seconds. If this score replaced the 26-second score in the original distribution, the mean would go from 16.9 seconds to 150.6, or from 3.30 seconds greater than the control mean to 137.0 seconds greater, because of only one very deviant score. In such cases, researchers frequently use the median score rather than the mean to represent the central tendency. Using the mean seems to give an unrepresentative estimate of central tendency because of the great influence of the one deviant score. However, using the median often severely limits any statistical tests that can be applied to the data.

The final measure of central tendency, almost never reported in psychological research, is the **mode,** or the most frequent score in the distribution. In the distribution of control scores in our experiment, it is 13, and in the distribution of experimental scores, it is 18.

Measures of Dispersion: Variability in Data

Measures of central tendency indicate the center of the scores, whereas measures of dispersion indicate how the scores are spread out about the center. The simplest measure of dispersion is the **range,** which is the difference between the highest and lowest scores in the distribution. For the control rats in the LSD experiment the range is 11 (20 − 9), and for the experimental rats it is 17 (26 − 9). The range indicates only the extreme scores, so it is rarely used.

The most useful measures of dispersion are the **standard deviation** and the **variance** of a distribution. The standard deviation is most useful as a descriptive statistic, whereas the variance of a distribution is employed in inferential statistics. As we shall see, the two are closely related.

One number that reflects the amount of spread that the scores exhibit around some central-tendency measure, usually the mean, is the *mean deviation*. This is calculated by taking the difference between the mean and every score in a distribution, summing these differences, and then dividing by the number of scores. However, we need to take the mean *absolute* difference (that is, to ignore the sign of the difference or whether the score was greater or less than the mean). The reason is that the sum of the deviations of scores about the mean is always zero, a defining characteristic of the mean (see Table A–1). Thus, the mean deviation must be the *absolute* mean deviation.

TABLE A–1
Calculation of the mean deviations and absolute mean deviations from two sets of scores. The sum of the deviations (differences) in calculating the mean deviation is zero, which is why it is necessary to use the absolute mean deviation.

Control Group			Experimental Group		
X	$(X - \bar{X})$	$\|X - \bar{X}\|$	X	$(X - \bar{X})$	$\|X - \bar{X}\|$
9	−4.60	4.60	9	−7.90	7.90
10	−3.60	3.60	13	−3.90	3.90
11	−2.60	2.60	13	−3.90	3.90
11	−2.60	2.60	14	−2.90	2.90
12	−1.60	1.60	14	−2.90	2.90
12	−1.60	1.60	15	−1.90	1.90
12	−1.60	1.60	16	− .90	.90
13	− .60	.60	16	− .90	.90
13	− .60	.60	16	− .90	.90
13	− .60	.60	17	+ .10	.10
13	− .60	.60	17	+ .10	.10
14	+ .40	.40	18	+1.10	.10
14	+ .40	.40	18	+1.10	1.10
14	+ .40	.40	18	+1.10	1.10
15	+1.40	1.40	18	+1.10	1.10
15	+1.40	1.40	19	+2.10	2.10
16	+2.40	2.40	19	+2.10	2.10
17	+3.40	3.40	20	+3.10	3.10
18	+4.40	4.40	22	+5.10	5.10
20	+6.40	6.40	26	+9.10	9.10

$\Sigma X = 272$ Total = 0.00 Total = 41.20 $\Sigma X = 338$ Total = 0.00 Total = 52.20
$\bar{X} = 13.60$ $\bar{X} = 16.90$

Absolute mean deviation $= \dfrac{41.20}{20} = 2.06$ Absolute mean deviation $= \dfrac{52.20}{20} = 2.62$

The mean deviations for our hypothetical experimental conditions in the LSD experiment are calculated in Table A–1. The symbol ‖ indicates the absolute value of a number, so $|-6| = 6$.

The absolute mean deviation of a set of scores is an adequate measure of dispersion and is based on the same logic involved in finding the mean of a distribution. However, the standard deviation and variance are preferred to the mean deviation because they have mathematical properties that make them much more useful in advanced statistical computations. The logic behind their calculation is quite similar to that of the mean deviation, which is why we have considered the mean deviation here. In calculating the mean deviation, we had to determine the absolute value of the difference of each score from the mean so that these differences would not sum to zero. Instead of taking the absolute difference, we could have gotten rid of the troublesome negative numbers by squaring the differences. This is exactly what is done in calculating the variance and standard deviation of a distribution.

The *variance* of a distribution is defined as *the sum of the squared deviations from the mean, divided by the number of scores*. In other words, each score is subtracted from the mean and squared; then all these values are summed and divided by the number of scores. The formula for the variance is

$$s^2 = \frac{\Sigma(X - \overline{X})^2}{n} \tag{A–1}$$

where s^2 represents the variance, X the individual scores, $\overline{X}$ the mean, and n the number of scores or observations. The *standard deviation* is simply *the square root of the variance*, and is therefore represented by s. So

$$s = \sqrt{\frac{\Sigma(X - \overline{X})^2}{n}} \tag{A–2}$$

Calculation of the standard deviations for the control and experimental conditions in the LSD experiment by the mean-deviation method is illustrated in Table A–2.

The formulas for the variance and standard deviation of a distribution shown in Equations A–1 and A–2 are rather cumbersome, and in practice, the equivalent computational formulas are used. The standard-deviation formula is

$$s = \sqrt{\frac{\Sigma X^2}{n} - \overline{X}^2} \tag{A–3}$$

where ΣX^2 is the sum of the squares of all the scores, $\overline{X}$ is the mean of the distribution, and n is the number of scores. Similarly, the formula for variance is

$$s^2 = \frac{\Sigma X^2}{n} - \overline{X}^2 \tag{A–4}$$

TABLE A–2
Calculation of the Standard Deviation, s, for the Control and Experimental Conditions by the Mean-Deviation Method.

Control Group			Experimental Group		
X	$(X-\bar{X})$	$(X-\bar{X})^2$	X	$(X-\bar{X})$	$(X-\bar{X})^2$
9	−4.60	21.16	9	−7.90	62.41
10	−3.60	12.96	13	−3.90	15.21
11	−2.60	6.76	13	−3.90	15.21
11	−2.60	6.76	14	−2.90	8.41
12	−1.60	2.56	14	−2.90	8.41
12	−1.60	2.56	15	−1.90	3.61
12	−1.60	2.56	16	− .90	.81
13	− .60	.36	16	− .90	.81
13	− .60	.36	16	− .90	.81
13	− .60	.36	17	+ .10	.01
13	− .60	.36	17	+ .10	.01
14	+ .40	.16	18	+1.10	1.21
14	+ .40	.16	18	+1.10	1.21
14	+ .40	.16	18	+1.10	1.21
15	1.40	1.96	18	+1.10	1.21
15	1.40	1.96	19	+2.10	4.41
16	2.40	5.76	19	+2.10	4.41
17	3.40	11.56	20	+3.10	9.61
18	4.40	19.36	22	+5.10	26.01
20	6.40	40.96	26	+9.10	82.81

$\Sigma X = 272$ Total $= 0.00$ $\Sigma(X-\bar{X})^2 = 138.80$ $\Sigma X = 338$ Total $= 0.00$ $\Sigma(X-\bar{X})^2 = 247.80$

$\bar{X} = 13.60$ $\bar{X} = 16.90$

$$s = \sqrt{\frac{\Sigma(X-\bar{X})^2}{n}}$$

$$s = \sqrt{\frac{\Sigma(X-\bar{X})^2}{n}}$$

$$s = \sqrt{\frac{138.80}{20}}$$

$$s = \sqrt{\frac{247.80}{20}}$$

$$s = 2.63$$

$$s = 3.52$$

The standard deviations for the experimental and control scores are calculated by the computational formula shown in Table A–3. The value in each case is the same as when the definitional formula is used.

To describe an array of data, psychologists usually present two descriptive statistics, the mean and the standard deviation. Although there are other measures of central tendency and dispersion, these are most useful for descriptive purposes. Variance is used extensively in inferential statistics (see Appendix B).

TABLE A-3
Calculation of the standard deviation, s, for the control and experimental conditions by using the computational formula (also called the raw-score method). The same values are obtained as when the definitional formula is used (see Table A-2), but the calculations are much easier to perform.

X	X²	X	X²
9	81	9	81
10	100	13	169
11	121	13	169
11	121	14	196
12	144	14	196
12	144	15	225
12	144	16	256
13	169	16	256
13	169	16	256
13	169	17	289
13	169	17	289
14	196	18	324
14	196	18	324
14	196	18	324
15	225	18	324
15	225	19	361
16	256	19	361
17	289	20	400
18	324	22	484
20	400	26	676

$\Sigma X = 272$ $\Sigma X^2 = 3838$ $\Sigma X = 338$ $\Sigma X^2 = 5960$

$$\bar{X} = 13.60 \qquad\qquad \bar{X} = 16.90$$

$$\bar{X}^2 = 184.96 \qquad\qquad \bar{X}^2 = 285.61$$

$$s = \sqrt{\frac{\Sigma X^2}{n} - \bar{X}^2} \qquad\qquad s = \sqrt{\frac{\Sigma X^2}{n} - \bar{X}^2}$$

$$s = \sqrt{\frac{3838}{20} - 184.96} \qquad\qquad s = \sqrt{\frac{5960}{20} - 285.61}$$

$$s = 2.63 \qquad\qquad s = 3.52$$

THE NORMAL DISTRIBUTION

In the histograms in Figure A–1 representing the running times of the rats in the two conditions of our hypothetical experiment, most of the scores pile up in the center and tail off toward the ends (or tails) of the distribution, especially for control subjects. Most psychological data tend to look like this when represented graphically; they often approximate the **normal curve** or **standard normal distribution,** where scores are most numerous in the middle, decline in frequency with distance from the middle, and do so in a fairly symmetrical way. A score ten points above the middle is about as common as a score ten points below it. Several examples of normal curves are shown in Figure A–2. First note that in all three distributions, the mean, median, and mode are the same. The main difference in the distributions is in their variability. The tall, thin curve A has a smaller variance (and, of course, standard deviation) than the other two, whereas the flat, broad curve C has a larger variance than the others. All three curves, though, are normal curves.

Each side of the normal curve has a point where the curve slightly reverses its direction; it starts bending outward more. This is called the *inflection point* and is labeled in the normal curve shown in Figure A–3. The inflection point in the curve is always one standard deviation from the mean, and the normal curve has the useful property that specific proportions of the distribution of scores it represents are contained within specific areas of the curve itself. About 68 percent of all scores are contained within one standard deviation of the mean (34 percent on each side). Similarly, almost 96 percent of the scores are contained within two standard deviations of the mean, and 99.74 percent of the scores are within three standard deviations. The percentage of each area is shown in Figure A–3. This is true of all normal curves, no matter how sharp or flat they are.

This property of normal curves is extremely useful because if we know an individual's score and the mean and standard deviation in the distribution of scores, we also know the person's relative rank. For example,

FIGURE A-2
Three examples of the normal curve that differ in variability. C has the greatest variability and A the least. The normal curve is a symmetrical distribution in which the mean, median, and mode all have the same value.

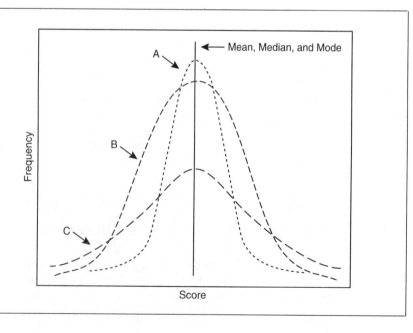

FIGURE A-3

This is the standard normal distribution that is presented in Figure B-1. There are two sides or tails to the distribution: positive and negative. If an experimenter simply asserts that there should be a difference between an experimental and a control condition but does not specify the direction of the difference, this is called a nondirectional hypothesis. If a $z = 2.67$ is found, it is necessary to look up the probability that this will occur in both the positive and negative tails of the distribution and add the two, since the experimenter has not specified whether the difference should be positive or negative. When the experimenter has specified the direction of difference, one need only look up the probability in one tail. Since the distribution is symmetrical, the probability that the null hypothesis can be rejected is half as great with a one-tailed as with a two-tailed test. The less certain one is about the outcome of an experiment, the greater the difference between conditions must be for it to be decided that it is not due to chance.

most IQ tests are devised so that the population mean is 100 and the standard deviation is 15. If a person has an IQ of 115, we know that he or she scored higher than 84 percent of all people on the test (50 percent of the people below the mean and 34 percent above). Similarly, a person with an IQ of 130 scored higher than almost 98 percent of all people, and a person with an IQ of 145 scored higher than 99.87 percent of the population. See whether you can arrive at these percentages by adding up the appropriate areas in Figure A–3.

Most distributions of scores in psychological data are, or at least are assumed to be, normal. (Often with small samples, as in our hypothetical data in Figure A–1, it is difficult to tell whether the distribution is normal.) Scores are compared across normal distributions with different means and variances in terms of **standard scores** or *z scores*. This score is simply the difference between an individual score and the mean expressed in units of standard deviations. So an IQ of 115 translates to a z score of 1.00, that is, $(115 - 100)/15$; and an IQ of 78 translates to a z score of -1.47, that is, $(78 - 100)/15$. Standard scores are useful because they allow comparison of the relative ranks of scores for a person across distributions in which the means and standard deviations vary greatly. Grades in courses should be calculated in terms of z scores if the means and standard deviations of the scores vary widely from one test to the next. Thus, a person's eventual rank in the class is calculated more faithfully by finding the mean of the z scores than by finding the mean of the raw scores of the tests.

When data in an experiment are said to be *normally distributed*, it means that, if they were graphed, they would form a normal distribution, as in Figure A–3. Thus *normal*, as it is used in psychological research, usually refers to a type of distribution (there are many other types of distributions) and is not a value judgment as to the goodness or badness of the scores.

Correlation Coefficient

In chapter 7, correlational research is described. The purpose of correlational research is to see how two or more attributes of an organism vary together. The strength and direction of a correlation are determined by the calculation of a correlation coefficient. We will consider just one: *Pearson product-moment correlation coefficient* or *r*. Shown in Box A–1 is the calculation formula for *r*, using the hypothetical data relating head size to memory performance discussed in chapter 7. Box A–2 repeats this analysis, using the computerized statistical package called MINITAB.

Regardless of how you calculate *r*, you should read the appropriate sections of chapter 7 that discuss the use and interpretation of a correlation coefficient.

BOX A–1 Computing Pearson *r*	Let us call one set of numbers in Table A–4 *X* scores and the other set *Y* scores. For example, head sizes might be *X* scores and words recalled *Y* scores. The formula for computing Pearson *r* from the raw scores in panels (a), (b), or (c) of Table 7–3 is as follows:

$$r = \frac{n \, \Sigma XY - (\Sigma X)(\Sigma Y)}{\sqrt{[n \, \Sigma X^2 - (\Sigma X)^2][n \, \Sigma Y^2 - (\Sigma Y)^2]}} \qquad \text{(A-5)}$$

The *n* refers to the number of subjects on which observations are taken (here, 10); the terms ΣX and ΣY are the totals of the *X* and *Y* scores, respectively; ΣX^2 and ΣY^2 are the sum of all the *X* (or *Y*) values after each is squared; and the $(\Sigma X)^2$ and $(\Sigma Y)^2$ are the total of all the *X* or *Y* values with the entire total or sum squared. This leaves the value ΣXY, or the sum of the cross-products. This is obtained very simply by multiplying each *X* value by its corresponding *Y* and then summing these products. You may see other formulas for calculation of Pearson *r* besides the raw-score formula in Equation A–5, but these will be equivalent (in general) to the one presented here. An illustration of how Pearson *r* is calculated using this raw-score formula is presented in Table A–4 using the data from the (a) column of Table 7–3 (chapter 7). You should try to work out the values for Pearson *r* for the (b) and (c) panels yourself, to make certain you understand how to calculate the values and to gain an intuitive feel for the concept of correlation. The values of *r* are given below the appropriate columns in Table 7–3.

TABLE A–4
Calculation of Pearson r for the Data in the First (A) Column of Table 7–3, by the Raw-Score Formula (Equation A–5).

Subject Number	X Head Size (cm.)	X^2	Y Words Recalled	Y^2	$X \cdot Y$
1	50.8	2580.64	17	289	863.60
2	63.5	4032.25	21	441	1330.50
3	45.7	2088.49	16	256	731.20
4	25.4	645.16	11	121	279.40
5	29.2	852.64	9	81	262.80
6	49.5	2450.25	15	225	742.50
7	38.1	1451.61	13	169	495.30
8	30.5	930.25	12	144	366.00
9	35.6	1267.36	14	196	498.40
10	58.4	3410.56	23	529	1343.20

$n = 10$ $\Sigma X = 426.70$ $\Sigma X^2 = 19,709.21$ $\Sigma Y = 151$ $\Sigma Y^2 = 2451$ $\Sigma XY = 6915.90$

$$r = \frac{n\Sigma XY - (\Sigma X)(\Sigma Y)}{\sqrt{[n\Sigma X^2 - (\Sigma X)^2][n\Sigma Y^2 - (\Sigma Y)^2]}}$$

$$r = \frac{10(6915.90) - (426.70)(151)}{\sqrt{[(10)(19,709.21) - (426.70)^2][(10)(2451) - (151)^2]}}$$

$$r = \frac{69,159.00 - 64,431.70}{\sqrt{[197,092.10 - 182,072.89][24,510 - 22,801]}}$$

$$r = \frac{4727.30}{\sqrt{[15,019.12][1709]}} = \frac{4727.30}{\sqrt{25,667,829.89}}$$

$$r = \frac{4727.30}{5066.34}$$

$$r = +.93$$

BOX A–2
Calculation of r by a Computer

One popular statistical package on many large computers is called MINITAB. The MINITAB program will compute r, as well as many other statistics. We have outlined a typical session on a computer in which MINITAB is used to calculate r for the data in Box A–1. The entries shaded are what you type into the computer, and the other information is what the computer presents to you. After you have signed on to the computer, you need to gain access to MINITAB, which in this case is done by typing MINITAB. (However, different computer systems may have other ways of accessing MINITAB; check with your computer center before trying to run MINITAB.) Then, you are likely to see some information about the MINITAB program, followed by "MTB." MTB means that you should enter the appropriate MINITAB command, and it is here that you need to tell MINITAB that you are entering data to be "read" for analysis. So, the appropriate command is: "READ INTO C1, C2." This tells

MINITAB that you are entering two columns of data (C1 and C2). Then MINITAB asks for the two columns by printing ''DATA,'' next to which you enter the two scores for a particular subject. You continue to enter pairs of scores until the data for all subjects have been entered (ten pairs in this case), after which you type ''END.'' You then enter the command ''CORRELATION BETWEEN C1 and C2,'' which tells MINITAB to compute the *r* between the ten pairs of scores. MINITAB tells you that ten rows of data were read (a handy check that you have entered the correct number of pairs of scores), and then prints out the correlation. The correlation computed by MINITAB is identical to the one in Table A–4. Next, MINITAB asks for additional commands. When you enter ''STOP,'' you leave the MINITAB program. You are now ready to sign off the computer. (You could have entered another MINITAB command besides ''STOP'' if you had additional statistical computations to perform.)

```
MINITAB RELEASE 82.1 *** COPYRIGHT - PENN STATE UNIV.
1982 APRIL 25, 1984 *** CONVERTED AT U. OF WISC. WAISMAN
CENTER STORAGE AVAILABLE 41099

MTB >  READ INTO C1, C2
DATA>  50.8 17
DATA>  63.5 21
DATA>  45.7 16
DATA>  25.4 11
DATA>  29.2 9
DATA>  49.5 15
DATA>  38.1 13
DATA>  30.5 12
DATA>  35.6 14
DATA>  58.4 23
DATA>  END
    10 ROWS READ
MTB >  CORRELATION BETWEEN C1 AND C2

    CORRELATION OF      C1 AND C2    = 0.933

MTB >  STOP

*** MINITAB *** STATISTICS DEPT * PENN STATE UNIV. * RE-
LEASE 82.1 * STORAGE AVAILABLE 41099
```

The results of a computer session with MINITAB. MINITAB has calculated the *r* for the data presented in Box A–1. Shaded entries are typed in by the user, and the other information is printed by the computer program.

There are several other statistical packages for computers (for example, SPSS and BMD) that may be available to you; whichever one is available, we recommend you become familiar with it. Computer analysis is faster and more accurate than doing statistical work by hand or step by step on a calculator.

INFERENTIAL STATISTICS

What statistical test should I use when . . .

I have one independent variable that has two levels?

Between-Subjects Design		Within-Subjects Design	
↓	↓	↓	↓
Ordinal Data	Interval/Ratio Data	Ordinal Data	Interval/Ratio Data
↓	↓	↓	↓
Mann-Whitney	Between-Subjects t	Wilcoxon	Within-Subjects t
↓	↓	↓	↓
Box B-2	Box B-4	Box B-3	Box B-5

I have one independent variable that has more than two levels?

Between-Subjects Design	Within-Subjects Design
↓	↓
Interval/Ratio Data	Interval/Ratio Data
↓	↓
One-Way Between-Subjects ANOVA	One-Way Within-Subjects ANOVA
↓	↓
Box B-6	Box B-7

I have two independent variables, each with at least two levels?

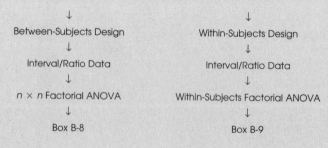

Between-Subjects Design	Within-Subjects Design
↓	↓
Interval/Ratio Data	Interval/Ratio Data
↓	↓
$n \times n$ Factorial ANOVA	Within-Subjects Factorial ANOVA
↓	↓
Box B-8	Box B-9

INFERENTIAL STATISTICS

STATISTICAL REASONING

Descriptive statistics are concerned with describing or summarizing data. The results from our LSD experiment (in appendix A) can be summarized by saying that the control group had a mean running time of 13.60 seconds and a standard deviation of 2.63, whereas the experimental rats injected with LSD had a mean of 16.90 seconds and a standard deviation of 3.52 seconds. On average, the experimental rats ran 3.30 seconds slower than the controls, but should we take this difference seriously? Perhaps it resulted from chance factors such as measurement error or a few rats in the control group having a particularly good day and thus feeling like running a bit faster. How can we judge whether the difference between the two conditions is real (reliable) or a fluke? Inferential statistics are used to answer this question.

In actual practice, answering this question is not too complicated. We choose an appropriate statistical test for the experimental situation, perform a few staightforward computations on a calculator (or computer), and then consult a special table. The table informs us of the probability that the difference we found between our conditions is a result of chance factors. If it is sufficiently unlikely to have occurred by chance, we conclude that the difference is statistically significant, or reliable. The computational procedures are often quite simple, but the logic behind them needs to be explained so you will understand how statistical inferences are made.

Sampling

A **population** is a complete set of measurements (or individuals or objects) having some common observable characteristic (see Box B–1). Examples of populations are all U.S. citizens of voting age, all albino rats that have had injections of LSD, and all people asked to remember a list of fifty words.

Of course, it is impossible to study the entire population in any of these cases. If we could measure the entire population of rats for running speed after either an injection of LSD or an injection of a chemically inert substance, we would have a better idea of the effects of LSD. (Any difference, of course, might still be attributable to measurement error.) But because it is almost always impractical to measure an entire population, we must sample from it. A **sample** is a subset of a population, and it is what we are usually examining when we compare experimental conditions. Thus, we make statistical inferences when we draw a conclusion about an entire population on the basis of only a sample of observations. We really want to know about the effects of LSD and the inert substance on rats in general, but we hope to draw this conclusion from a sample of, say, twenty rats in each condition.

Technically, we can only *generalize* about the population from which we have sampled, but if we took this statement literally, experimental research would hardly be worth doing. If we received fifty rats from a supply house, and we selected a sample of forty and randomly assigned them to the two conditions of our experiment, would our conclusions be true only of the population of fifty rats? Well, perhaps technically, but no one would

---

BOX B-1
Statistical Notation

Characteristics of a population of scores are called *parameters,* and characteristics of a sample of scores drawn from a larger population are *statistics.* The mean of an entire population of scores is a parameter, and the mean of a sample is a statistic. Different symbols are used for population parameters and sample statistics. Some of the most frequent are listed here. Several of the concepts have already been explained, and the others will be discussed in the next few pages.

N = number of scores in a population

n = number of scores in a sample

μ = population mean (μ is pronounced mu)

$\bar{X}$ = sample mean

σ^2 = population variance (σ is pronounced sigma)

s^2 = sample variance $\dfrac{\Sigma(X - \bar{X})^2}{n}$

$\hat{s}^2$ = unbiased estimate of population variance $\dfrac{\Sigma(X - \bar{X})^2}{n - 1}$

σ = population standard deviation

s = sample standard deviation

$\hat{s}$ = sample standard deviation based on the unbiased variance estimate

$\sigma_{\bar{X}}$ = standard error of the mean $\dfrac{\sigma}{\sqrt{N}}$

$s_{\bar{X}}$ = estimated standard error of the mean $\dfrac{s}{\sqrt{n}}$ or $\dfrac{s}{\sqrt{n - 1}}$

care about the result if this were so, and we would not have wasted our time doing the experiment. We at least want to assume that the results are characteristic of that strain of rats, and, perhaps, that these results also generalize to other species, including human beings. The problem is the same in research with human beings. Suppose you are a researcher at the University of Toronto interested in some aspect of social behavior. You prepare your experiment, which has three conditions, and you plan to use students from introductory psychology courses as subjects, a common practice. You display a sign-up sheet, randomly assign the volunteers to the three experimental conditions when they show up, and collect your data. To whom do your conclusions generalize? To introductory psychology students at the University of Toronto who volunteered for your experiment? If so, who cares about what you found? In practice, psychologists assume that their results generalize more widely than to the limited population from which they sampled for their experiment.

The Distribution of Sample Means.   One way we could check on the reliability of our hypothetical LSD experiment would be to perform the experiment repeatedly using new groups of rats. Of course, obtaining exactly the same mean running times for the experimental and control conditions in these replications would be unlikely. The means in seconds for the experimental and control conditions in four replications might be 17.9 and 12.5, 16.0 and 13.4, 16.6 and 14.5, and 15.4 and 15.1. Because the experimental rats that receive the LSD always run slower than the control rats, we would have more confidence in our original finding, although the difference is rather small in the last replication. If we repeated the experiment like this and plotted the distribution of the sample means obtained in the two conditions, the distributions would tend to be normal, and they would have all the characteristics of a normal distribution, such as a certain proportion of the scores falling under a certain part of the curve. A plot of the difference between the sample means in each experiment would also be normally distributed.

To give you a better idea of the **distribution** of sample means concept, let us borrow an example from a class demonstration by Horowitz (1974, pp. 179–182). Horowitz manufactured a population of 1,000 normally distributed scores so that the mean and standard deviation of the entire population would be known, which is almost never the case in actual research situations. His 1,000 scores ranged from 0 to 100 and had a mean of 50 and a standard deviation of 15.8. The scores were listed on 1,000 slips of paper and placed in a container. Horowitz had ninety-six students take samples of ten slips from the container and calculate the mean. On each draw from the container, the student took out a slip, noted its number, and then replaced the slip. The slips were then somewhat mixed up in the container, another slip was drawn, and so on. After each student calculated the mean of the ten scores in his or her sample, Horowitz collected all ninety-six sample means and plotted their distribution, which is represented in Table B–1. The intervals between which means might fall are on the left and the number of means falling within each interval is on the right. Notice that the distribution is almost perfectly symmetrical, with almost as many scores in any interval a certain distance below the true mean of the population

> **TABLE B–1**
> The Distribution of sample means for the 96 samples taken by students in Horowitz's class. Each sample mean was based on 10 observations. (After Horowitz, 1974, *Elements of Statistics for Psychology and Education*, Table 8.1. Copyright 1974 by McGraw-Hill. Reprinted with permission.)
>
> | INTERVAL | FREQUENCY | |
> | --- | --- | --- |
> | 62.0–63.9 | 1 | |
> | 60.0–61.9 | 1 | |
> | 58.0–59.9 | 3 | |
> | 56.0–57.9 | 7 | |
> | 54.0–55.9 | 9 | |
> | 52.0–53.9 | 12 | |
> | 50.0–51.9 | 15 | Mean of sample means = 49.99 |
> | 48.0–49.9 | 15 | Standard deviation (s) of |
> | 46.0–47.9 | 13 | sample means = 5.01 |
> | 44.0–45.9 | 9 | |
> | 42.0–43.9 | 6 | |
> | 40.0–41.9 | 3 | |
> | 38.0–39.9 | 1 | |
> | 36.0–37.9 | 1 | |
> | 96 samples | | |

(50) as above it. Also, the mean of the ninety-six sample means (49.99) is quite close to the actual mean of the population (50). The main thing you should notice in Table B–1 is the great variability among the sample means. Although each sample of ten was presumably random, not biased in any way, and came from the same population, one sample had a mean of 37.8, while another had a mean of 62.3. If you did an experiment and found two very different sample means, and you tried to decide whether they came from the same underlying distribution or two different distributions, you might think that such a large difference indicated that they came from different distributions. In other words, you would think that the experimental treatment produced scores reliably different (from a different distribution) than the control scores. Usually this is a good rule—the larger the difference between means in the conditions, the more likely the means are to be reliably different—but as we have seen, even random sampling from a known distribution can produce sample means that differ greatly from each other and from the true population mean, which is known in this case. While pondering small differences between means, keep this lesson in mind. Is the 3.30-second difference between experimental and control means in our hypothetical LSD experiment really reliable?

The Standard Error of the Mean.   The **standard error of the mean** is the standard deviation of a distribution of sample means. In the data in Table B–1, it is 5.01. The standard error of the mean gives us some idea as to the amount of variability in the distribution of sample means, or how likely it is that the value of any particular sample mean is in error. Large standard errors indicate great variability, whereas small ones tell us that a particular sample mean is likely to be quite close to the actual population mean. Thus, the standard error of the mean is a very useful number.

You might be wondering why we bother to tell you about the standard error of the mean if in order to calculate it you must repeat an experiment numerous times to get the distribution of sample means and then calculate its standard deviation. Fortunately, you do not. The formula for finding the standard error of the mean (represented by $\sigma_{\bar{x}}$) is simply the standard deviation of the population (σ) divided by the square root of the number of observations ($\sqrt{n}$). Or

$$\sigma_{\bar{x}} = \frac{\sigma}{\sqrt{n}} \tag{B–1}$$

Now, if you are still with us you might well be thinking, "Terrific. What good does this do me if the standard deviation of the population, the numerator in equation B–1, is never known?" That question has occurred to statisticians, too, so they have devised a method for estimating the standard deviation of the population from the standard deviation of a sample. If you look back at equation A–2, in appendix A, where the formula for the standard deviation of a sample (s) appears, and simply replace the n in the denominator by $n - 1$, you have the formula for getting an unbiased estimate of σ, the standard deviation of the population. The equation for finding the standard error of distribution of sample means (called the standard error of the mean, or $s_{\bar{x}}$) is

$$\text{Estimated } \sigma_{\bar{x}} = s_{\bar{x}} = \frac{s}{\sqrt{n - 1}} \tag{B–2}$$

Because the standard error of the mean indicates our error in assuming that our sample mean represents the population mean, we want it to be as small as possible. Equations B–1 and B–2 tell us how to do this: Increase the size of the sample, n, which increases the denominator in the equation. The greater is n, the sample size, the smaller will be the standard error of the mean, $s_{\bar{x}}$. In a population involving 1,000 scores, the sample mean should be closer to the population mean if there are 500 observations in the sample rather than only 10.

Horowitz drove this point home to the ninety-six students in his class by having them repeat the exercise of drawing slips from the population of 1,000 scores and calculating the mean again, but this time he had them sample fifty slips rather than only ten. The resulting distribution of sample means is shown in Table B–2. This time, with larger samples, there is much less variability in the sample means. They are much closer to the actual population mean of 50. The standard deviation of the distribution of sample means, or the standard error of the mean, is 2.23, as opposed to 5.01 when the sample size was only 10. If $n = 100$ in a sample from the 1,000 scores, the standard error of the mean would be 1.59; with a sample of 500 it would be .71, and with 1,000 scores in a sample it would be only .50. (These were calculated from equation B–1 because the standard deviation, σ, is known for the entire population.) The reason we might not get the population

TABLE B-2
The distribution of sample means for the 96 samples taken by students when sample size (*n*) = 50. The distribution is again normal, as in Table B-1, but when each sample is based on a larger sample size, as it is here, the variability of the distribution (represented by the standard error of the mean) is much smaller. (After Horowitz, 1974, *Elements of Statistics for Psychology and Education*, Table 8.2. Copyright 1974 by McGraw-Hill. Reprinted with permission.)

INTERVAL	FREQUENCY	
55.0–55.9	1	
54.0–54.9	3	
53.0–53.9	5	
52.0–52.9	9	
51.0–51.9	13	
50.0–50.9	17	
49.0–49.9	16	Mean of sample means = 49.95
48.0–48.9	14	Standard deviation (*s*) of sample means = 2.23
47.0–47.9	9	
46.0–46.9	6	
45.0–45.9	2	
44.0–44.9	1	
	96 samples	

mean even with a sample of 1,000 is that the sampling was done with *replacement*; that is, after a slip was drawn it was returned to the container and it might have been drawn again and again, but some slips were never drawn.

The lesson to be learned is that we should always try to maximize the number of observations—the sample size—in experimental conditions so that the statistics obtained will be as close as possible to the population parameters.

Testing Hypotheses

Scientists set up experiments to test hypotheses. The conventional statistical logic for testing hypotheses goes something like this. An experimenter arranges conditions, such as the experimental (LSD) and control (placebo) in our experiment with rats in order to test an **experimental hypothesis.** The experimental hypothesis in this case is that LSD will have some effect on running speed. This is tested against the **null hypothesis,** which maintains that the two conditions do not differ in their effects on running speed. In other words, the experimental hypothesis holds that the samples of running speeds come from two different underlying populations (that is, populations with different distributions), and the null hypothesis maintains that the two samples come from the same distribution. Statistical tests allow us to find the likelihood with which the null hypothesis can be rejected. How unlikely must a null hypothesis be to be rejected? If an experimental result differs from that to be expected by the null hypothesis (so much so that a difference that great would be expected on the basis of chance only 5 times in 100), we conclude that the null hypothesis can be rejected. This .05 **level of significance** is just a convention; many psychologists prefer a more conservative .01 level for rejection, so that a null hypothesis is rejected only if the experimental result is likely to occur by chance in one case in 100. At any rate, the experimental hypothesis is tested, in a sense, indirectly. It is not affirmed, but the null hypothesis is rejected.

The logic of pitting an experimental hypothesis against the null hypothesis has come under attack in recent years for several reasons. Some argue that it gives a misleading idea about how scientists operate. For one thing, not many researchers wander about the world losing any sleep over or investing any thought into the null hypothesis. In general, experiments are set up to test our theories, and what is of primary concern is how the results can be interpreted or accounted for by our theories. Of special interest is the case in which important experimental results seem irreconcilable with the major theories of a phenomenon. Experiments are important because of what they tell us about our theories and ideas—this is why we designed them in the first place—and not about rejection of the null hypothesis. But the logic of testing hypotheses against the null hypothesis is widely used as an introduction, however oversimplified to the way scientific inference proceeds. Thus we present it here.

Testing Hypotheses: Parameters Known.   The logic of testing hypotheses against the null hypothesis can be aptly illustrated in cases in which the parameters of a population are known and we wish to determine whether a particular sample comes from the population. Such cases are quite unusual in actual research, of course, because population parameters are rarely known. Suppose you were interested in whether the members of your experimental-psychology class were reliably above the national mean in intelligence as measured by IQ tests (or reliably below, as the case may be). We know the population parameters in this case; the mean is 100 and the standard deviation is 15. You could test your class easily enough by giving them the short form of some intelligence test, such as the Otis, developed for group testing. Suppose you randomly sampled 25 people from your class of 100 and found the mean IQ of the sample to be 108 with a standard deviation of 5.

How do we go about testing the experimental hypothesis that the class is reliably brighter than the population as a whole? First let us consider the hypotheses. The experimental hypothesis is that the students are brighter than people in the nation as a whole, or that the IQ scores of the students sampled come from a different population than randomly selected people. The null hypothesis is that there is no reliable difference between our sample and the national mean, or that the students in the class are a sample from the same national population. If the null hypothesis were actually the case, the difference between the sample mean of 108 and the population parameter mean (μ) of 100 would result from random factors. Certainly this is not implausible, because we have seen from our discussion of the distribution of sample means how much a sample mean can differ from a population parameter, even when the sample is selected in an unbiased manner. Remember Horowitz's classroom demonstration, the results of which are portrayed in Tables B–1 and B–2.

The normal curve, the distribution of sample means, and z scores can help us determine how likely it is that the null hypothesis is false. When unbiased samples are taken from a larger population, the means of these samples are normally distributed. With normal distributions we can specify what proportion of the distribution falls under each part of the curve (as shown in Figure A–3 in Appendix A). Remember also that the z scores are the calculation of any score in a normal distribution in standard deviation units from the mean.

All this by way of review. Now how does this help us? What we do in testing the hypothesis that the sample is actually from a population with a mean IQ greater that the population at large is to treat the sample mean as an individual score (in terms of our earlier discussion) and calculate a z score on the basis of the deviation of the sample mean from the population mean. In our case, we know the population mean is 100 and the class mean of the randomly selected students is 108. To calculate the z score, we also need to know the standard error of the mean, the standard deviation of the distribution of sample means. The equation for the z score here is

$$z = \frac{\overline{X} - \mu}{\sigma_{\overline{x}}} \qquad (B–3)$$

The standard error of the mean ($\sigma_{\overline{x}}$) is found by dividing the standard deviation of the population (σ) by $\sqrt{n}$ (see equation B–1), so $\sigma_{\overline{x}}$ is $15/\sqrt{25}$, or 3. Thus z is $(108 - 100)/3$, or 2.67. This result, 2.67, allows us to reject the null hypothesis with reasonable confidence and conclude in favor of the alternative hypothesis, that the class is actually superior in IQ to the population at large. We establish this by asking the question: How likely is a z score of 2.67 when a sample mean is drawn from a larger population whose mean is actually 100? The answer is that it will occur only .0038 of the time, or 38 times in 10,000. (In the next paragraph we will discuss how this was calculated.) The custom in rejecting the null hypothesis is that if it could only occur 1 time in 20 by chance, we would reject it, so the difference in the class sample mean is *reliably different* or **significantly different** from the mean of the population.

To explain how this rather remarkable conclusion is reached, we need to refer again to the special property of the normal curve, which is that a certain proportion of cases fall under each part of the curve. Looking at Figure B–1, we see that having a z score of ± 2.00 is highly improbable. Greater scores in either direction occur only 2.15 percent of the time. In other words, the probability of such an occurrence is .0215. This is also below the 5 percent or .05 level of significance, so any mean score two or more standard deviations from the population mean is considered, using the logic we have outlined here, significantly different from the population mean. In fact, the critical z value for rejecting the null hypothesis at the .05 level of significance, is ± 1.96. Table C–1 (in appendix C) presents (1) z scores from zero to four, with (2) the amount of area between the mean and z, and (3) most important, the amount of area beyond z. The amount of area beyond z is the probability of finding a score that distant from the mean on the basis of chance alone. Once again, when this probability falls below .05, as it does with z scores of ± 1.96 (or more), we reject the null hypothesis. Notice that with a z of 2.67, as in our IQ example, the probability of such a rare occurrence is only .0038 (see Figure B–1).

The statistical problem we have just considered—comparing a sample mean to a population parameter to see whether the sample came from that population—is rather artificial, because population parameters are rarely known. But this example does exhibit characteristics of most common statistical tests. In all tests, some computations are performed on the data or raw scores, a value is found as in the z score just calculated, and then this value is compared with a distribution of values so that we can determine the likelihood that such a value could be obtained if the null hypothesis were in fact true. This distribution tells us, then, with what probability our result could be attributed to random variation. If the probability is less than 5 cases in 100 ($p < .05$), then we say the null hypothesis can be rejected. This probability is sometimes called the **alpha (α) level** and, as already mentioned, some psychologists prefer values of .01 or even smaller so that they can be more certain that the null hypothesis should be rejected.

Our z-score test can also serve to introduce you very briefly to other important statistical concepts. First, let us consider two types of errors that can be made by applying statistical tests to experimental data. A **type 1 error** is rejection of the null hypothesis when it is actually true, and the probability that this error will occur is indexed by the alpha level, which the experimenter selects. If the alpha level is $p = .05$, then we shall mistakenly reject the null hypothesis in 5 cases in 100. This illustrates the probabilistic nature of inferential statistics; we are not absolutely certain that a null hypothesis can be rejected, only reasonably certain. Thus the lower α level or p level we use in determining statistical significance, the less chance we have of making a type 1 error. However, this increases the probability of a **type 2 error,** which occurs when we *fail* to reject the null hypothesis when it is actually *false.* Thus by setting α levels at different points we systematically decrease and increase the two types of errors.

Scientists are generally conservative in such matters, so the α level is usually kept fairly small, such as .05 or .01 (rather than, say, .10 or .15). Thus we minimize the error of rejecting the null hypothesis when it is true, or claiming a difference in our results when a difference is not there. As a consequence, though, we increase the probability of type 2 errors. A *conservative* statistical test minimizes type 1 errors, whereas more *liberal* statis-

FIGURE B-1
Proportions of scores in specific areas under the normal curve. The inflection points are one standard deviation from the mean.

tical tests increase the probability of a type 1 error but decrease that of a type 2 error.

Unfortunately, we can never know positively in our experimental situations whether we are committing type 1 or type 2 errors. We find this out primarily by doing experimental replications of our results, but also by calculating the power of a statistical test. The *power* of a test is the probability of rejecting the null hypothesis when it is actually false; thus we always want to maximize the power of our statistical tests. This is not the place to describe how the power of tests is calculated, but we will note the two main factors that influence power. Look back to the z-score formula in equation B–3. Whatever would make the z score larger would increase the power of the statistical test, or the likelihood of rejecting the null hypothesis. The value μ, the population mean, is fixed. Thus only two changes in the values of equation B–3 can affect z. One is the difference between the sample mean and the population mean $(\bar{X} - \mu)$ and the other is n, the size of the sample. If the discrepancy between μ and $\bar{X}$ is increased (or in other cases, if the difference between sample means in an experimental comparison is increased), the probability of rejecting the null hypothesis is also increased.

However, there is nothing we can do about the size of the difference between means; it is fixed. We can increase the power of our statistical tests by increasing the sample size. The reason is that with larger samples we can be more confident that our sample means represent the mean of the populations from which they are drawn, and thus we can be more confident that any difference between a sample mean and a population mean (or between two sample means) is reliable. Sample size can have a great effect on the power of a test, as shown in Table B–3. Presented there are the z scores and p values for our difference between a sample mean of 108 IQ points and the population mean of 100 as the sample size varies. As the sample size varies, so will our conclusion as to whether the sample came from a national population or a more restricted, high-IQ population. If we assume that the null hypothesis is actually false here, then by increasing sample size we decrease the probability of a type 2 error, or increase the power of the test we are using.

One final issue to consider is the *directionality* of statistical tests. According to conventional logic involved in testing an alternative hypothesis against the null hypothesis, the alternative hypothesis may be **directional** or **nondirectional.** If an experimental and a control group are in an experiment, a nondirectional alternative hypothesis would be that the two groups differ in performance on the dependent variable. A directional hypothesis would, in addition, state the predicted direction of the difference; for example, the experimental group might be predicted to do better than the control.

This distinction is important, because if the alternative hypothesis is directional, a **one-tailed (or *one-sided*) statistical test** is used, but if the alternative hypothesis is nondirectional, a **two-tailed (*two-sided*) test** is used. One versus two "tails" refers to whether we consider one or both tails of the distribution when we look up a p level associated with the result of a statistical test (say, $z = 1.69$).

TABLE B–3
How varying sample size (n) affects the power of a statistical test, or how likely it is that the null hypothesis can be rejected when the test is used. The example is from the z score (calculated in the text) on a mean sample IQ of 108, where

$$z = \frac{\bar{X} - \mu}{\sigma_{\bar{x}}}$$

If the mean difference remains the same but n increases, z increases because

$$\sigma_{\bar{x}} = \frac{\sigma}{\sqrt{n}}$$

n	$\bar{X} - \mu$	$\sigma_{\bar{x}}$	z	p†
2	8	13.14	.61	.2709
5	8	6.70	1.19	.1170
7	8	5.67	1.41	.0793
10	8	4.74	1.69	.0455*
12	8	4.33	1.85	.0322*
15	8	3.88	2.06	.0197*
17	8	3.64	2.20	.0139*
20	8	3.35	2.38	.0087*
25	8	3.00	2.67	.0038*
50	8	2.12	3.77	.0001*
75	8	1.73	4.62	<.00003*
100	8	1.50	5.33	<.00003*

*All these values meet the conventional level of statistical significance, $p < .05$ (one-tailed).
†p values are one-tailed.

Examine Figure B–1 once again. We took a sample ($n = 25$) of students, determined that the mean IQ of the sample was 108, and calculated a $z = +2.67$ in testing to see whether this was different from the mean population IQ of 100. If we had no prior expectation of how the sample IQ should deviate from the normal population—if we thought it could be either higher or lower—this would have a nondirectional hypothesis. In fact, we did expect the sample IQ to be greater than 100, so we tested a directional hypothesis and thus used a one-tailed test. This means we looked up the resulting z score in only one tail of the normal distribution, that greater than zero. A $z = +2.67$ leads to a one-tailed p value of .0038. If the hypothesis were nondirectional, then we have no a priori right to expect the resultant z score to be greater instead of less than zero. The z score could be in the positive or negative tail. Because the difference could have occurred in either direction, we use a two-tailed test. In practice, the two tails of the distribution are symmetrical, so we simply double the p level for the one-tailed test. In our example, if the hypothesis had been nondirectional, p would equal $2 \times .0038$, or .0076, still well below .05.

Two-tailed tests are more conservative and less powerful than one-tailed tests: it is harder to reject the null hypothesis. If we are uncertain about the outcome of an experiment, we need a greater value of the statistic to allow us to declare a difference. In practice, most investigators prefer to use the more conservative two-tailed test with sufficient power ensured by fairly large sample sizes.

In the remainder of this appendix, we show you how to calculate several statistical tests. We believe it is important for you to do some of these calculations by hand or with a calculator. When you carefully work through the calculations, you become familiar with the logic and components of the statistical test. However, as we noted in appendix A (see Box A–2), many statistical tests can be done automatically by sophisticated calculators and computers. All you need to do is access a particular statistical program and then enter your data. Most of the statistical tests outlined in this appendix can be done by the computer package, MINITAB. We suggest you become familiar with the statistical capabilities of the computing equipment available to you. Computers can conduct statistical tests faster and more accurately than you can, and they relieve some of the tedium associated with the more complex statistical tests that require numerous complicated calculations.

Tests for Differences Between Two Groups

A variety of statistical tests exist for almost every purpose. At present, we are interested in discussing tests that assess the reliability of a difference between two groups or conditions. How do we pick an appropriate test from all those available? There is no hard-and-fast rule. Tests vary in the assumptions they make, their power, and the types of situation for which they are appropriate. Perhaps the most popular test for the difference between two means in psychological research is the *t* **test.** Because the *t* test provides the same estimate of reliability as does the simple analysis of variance (discussed next), we will first concentrate on two other tests, the Mann-Whitney *U* test and the Wilcoxon signed-ranks test. These tests also are useful in introducing yet another type of statistical test.

The Mann-Whitney and Wilcoxon tests are **nonparametric statistics** as opposed to **parametric statistics.** Parametric statistical tests, such as analysis of variance and *t*, are those that make assumptions about the underlying population parameters of the samples on which the tests are performed. Common assumptions of parametric tests are that the variances of the underlying populations being compared are equivalent, that the underlying distributions are normal, and that the level of measurement is at least an interval scale. If these assumptions are not met, the test may be inappropriate. But how can we ever know whether the assumptions underlying the test are met if we do not know the population parameters? Usually we cannot, except by estimating population parameters from sample statistics. However, if we turn to nonparametric statistical tests, the problem does not arise, because these tests make no assumptions about the underlying population parameters. This is why these tests are often called distribution-free statistics. Because the parameters cannot be known anyway, this provides an important reason for using nonparametric tests. Another reason is that these tests are generally very easy to calculate and can often even be done by hand. However, nonparametric tests are usually less powerful than parametric tests used in the same situation; that is, they are less likely to allow the null hypothesis to be rejected.

The **Mann-Whitney** *U* **test** is used when we want to compare two samples and decide whether they come from the same or different underlying populations. It is used when the two samples are composed of different subjects—between-subjects designs. The underlying rationale for the Mann-Whitney test will not be discussed here. The logic is the same as in other statistical tests in which a value is computed from the test and compared with a distribution of values to determine whether the null hypothesis should be rejected. The way in which the Mann-Whitney test is applied to data is outlined in Box B–2, where the reliability of the difference between the two samples in our hypothetical LSD experiment is tested.

The **Wilcoxon signed-ranks test** is also used in testing for the difference between two samples, but in this case the design must be a *related-measures design*. In other words, either the same subjects must serve in both the experimental and control groups (a within-subjects design), or the subjects must be matched in some way. Of course, precautions must be taken in within-subjects designs to ensure that a variable such as practice or fatigue is not confounded with the variable of interest.

BOX B–2
Calculation of a
Mann-Whitney
U Test

These data are from our hypothetical experiment involving the effects of LSD on the running speeds of rats. Using the Mann-Whitney *U* test to test the reliability of the difference between our two samples, we follow these steps:

Step 1.   Rank all the numbers for *both groups* together, beginning with the smallest number. Assign it the lowest rank.

CONTROL (PLACEBO)		EXPERIMENTAL (LSD)	
Latency (sec.)	Rank	Latency (sec.)	Rank
9	1.5	9	1.5
10	3	13	11.5
11	4.5	13	11.5
11	4.5	14	17
12	7	14	17
12	7	15	21
12	7	16	24.5
13	11.5	16	24.5
13	11.5	16	24.5
13	11.5	17	28
13	11.5	17	28
14	17	18	32
14	17	18	32
14	17	18	32
15	21	18	32
15	21	19	35.5
16	24.5	19	35.5
17	28	20	37.5
18	32	22	39
20	37.5	26	40
	Σ rank$_1$ 295.5		Σ rank$_2$ 524.5

Note: When scores are tied, assign the mean value of the tied ranks to each. Thus, for both 9-second times in this example, the rank 1.5 is assigned (the mean of 1 and 2).

Step 2. The equations for finding U and U' are as follows, where n_1 is the size of the smaller sample, n_2 is the size of the larger sample, ΣR_1 is the sum of the ranks of the smaller sample, and ΣR_2 is the sum of the ranks of the larger sample. The subscripts are important only if the sample sizes are unequal, which is not the case here.

$$U = n_1 n_2 + \frac{n_1(n_1 + 1)}{2} - \Sigma R_1$$

$$U = (20)(20) + \frac{(20)(21)}{2} - 295.5$$

$$U = 400 + 210 - 295.5$$

$$U = 314.5$$

$$U' = n_1 n_2 + \frac{n_2(n_2 + 1)}{2} - \Sigma R_2$$

$$U' = (20)(20) + \frac{(20)(21)}{2} - 524.5$$

$$U' = 85.5$$

Actually, it is only necessary to compute U or U', because the other can be found according to the equation:

$$U = n_1 n_2 - U'$$

or

$$U' = n_1 n_2 - U$$

Step 3. Take U or U', whichever value is *smaller*, and look at Table C–2 (in appendix C) to see whether the difference between the two groups is reliable. The values in the table are recorded by different sample sizes. In this case, both sample sizes are 20, so the critical value from the table is 88. For the difference between the two groups to be judged reliable, the U or U' from the experiment must be *less than* the appropriate value shown in Table C–2. Because 85.5 is less than 88, we can conclude that the difference between the two groups is reliable at the .001 level of significance.

Note: Table C–2 is only appropriate when the sizes of the two samples are between 8 and 21. For other cases, consult an advanced text.

Before considering the signed-ranks test, let us examine its simpler cousin, the sign test, which is appropriate in the same situations. The sign test is the essence of simplicity. Suppose we have twenty-six subjects serving in both conditions of an experiment, and we predict that when subjects are in the experimental condition they will do better than when they are in the control condition. Now suppose that nineteen subjects actually do better in the experimental condition than in the control, and the reverse is true for the other seven. Is this difference reliable? The sign test yields an answer to this question without our needing to know what the actual scores were. Under the null hypothesis, we might expect thirteen subjects to perform better in the experimental condition and thirteen to perform better in the control. The sign test allows us to compute the exact probability that the null hypothesis is false when there are nineteen cases in the predicted direction but also seven reversals or exceptions. The null hypothesis can be rejected in this case with a .014 significance level (one-tailed); with a non-directional prediction, p equals .028 (two-tailed). In Table C–3 (in appendix C) are the α levels (one-tailed) for situations with sample sizes from three to forty-two when there are x number of exceptions to the predicted hypothesis. So, for example, when there are sixteen subjects in the experiment (remember, in both conditions) and thirteen show the predicted pattern of results whereas three exhibit reversals, we can reject the null hypothesis at the .011 level of significance (one-tailed).

The sign test uses very little of the data from an experiment, just whether the subjects performed better or worse in one condition than in another. For the sign test, the direction of the difference and not its magnitude is what matters. The sign test therefore wastes much of the information gathered in an experiment and is not a very powerful statistical test. The Wilcoxon signed-ranks test is used as the sign test in situations where the same (or matched) subjects are in two conditions and the direction of the difference is taken into account, too. For this reason it is also called the *sized sign test.* The Wilcoxon test is more powerful than the sign test. Box B–3 shows how the Wilcoxon signed-ranks test is used.

In Boxes B–4 and B–5 we present the corresponding t tests for the analyses presented in the previous two boxes. The t test is a parametric test, which means that we assume that the underlying distributions are roughly normal in shape. Furthermore, the t test and other parametric tests were designed to be used on data that are at least interval in nature. The U test and the sign test require only ordinal data. The t tests are essentially based on z scores having to do with the standard error of the difference between means. Thus, even if the computational formulas appear unusual at first, the underlying logic is the same as that discussed earlier in this chapter.

BOX B–3 Calculation of the Wilcoxon Signed- Ranks Test	Imagine an experiment designed to test whether Professor von Widget's memory course really works. A group of thirty subjects is presented with fifty words to remember. Then the subjects are randomly separated into two groups, and a check indicates that the groups do not differ reliably in terms of the mean number of words recalled. The experimental group is given Professor von Widget's three-week course, and the control group is not. Then all thirty subjects are tested again on another fifty-word list. The controls show no improvement from one list to another. The question is whether the experimental subjects' memories were reliably improved. (Note: We could—and should—also compare the experimental subjects' performance on the second test with that of the controls. The Mann-Whitney test is appropriate for this comparison. Do you know why?) We use the Wilcoxon signed-ranks test to assess whether the experimental subjects improved reliably from the first test to the second.

Step 1. Place the data in a table (such as the one that follows) where both scores for each subject (before and after the memory course) are paired together. Find and record the difference between the pairs.

MEAN NUMBER OF WORDS RECALLED				
Subject	Before	After	Difference	Rank
1	11	17	+ 6	14
2	18	16	− 2	5.5
3	9	21	+12	15
4	15	16	+ 1	2.5
5	14	17	+ 3	8.5
6	12	15	+ 3	8.5
7	17	16	− 1	2.5
8	16	17	+ 1	2.5
9	15	20	+ 5	13
10	19	16	− 3	8.5
11	12	13	+ 1	2.5
12	16	14	− 2	5.5
13	10	14	+ 4	11.5
14	17	20	+ 3	8.5
15	6	10	+ 4	11.5
	$\bar{X} = 13.80$	$\bar{X} = 16.07$		

Step 2. Rank the values of the differences according to size, beginning with the smallest. *Ignore the sign.* Use the absolute values of the numbers. For tied ranks, assign each the mean value of the ranks. (See the right-hand column of the table here.)

Step 3. Add the ranks for all the difference values that are negative (5.5 + 2.5 + 8.5 + 5.5 = 22.0) and positive (14 + 15 + 2.5 + 8.5 + 8.5 + 2.5 + 13 + 2.5 + 11.5 + 8.5 + 11.5 = 98.0). These are the signed-rank values.

Step 4. Take the signed-rank value that is smallest (22) and go to Table C–4 in Appendix C. Look up the number of pairs of observations (listed as *n* on the left). There are 15 in this case. Then look at the number under the desired level of significance. The direction of the outcome was predicted (we expected the memory course to help rather than hurt recall of words), so let us choose the value under the .025 level of significance for a one-tailed test. This value is 25. If the smaller of the two values from the experiment is *below* the appropriate value in the table, then the result is reliable. Since 22 is below 25, we can conclude that Professor von Widget's course really did help subjects recall words.

Note: Remember that the controls showed no improvement in performance from one test to the other. This is a crucial bit of information, for otherwise we could not rule out two plausible competing hypotheses—one is that the improvement on the second list was simply owing to practice on the first, and the other is that the second list was easier than the first.

BOX B-4
Calculation of a
Between-Subjects
t Test

These are hypothetical experimental data previously discussed (see Box B–2). The calculation formula is

$$t = \frac{\bar{X}_1 - \bar{X}_2}{\sqrt{\left[\frac{\Sigma X_1^2 - \frac{(\Sigma X_1)^2}{n_1} + \Sigma X_2^2 - \frac{(\Sigma X_2)^2}{n_2}}{n_1 + n_2 - 2}\right]\left[\frac{1}{n_1} + \frac{1}{n_2}\right]}}$$

$\bar{X}_1$ = mean of group 1
$\bar{X}_2$ = mean of group 2
n_1 = number of scores in group 1
n_2 = number of scores in group 2

ΣX_1^2 = sum of squared scores in group 1
ΣX_2^2 = sum of squared scores in group 2
$(\Sigma X_1)^2$ = square of group-1 sum
$(\Sigma X_2)^2$ = square of group-2 sum

CONTROL (PLACEBO)				EXPERIMENTAL (LSD)			
X	X²	X	X²	X	X²	X	X²
9	81	13	169	9	81	17	289
10	100	14	196	13	169	18	324
11	121	14	196	13	169	18	324
11	121	14	196	14	196	18	324
12	144	15	225	14	196	18	324
12	144	15	225	15	225	19	361
12	144	16	256	16	256	19	361
13	169	17	289	16	356	20	400
13	169	18	324	16	356	22	484
13	169	20	400	17	289	26	676
$\Sigma X = 272$		$\Sigma X^2 = 3838$		$\Sigma X = 338$		$\Sigma X^2 = 5960$	
$\bar{X} = 13.60$				$\bar{X} = 16.90$			

Step 1. After calculating ΣX, ΣX^2, and $\bar{X}$ for each group (by the way, there is no need to rank order our data), we need to calculate $(\Sigma X)^2/n$ for each group: $(272)^2/20 = 3699.20$ and $(338)^2/20 = 5712.20$. Then we need to determine $\Sigma X^2 - (\Sigma X)^2/n$ for each group: $3838 - 3699.2 = 138.8$ and $5960 - 5712.2 = 247.8$

Step 2. Now we add the two group figures we obtained in the last step: $247.8 + 138.8$, and divide this sum by $n_1 + n_2 - 2$: $386.6/38 = 10.17$.

Step 3. The quotient obtained in Step 2 (10.17) is multiplied by

$$\left[\frac{1}{n_1} + \frac{1}{n_2}\right]: (10.17)(2/20) = 1.02.$$

Step 4. We now take the square root of the product obtained in Step 3: $\sqrt{1.02} = 1.01$.

Step 5. We find the absolute difference between the mean scores of the two groups (by subtracting one from the other, and ignoring the sign): $16.90 - 13.60 = 3.30$.

Step 6. t = the difference between means (Step 5) divided by the results of Step 4: $3.30/1.01 = 3.27$. So, our $t = 3.27$. To evaluate this, we look in the tabled values of t in Table C–5 in appendix C. We enter this table with the number of degrees of freedom (df) in our experiment, which means the number of scores that are free to vary. For a between-subjects t, the degrees of freedom are $n_1 + n_2 - 2$, in this case $df = 38$. For $p = .05$ and $df = 38$, the critical value of t is 2.04 in our table (always take the next lowest df to calculate the critical value). Our obtained t exceeds the critical value, so we can reject the hypothesis that our two groups have the same running scores; that is, LSD had an effect on the behavior of our subjects.

BOX B–5
Calculation of a
Within-Subjects t
Test

The hypothetical data are from Professor Widget's experiment (see Box B–3). The computational formula for the within-subjects t test is as follows:

$$t = \sqrt{\frac{n - 1}{[n\Sigma D^2/(\Sigma D)^2] - 1}}$$

where n = number of subjects; and D = difference in the scores of a given subject (or matched subject pair) in the two conditions.

		MEAN NUMBER OF WORDS RECALLED		
Subject	**Before**	**After**	**Difference**	D^2
1	11	17	+ 6	36
2	18	16	− 2	4
3	9	21	+12	144
4	15	16	+ 1	1
5	14	17	+ 3	9
6	12	15	+ 3	9
7	17	16	− 1	1
8	16	17	+ 1	1
9	15	20	+ 5	25
10	19	16	− 3	9
11	12	13	+ 1	1
12	16	14	− 2	4
13	10	14	+ 4	16
14	17	20	+ 3	9
15	6	10	+ 4	16
	$\bar{X} = 13.80$	$\bar{X} = 16.07$	$\Sigma D = 35$	$\Sigma D^2 = 285$
			$(\Sigma D)^2 = 1,225$	

Step 1.   After you arrange the scores for each subject in pairs as shown in this table, record the difference between each pair and then square each of these difference scores.

Step 2.   Add the difference scores across subjects, which yields ΣD, then square this sum to get $(\Sigma D)^2$: $\Sigma D = 35$; and $(\Sigma D)^2 = 1,225$.

Step 3. Calculate the sum of the squared difference scores to get $\Sigma D^2 = 285$.

Step 4. Multiply ΣD^2 (Step 3) by the number of subjects: $285 \times 15 = 4{,}275$.

Step 5. Divide the product found in Step 4 by $(\Sigma D)^2$: $4{,}275/1{,}225 = 3.49$, and then subtract 1 from the result: $3.49 - 1 = 2.49$.

Step 6. Divide the number of subjects less 1 $(n - 1)$ by the result of Step 5: $14/2.49 = 5.62$.

Step 7. $t = \sqrt{5.62} = 2.37$.

Step 8. To evaluate t, compare it to the critical values shown in Table C–5 in appendix C. Enter the table with $n - 1$ df, and for this study $df = 14$. With $df = 14$, the critical value of t is 2.145 for $p = .05$. The obtained t exceeds the critical value, so we can conclude that von Widget's course really did affect word recall.

Magnitude of Effect. In summary, calculating a statistic such as z or t allows us to determine whether the results are owing to chance factors. Determining the α level of a difference, as in Box B–4, tells us that the difference is significant statistically, and we can reject the null hypothesis. An interesting characteristic of t (and the F test that we discuss next) is that the value of t needed to reject the null hypothesis decreases as the degrees of freedom increase. This means that the power of t increases with sample size just as z (see Table B–3). It is also the case, as the formula for the independent groups t in Box B–4 indicates, that as we hold the difference between means constant, increasing the sample size (n) will increase the value of t by making the denominator smaller. This too will allow us to have more power and reject more null hypotheses. In some cases, then, it is possible that very small differences between means will be statistically significant. Usually when we do an experiment, we want substantial differences between means—a big effect of the independent variable. With a very powerful experiment, however, we can detect differences between means that are exceptionally small. In the latter instance, we may not know whether the difference is owing to a powerful independent variable or a very powerful statistical test.

How do we know when we have a powerful independent variable? To determine the **magnitude of effect** of the independent variable, we need a way of showing the degree to which belonging in a particular group predicts the behavior. In the example in Box B–4, we would like to have a calculation that would allow us to have some idea as to whether a rat had received a placebo or LSD. The information we need is a correlation coefficient, because we want to predict what happened to a rat in much the same way we would want to predict a memory score based on head size as in Box A–1. After we have conducted a t test, we can then calculate a correlation to assess the magnitude of the effect. The correlation coefficient that would be appropriate here is r_{pb}, which is called the **point-biserial** correlation. The formula is

$$r_{pb} = \sqrt{t^2/(t^2 + df)} \qquad (B-4)$$

The value of r_{pb} can be between 0 and +1.00. By convention, values up to .3 are considered to be small, a value from .31 to .5 is moderate, and values over .5 are appreciable (Thompson & Buchanan, 1979). For the data in Box B–4, $t = 3.27$ and $df = 38$, which yields by formula B–4, $r_{pb} = .47$. This would be deemed a moderate effect. The same formula for r_{pb} could be used for the results in Box B–5. Why don't you determine what it is?

There are other measures of magnitude of effect, but we will not present the ones that are used with the F test, a discussion of which follows. The logic is the same regardless of the statistical test: the inferential statistics tell us how sure we may be that the null hypothesis is wrong. On the other hand, the correlation coefficients, such as r_{pb}, measure the magnitude of the effect of the independent variable—the degree to which the null hypothesis is wrong (Thompson & Buchanan, 1979).

Measures of magnitude of effect have another important use, which is also related to the fact that rejecting the null hypothesis is dependent on sample size. Suppose we conduct an experiment and discover that the value of t is not large enough to reject the null hypothesis even though the difference between means is not zero (that is, they differ). One reason that the t value is small could be owing to a sample size that is too small to detect a statistically significant difference between the means. In this case, a prudent researcher would calculate the appropriate measure of magnitude of effect, such as r_{pb}. If the coefficient yields a moderate or appreciable value, then it might be wise to increase the sample size in the experiment in order to reject the null hypothesis. Getting statistically significant results is important, but it is really only "half the battle." Significant results that are very small are not particularly exciting. Appreciable effects that are not statistically significant probably mean that you are on to something, and an increase in statistical power is warranted.

The Analysis of Variance

Most psychological research has progressed beyond the stage where there are only two conditions, an experimental and a control that are compared with each other. Investigators typically have more than two conditions in psychological research. In our example of the effects of LSD on running speed of rats, it may be quite useful to vary the amount of LSD administered to the rats. Perhaps low dosages and high dosages produce different effects. We could not determine this from the two-group design where one group received LSD in some amount and the other did not. To evaluate the results of such an experiment with multiple groups, we must use the analysis of variance. A simple analysis of variance is used in situations where one factor or independent variable (such as amount of LSD) is varied systematically, and thus is usually called a *one-factor analysis of variance*.

Often researchers are interested in varying more than one factor. They may want to vary two or more factors simultaneously. In such complex or multifactor experimental designs, the analysis of variance is also appropriate, but it is more complex. In this section, we introduce you to the logic of both simple and multifactor analyses of variance (abbreviated *ANOVA*).

Simple Analysis of Variance.   The heart of the analysis-of-variance procedure is a comparison of variance estimates. We have already discussed the concept of variance and how it is estimated from one particular sample of observations. You should refer back to the section on measures of dispersion if the concept of variance is unclear. Recall that the equation for the unbiased estimate of the population variance is

$$\hat{s}^2 = \frac{\Sigma(X - \bar{X})^2}{n - 1} \tag{B–5}$$

and that when the deviation of scores from the mean is large, the variance will be great. Similarly, when the deviations from the mean are small, the variance will be small.

In the analysis of variance, two independent estimates of variance are obtained. One is based on the variability between the different experimental groups—how much the means of the different groups differ from one another. Actually, the variance is computed as to how much the individual group means differ from the overall mean of all scores in the experiment. The greater the difference among the means of the groups, the greater will be the **between-groups variance.**

The other estimate of variance is the **within-groups variance.** This is the concept we discussed in considering estimates of variance from individual samples. Now we are concerned with finding an estimate of within-groups variance that is representative of all the individual groups, so we take the mean of the variances of these groups. The within-groups variance gives us an estimate of how much the subjects in the groups differ from one another (or the mean of the group). Two variance estimates are obtained, one for the variance within groups and one for the variance between groups. Now what good does this do?

The basic logic of testing to see whether the scores of the different groups or conditions are reliably different is as follows. The null hypothesis is that all the subjects in the various conditions are drawn from the same underlying population; the experimental variable has no effect. If the null hypothesis were true and all the scores in the different groups came from the same population, then the between-groups variance should be the same as the within-groups variance. The means of the different groups should differ from one another no more nor less than do the scores within the groups. For us to reject the null hypothesis, then, the means of the different groups must vary from one another more than the scores vary within the groups. The greater the variance (differences) between the groups of the experiment, the more likely the independent variable is to have had an effect, especially if the within-groups variance is low.

The person who originated this logic was the eminent British statistician R. A. Fisher, and the test is referred to as an F test in his honor. The F test is simply a ratio of the between-groups variance estimate to the within-groups variance estimate, so

$$F = \frac{\text{between-groups variance}}{\text{within-groups variance}} \qquad \text{(B–6)}$$

According to the logic just outlined, the F ratio under the null hypothesis should be 1.00, because the between-groups variance should be the same as the within-groups variance. The greater the between-groups variance is than the within-groups variance and, consequently, the greater the F ratio is than 1.00, the more confident we can be in rejecting the null hypothesis. Exactly how much greater the F ratio must be than 1.00 depends on the **degrees of freedom** in the experiment, or how free the measures are to vary. This depends both on the number of groups or conditions in the experiment and on the number of observations in each group. The greater the number of degrees of freedom, the smaller need be the value of the F ratio to be judged a reliable effect, as you can see from examining Table C–6 in appendix C. Follow the computational example in Box B–6 carefully to get a feel for the analysis of variance.

BOX B–6 Computing Simple Analysis of Variance: One Variable— Between Subjects	This ANOVA is often called a *one-way ANOVA* because there is only *one* independent variable. Imagine you have just performed an experiment testing the effects of LSD on the running speeds of rats, but that there were three levels of LSD administered, rather than two as in our earlier example. Ten rats received no LSD, ten others received a small amount, and a third group received a great amount. Thus the experiment uses a between-subjects design where amount of LSD (none, small, large) is the independent variable and running time is the dependent variable. First calculate the sum of the scores (ΣX) and the sum of the squared values of the scores (ΣX^2).

	AMOUNT OF LSD		
	None	**Small**	**Large**
	13	17	26
	11	15	20
	14	16	29
	18	20	31
	12	13	17
	14	19	25
	10	18	26
	13	17	23
	16	19	25
	12	21	27
ΣX =	133	175	249
$\bar{X}$ =	13.30	17.50	24.90
ΣX^2 =	1819	3115	6351
$\Sigma\Sigma X$ =	557	$\Sigma\Sigma X^2$ = 11285	

A basic quantity in calculating analysis of variance is the *sum of squares,* which is an abbreviation for the *sum of squared deviations from the mean.* If you look back to equation A–1 (in appendix A), which defines the variance of a sample, you will see that the sum of squares is the numerator. Three sum of squares are of interest. First, there is the total sum of squares (*SS* Total), which is the sum of the squared deviations of the individual scores from the grand mean or the mean of all scores in all groups in the experiment. Second, there is the sum of squares between groups (*SS* Between), which is the sum of the squared deviations of the group means from the grand mean. Third, the sum of squares within groups (*SS* Within) is the mean of the sum of the squared deviations of the individual scores within groups or conditions from the group means. It turns out that *SS* Total = *SS* Between + *SS* Within, so that in practice only two sums of squares need be calculated; the third can be found by subtraction.

These sums of squares could be calculated by taking the deviations from the appropriate means, squaring them, and then finding the sum, but such a method would take much time and labor. Fortunately, there are computational formulas that allow the calculations to be done more easily, especially if the values of ΣX and ΣX^2 have been found for each group, as in the present data. The formula for finding the total sum of squares is

$$SS \text{ Total} = \Sigma\Sigma X^2 - \frac{T^2}{N} \tag{B–7}$$

where $\Sigma\Sigma X^2$ means that each score within each group is squared (X^2) and all these squared values are added together, so ΣX^2. There are two summation signs, one for summing the squared values within groups and one for then summing these ΣX^2 across the different groups. The T is the total of all scores, and N is the total number of scores in the experiment. So *SS* Total in our example is calculated in the following way:

$$SS \text{ Total} = \Sigma\Sigma X^2 - \frac{T^2}{N}$$

$$SS \text{ Total} = 1819 + 3115 + 6351 - \frac{(133 + 175 + 249)^2}{30}$$

$$SS \text{ Total} = 11,285 - \frac{310,249}{30}$$

$$SS \text{ Total} = 11,285 - 10,341.63$$

$$SS \text{ Total} = 943.37$$

The between-groups sum of squares is calculated with the following formula:

$$SS \text{ Between} = \Sigma \frac{(\Sigma X)^2}{n} - \frac{T^2}{N} \tag{B–8}$$

The first part of the formula means that the sum of the values for each group is squared and then divided by the number of observations on which it is based, or $(\Sigma X)^2/n$; then these values are summed across groups, so $\Sigma(\Sigma X)^2/n$. The second part of the formula is the same as the *SS* Total:

$$SS \text{ Between} = \Sigma \frac{(\Sigma X)^2}{n} - \frac{T^2}{N}$$

$$SS \text{ Between} = \frac{17,689}{10} + \frac{30,625}{10} + \frac{62,001}{10} - 10,341.63$$

$$SS \text{ Between} = 11,031.50 - 10,341.63$$

$$SS \text{ Between} = 689.87$$

The sum of squares within groups can be found by subtracting SS Between from SS Total, so SS Within = 943.37 − 689.87 = 253.50. As a check, we should also calculate it directly. This is done by computing an SS Total (as in equation B–7) for each group and summing all these sums of squares for the individual groups. Unless we have made an error, this quantity should equal SS Within obtained by subtraction. Note that

$$\frac{(\Sigma\Sigma X)^2}{N} \text{ or } \frac{T^2}{N}$$

is called the *correction term* because it is taken out of most SS.

After we have obtained the various sums of squares, it is convenient to construct an analysis-of-variance table such as the one that follows. In the far left column appears the source of variance, or source. Keep in mind that there are two primary sources of variance we are interested in comparing—between groups and within groups.

In the next column are the number of degrees of freedom (*df*). These can be thought of as the number of scores that are free to vary, given that the total is fixed. For the degrees of freedom between groups, if the overall total is fixed, all groups are free to vary except one. Thus, the between-groups *df* is the number of groups minus one. In our example, then, it is 3 − 1 = 2. The within-groups *df* is equal to the total number of scores minus the number of groups, because there is one score in each group that cannot vary if the group total is fixed. So within-groups *df* is 30 − 3 = 27. The total *df* = between-groups *df* + within-groups *df*.

The third column includes the **sum of squares** (*SS*), which have already been calculated. The fourth column represents the *mean squares* (*MS*), which are found by dividing the *SS* by the *df* for each row. Each mean square is an estimate of the population variance if the null hypothesis is true. But if the independent variable had an effect, the between-groups mean square should be larger than the within-groups mean square.

As discussed in the text, these two values are compared by computing an *F* ratio, which is found by dividing the *MS* Between by the *MS* Within. Once the *F* value is calculated, it is necessary to determine whether the value reaches an acceptable level of statistical significance. By looking at Table C–6 in appendix C, we can see that for 2 and 26 degrees of freedom (the closest we can get to 2 and 27), an *F* value of 9.12 is needed for the .001 level of significance. Our *F* value surpasses 9.12, so we can conclude that the groups varied reliably in running speed because of variation in the independent variable—amount of LSD injected.

Source	df	SS	MS	F	p
Between-groups	2	689.87	344.94	36.73	<.001
Within-groups	27	253.50	9.39		
Total	29	943.37			

Note: If you compute analyses of variance with the aid of a calculator, watch out for errors. If you come up with a negative sum of squares within-groups (by subtracting SS Between from SS Total), you will know you made an error. You cannot have a negative sum of squares. You should compute SS Within both by subtraction and directly, anyway, as a check. One common error is to confuse ΣX^2 (square each number and then sum the squares) with $(\Sigma X)^2$, which is the square of the total of the scores.

BOX B–7
Within-Subjects (Treatments × Subjects) ANOVA—One Variable (One-way ANOVA)

We could have conducted the previous three-level LSD study with a within-subjects rather than a between-subjects design. Of course, we would have counterbalanced the order of administering dosages across subjects. Let us assume that we used nine subjects in our within-subjects LSD study: Three subjects received the dose order None-Large-Small; three received the doses in the Small-None-Large order; and three were dosed in the order Large-Small-None. After each dose of LSD, the rats' running time in the straight alley was recorded. We could analyze the effects of order by a two-factor, within-subjects ANOVA (see Box B–9), but for the purposes of this illustration, we will ignore the effects of treatment order.

In a within-subjects ANOVA, we need to calculate the following kinds of variability:

SS Total—This is the variation about the mean of all the scores. *SS* Total is the sum of the remaining sums of squares.

SS Treatment—This is the difference among the treatment conditions and is calculated like *SS* Between in the previous ANOVA.

SS Subjects—This estimates the differences among individuals in our experiment and is used to calculate the next *SS*.

SS Error or *SS Treatment* × *Subject*—This represents the random variability that would occur in the scores of the same individuals in the same conditions. This interaction gives the ANOVA the name **Treatments × Subjects.** Usually, this *SS* is called *error variance*, and it is the denominator of the *F* ratio of the treatment effect.

We will use the hypothetical data from the first nine subjects of the LSD study shown in Box B–6. We will assume the ordering of treatments as mentioned earlier. You should set up your data table as follows, so that the scores for each subject are in a row. Leave room so that a given subject's total score summed across treatments can appear in the table. You might also want to leave room for the squares of the scores and the squares of the subjects' totals.

RUNNING TIMES					
	Amount of LSD			Subject Total	Subject Total Squared
Subject	None	Small	Large		
1	13	17	26	56	3136
2	11	15	20	46	2116
3	14	16	29	59	3481
4	18	20	31	69	4761
5	12	13	17	42	1764
6	14	19	25	58	3364
7	10	18	26	54	2916
8	13	17	23	53	2809
9	16	19	25	60	3600
$\Sigma X =$	121	154	222	497	
$\Sigma X^2 =$	1675	2674	5622		27497
	$\Sigma\Sigma X = 497$	$\Sigma\Sigma X^2 = 9971 \ (1675 + 2674 + 5622)$			

Step 1.   When you calculate $\Sigma\Sigma X$ by adding the three treatment totals (121 + 154 + 222), you can check your accuracy by adding up the subject totals, the sum of which should equal $\Sigma\Sigma X$. Calculate ΣX^2 for each treatment, $\Sigma\Sigma X^2$, and the sum of the squares of the subject totals (last column).

Step 2.   Calculation of the correction term, C

$C = (\Sigma\Sigma X)^2/N$, where $N =$ the total number of scores in the table (9 subjects $\times$ 3 scores for each subject)
$= 497^2/27$
$= 247009/27$
$= 9148.48$

Step 3. SS Total $= \Sigma\Sigma X^2 -$ Step 2
$= 9971 - 9148.48$
$= 822.52$

Step 4. SS Treatments $= SS$ Dose. SS Dose is calculated by summing the squares of the treatment totals, dividing that sum by the number of scores in each treatment, and then subtracting C (Step 2).

SS Dose $= \dfrac{121^2 + 154^2 + 222^2}{9} -$ Step 2
$= 87419/9 -$ Step 2
$= 9737.89 - 9148.48$
$= 589.41$

Step 5. SS Subject $=$ Sum of the squared subject totals (final column in the table) divided by the number of scores per subject (3) minus C.
$= 27947/3 -$ Step 2
$= 9315.67 - 9148.48$
$= 167.19$

Step 6. SS Error $= SS$ Total $- SS$ Dose $- SS$ Subject
$=$ Step 3 $-$ Step 4 $-$ Step 5
$= 822.52 - 589.41 - 167.19$
$= 65.92$

Step 7.   Determination of *df*

$$df \text{ Total} = \# \text{ scores} - 1 = 26$$
$$df \text{ Dose} = \# \text{ treatments} - 1 = 2$$
$$df \text{ Subject} = \# \text{ subjects} - 1 = 8$$
$$df \text{ Error} = (df \text{ Dose})(df \text{ Subject}) = 16$$

Step 8.   Determination of *MS*

$$MS \text{ Dose} = SS \text{ Dose}/df \text{ Dose} = 589.41/2 = 294.71$$
$$MS \text{ Error} = SS \text{ Error}/df \text{ Error} = 65.92/16 = 4.12$$

Step 9. $F = MS \text{ Dose}/MS \text{ Error} = 294.71/4.12 = 71.53$

Step 10.   Summary Table

Source	SS	df	MS	F
Subjects	167.19	8		
Dose	589.41	2	294.71	71.53
Error	65.92	16	4.12	
Total	822.52	26		

We determine the significance of the *F* ratio by entering Table C–6 (in appendix C) with 2 and 16 degrees of freedom. Our obtained *F* greatly exceeds those needed for significance with 2 and 16 *df,* so we can conclude that dose level of LSD influenced the running times of our rats.

If the simple analysis of variance yields a significant *F* ratio, there is still more we would like to know, in particular, which of the individual conditions vary among themselves. This is especially important in cases where manipulation of the independent variable is qualitative in nature. *Quantitative* variation of an independent variable is when the quantity of an independent variable is manipulated (for example, amount of LSD), whereas *qualitative* variation is when conditions vary but not in some easily specified quantitative manner. An example of qualitative variation is an instructional manipulation in which the different conditions vary in terms of the instructions given at the beginning of the experiment. In such situations, it is not enough simply to say that the conditions vary reliably from one to another. It is of interest to know which particular conditions differ. To answer this question, we need to perform tests after the simple analysis of variance. In these follow-up tests (generally called post hoc tests), the conditions of the experiment are taken two at a time and compared so that we can see which pairs are reliably different. There are several statistical tests for this purpose. We could perform analyses of variance on groups taken as pairs, which is equivalent to performing *t* tests, but usually other tests are done. These include the Newman-Keuls test, the Scheffé test, Duncan's multiple-range test, Tukey's HSD (Honestly Significant Differences) test, and Dunnett's test. These tests vary in their assumptions and their power. You should consult statistical texts when you need to use a follow-up test. Follow-up tests are also used when manipulation of the independent variable is quantitative in nature. These are called *trend tests* (we will not discuss them here).

Multifactor Analysis of Variance. To discover the multiple determinants of behavior and how they interact, we must perform experiments in which more than one factor is varied simultaneously. The appropriate procedure for analyzing results of such experiments is the *multifactor analysis of variance*. There may be any number of factors in the experiment, but it is rare to find more than four variables of interest manipulated simultaneously. When there are two factors, the analysis is referred to as a two-way ANOVA; when there are three factors, it is a three-way ANOVA; and so on.

The importance of such complex designs involving more than one factor is that they allow the experimenter to assess how different factors may *interact* to produce a result. Recall that an interaction occurs when the effect of one experimental variable is influenced by the level of the other experimental variable. When performing a complex analysis of variance, we find out the separate effects of each factor in the experiment (called **main effects**), and also how the variables affect one another (called **interaction effects,** or simply *interactions*).

In the following two boxes, we present some recipes for complex ANOVAs. Because of space limitations, we have refrained from presenting much of the logic behind these tests. However, you should find the examples useful in analyzing your own results even if you have not had a formal course in statistics.

BOX B-8
Calculation of a
2 × 2 ANOVA

This is a between-subjects design. The data are from a memory experiment in which subjects had to remember words of either high imagery (cigar) or low imagery (democracy). Some subjects simply said the words to themselves as they were presented (rote rehearsal), and the other subjects tried to get a mental image of the words (elaborative rehearsal).

	HIGH-IMAGERY WORDS		LOW-IMAGERY WORDS	
	Rote Rehearsal	Elaborative Rehearsal	Rote Rehearsal	Elaborative Rehearsal
	5	8	4	7
	7	8	1	6
	6	9	5	3
	4	7	6	3
	4	10	4	5
	9	10	3	6
	7	8	4	2
	5	9	4	4
	5	8	5	5
	6	9	3	4
ΣX =	58	86	39	45
ΣX^2 =	358	748	169	225

$$\Sigma\Sigma X^2 = (358 + \ldots + 225) = 1500 \qquad \Sigma\Sigma X = 228$$

Step 1. Square the grand sum ($\Sigma\Sigma X = 228$) and divide by the total number of scores (40). $(\Sigma\Sigma X)^2/N = (228)^2/40 = 1299.6$. This is the correction term.

Step 2. SS Total $= \Sigma\Sigma X^2 - (\Sigma\Sigma X)^2/N$. Subtract the results of Step 1 from 1500. SS Total $= 200.4$.

Step 3. SS Imagery. Get the sum of all scores in each imagery condition, square each sum, then divide each sum by the number of scores yielding each sum, add the two quotients, and then subtract the results of Step 1 from the last sum.

$$SS \text{ Imagery} = (58 + 86)^2/20 + (39 + 45)^2/20 - \text{Step 1}$$

$$= \frac{144^2 + 84^2}{20} - 1299.6$$

$$= 1389.6 - 1299.6$$

$$= 90$$

Step 4. SS Rehearsal. This is calculated in the same manner as Step 3, except that you base your calculations on the grand sum of each type of rehearsal.

$$SS \text{ Rehearsal} = \frac{(86 + 45)^2 + (58 + 39)^2}{20} - \text{Step 1}$$

$$= 1328.5 - 1299.6$$

$$= 28.9$$

Step 5. SS Imagery $\times$ Rehearsal. Square each group sum and add the squares. Then divide each sum by the number of scores in each sum. From the last result, subtract the SS Imagery (Step 3), SS Rehearsal (Step 4), and Step 1.

$$SSI \times R = \frac{58^2 + 86^2 + 39^2 + 45^2}{10} - \text{Step 1} - \text{Step 3} - \text{Step 4}$$

$$= 14306/10 - 1299.6 - 90 - 28.9$$

$$= 12.1$$

Step 6. SS Error. Subtract each of your treatments SS from SS Total.

$$SS \text{ Error} = 200.4 - 90 - 28.9 - 12.1$$

$$= 69.4$$

Step 7. Determining degrees of freedom

df Total $=$ the number of measures less one $(40 - 1) = 39$
df Imagery $=$ number of levels of Imagery less one $(2 - 1) = 1$
df Rehearsal $=$ number of levels of Rehearsal less one $(2 - 1) = 1$
df I $\times$ R $= df$ Imagery $\times$ df Rehearsal $(1 \times 1) = 1$
df Error $= df$ Total $- df$ Imagery $- df$ Rehearsal $- df$ I $\times$ R
$(39 - 1 - 1 - 1) = 36$

Step 8. Summary table. Calculate mean squares (MS) by dividing SS by the number of df. Then calculate the F ratios by dividing the treatment MS by the MS Error.

SUMMARY TABLE OF A 2 × 2 ANOVA					
Source	SS	df	MS	F	p
Imagery	90.0	1	90.0	46.6	<.05
Rehearsal	28.9	1	28.9	15.0	<.05
Imagery × Rehearsal	12.1	1	12.1	6.3	<.05
Error	69.4	36	1.9		

Step 9.   To determine the significance of the F ratio, enter statistical Table C–6 with the df for the numerator (in this case it is always 1), and with the df for the denominator (df Error), which is 36, for any effect you are interested in.

We can conclude that the type of words and type of rehearsal both influenced recall. But we should note that the effects of word type were dependent on the type of rehearsal (that is, we obtained an interaction).

BOX B-9
Factorial ANOVA with Repeated Measures (Within-Subjects)

	ROTE REHEARSAL Retention Interval		ELABORATE REHEARSAL Retention Interval		SUBJECT TOTAL	REHEARSAL TOTAL		RETENTION TOTAL	
Subject	2 sec	12 sec	2 sec	12 sec		Rote	Elab.	2 sec	12 sec
1	15	3	11	11	40	18	22	26	14
2	20	15	19	18	72	35	37	39	33
3	18	2	18	19	57	20	37	36	21
4	15	13	16	15	59	28	31	31	28
5	10	1	17	12	40	11	29	27	13
6	14	5	16	13	48	19	29	30	18
7	17	6	19	18	60	23	37	36	24
8	19	12	16	19	66	31	35	35	31
9	11	4	9	12	36	15	21	20	16
10	17	10	14	7	48	27	21	31	17
11	18	11	18	10	57	29	28	36	21
12	18	4	20	19	61	22	39	38	23
13	16	9	19	18	62	25	37	35	27
14	18	6	19	17	60	24	36	37	23
15	10	5	10	7	32	15	17	20	12
16	16	5	19	18	58	21	37	35	23
$\Sigma X =$ 252		111	260	233	856	363	493	512	344
$\Sigma X^2 =$ 4114		1033	4408	3669	47776	24820		24910	

$$\Sigma\Sigma X = 856 \qquad \Sigma\Sigma X^2 = 13224$$

In a within-subjects ANOVA, we need to calculate both column (treatment) and row (subject) totals, because subjects are serving as their own control condition. In fact, our error variance is estimated by the interaction of subjects within treatments (see box B–7). Arrange your data table so that the scores of a single subject are in a row. It is usually a good idea to leave room so that treatment totals for a single subject may be placed in the table. We will analyze the data from Experiment 1 by Elmes and Bjork (1975). In their study, subjects either rote or elaboratively rehearsed words, and then they performed a distracting math task for 2 or 12 seconds before attempting to recall the words. Thus, this is a 2×2 within-subjects design. The individual subjects' total recall scores are shown in the table that begins this box.

Step 1. Determine the total score/subject (row) and total score/treatment combination (column). Find each subject's total score for every independent variable. The subject totals for a particular independent variable (for example, subject #1 has rehearsal totals of 18 and 22) should add up to that subject's total score (in this case, 40). Determine each treatment total by adding the appropriate column sums; check your answer by also adding the subject totals for that level of the independent variable. For example, the Rote Rehearsal total = 252 + 111 = 363 (sum of columns 1 and 2, which is equal to the sum of column 6).

Step 2. Determine the correction term (C). $C = (\Sigma\Sigma X)^2/N$, where $N =$ the number of measures in the table. $N = 16$ subjects $\times$ 4 scores = 64.

$$\begin{aligned} C &= 856^2/64 \\ &= 732736/64 \\ &= 11449 \end{aligned}$$

Step 3. SS Total $= \Sigma\Sigma X^2 -$ Step 2
$$\begin{aligned} &= 13224 - 11449 \\ &= 1775 \end{aligned}$$

Step 4. SS Subjects. Square each subject's total score (column 5), add the squares, and divide that total by the number of scores for each subject (4), then subtract the results of Step 2.

$$\begin{aligned} SS \text{ Subject} &= 47776/4 - \text{Step 2} \\ &= 11944 - 11449 \\ &= 495 \end{aligned}$$

Step 5. SS Rehearsal $= (363^2 + 493^2)/32 -$ Step 2
$$\begin{aligned} &= 374818/32 - \text{Step 2} \\ &= 11713.06 - 11449 \\ &= 264.06 \end{aligned}$$

Step 6. MS Rehearsal. Divide the SS Rehearsal by the df for Rehearsal. The df Rehearsal = the number of levels of Rehearsal − 1.

$$\begin{aligned} df \text{ Rehearsal} &= 2 - 1 \\ MS \text{ Rehearsal} &= 264.06/1 \\ &= 264.06 \end{aligned}$$

Step 7. *SS* Error Rehearsal. The error term for Rehearsal is the interaction of subjects with rehearsal. Square the subject totals for each level of Rehearsal (columns 6 and 7), add the squares, divide by the number of scores needed to get each sum (2 in this case), then subtract *C* (Step 2), *SS* Subject (Step 4), and *SS* Rehearsal (Step 5).

$$SS \text{ Error Rehearsal} = \frac{18^2 + 22^2 + \ldots + 21^2 + 37^2}{2} - \text{Steps 2, 4, and 5}$$

$$= 24820/2 - \text{Steps 2, 4, and 5}$$
$$= 12410 - 11449 - 495 - 264.06$$
$$= 201.94$$

Step 8. *MS* Error Rehearsal. Divide *SS* Error Rehearsal by *df* Error Rehearsal.

$$df = (\#\text{Subject} - 1)(df \text{ Rehearsal}) = (15)(1)$$
$$MS \text{ Error Rehearsal} = 201.94/15$$
$$= 13.46$$

Step 9. *F* Rehearsal = *MS* Rehearsal/*MS* Error Rehearsal
$$= \text{Step 6/Step 8}$$
$$= 264.06/13.46$$
$$= 19.62$$

Step 10. Repeat Steps 5–9 to find the *F* for Retention Interval (RI)

$$SS \text{ RI} = (512^2 + 344^2)/32 - \text{Step 2}$$
$$= 441.00$$
$$MS \text{ RI} = 441.00/(2 - 1)$$
$$= 441.00$$

$$SS \text{ Error RI} = \frac{26^2 + 14^2 + \ldots + 35^2 + 23^2}{2} - \text{Step 2, Step 4, and } SS \text{ RI}$$

$$= 24910/2 - C - SS \text{ Subject} - SS \text{ RI}$$
$$= 12455 - 11449 - 495 - 441$$
$$= 70$$

$$MS \text{ Error RI} = SS \text{ Error RI}/(16 - 1)(2 - 1)$$
$$= 70/15$$
$$= 4.67$$

$$F \text{ RI} = 441.00/4.67$$
$$= 94.43$$

Step 11. $SS \text{ Rehearsal} \times \text{RI} = \dfrac{252^2 + 111^2 + 260^2 + 233^2}{16} - C$

$$- SS \text{ Reh} - SS \text{ RI}$$
$$= 12357.13 - 11449 - 264.06 - 441.00$$
$$= 203.07$$

Step 12. $MS \text{ Rehearsal} \times \text{RI} = 203.07/(df \text{ Rehearsal})(df \text{ RI})$
$$= 203.07/1$$
$$= 203.07$$

Step 13. SS Error Rehearsal × RI. Calculate this triple interaction by subtracting all the SS you have calculated from SS Total.

$$
\begin{aligned}
SS \text{ Error Rehearsal} \times \text{RI} &= SS \text{ Total} - SS \text{ Subject} - SS \text{ Rehearsal} - SS \text{ RI} \\
&\quad - SS \text{ Rehearsal} \times \text{RI} - SS \text{ Error Rehearsal} \\
&\quad - SS \text{ Error RI} \\
&= 1775 - 495 - 264.06 - 441 - 203.07 \\
&\quad - 204.94 - 70 \\
&= 99.93
\end{aligned}
$$

Step 14. MS Error Rehearsal × RI = 99.93/(#Subject − 1)(df Rehearsal)(df RI)
$$
\begin{aligned}
&= 99.93/15 \\
&= 6.66
\end{aligned}
$$

Step 15. F Rehearsal × RI = MS Rehearsal × RI/MS Error Rehearsal × RI
$$
\begin{aligned}
&= 203.07/6.66 \\
&= 30.49
\end{aligned}
$$

Step 16.   Summary table of 2 × 2 within-subjects ANOVA

Source	SS	df	MS	F
Subjects	495.00	15		
Rehearsal	264.06	1	264.06	19.62
Error Reh	201.94	15	13.46	
Retention Interval	441.00	1	441.00	94.43
Error RI	70.00	15	4.67	
Reh × RI	203.07	1	203.07	30.49
Error Reh × RI	99.93	15	6.66	
Total	1775.00	63		

To determine significance, enter table C–6 with the appropriate degrees of freedom for each F ratio. (In this case, the $df = 1$ and 15). Note that both rehearsal and retention interval had significant effects on recall, and that the effects of type of rehearsal are dependent on the length of the retention interval.

STATISTICAL TABLES

STATISTICAL TABLES

TABLE C-1
Proportions of Area under the Normal Curve

Column A gives the positive z score.

Column B gives the area between the mean and z. Because the curve is symmetrical, areas for negative z scores are the same as for positive ones.

Column C gives the area that is beyond z.

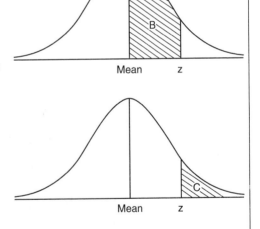

How to Use Table C-1: The values in this table represent the proportion of areas in the standard normal curve, which has a mean of 0, a standard deviation of 1.00, and a total area equal to 1.00. The raw scores must first be transformed into a z score. Column A represents this z score, Column B represents the distance between the mean of the standard normal distribution (0) and the z score, and Column C represents the proportion of the area beyond a given z.

TABLE C-1
(Continued)

(A) z	(B) area between mean and z	(C) area beyond z	(A) z	(B) area between mean and z	(C) area beyond z	(A) z	(B) area between mean and z	(C) area beyond z
0.00	.0000	.5000	0.45	.1736	.3264	0.90	.3159	.1841
0.01	.0040	.4960	0.46	.1772	.3228	0.91	.3186	.1814
0.02	.0080	.4920	0.47	.1808	.3192	0.92	.3212	.1788
0.03	.0120	.4880	0.48	.1844	.3156	0.93	.3238	.1762
0.04	.0160	.4840	0.49	.1879	.3121	0.94	.3264	.1736
0.05	.0199	.4801	0.50	.1915	.3085	0.95	.3289	.1711
0.06	.0239	.4761	0.51	.1950	.3050	0.96	.3315	.1685
0.07	.0279	.4721	0.52	.1985	.3015	0.97	.3340	.1660
0.08	.0319	.4681	0.53	.2019	.2981	0.98	.3365	.1635
0.09	.0359	.4641	0.54	.2054	.2946	0.99	.3389	.1611
0.10	.0398	.4602	0.55	.2088	.2912	1.00	.3413	.1587
0.11	.0438	.4562	0.56	.2123	.2877	1.01	.3438	.1562
0.12	.0478	.4522	0.57	.2157	.2843	1.02	.3461	.1539
0.13	.0517	.4483	0.58	.2190	.2810	1.03	.3485	.1515
0.14	.0557	.4443	0.59	.2224	.2776	1.04	.3508	.1492
0.15	.0596	.4404	0.60	.2257	.2743	1.05	.3531	.1469
0.16	.0636	.4364	0.61	.2291	.2709	1.06	.3554	.1446
0.17	.0675	.4325	0.62	.2324	.2676	1.07	.3577	.1423
0.18	.0714	.4286	0.63	.2357	.2643	1.08	.3599	.1401
0.19	.0753	.4247	0.64	.2389	.2611	1.09	.3621	.1379
0.20	.0793	.4207	0.65	.2422	.2578	1.10	.3643	.1357
0.21	.0832	.4168	0.66	.2454	.2546	1.11	.3665	.1335
0.22	.0871	.4129	0.67	.2486	.2514	1.12	.3686	.1314
0.23	.0910	.4090	0.68	.2517	.2483	1.13	.3708	.1292
0.24	.0948	.4052	0.69	.2549	.2451	1.14	.3729	.1271
0.25	.0987	.4013	0.70	.2580	.2420	1.15	.3749	.1251
0.26	.1026	.3974	0.71	.2611	.2389	1.16	.3770	.1230
0.27	.1064	.3936	0.72	.2642	.2358	1.17	.3790	.1210
0.28	.1103	.3897	0.73	.2673	.2327	1.18	.3810	.1190
0.29	.1141	.3859	0.74	.2704	.2296	1.19	.3830	.1170
0.30	.1179	.3821	0.75	.2734	.2266	1.20	.3849	.1151
0.31	.1217	.3783	0.76	.2764	.2236	1.21	.3869	.1131
0.32	.1255	.3745	0.77	.2794	.2206	1.22	.3888	.1112
0.33	.1293	.3707	0.78	.2823	.2177	1.23	.3907	.1093
0.34	.1331	.3669	0.79	.2852	.2148	1.24	.3925	.1075
0.35	.1368	.3632	0.80	.2881	.2119	1.25	.3944	.1056
0.36	.1406	.3594	0.81	.2910	.2090	1.26	.3962	.1038
0.37	.1443	.3557	0.82	.2939	.2061	1.27	.3980	.1020
0.38	.1480	.3520	0.83	.2967	.2033	1.28	.3997	.1003
0.39	.1517	.3483	0.84	.2995	.2005	1.29	.4015	.0985
0.40	.1554	.3446	0.85	.3023	.1977	1.30	.4032	.0968
0.41	.1591	.3409	0.86	.3051	.1949	1.31	.4049	.0951
0.42	.1628	.3372	0.87	.3078	.1922	1.32	.4066	.0934
0.43	.1664	.3336	0.88	.3106	.1894	1.33	.4082	.0918
0.44	.1700	.3300	0.89	.3133	.1867	1.34	.4099	.0901

TABLE C-1
(Continued)

(A) z	(B) area between mean and z	(C) area beyond z	(A) z	(B) area between mean and z	(C) area beyond z	(A) z	(B) area between mean and z	(C) area beyond z
1.35	.4115	.0885	1.80	.4641	.0359	2.25	.4878	.0122
1.36	.4131	.0869	1.81	.4649	.0351	2.26	.4881	.0119
1.37	.4147	.0853	1.82	.4656	.0344	2.27	.4884	.0116
1.38	.4162	.0838	1.83	.4664	.0336	2.28	.4887	.0113
1.39	.4177	.0823	1.84	.4671	.0329	2.29	.4890	.0110
1.40	.4192	.0808	1.85	.4678	.0322	2.30	.4893	.0107
1.41	.4207	.0793	1.86	.4686	.0314	2.31	.4896	.0104
1.42	.4222	.0778	1.87	.4693	.0307	2.32	.4898	.0102
1.43	.4236	.0764	1.88	.4699	.0301	2.33	.4901	.0099
1.44	.4251	.0749	1.89	.4706	.0294	2.34	.4904	.0096
1.45	.4265	.0735	1.90	.4713	.0287	2.35	.4906	.0094
1.46	.4279	.0721	1.91	.4719	.0281	2.36	.4909	.0091
1.47	.4292	.0708	1.92	.4726	.0274	2.37	.4911	.0089
1.48	.4306	.0694	1.93	.4732	.0268	2.38	.4913	.0087
1.49	.4319	.0681	1.94	.4738	.0262	2.39	.4916	.0084
1.50	.4332	.0668	1.95	.4744	.0256	2.40	.4918	.0082
1.51	.4345	.0655	1.96	.4750	.0250	2.41	.4920	.0080
1.52	.4357	.0643	1.97	.4756	.0244	2.42	.4922	.0078
1.53	.4370	.0630	1.98	.4761	.0239	2.43	.4925	.0075
1.54	.4382	.0618	1.99	.4767	.0233	2.44	.4927	.0073
1.55	.4394	.0606	2.00	.4772	.0228	2.45	.4929	.0071
1.56	.4406	.0594	2.01	.4778	.0222	2.46	.4931	.0069
1.57	.4418	.0582	2.02	.4783	.0217	2.47	.4932	.0068
1.58	.4429	.0571	2.03	.4788	.0212	2.48	.4934	.0066
1.59	.4441	.0559	2.04	.4793	.0207	2.49	.4936	.0064
1.60	.4452	.0548	2.05	.4798	.0202	2.50	.4938	.0062
1.61	.4463	.0537	2.06	.4803	.0197	2.51	.4940	.0060
1.62	.4474	.0526	2.07	.4808	.0192	2.52	.4941	.0059
1.63	.4484	.0516	2.08	.4812	.0188	2.53	.4943	.0057
1.64	.4495	.0505	2.09	.4817	.0183	2.54	.4945	.0055
1.65	.4505	.0495	2.10	.4821	.0179	2.55	.4946	.0054
1.66	.4515	.0485	2.11	.4826	.0174	2.56	.4948	.0052
1.67	.4525	.0475	2.12	.4830	.0170	2.57	.4949	.0051
1.68	.4535	.0465	2.13	.4834	.0166	2.58	.4951	.0049
1.69	.4545	.0455	2.14	.4838	.0162	2.59	.4952	.0048
1.70	.4554	.0446	2.15	.4842	.0158	2.60	.4953	.0047
1.71	.4564	.0436	2.16	.4846	.0154	2.61	.4955	.0045
1.72	.4573	.0427	2.17	.4850	.0150	2.62	.4956	.0044
1.73	.4582	.0418	2.18	.4854	.0146	2.63	.4957	.0043
1.74	.4591	.0409	2.19	.4857	.0143	2.64	.4959	.0041
1.75	.4599	.0401	2.20	.4861	.0139	2.65	.4960	.0040
1.76	.4608	.0392	2.21	.4864	.0136	2.66	.4961	.0039
1.77	.4616	.0384	2.22	.4868	.0132	2.67	.4962	.0038
1.78	.4625	.0375	2.23	.4871	.0129	2.68	.4963	.0037
1.79	.4633	.0367	2.24	.4875	.0125	2.69	.4964	.0036

TABLE C-1
(Continued)

(A) z	(B) area between mean and z	(C) area beyond z	(A) z	(B) area between mean and z	(C) area beyond z	(A) z	(B) area between mean and z	(C) area beyond z
2.70	.4965	.0035	2.95	.4984	.0016	3.20	.4993	.0007
2.71	.4966	.0034	2.96	.4985	.0015	3.21	.4993	.0007
2.72	.4967	.0033	2.97	.4985	.0015	3.22	.4994	.0006
2.73	.4968	.0032	2.98	.4986	.0014	3.23	.4994	.0006
2.74	.4969	.0031	2.99	.4986	.0014	3.24	.4994	.0006
2.75	.4970	.0030	3.00	.4987	.0013	3.25	.4994	.0006
2.76	.4971	.0029	3.01	.4987	.0013	3.30	.4995	.0005
2.77	.4972	.0028	3.02	.4987	.0013	3.35	.4996	.0004
2.78	.4973	.0027	3.03	.4988	.0012	3.40	.4997	.0003
2.79	.4974	.0026	3.04	.4988	.0012	3.45	.4997	.0003
2.80	.4974	.0026	3.05	.4989	.0011	3.50	.4998	.0002
2.81	.4975	.0025	3.06	.4989	.0011	3.60	.4998	.0002
2.82	.4976	.0024	3.07	.4989	.0011	3.70	.4999	.0001
2.83	.4977	.0023	3.08	.4990	.0010	3.80	.4999	.0001
2.84	.4977	.0023	3.09	.4990	.0010	3.90	.49995	.00005
2.85	.4978	.0022	3.10	.4990	.0010	4.00	.49997	.00003
2.86	.4979	.0021	3.11	.4991	.0009			
2.87	.4979	.0021	3.12	.4991	.0009			
2.88	.4980	.0020	3.13	.4991	.0009			
2.89	.4981	.0019	3.14	.4992	.0008			
2.90	.4981	.0019	3.15	.4992	.0008			
2.91	.4982	.0018	3.16	.4992	.0008			
2.92	.4982	.0018	3.17	.4992	.0008			
2.93	.4983	.0017	3.18	.4993	.0007			
2.94	.4984	.0016	3.19	.4993	.0007			

TABLE C–2
Critical Values of the *U* Statistic of the Mann-Whitney *U* Test

To use these four subtables, first decide what level of significance you want with either a one- or a two-tailed test. For example, if you want $p = .05$, two-tailed, use subtable c. Then locate the number of cases or measures (*n*) in both groups in the particular subtable you have chosen. The *U* value you have calculated must be *less* than that at the appropriate place in the table. For example, if you had 18 subjects in each group of an experiment, and calculated $U = 90$, you could conclude that the null hypothesis can be rejected because the critical *U* value with groups of these sizes is 99 (see subtable c).

(a) Critical Values of *U* for a One-Tailed Test at .001 or for a Two-Tailed Test at .002

n_1 \ n_2	9	10	11	12	13	14	15	16	17	18	19	20
1												
2												
3									0	0	0	0
4		0	0	0	1	1	1	2	2	3	3	3
5	1	1	2	2	3	3	4	5	5	6	7	7
6	2	3	4	4	5	6	7	8	9	10	11	12
7	3	5	6	7	8	9	10	11	13	14	15	16
8	5	6	8	9	11	12	14	15	17	18	20	21
9	7	8	10	12	14	15	17	19	21	23	25	26
10	8	10	12	14	17	19	21	23	25	27	29	32
11	10	12	15	17	20	22	24	27	29	32	34	37
12	12	14	17	20	23	25	28	31	34	37	40	42
13	14	17	20	23	26	29	32	35	38	42	45	48
14	15	19	22	25	29	32	36	39	43	46	50	54
15	17	21	24	28	32	36	40	43	47	51	55	59
16	19	23	27	31	35	39	43	48	52	56	60	65
17	21	25	29	34	38	43	47	52	57	61	66	70
18	23	27	32	37	42	46	51	56	61	66	71	76
19	25	29	34	40	45	50	55	60	66	71	77	82
20	26	32	37	42	48	54	59	65	70	76	82	88

TABLE C-2
(Continued)

(b) Critical Values of *U* for a One-Tailed Test at .01 or for a Two-Tailed Test at .02

n_1 \ n_2	9	10	11	12	13	14	15	16	17	18	19	20
1												
2					0	0	0	0	0	0	1	1
3	1	1	1	2	2	2	3	3	4	4	4	5
4	3	3	4	5	5	6	7	7	8	9	9	10
5	5	6	7	8	9	10	11	12	13	14	15	16
6	7	8	9	11	12	13	15	16	18	19	20	22
7	9	11	12	14	16	17	19	21	23	24	26	28
8	11	13	15	17	20	22	24	26	28	30	32	34
9	14	16	18	21	23	26	28	31	33	36	38	40
10	16	19	22	24	27	30	33	36	38	41	44	47
11	18	22	25	28	31	34	37	41	44	47	50	53
12	21	24	28	31	35	38	42	46	49	53	56	60
13	23	27	31	35	39	43	47	51	55	59	63	67
14	26	30	34	38	43	47	51	56	60	65	69	73
15	28	33	37	42	47	51	56	61	66	70	75	80
16	31	36	41	46	51	56	61	66	71	76	82	87
17	33	38	44	49	55	60	66	71	77	82	88	93
18	36	41	47	53	59	65	70	76	82	88	94	100
19	38	44	50	56	63	69	75	82	88	94	101	107
20	40	47	53	60	67	73	80	87	93	100	107	114

TABLE C–2
(Continued)

(c) Critical Values of *U* for a One-Tailed Test at .025 or for a Two-Tailed Test at .05

n_1 \ n_2	9	10	11	12	13	14	15	16	17	18	19	20
1												
2	0	0	1	1	1	1	1	1	2	2	2	2
3	2	3	3	4	4	5	5	6	6	7	7	8
4	4	5	6	7	8	9	10	11	11	12	13	13
5	7	8	9	11	12	13	14	15	17	18	19	20
6	10	11	13	14	16	17	19	21	22	24	25	27
7	12	14	16	18	20	22	24	26	28	30	32	34
8	15	17	19	22	24	26	29	31	34	36	38	41
9	17	20	23	26	28	31	34	37	39	42	45	48
10	20	23	26	29	33	36	39	42	45	48	52	55
11	23	26	30	33	37	40	44	47	51	55	58	62
12	26	29	33	37	41	45	49	53	57	61	65	69
13	28	33	37	41	45	50	54	59	63	67	72	76
14	31	36	40	45	50	55	59	64	67	74	78	83
15	34	39	44	49	54	59	64	70	75	80	85	90
16	37	42	47	53	59	64	70	75	81	86	92	98
17	39	45	51	57	63	67	75	81	87	93	99	105
18	42	48	55	61	67	74	80	86	93	99	106	112
19	45	52	58	65	72	78	85	92	99	106	113	119
20	48	55	62	69	76	83	90	98	105	112	119	127

| TABLE C–2 |
| (Continued) |

(d) Critical Values of U for a One-Tailed Test at .05 or for a Two-Tailed Test at .10

n_1 \ n_2	9	10	11	12	13	14	15	16	17	18	19	20
1											0	0
2	1	1	1	2	2	2	3	3	3	4	4	4
3	3	4	5	5	6	7	7	8	9	9	10	11
4	6	7	8	9	10	11	12	14	15	16	17	18
5	9	11	12	13	15	16	18	19	20	22	23	25
6	12	14	16	17	19	21	23	25	26	28	30	32
7	15	17	19	21	24	26	28	30	33	35	37	39
8	18	20	23	26	28	31	33	36	39	41	44	47
9	21	24	27	30	33	36	39	42	45	48	51	54
10	24	27	31	34	37	41	44	48	51	55	58	62
11	27	31	34	38	42	46	50	54	57	61	65	69
12	30	34	38	42	47	51	55	60	64	68	72	77
13	33	37	42	47	51	56	61	65	70	75	80	84
14	36	41	46	51	56	61	66	71	77	82	87	92
15	39	44	50	55	61	66	72	77	83	88	94	100
16	42	48	54	60	65	71	77	83	89	95	101	107
17	45	51	57	64	70	77	83	89	96	102	109	115
18	48	55	61	68	75	82	88	95	102	109	116	123
19	51	58	65	72	80	87	94	101	109	116	123	130
20	54	62	69	77	84	92	100	107	115	123	130	138

TABLE C-3
Distribution for the Sign Test

This table shows alpha levels of the sign test for pairs of observations ranging from 3 to 42. The symbol x denotes the number of exceptions (the number of times the difference between conditions is in the unexpected direction), and the p level indicates the probability that that number of exceptions could occur by chance. If, out of 28 paired observations, 20 are ordered in the expected direction and only 8 are exceptions, the probability that this could occur by chance is .018.

x	p	x	p	x	p	x	p	x	p	x	p
n = 3		n = 12		n = 19		n = 25		n = 31		n = 37	
0	.125	1	.003	3	.002	5	.002	7	.002	10	.004
n = 4		2	.019	4	.010	6	.007	8	.005	11	.010
0	.062	3	.073	5	.032	7	.022	9	.015	12	.024
1	.312	4	.194	6	.084	8	.051	10	.035	13	.049
n = 5		n = 13		7	.180	9	.115	11	.075	14	.094
0	.031	1	.002	n = 20		10	.212	12	.141	15	.162
1	.188	2	.011	3	.001	n = 26		n = 32		n = 38	
n = 6		3	.016	4	.006	6	.005	8	.004	10	.003
0	.016	4	.133	5	.021	7	.014	9	.010	11	.007
1	.109	n = 14		6	.058	8	.038	10	.025	12	.017
2	.344	1	.001	7	.132	9	.084	11	.055	13	.036
n = 7		2	.006	n = 21		10	.163	12	.108	14	.072
0	.008	3	.029	4	.004	n = 27		13	.189	15	.128
1	.062	4	.090	5	.013	6	.003	n = 33		n = 39	
2	.227	5	.212	6	.039	7	.010	8	.002	11	.005
n = 8		n = 15		7	.095	8	.026	9	.007	12	.012
0	.004	1	.000	8	.192	9	.061	10	.018	13	.027
1	.035	2	.004	n = 22		10	.124	11	.040	14	.054
2	.145	3	.018	4	.002	11	.221	12	.081	15	.100
n = 9		4	.059	5	.008	n = 28		13	.148	16	.168
0	.002	5	.151	6	.026	6	.002	n = 34		n = 40	
1	.020	n = 16		7	.067	7	.006	9	.005	11	.003
2	.090	2	.002	8	.143	8	.018	10	.012	12	.008
3	.254	3	.011	n = 23		9	.044	11	.029	13	.019
n = 10		4	.038	4	.001	10	.092	12	.061	14	.040
0	.001	5	.105	5	.005	11	.172	13	.115	15	.077
1	.011	6	.227	6	.017	n = 29		14	.196	16	.134
2	.055	n = 17		7	.047	7	.004	n = 35		n = 41	
3	.172	2	.001	8	.105	8	.012	9	.003	11	.002
n = 11		3	.006	9	.202	9	.031	10	.008	12	.006
0	.000	4	.025	n = 24		10	.068	11	.020	13	.014
1	.006	5	.072	5	.008	11	.132	12	.045	14	.030
2	.033	6	.166	6	.011	n = 30		13	.088	15	.059
3	.113	n = 18		7	.032	7	.003	14	.155	16	.106
4	.274	3	.004	8	.076	8	.008	n = 36		17	.174
		4	.015	9	.154	9	.021	9	.002	n = 42	
		5	.048			10	.049	10	.006	12	.004
		6	.119			11	.100	11	.014	13	.010
		7	.240			12	.181	12	.033	14	.022
								13	.066	15	.044
								14	.121	16	.082
								15	.203	17	.140

TABLE C–4
Critical Values of Wilcoxon's *T* Statistic for the Matched-Pairs Signed-Ranks Test

In using this table, first locate the number of *pairs* of scores in the *n* column. The critical values for several levels of significance are listed in the columns to the right. For example, if *n* were 15 and the computed value 19, we could conclude that since 19 is less than 25, the difference between conditions is significant beyond the .02 level of significance for a two-tailed test.

	LEVEL OF SIGNIFICANCE FOR ONE-TAILED TEST		
	.025	.01	.005
	LEVEL OF SIGNIFICANCE FOR TWO-TAILED TEST		
n	.05	.02	.01
6	1	—	—
7	2	0	—
8	4	2	0
9	6	3	2
10	8	5	3
11	11	7	5
12	14	10	7
13	17	13	10
14	21	16	13
15	25	20	16
16	30	24	19
17	35	28	23
18	40	33	28
19	46	38	32
20	52	43	37
21	59	49	43
22	66	56	49
23	73	62	55
24	81	69	61
25	90	77	68

TABLE C–5
Critical Values of t

To find the appropriate value of t, read across the row that contains the number of degrees of freedom in your experiment. The columns are determined by the level of significance you have chosen. The value of t you obtain must be *greater* than that in the table in order to be significant. For example, with $df = 15$ and $p = .05$ (two-tailed test), your t value must be greater than 2.131.

	LEVEL OF SIGNIFICANCE FOR ONE-TAILED TEST					
	.10	.05	.025	.01	.005	.0005
	LEVEL OF SIGNIFICANCE FOR TWO-TAILED TEST					
df	.20	.10	.05	.02	.01	.001
1	3.078	6.314	12.706	31.821	63.657	636.619
2	1.886	2.920	4.303	6.965	9.925	31.598
3	1.638	2.353	3.182	4.541	5.841	12.941
4	1.533	2.132	2.776	3.747	4.604	8.610
5	1.476	2.015	2.571	3.365	4.032	6.859
6	1.440	1.943	2.447	3.143	3.707	5.959
7	1.415	1.895	2.365	2.998	3.449	5.405
8	1.397	1.860	2.306	2.896	3.355	5.041
9	1.383	1.833	2.262	2.821	3.250	4.781
10	1.372	1.812	2.228	2.764	3.169	4.587
11	1.363	1.796	2.201	2.718	3.106	4.437
12	1.356	1.782	2.179	2.681	3.055	4.318
13	1.350	1.771	2.160	2.650	3.012	4.221
14	1.345	1.761	2.145	2.624	2.977	4.140
15	1.341	1.753	2.131	2.602	2.947	4.073
16	1.337	1.746	2.120	2.583	2.921	4.015
17	1.333	1.740	2.110	2.567	2.898	3.965
18	1.330	1.734	2.101	2.552	2.878	3.922
19	1.328	1.729	2.093	2.539	2.861	3.883
20	1.325	1.725	2.086	2.528	2.845	3.850
21	1.323	1.721	2.080	2.518	2.831	3.819
22	1.321	1.717	2.074	2.508	2.819	3.792
23	1.319	1.714	2.069	2.500	2.807	3.767
24	1.318	1.711	2.064	2.492	2.797	3.745
25	1.316	1.708	2.060	2.485	2.787	3.725
26	1.315	1.706	2.056	2.479	2.779	3.707
27	1.314	1.703	2.052	2.473	2.771	3.690
28	1.313	1.701	2.048	2.467	2.763	3.674
29	1.311	1.699	2.045	2.462	2.756	3.659
30	1.310	1.697	2.042	2.457	2.750	3.646
40	1.303	1.684	2.021	2.423	2.704	3.551
60	1.296	1.671	2.000	2.390	2.660	3.460
120	1.289	1.658	1.980	2.358	2.617	3.373
∞	1.282	1.645	1.960	2.326	2.576	3.291

TABLE C-6
Critical Values of the F Distribution

Find the appropriate values in the table by looking up the degrees of freedom in the numerator and denominator of the F ratio. After you have decided on the level of significance desired, the obtained F ratio must be *greater* than that in the table. For example, with $p = .05$ and 9 *df* in the numerator and 28 in the denominator, your F value must be greater than 2.24 to be reliable.

df for denom.	α	1	2	3	4	5	6	7	8	9
3	.25	2.02	2.28	2.36	2.39	2.41	2.42	2.43	2.44	2.44
	.10	5.54	5.46	5.39	5.34	5.31	5.28	5.27	5.25	5.24
	.05	10.1	9.55	9.28	9.12	9.01	8.94	8.89	8.85	8.81
	.025	17.4	16.0	15.4	15.1	14.9	14.7	14.6	14.5	14.5
	.01	34.1	30.8	29.5	28.7	28.2	27.9	27.7	27.5	27.4
	.001	167	148	141	137	135	133	132	131	130
4	.25	1.81	2.00	2.05	2.06	2.07	2.08	2.08	2.08	2.08
	.10	4.54	4.32	4.19	4.11	4.05	4.01	3.98	3.95	3.94
	.05	7.71	6.94	6.59	6.39	6.26	6.16	6.09	6.04	6.00
	.025	12.2	10.6	9.98	9.60	9.36	9.20	9.07	8.98	8.90
	.01	21.2	18.0	16.7	16.0	15.5	15.2	15.0	14.8	14.7
	.001	74.1	61.2	56.2	53.4	51.7	50.5	49.7	49.0	48.5
5	.25	1.69	1.85	1.88	1.89	1.89	1.89	1.89	1.89	1.89
	.10	4.06	3.78	3.62	3.52	3.45	3.40	3.37	3.34	3.32
	.05	6.61	5.79	5.41	5.19	5.05	4.95	4.88	4.82	4.77
	.025	10.0	8.43	7.76	7.39	7.15	6.98	6.85	6.76	6.68
	.01	16.3	13.3	12.1	11.4	11.0	10.7	10.5	10.3	10.2
	.001	47.2	37.1	33.2	31.1	29.8	28.8	28.2	27.6	27.2
6	.25	1.62	1.76	1.78	1.79	1.79	1.78	1.78	1.78	1.77
	.10	3.78	3.46	3.29	3.18	3.11	3.05	3.01	2.98	2.96
	.05	5.99	5.14	4.76	4.53	4.39	4.28	4.21	4.15	4.10
	.025	8.81	7.26	6.60	6.23	5.99	5.82	5.70	5.60	5.52
	.01	13.8	10.9	9.78	9.15	8.75	8.47	8.26	8.10	7.98
	.001	35.5	27.0	23.7	21.9	20.8	20.0	19.5	19.0	18.7
7	.25	1.57	1.70	1.72	1.72	1.71	1.71	1.70	1.70	1.69
	.10	3.59	3.26	3.07	2.96	2.88	2.83	2.78	2.75	2.72
	.05	5.59	4.74	4.35	4.12	3.97	3.87	3.79	3.73	3.68
	.025	8.07	6.54	5.89	5.52	5.29	5.12	4.99	4.90	4.82
	.01	12.2	9.55	8.45	7.85	7.46	7.19	6.99	6.84	6.72
	.001	29.2	21.7	18.8	17.2	16.2	15.5	15.0	14.6	14.3
8	.25	1.54	1.66	1.67	1.66	1.66	1.65	1.64	1.64	1.63
	.10	3.46	3.11	2.92	2.81	2.73	2.67	2.62	2.59	2.56
	.05	5.32	4.46	4.07	3.84	3.69	3.58	3.50	3.44	3.39
	.025	7.57	6.06	5.42	5.05	4.82	4.65	4.53	4.43	4.36
	.01	11.3	8.65	7.59	7.01	6.63	6.37	6.18	6.03	5.91
	.001	25.4	18.5	15.8	14.4	13.5	12.9	12.4	12.0	11.8
9	.25	1.51	1.62	1.63	1.63	1.62	1.61	1.60	1.60	1.59
	.10	3.36	3.01	2.81	2.69	2.61	2.55	2.51	2.47	2.44
	.05	5.12	4.26	3.86	3.63	3.48	3.37	3.29	3.23	3.18
	.025	7.21	5.71	5.08	4.72	4.48	4.32	4.20	4.10	4.03
	.01	10.6	8.02	6.99	6.42	6.06	5.80	5.61	5.47	5.35
	.001	22.9	16.4	13.9	12.6	11.7	11.1	10.7	10.4	10.1

TABLE C–6
(Continued)

df for denom.	α	1	2	3	4	5	6	7	8	9
10	.25	1.49	1.60	1.60	1.59	1.59	1.58	1.57	1.56	1.56
	.10	3.29	2.92	2.73	2.61	2.52	2.46	2.41	2.38	2.35
	.05	4.96	4.10	3.71	3.48	3.33	3.22	3.14	3.07	3.02
	.025	6.94	5.46	4.83	4.47	4.24	4.07	3.95	3.85	3.78
	.01	10.0	7.56	6.55	5.99	5.64	5.39	5.20	5.06	4.94
	.001	21.0	14.9	12.6	11.3	10.5	9.92	9.52	9.20	8.96
11	.25	1.47	1.58	1.58	1.57	1.56	1.55	1.54	1.53	1.53
	.10	3.23	2.86	2.66	2.54	2.45	2.39	2.34	2.30	2.27
	.05	4.84	3.98	3.59	3.36	3.20	3.09	3.01	2.95	2.90
	.025	6.72	5.26	4.63	4.28	4.04	3.88	3.76	3.66	3.59
	.01	9.65	7.21	6.22	5.67	5.32	5.07	4.89	4.74	4.63
	.001	19.7	13.8	11.6	10.4	9.58	9.05	8.66	8.35	8.12
12	.25	1.46	1.56	1.56	1.55	1.54	1.53	1.52	1.51	1.51
	.10	3.18	2.81	2.61	2.48	2.39	2.33	2.28	2.24	2.21
	.05	4.75	3.89	3.49	3.26	3.11	3.00	2.91	2.85	2.80
	.025	6.55	5.10	4.47	4.12	3.89	3.73	3.61	3.51	3.44
	.01	9.33	6.93	5.95	5.41	5.06	4.82	4.64	4.50	4.39
	.001	18.6	13.0	10.8	9.63	8.89	8.38	8.00	7.71	7.48
13	.25	1.45	1.55	1.55	1.53	1.52	1.51	1.50	1.49	1.49
	.10	3.14	2.76	2.56	2.43	2.35	2.28	2.23	2.20	2.16
	.05	4.67	3.81	3.41	3.18	3.03	2.92	2.83	2.77	2.71
	.025	6.41	4.97	4.35	4.00	3.77	3.60	3.48	3.39	3.31
	.01	9.07	6.70	5.74	5.21	4.86	4.62	4.44	4.30	4.19
	.001	17.8	12.3	10.2	9.07	8.35	7.86	7.49	7.21	6.98
14	.25	1.44	1.53	1.53	1.52	1.51	1.50	1.49	1.48	1.47
	.10	3.10	2.73	2.52	2.39	2.31	2.24	2.19	2.15	2.12
	.05	4.60	3.74	3.34	3.11	2.96	2.85	2.76	2.70	2.65
	.025	6.30	4.86	4.24	3.89	3.66	3.50	3.38	3.29	3.21
	.01	8.86	6.51	5.56	5.04	4.69	4.46	4.28	4.14	4.03
	.001	17.1	11.8	9.73	8.62	7.92	7.43	7.08	6.80	6.58
15	.25	1.43	1.52	1.52	1.51	1.49	1.48	1.47	1.46	1.46
	.10	3.07	2.70	2.49	2.36	2.27	2.21	2.16	2.12	2.09
	.05	4.54	3.68	3.29	3.06	2.90	2.79	2.71	2.64	2.59
	.025	6.20	4.77	4.15	3.80	3.58	3.41	3.29	3.20	3.12
	.01	8.68	6.36	5.42	4.89	4.56	4.32	4.14	4.00	3.89
	.001	16.6	11.3	9.34	8.25	7.57	7.09	6.74	6.47	6.26
16	.25	1.42	1.51	1.51	1.50	1.48	1.47	1.46	1.45	1.44
	.10	3.05	2.67	2.46	2.33	2.24	2.18	2.13	2.09	2.06
	.05	4.49	3.63	3.24	3.01	2.85	2.74	2.66	2.59	2.54
	.025	6.12	4.69	4.08	3.73	3.50	3.34	3.22	3.12	3.05
	.01	8.53	6.23	5.29	4.77	4.44	4.20	4.03	3.89	3.78
	.001	16.1	11.0	9.00	7.94	7.27	6.81	6.46	6.19	5.98
17	.25	1.42	1.51	1.50	1.49	1.47	1.46	1.45	1.44	1.43
	.10	3.03	2.64	2.44	2.31	2.22	2.15	2.10	2.06	2.03
	.05	4.45	3.59	3.20	2.96	2.81	2.70	2.61	2.55	2.49
	.025	6.04	4.62	4.01	3.66	3.44	3.28	3.16	3.06	2.98
	.01	8.40	6.11	5.18	4.67	4.34	4.10	3.93	3.79	3.68
	.001	15.7	10.7	8.73	7.68	7.02	6.56	6.22	5.96	5.75

df for numerator

TABLE C-6 (Continued)

df for denom.	α	\multicolumn{9}{c}{df for numerator}
		1	**2**	**3**	**4**	**5**	**6**	**7**	**8**	**9**
18	.25	1.41	1.50	1.49	1.48	1.46	1.45	1.44	1.43	1.42
	.10	3.01	2.62	2.42	2.29	2.20	2.13	2.08	2.04	2.00
	.05	4.41	3.55	3.16	2.93	2.77	2.66	2.58	2.51	2.46
	.025	5.98	4.56	3.95	3.61	3.38	3.22	3.10	3.01	2.93
	.01	8.29	6.01	5.09	4.58	4.25	4.01	3.84	3.71	3.60
	.001	15.4	10.4	8.49	7.46	6.81	6.35	6.02	5.76	5.56
19	.25	1.41	1.49	1.49	1.47	1.46	1.44	1.43	1.42	1.41
	.10	2.99	2.61	2.40	2.27	2.18	2.11	2.06	2.02	1.98
	.05	4.38	3.52	3.13	2.90	2.74	2.63	2.54	2.48	2.42
	.025	5.92	4.51	3.90	3.56	3.33	3.17	3.05	2.96	2.88
	.01	8.18	5.93	5.01	4.50	4.17	3.94	3.77	3.63	3.52
	.001	15.1	10.2	8.28	7.26	6.62	6.18	5.85	5.59	5.39
20	.25	1.40	1.49	1.48	1.47	1.45	1.44	1.43	1.42	1.41
	.10	2.97	2.59	2.38	2.25	2.16	2.09	2.04	2.00	1.96
	.05	4.35	3.49	3.10	2.87	2.71	2.60	2.51	2.45	2.39
	.025	5.87	4.46	3.86	3.51	3.29	3.13	3.01	2.91	2.84
	.01	8.10	5.85	4.94	4.43	4.10	3.87	3.70	3.56	3.46
	.001	14.8	9.95	8.10	7.10	6.46	6.02	5.69	5.44	5.24
22	.25	1.40	1.48	1.47	1.45	1.44	1.42	1.41	1.40	1.39
	.10	2.95	2.56	2.35	2.22	2.13	2.06	2.01	1.97	1.93
	.05	4.30	3.44	3.05	2.82	2.66	2.55	2.46	2.40	2.34
	.025	5.79	4.38	3.78	3.44	3.22	3.05	2.93	2.84	2.76
	.01	7.95	5.72	4.82	4.31	3.99	3.76	3.59	3.45	3.35
	.001	14.4	9.61	7.80	6.81	6.19	5.76	5.44	5.19	4.99
24	.25	1.39	1.47	1.46	1.44	1.43	1.41	1.40	1.39	1.38
	.10	2.93	2.54	2.33	2.19	2.10	2.04	1.98	1.94	1.91
	.05	4.26	3.40	3.01	2.78	2.62	2.51	2.42	2.36	2.30
	.025	5.72	4.32	3.72	3.38	3.15	2.99	2.87	2.78	2.70
	.01	7.82	5.61	4.72	4.22	3.90	3.67	3.50	3.36	3.26
	.001	14.0	9.34	7.55	6.59	5.98	5.55	5.23	4.99	4.80
26	.25	1.38	1.46	1.45	1.44	1.42	1.41	1.39	1.38	1.37
	.10	2.91	2.52	2.31	2.17	2.08	2.01	1.96	1.92	1.88
	.05	4.23	3.37	2.98	2.74	2.59	2.47	2.39	2.32	2.27
	.025	5.66	4.27	3.67	3.33	3.10	2.94	2.82	2.73	2.65
	.01	7.72	5.53	4.64	4.14	3.82	3.59	3.42	3.29	3.18
	.001	13.7	9.12	7.36	6.41	5.80	5.38	5.07	4.83	4.64
28	.25	1.38	1.46	1.45	1.43	1.41	1.40	1.39	1.38	1.37
	.10	2.89	2.50	2.29	2.16	2.06	2.00	1.94	1.90	1.87
	.05	4.20	3.34	2.95	2.71	2.56	2.45	2.36	2.29	2.24
	.025	5.61	4.22	3.63	3.29	3.06	2.90	2.78	2.69	2.61
	.01	7.64	5.45	4.57	4.07	3.75	3.53	3.36	3.23	3.12
	.001	13.5	8.93	7.19	6.25	5.66	5.24	4.93	4.69	4.50
30	.25	1.38	1.45	1.44	1.42	1.41	1.39	1.38	1.37	1.36
	.10	2.88	2.49	2.28	2.14	2.05	1.98	1.93	1.88	1.85
	.05	4.17	3.32	2.92	2.69	2.53	2.42	2.33	2.27	2.21
	.025	5.57	4.18	3.59	3.25	3.03	2.87	2.75	2.65	2.57
	.01	7.56	5.39	4.51	4.02	3.70	3.47	3.30	3.17	3.07
	.001	13.3	8.77	7.05	6.12	5.53	5.12	4.82	4.58	4.39

**TABLE C–6
(Continued)**

df for denom.	α	1	2	3	4	5	6	7	8	9
40	.25	1.36	1.44	1.42	1.40	1.39	1.37	1.36	1.35	1.34
	.10	2.84	2.44	2.23	2.09	2.00	1.93	1.87	1.83	1.79
	.05	4.08	3.23	2.84	2.61	2.45	2.34	2.25	2.18	2.12
	.025	5.42	4.05	3.46	3.13	2.90	2.74	2.62	2.53	2.45
	.01	7.31	5.18	4.31	3.83	3.51	3.29	3.12	2.99	2.89
	.001	12.6	8.25	6.60	5.70	5.13	4.73	4.44	4.21	4.02
60	.25	1.35	1.42	1.41	1.38	1.37	1.35	1.33	1.32	1.31
	.10	2.79	2.39	2.18	2.04	1.95	1.87	1.82	1.77	1.74
	.05	4.00	3.15	2.76	2.53	2.37	2.25	2.17	2.10	2.04
	.025	5.29	3.93	3.34	3.01	2.79	2.63	2.51	2.41	2.33
	.01	7.08	4.98	4.13	3.65	3.34	3.12	2.95	2.82	2.72
	.001	12.0	7.76	6.17	5.31	4.76	4.37	4.09	3.87	3.69
120	.25	1.34	1.40	1.39	1.37	1.35	1.33	1.31	1.30	1.29
	.10	2.75	2.35	2.13	1.99	1.90	1.82	1.77	1.72	1.68
	.05	3.92	3.07	2.68	2.45	2.29	2.17	2.09	2.02	1.96
	.025	5.15	3.80	3.23	2.89	2.67	2.52	2.39	2.30	2.22
	.01	6.85	4.79	3.95	3.48	3.17	2.96	2.79	2.66	2.56
	.001	11.4	7.32	5.79	4.95	4.42	4.04	3.77	3.55	3.38
∞	.25	1.32	1.39	1.37	1.35	1.33	1.31	1.29	1.28	1.27
	.10	2.71	2.30	2.08	1.94	1.85	1.77	1.72	1.67	1.63
	.05	3.84	3.00	2.60	2.37	2.21	2.10	2.01	1.94	1.88
	.025	5.02	3.69	3.12	2.79	2.57	2.41	2.29	2.19	2.11
	.01	6.63	4.61	3.78	3.32	3.02	2.80	2.64	2.51	2.41
	.001	10.8	.91	5.42	4.62	4.10	3.74	3.47	3.27	3.10

df for numerator

TABLE C-7
Random Numbers

	1	2	3	4	5	6	7	8	9
1	32942	95416	42339	59045	26693	49057	87496	20624	14819
2	07410	99859	83828	21409	29094	65114	36701	25762	12827
3	59981	68155	45673	76210	58219	45738	29550	24736	09574
4	46251	25437	69654	99716	11563	08803	86027	51867	12116
5	65558	51904	93123	27887	53138	21488	09095	78777	71240
6	99187	19258	86421	16401	19397	83297	40111	49326	81686
7	35641	00301	16096	34775	21562	97983	45040	19200	16383
8	14031	00936	81518	48440	02218	04756	19506	60695	88494
9	60677	15076	92554	26042	23472	69869	62877	19584	39576
10	66314	05212	67859	89356	20056	30648	87349	20389	53805
11	20416	87410	75646	64176	82752	63606	37011	57346	69512
12	28701	56992	70423	62415	40807	98086	58850	28968	45297
13	74579	33844	33426	07570	00728	07079	19322	56325	84819
14	62615	52342	82968	75540	80045	53069	20665	21282	07768
15	93945	06293	22879	08161	01442	75071	21427	94842	26210
16	75689	76131	96837	67450	44511	50424	82848	41975	71663
17	02921	16919	35424	93209	52133	87327	95897	65171	20376
18	14295	34969	14216	03191	61647	30296	66667	10101	63203
19	05303	91109	82403	40312	62191	67023	90073	83205	71344
20	57071	90357	12901	08899	91039	67251	28701	03846	94589
21	78471	57741	13599	84390	32146	00871	09354	22745	65806
22	89242	79337	59293	47481	07740	43345	25716	70020	54005
23	14955	59592	97035	80430	87220	06392	79028	57123	52872
24	42446	41880	37415	47472	04513	49494	08860	08038	43624
25	18534	22346	54556	17558	73689	14894	05030	19561	56517
26	39284	33737	42512	86411	23753	29690	26096	81361	93099
27	33922	37329	89911	55876	28379	81031	22058	21487	54613
28	78355	54013	50774	30666	61205	42574	47773	36027	27174
29	08845	99145	94316	88974	29828	97069	90327	61842	29604
30	01769	71825	55957	98271	02784	66731	40311	88495	18821
31	17639	38284	59478	90409	21997	56199	30068	82800	69692
32	05851	58653	99949	63505	40409	85551	90729	64938	52403
33	42396	40112	11469	03476	03328	84238	26570.	51790	42122
34	13318	14192	98167	75631	74141	22369	36757	89117	54998
35	60571	54786	26281	01855	30706	66578	32019	65884	58485
36	09531	81853	59334	70929	03544	18510	89541	13555	21168
37	72865	16829	86542	00396	20363	13010	69645	49608	54738
38	56324	31093	77924	28622	83543	28912	15059	80192	83964
39	78192	21626	91399	07235	07104	73652	64425	85149	75409
40	64666	34767	97298	92708	01994	53188	78476	07804	62404
41	82201	75694	02808	65983	74373	66693	13094	74183	73020
42	15360	73776	40914	85190	54278	99054	62944	47351	89098
43	68142	67957	70896	37983	20487	95350	16371	03426	13895
44	19138	31200	30616	14639	44406	44236	57360	81644	94761
45	28155	03521	36415	78452	92359	81091	56513	88321	97910
46	87971	29031	51780	27376	81056	86155	55488	50590	74514
47	58147	68841	53625	02059	75223	16783	19272	61994	71090
48	18875	52809	70594	41649	32935	26430	82096	01605	65846
49	75109	56474	74111	31966	29969	70093	98901	84550	25769
50	35983	03742	76822	12073	59463	84420	15868	99505	11426

REFERENCES

Adams, J. A. (1972). Research and the future of engineering psychology. *American Psychologist, 27,* 615–622.

American Psychological Association. (1972). Guidelines for psychologists for the use of drugs in research. *American Psychologist, 27,* 336.

American Psychological Association. (1981a). Ethical principles of psychologists. *American Psychologist, 36,* 633–638.

American Psychological Association. (1981b). Guidelines for the use of animals in school-science behavior projects. *American Psychologist, 36,* 686.

American Psychological Association. (1982). *Ethical principles in the conduct of research with human behavior.* Washington, DC: Author.

American Psychological Association. (1987). *Casebook on ethical issues.* Washington, DC: Author.

American Psychological Association. (1989). Ethical principles of psychologists. *American Psychologist, 45,* 390–395.

American Psychological Association. (1994). *Publication manual of the American Psychological Association* (4th ed.). Washington, DC: Author.

Anderson, N. H. (1981). *Foundations of information integration theory.* New York: Academic Press.

Atkinson, R. C. (1975). Mnemotechnics and second-language learning. *American Psychologist, 30,* 821–828.

Bachman, J. D., & Johnston, L. D. (1979). The freshman. *Psychology Today, 13,* 78–87.

Banaji, M. R., & Crowder, R. G. (1989). The bankruptcy of everyday memory. *American Psychologist, 44,* 1185–1193.

Barber, T. X. (1976). *Pitfalls in human research: Ten pivotal points.* New York: Pergamon.

Barefoot, J. C., Hoople, H., & McClay, D. (1972). Avoidance of an act which would violate personal space. *Psychonomic Science, 28,* 205–206.

Barker, R. G. (1968). *Ecological psychology.* Stanford, CA: Stanford University Press.

Barker, R. G., & Wright, H. F. (1951). *One boy's day.* New York: Harper and Row.

Begg, I. M., Anas, A., & Farinacci, S. (1992). Dissociation of process in belief: Source recollection, statement familiarity, and the illusion of truth. *Journal of Experimental Psychology: General, 121,* 446–458.

Bem, D. J. (1987). Writing the empirical journal article. In M. P. Zanna & J. M. Darley (Eds.), *The compleat academic: A practical guide for the beginning social scientist.* New York: Random House.

Berkowitz, L., & Donnerstein, E. (1982). External validity is more than skin deep. *American Psychologist, 37,* 245–257.

Best, J. B. (1989). *Cognitive psychology* (2nd ed.). St. Paul, MN: West.

Blaauw, G. J. (1982). Driving experience and task demands in simulator and instrumented car: A validation study. *Human Factors, 24,* 473–486.

Blaney, R. H. (1986). Affect and memory: A review. *Psychological Bulletin, 99,* 229–246.

Boice, R. (1983). Observational skills. *Psychological Bulletin, 93,* 3–29.

Boring, E. G. (1950). *A history of experimental psychology.* New York: Appleton Century-Crofts.

Boring, E. G. (1954). The nature and history of experimental control. *American Journal of Psychology, 67,* 573–589.

Boring, E. G. (1961). The beginning and growth of measurement in psychology, *Isis, 52,* 238–257.

Bowd, A. D. (1980). Ethical reservations about psychological research with animals. *Psychological Record, 30,* 201–210.

Bower, G. H. (1972). Mental imagery and associative learning. In L. Gregg (Ed.), *Cognition in learning and memory.* New York: Wiley.

Bradley, M. T., & Rettinger, J. (1992). Awareness of crime-relevant information and the guilty knowledge test. *Journal of Applied Psychology, 77,* 55–59.

Brady, J. V. (1958). Ulcers in "executive" monkeys. *Scientific American, 199,* 92–100.

Brady, J. V., Porter, R. W., Conrad, D. G., & Mason, J. W. (1958). Avoidance behavior and the development of gastroduodenal ulcers. *Journal of the Experimental Analysis of Behavior, 1,* 69–72.

Brennen, T., Baguley, T., Bright, J., & Bruce, V. (1990). Resolving semantically induced tip-of-the-tongue states. *Memory & Cognition, 18,* 339–347.

Broad, W., & Wade, N. (1982). *Betrayers of the truth.* New York: Simon and Schuster.

Broadbent, D. E. (1971). *Decision and stress.* London: Academic Press.

Broadbent, D. E. (1973). *In defence of empirical psychology.* London: Methuen.

Brown, R., & McNeill, D. (1966). The "tip-of-the-tongue" phenomenon. *Journal of Verbal Learning and Verbal Behavior, 5,* 325–327.

Butters, N., & Cermak, L. S. (1986). A case study of the forgetting of autobiographical knowledge: Implications for the study of retrograde amnesia. In D. Rubin (Ed.), *Autobiographical memory* (pp. 253–272). New York: Cambridge University Press.

Campbell, D. T., & Erlebacher, A. (1970a). How regression artifacts can mistakenly make compensatory education look harmful. In J. Helmuth (Ed.), *Compensatory education: A national debate: Vol. 3 Disadvantaged child.* New York: Brunner/Mazel.

Campbell, D. T., & Erlebacher, A. (1970b). Reply to the replies. In J. Helmuth (Ed.), *Compensatory education: A national debate: Vol. 3. Disadvantaged child.* New York: Brunner/Mazel.

Campbell, D. T., & Stanley, J. C. (1963). *Experimental and quasi-experimental designs for research.* Chicago: Rand McNally.

Carver, C. S., Coleman, A. E., & Glass, D. C. (1976). The coronary-prone behavior pattern and the suppression of fatigue on a treadmill test. *Journal of Personality and Social Psychology, 33,* 460–466.

Chaplin, J. P. (1968). *Dictionary of psychology.* New York: Dell.

Cicirelli, V. (1970). The relevance of the regression artifact problem to the Westinghouse-Ohio evaluation of Head Start: A reply to Campbell and Erlebacher. In J. Helmuth (Ed.), *Compensatory education: A national debate: Vol. 3 Disadvantaged child.* New York: Brunner/Mazel.

Cicirelli, V., & Granger, R. (1969, June). *The impact of Head Start: An evaluation of the effects of Head Start on children's cognitive and affective development.* A report presented to the Office of Economic Opportunity pursuant to Contract B89–4356. Westinghouse Learning Corporation, Ohio University. (Distributed by Clearinghouse for Federal Scientific and Technical Information, U.S. Department of Commerce, National Bureau of Standards, Institute for Applied Technology, PB 184–328.)

Cohen, J. D., Dunbar, K., & McClelland, J. L. (1990). On the control of automatic processes: A parallel distributed processing account of the Stroop effect. *Psychological Review, 97*, 332–361.

Colasanto, D. (1989, October). Earthquake fails to shake composure of many Bay Area residents. *Gallup Report, 289*, 21–23.

Cole, M., Gay, J., Glick, J. A., & Sharp, D. W. (1971). *The cultural context of learning and thinking*. New York: Basic Books.

Comish, S. E. (1987). Recognition of facial stimuli following an intervening task involving the Identi-kit. *Journal of Applied Psychology, 72*, 488–491.

Cook, T. D., & Campbell, D. T. (1979). *Quasi-experimentation: Design and analysis for field settings*. Chicago: Rand McNally.

Craik, F. I. M., & Lockhart, R. S. (1972). Levels of processing: A framework for memory research. *Journal of Verbal Learning and Verbal Behavior, 11*, 671–684.

Crowder, R. G., & Wagner, R. K. (1992). *The psychology of reading*. New York: Oxford University Press.

D'Amato, M. R. (1970). *Experimental psychology: Methodology, psychophysics, and learning*. New York: McGraw-Hill.

Darley, J. M., & Zanna, M. P. (1987). The hiring process in academia. In M. P. Zanna and J. M. Darley (Eds.), *The compleat academic*. Hillsdale, NJ: Erlbaum.

DeGreene, K. B. (Ed.). (1970). *Systems psychology*. New York: McGraw-Hill.

Desharnais, R., Godin, G., Joblin, J., & Valois, P. (1990). Optimism and health relevant cognitions after a myocardial infarction. *Psychological Reports, 67*, 1131–1135.

Devenport, L. D., & Devenport, J. D. (1990). The laboratory animal dilemma: A solution in our backyards. *Psychological Science, 1*, 215–216.

Dewing, K., & Hetherington, P. (1974). Anagram solving as a function of word imagery. *Journal of Experimental Psychology, 102*, 764–767.

Dipboye, R. L., & Flanagan, M. F. (1979). Research settings in industrial and organizational psychology. *American Psychologist, 34*, 141–150.

Dollard, J., & Miller, N. E. (1950). *Personality and psychotherapy*. New York: McGraw-Hill.

Duncan, K. D., & Praetorius, N. (1992). Flow displays representing complex-plant for diagnosis and process-control. *Reliability Engineering & System Safety, 36*, 239–244.

Edwards, A. L. (1953). The relationship between the judged desirability of a trait and the probability that the trait will be endorsed. *Journal of Applied Psychology, 37*, 90–93.

Edwards, A. L. (1957). *The social desirability variable in personality research*. New York: Dryden.

Egeth, H., Blecker, D. L., & Kamlet, A. S. (1969). Verbal interference in a perceptual comparison task. *Perception & Psychophysics, 6*, 355–356.

Eibl-Eibesfeldt, I. (1970). *Ethology: The biology of behavior*. New York: Holt, Rinehart & Winston.

Eibl-Eibesfeldt, I. (1972). Similarities and differences between cultures in expressive movements. In R. A. Hinde (Ed.), *Non-verbal communication*. Cambridge, England: Cambridge University Press.

Elmes, D. G. (1978). *Readings in experimental psychology*. Chicago: Rand McNally.

Elmes, D. G. (1988, May 8). Cheap-shot prize goes to Proxmire. *Roanoke Times & World News*, p. F3.

Elmes, D. G., & Bjork, R. A. (1975). The interaction of encoding and rehearsal processes in the recall of repeated and nonrepeated items. *Journal of Verbal Learning and Verbal Behavior, 14*, 30–42.

Elmes, D. G., Chapman, P. F., & Selig, C. W. (1984). Role of mood and connotation in the spacing effect. *Bulletin of the Psychonomic Society, 22*, 186–188.

Eron, L. D. (1982). Parent-child interaction, television violence, and aggression of children. *American Psychologist, 37,* 197–211.

Eron, L. D., Huesmann, L. R., Lefkowitz, M. M., & Walder, L. O. (1972). Does television violence cause aggression? *American Psychologist, 27,* 253–263.

Evans, J. W., & Schiller, J. (1970). How preoccupation with possible regression artifacts can lead to a faulty strategy for the evaluation of social action programs: A reply to Campbell and Erlebacher. In J. Helmuth (Ed.), *Compensatory education: A national debate: Vol. 3. Disadvantaged child.* New York: Brunner/Mazel.

Eysenck, H. J., & Eaves, L. J. (1981). *The cause and effects of smoking.* New York: Gage.

Fechner, G. (1860/1966). *Elements of psychophysics,* Vol. 1. (H. E. Adler, D. H. Howes, and E. G. Boring, Eds. and Trans.). New York: Holt, Rinehart and Winston.

Feingold, B. F. (1975). Hyperkinesis and learning disabilities linked to artificial food flavors and colors. *American Journal of Nursing, 75,* 797–803.

Festinger, L. (1957). *A theory of cognitive dissonance.* Stanford, CA: Stanford University Press.

Festinger, L., Riecken, H. W., & Schachter, S. (1956). *When prophecy fails.* Minneapolis: University of Minnesota Press.

Ficken, M. S. (1990). Acoustic characteristics of alarm calls associated with predation risk in chickadees. *Animal Behaviour, 39,* 400–401.

Fingerman, P., & Levine, M. (1974). Nonlearning: The completeness of the blindness. *Journal of Experimental Psychology, 102,* 720–721.

Fleming, R., Leventhal, H., Glynn, K., & Ershler, J. (1989). The role of cigarettes in the initiation and progression of early substance abuse. *Addictive Behaviors, 14,* 261–272.

Fossey, D. (1972). Living with mountain gorillas. In T. B. Allen (Ed.), *The marvels of animal behavior.* Washington, DC: National Geographic Society.

Freedle, R., & Kostin, I. (1994). Can multiple-choice reading tests be construct-valid? A reply to Katz, Lautenschlager, Blackburn, and Harris. *Psychological Science, 5,* 107–110.

Gabrenya, W. K., Latané, B., & Wang, Y. (1983). Social loafing in cross-cultural perspective: Chinese on Taiwan. *Journal of Cross-Cultural Psychology, 14,* 368–384.

Gallup, G. G., & Suarez, S. D. (1985). Alternatives to the use of animals in psychological research. *American Psychologist, 40,* 1104–1111.

Garner, W. R., Hake, H., & Eriksen, C. W. (1956). Operationism and the concept of perception. *Psychological Review, 63,* 149–159.

Glenberg, A. M. (1988). *Learning from data.* San Diego: Harcourt Brace Jovanovich.

Goldstein, G., & Hersen, M. (Eds.). (1990). *Handbook of psychological assessment* (2nd ed.). New York: Pergamon.

Graessle, O. A., Ahbel, K., & Porges, S. W. (1978). Effects of mild prenatal decompressions on growth and behavior in the rat. *Bulletin of the Psychonomic Society, 12,* 329–331.

Green, D. M., & Swets, J. A. (1966). *Signal detection theory and psychophysics.* New York: Wiley.

Greenough, W. T. (1992). Animal rights replies distort(ed) and misinform(ed). *Psychological Science, 3,* 142.

Gregory, R. (1970). *The intelligent eye.* New York: McGraw-Hill.

Guilford, J. P. (1967). *The nature of human intelligence.* New York: McGraw-Hill.

Guttman, L. L. (1944). A basis for scaling quantitative data. *American Sociological Review, 9,* 139–150.

Guttman, L. L. (1950). The basis for scalogram analysis. In S. A. Stouffer, L. L. Guttman, E. A. Suchman, P. W. Lazarsfield, J. A. Star, & J. A. Clausen, *Studies in social psychology—World War II* (Vol. 4). Princeton, NJ: Princeton University Press.

Hanson, N. R. (1958). *Patterns of discovery.* Cambridge: Cambridge University Press.

Harkins, S. G., Latané, B., & Williams, K. (1980). Social loafing: Allocating effort or taking it easy? *Journal of Experimental Social Psychology, 16,* 457–465.

Harlow, H. F. (1959, June). Love in infant monkeys. *Scientific American, 200(6),* 68–74.

Harlow, H. F., Gluck, J. P., & Suomi, S. J. (1972). Generalization of behavioral data between nonhuman and human animals. *American Psychologist, 27,* 709–716.

Harré, R. (1983). *Great scientific experiments.* Oxford: Oxford University Press.

Hart, B. M., Allen, K. E., Buell, J. S., Harris, F. R., & Wolf, M. M. (1964). Effects of social reinforcement on operant crying. *Journal of Experimental Child Psychology, 1,* 145–153.

Hicks, R. A., & Kilcourse, J. (1983). Habitual sleep duration and the incidence of headaches in college students. *Bulletin of the Psychonomic Society, 21,* 119.

Hintzman, D. L., Carre, F. A., Eskridge, V. L., Owens, A. M., Shaff, S. S., & Sparks, M. E. (1972). "Stroop" effect: Input or output phenomenon? *Journal of Experimental Psychology, 95,* 458–459.

Hoff, C. (1980). Immoral and moral uses of animals. *New England Journal of Medicine, 302,* 115–118.

Homans, G. C. (1965). Group factors in worker productivity. In H. Proshansky and L. Seidenberg (Eds.), *Basic studies in social psychology.* New York: Holt.

Horowitz, L. M. (1974). *Elements of statistics for psychology and education.* New York: McGraw-Hill.

Howard, D. V., & Wiggs, C. L. (1993). Aging and learning: Insights from implicit and explicit tests. In J. Cerella, W. J. Hoyer, J. Rybash, & M. Commons (Eds.), *Adult age differences: Limits on loss.* New York: Academic Press.

Huesmann, L. R., Eron, L. D., Leftkowitz, M. M., & Walder, L. O. (1973). Television violence and aggression: The causal effect remains. *American Psychologist, 28,* 617–620.

Huff, D. (1954). *How to lie with statistics.* New York: Norton.

Hurlburt, R. L. (1994). *Comprehending behavioral statistics.* Pacific Grove, CA: Brooks/Cole.

Hyman, R. (1964). *The nature of psychological inquiry.* Englewood Cliffs, NJ: Prentice-Hall.

Imber, S. D., Glanz, L. M., Elkin, I., Sotsky, S. M., Boyer, J. L., & Leber, W. R. (1986). Ethical issues in psychotherapy research: Problems in a collaborative clinical study. *American Psychologist, 41,* 137–146.

Jarrad, L. E. (1963). Effects of d-lysergic acid diethylamide on operant behavior in the rat. *Psychopharmacologia, 5,* 39–46.

Jensen, A. R. (1969). How much can we boost I.Q. and scholastic achievement? *Harvard Educational Review, 39,* 1–123.

Johnson-Laird, P. N. (1988). *The computer and the mind: An introduction to cognitive science.* Cambridge: Harvard University Press.

Jones, R. F. (1982). *Ancients and moderns.* New York: Dover.

Judd, C. M., Smith, E. R., & Kidder, L. H. (1991). *Research methods in social relations* (6th ed.). Fort Worth: Holt, Rinehart and Winston.

Kantowitz, B. H. (1974). Double stimulation. In B. H. Kantowitz (Ed.), *Human information processing—Tutorials in performance and cognition.* Hillsdale, NJ: Erlbaum.

Kantowitz, B. H. (1990). Can cognitive theory guide human factors measurement? *Proceedings of the Human Factors Society, 34,* 1258–1262.

Kantowitz, B. H. (1992a). Selecting measures for human factors research. *Human Factors, 34,* 387–398.

Kantowitz, B. H. (1992b). Heavy vehicle driver workload assessment: Lessons from aviation. *Proceedings of the Human Factors Society, 36,* 1113–1117.

Kantowitz, B. H. (1994, January). *Evaluating driver workload in a heavy vehicle simulator.* Paper presented at INEL Workload Transition Workshop, Idaho Falls, ID.

Kantowitz, B. H., & Caspar, P. A. (1988). Human workload in aviation. In E. Weiner & D. Nagel (Eds.), *Human factors in aviation.* New York: Academic Press, 157–187.

Kaplan, R. M., & Saccuzzo, D. P. (1982). *Psychological testing: Principles, applica-*

tions, and issues. Monterey, CA: Brooks/Cole.

Katz, D. (1979, February 7). Paying the price for drug development. *Roanoke Times & World News.*

Katz, S., Lautenschlager, G., Blackburn, A., & Harris, F. (1990). Answering reading comprehension items without passages on the SAT. *Psychological Science, 1,* 122–127.

Kelloway, K. K., & Barling, J. (1993). Members' participation in local union activities: Measurement, prediction, and replication. *Journal of Applied Psychology, 78,* 262–279.

Kendler, H. H. (1981). *Psychology: A science in conflict.* New York: Oxford.

Kerlinger, F. (1986). *Foundations of behavioral research.* New York: Holt, Rinehart & Winston.

Kinsey, A. C., Pomeroy, W. B., & Martin, C. E. (1953). *Sexual behavior in the human female.* Philadelphia: Saunders.

Kinzel, A. F. (1970). Body-buffer zone in violent prisoners. *The American Journal of Psychiatry, 127,* 59–64.

Kirk, R. R. (1982). *Experimental design: Procedures for the behavioral sciences* (2nd ed.). Belmont, CA: Brooks/Cole.

Kohn, A. (1986). *False prophets.* New York: Basil Blackwell.

Kravitz, D. A., & Martin B. (1986). Ringelmann rediscovered: The original article. *Journal of Personality and Social Psychology, 50,* 936–941.

Kuhn, T. S. (1962). *The structure of scientific revolutions.* Chicago: University of Chicago Press.

Latané, B. (1981). The psychology of social impact. *American Psychologist, 36,* 343–356.

Latané, B., & Darley, J. M. (1970). *The unresponsive bystander—Why doesn't he help?* New York: Appleton-Century-Crofts.

Latané, B., Williams, K., & Harkins, S. (1979). Many hands make light the work: Causes and consequences of social loafing. *Journal of Personality and Social Psychology, 37,* 822–832.

Leon, G. R. (1990). *Case histories of psychopathology* (4th ed.). Boston: Allyn and Bacon.

Lester, B. M., & Brazelton, T. B. (1982). Cross-cultural assessment of neonatal behavior. In D. A. Wagner & H. W. Stevenson (Eds.), *Cultural perspectives on child development.* San Francisco: Freeman.

Levin, I. P., Louviere, J. J., & Schepanski, A. A. (1983). External validity tests of laboratory studies of information integration. *Organizational Behavior and Human Performance, 31,* 173–193.

Likert, R. (1932). A technique for the measurement of attitudes. *Archives of Psychology, 140,* 44–53.

Lovelace, E. A., & Twohig, P. T. (1990). Healthy older adult's perception of their memory function and use of mnemonics. *Bulletin of the Psychonomic Society, 28,* 115–118.

Luchins, A. S. (1942). Mechanization in problem solving: The effect of Einstellung. *Psychological Monographs, 54* (6, Whole No. 181).

MacLeod, C. M. (1991). Half a century of research on the Stroop effect: An integrative review. *Psychological Bulletin, 109,* 163–203.

Marks, L. E. (1974). *Sensory process: The new psychophysics.* New York: Academic Press.

Marriot, P. (1949). size of working groups and output. *Occupational Psychology, 23,* 47–57.

Martin, P., & Bateson, P. (1993). *Measuring behaviour: An introductory guide* (2nd. ed.) Cambridge: Cambridge University Press.

Masling, J. (1966). Role-related behavior of the subject and psychologist and its effects upon psychological data. *Nebraska symposium on motivation* (Vol. 14). Lincoln: University of Nebraska Press.

Massaro, D. W. (1975). *Experimental psychology and information processing.* Chicago: Rand McNally.

Mayer, R. E. (1977). Problem-solving performance with task overload: Effects of self-pacing and trait anxiety. *Bulletin of the Psychonomic Society, 9,* 283–286.

Mayr, E. (1982). *The growth of biological thought.* Cambridge, MA: Belknap Press.

Mayzner, M. S., & Tresselt, M. E. (1966). Anagram solution times: A function of multiple solution anagrams. *Journal of Experimental Psychology, 71,* 66–73.

McCall, R. B. (1990). *Fundamental statistics for the behavioral sciences* (5th ed.). San Diego: Harcourt Brace.

McSweeny, A. J. (1978). The effects of response cost on the behavior of a million persons: Charging for directory assistance in Cincinnati. *Journal of Applied Behavior Analysis, 11,* 47–51.

Melton, G., & Gray, J. (1988). Ethical dilemmas in AIDS research: Individual privacy and public health. *American Psychologist, 43,* 60–64.

Milgram, S. (1963). Behavioral study of obedience. *Journal of Abnormal and Social Psychology, 67,* 371–378.

Milgram, S. (1977). Ethical issues in the study of obedience. In B. Milgram (Ed.), *The individual in a social world* (pp. 188–199). Reading, MA: Addison-Wesley.

Mill, J. S. (1930). *A system of logic.* London: Longmans Green. (Original work published 1843).

Miller, D. B. (1977). Roles of naturalistic observation in comparative psychology. *American Psychologist, 32,* 211–219.

Miller, N. E. (1985). The value of behavioral research on animals. *American Psychologist, 40,* 423–440.

Mook, D. G. (1983). In defense of external invalidity. *American Psychologist, 38,* 379–387.

Moscovitch, M. (1982). Multiple dissociations of functions in the amnesiac syndrome. In L. Cermak (Ed.), *Human memory and amnesia.* Hillsdale, NJ: Erlbaum.

Neisser, U. (1976). *Cognition and reality: Principles and implications of cognitive psychology.* San Francisco: Freeman.

Neisser, U. (1978). Memory: What are the important questions? In M. M. Gruneberg, P. E. Morris, & R. N. Sykes (Eds.), *Practical aspects of memory* (pp. 3–24). London: Academic Press.

Neisser, U. (1981). John Dean's memory, *Cognition, 9,* 1–22.

Neisser, U. (1982). *Memory observed: Remembering in natural contexts.* San Francisco: Freeman.

Nissen, M. J., Ross, J. L., Willingham, D. B., MacKenzie, T. B., & Schacter, D. L. (1988). Memory and awareness in a patient with multiple personality disorder. *Brain and Cognition, 8,* 117–134.

Notterman, J. M., & Mintz, D. E. (1965). *Dynamics of response.* New York: Wiley.

Orne, M. T. (1962). On the social psychology of the psychological experiment: With particular reference to demand characteristics and their implications. *American Psychologist, 17,* 776–783.

Orne, M. T. (1969). Demand characteristics and the concept of quasi-controls. In R. Rosenthal & R. L. Rosnow (Eds.), *Artifact in behavioral research.* New York: Academic Press.

Orne, M. T., & Evans, T. J. (1965). Social control in the psychological experiment: Antisocial behavior and hypnosis. *Journal of Personality and Social Psychology, 1,* 189–200.

Paivio, A. (1975). Perceptual comparisons through the mind's eye. *Memory & Cognition, 3,* 635–647.

Parsons, H. M. (1974). What happened at Hawthorne? *Science, 183,* 922–931.

Pavlov, I. P. (1963). *Lectures on conditioned reflexes.* New York: International Publishers.

Peirce, C. S. (1877). The fixation of belief. *Popular Science Monthly, 12,* 1–15. Reprinted in E. C. Moore (Ed.). (1972). *Charles S. Peirce: The essential writings.* New York: Harper & Row.

Perlmutter, M., & Myers, N. A. (1979). Development of recall in two- to four-year old children. *Developmental Psychology, 15,* 73–83.

Phillips, D. P. (1972). Deathday and birthday: An unexpected connection. In J. Tanur, F. Mosteller, W. H. Kruskal, R. F. Link, R. S. Peters, & G. R. Rising (Eds.), *Statistics: A guide to the unknown.* San Francisco: Holden Day.

Phillips, D. P. (1977). Motor vehicle fatalities increase just after publicized suicide stories. *Science, 196,* 1464–1465.

Phillips, D. P. (1978). Airplane accident fatalities increase just after stories about murder and suicide. *Science, 201,* 148–150.

Phillips, D. P. (1983). The impact of mass media violence on U.S. homicides. *American Sociological Review, 48,* 560–568.

Piaget, J., & Inhelder, B. (1969). *The psychology of the child.* London: Routledge & Kegan Paul.

Piliavin, I. M., Piliavin, J. A., & Rodin, J. (1975). Costs, diffusion and the stigmatized victim. *Journal of Personality and Social Psychology, 32,* 429–438.

Platt, J. R. (1964). Strong inference. *Science, 146,* 347–353.

Plous, S. (1991). An attitude survey of animal rights activists. *Psychological Science, 2,* 194–196.

Popper, K. R. (1961). *The logic of scientific discovery.* New York: Basic Books.

Poulton, E. C. (1982). Influential companions: Effects of one strategy on another in the within-subjects designs of cognitive psychology. *Psychological Bulletin, 9,* 673–690.

Pratkanis, A. R., Greenwald, A. G., Leippe, M. R., & Baumgardner, M. H. (1988). In search of reliable persuasion effects: The sleeper effect is dead. Long live the sleeper effect. *Journal of Personality and Social Psychology, 54,* 203–218.

Putnam, F. W., Guroff, J. J., Silberman, E. K., Barban, L., & Post, R. M. (1986). The clinical phenomenology of multiple personality disorder: 100 recent cases. *Journal of Clinical Psychiatry, 47,* 285–293.

Read, J. D. (1983). Detection of Fs in a single statement: The role of phonetic recoding. *Memory & Cognition, 11,* 390–399.

Reckase, M. D. (1990). Scaling techniques. In G. Goldstein & M. Hersen (Eds.), *Handbook of psychological assessment* (2nd ed.). New York: Pergamon, 41–56.

Riccio, D. C., Ackil, J., & Burch–Vernon, A. (1992). Forgetting of stimulus attributes: Methodological implications for assessing associative phenomena. *Psychological Bulletin, 112,* 433–445.

Richman, C. L., Mitchell, D. B., & Reznick, J. S. (1979). Mental travel: Some reservations, *Journal of Experimental Psychology: Human Perception and Performance, 5,* 13–18.

Ringelmann, M. (1913). Recherches sur les moteurs animes: Travail de l'homme. *Annales de l'Institut National Agronomique,* 2e series-tome XII, 1–40.

Roberts, C. (1971). Debate I. Animal experimentation and evolution. *American Scholar, 40,* 497–503.

Roediger, H. L., & McDermott, K. B. (1994). Unpublished data.

Roediger, H. L., & Neely, J. H. (1982). Retrieval blocks in episodic and semantic memory. *Canadian Journal of Psychology, 36,* 213–242.

Rogosa, D. (1980). A critique of the cross-lagged correlation. *Psychological Bulletin, 88,* 245–248.

Rollin, B. E. (1985). The moral status of research animals in psychology. *American*

Psychologist, 40, 920–926.

Rose, T. L. (1978). The functional relationship between artificial food colors and hyperactivity. *Journal of Applied Behavior Analysis, 11,* 439–446.

Rosenberg, M. J. (1969). The conditions and consequences of evaluation apprehension. In R. Rosenthal & R. L. Rosnow (Eds.), *Artifact in behavioral research.* New York: Academic Press.

Rosnow, R. L., & Rosenthal, R. (1970). Volunteer effects in behavioral research. In *New directions in psychology 4.* New York: Holt, Rinehart & Winston.

Rowland, L. W. (1939). Will hypnotized persons try to harm themselves or others? *Journal of Abnormal and Social Psychology, 34,* 114–117.

Ruback, R. B., & Snow, J. N. (1993). Territoriality and nonconscious racism at water fountains: Intruders and drinkers (blacks and whites) are affected by race. *Environment and Behavior, 25,* 250–267.

Saari, L. M., & Latham, G. P. (1982). Employee reactions to continuous and variable ratio reinforcement schedules involving a monetary incentive. *Journal of Applied Psychology, 67,* 506–508.

Sacks, O. (1985). *The man who mistook his wife for a hat and other clinical tales.* New York: Summit.

Scarborough, D. L. (1972). Stimulus modality effects on forgetting in short-term memory. *Journal of Experimental Psychology, 95,* 285–289.

Scarr, S. (1988). Race and gender as psychological variables: Social and ethical issues. *American Psychologist, 43,* 56–59.

Schachter, S. (1982). Don't sell habit-breakers short. *Psychology Today, 16,* 27–33.

Schaie, K. W. (1977). Quasi-experimental designs in the psychology of aging. In J. E. Birren & K. W. Schaie (Eds.), *Handbook of the psychology of aging.* New York: Van Nostrand.

Scheier, M. F., & Carver, C. S. (1985). Optimism, coping, and health: Assessment and implications of generalized outcome expectancies. *Health Psychology, 4,* 219–247.

Schneider, D. J. (1988). *Introduction to social psychology.* New York: Harcourt Brace Jovanovich.

Schooler, J. W., Ohlsson, S., & Brooks, K. (1993). Thoughts beyond words: When language overshadows insight. *Journal of Experimental Psychology: General, 122,* 166–183.

Schreibman, L., O'Neill, R. E., & Koegel, R. L. (1983). Behavioral training for siblings of autistic children. *Journal of Applied Behavioral Analysis, 16,* 129–138.

Sellin, T., & Wolfgang, M. E. (1964). *The measurement of delinquency.* New York: Wiley.

Sidman, M. (1960). *Tactics of scientific research.* New York: Basic Books.

Sieber, J. E., & Stanley, B. (1988). Ethical and professional dimensions of socially sensitive research. *American Psychologist, 43,* 49–55.

Singer, P. (1978). Animal experimentation: Philosophical perspectives. In W. T. Reich (Ed.). *Encyclopedia of bioethics.* New York: Free Press.

Skinner, B. F. (1963). The flight from the laboratory. In M. Marx (Ed.) *Theories in Contemporary Psychology.* New York: MacMillan.

Smith, M. C. (1983). Hypnotic memory enhancement: Does it work? *Psychological Bulletin, 94,* 387–407.

Sternberg, R. J. (1992, September). How to win acceptances by psychological journals: 21 tips for better writing. *APS Observer,* 12–18.

Sternberg, R. J. (1993). *The psychologist's companion* (3rd ed.). New York: Cambridge University Press.

Stevens, S. S. (1961). The psychophysics of sensory functions. In W. A. Rosenblith (Ed.), *Sensory communication.* Cambridge: M.I.T. Press.

Stevens, S. S. (1966). A metric for the social consensus. *Science, 151,* 530–541.

St. James, J. D. (1990). Observations on the microstructure of response conflict. *Perception & Psychophysics, 48,* 517–524.

Stroop, J. R. (1935). Studies of interference in serial verbal reactions. *Journal of Experimental Psychology, 18,* 643–662.

Thios, S. J., & D'Agostino, P. R. (1976). Effects of repetition as a function of study-phase retrieval. *Journal of Verbal Learning and Verbal Behavior, 15,* 529–536.

Thompson, J. B., & Buchanan, W. (1979). *Analyzing psychological data.* New York: Scribner's.

Timberlake, W., & Silva, F. J. (1994). Observation of behavior, inference of function, and the study of learning. *Psychonomic Bulletin & Review, 1,* 73–88.

Todd, C. M., & Perlmutter, M. (1980). Reality recalled by school children. In M. Perlmutter (Ed.), *Children's memory: New directions for child development, 10.* San Francisco: Jossey-Bass, 69–85.

Tulving, E., & Pearlstone, Z. (1966). Availability versus accessibility of information in memory for words. *Journal of Verbal Learning and Verbal Behavior, 5,* 381–391.

Tversky, B., & Teiffer, E. (1976). Development of strategies for recall and recognition. *Developmental Psychology, 12,* 406–410.

Underwood, B. (1957). *Psychological research.* New York: Appleton.

Underwood, B. J. (1975). Individual differences as a crucible in theory construction. *American Psychologist, 30,* 128–134.

Uttal, W. R. (1978). *The psychology of mind.* Hillsdale, NJ: Erlbaum.

Velten, E. A. (1968). A laboratory task for the induction of mood states. *Behavior Research and Therapy, 6,* 473–478.

Walters, C., Shurley, J. T., & Parsons, O. A. (1962). Differences in male and female responses to underwater sensory deprivation: An exploratory study. *Journal of Nervous and Mental Disease, 135,* 302–310.

Warren, R. M. (1963). Are loudness judgments based on distance estimates? *Journal of the Acoustical Society of America, 35,* 613–614.

Wason, P. C. (1977). 'On the failure to eliminate hypotheses . . .'—A second look. In P. N. Johnson-Laird & P. C. Wason (Eds.), *Thinking: Readings in cognitive science.* Cambridge: Cambridge University Press.

Webb, E. J., Campbell, D. T., Schwartz, R. D., & Sechrist, L. (1981). *Unobstrusive measures: Nonreactive research in the social sciences.* Chicago: Rand McNally.

Weber, S. J., & Cook, T. D. (1972). Subject effects in laboratory research: An examination of subject roles, demand characteristics, and valid inference. *Psychological Bulletin, 77,* 273–295.

Weisberg, H. F., Krosnick, J. A., & Bowen, B. D. (1989). *An introduction to survey research and data analysis* (2nd ed.). Glenview, IL: Scott, Foresman.

Weiss, J. M. (1968). Effects of coping responses on stress. *Journal of Comparative and Physiological Psychology, 65,* 251–260.

Weiss, J. M. (1971). Effects of coping behavior in different warning signal conditions on stress pathology in rats. *Journal of Comparative and Physiological Psychology, 77,* 1–13.

White, R. J. (1971). Debate II. Antivivisection: The reluctant hydra. *American Scholar, 40,* 503–512.

Wildman, B. G., & Erickson, M. T. (1977). Methodological problems in behavioral observation. In J. D. Cone and R. P. Hawkins (Eds.), *Behavioral assessment.* New York: Brunner/Mazel.

Willerman, L., Schultz, R., Rutledge, J. N., & Bigler, E. D. (1991). *In vivo* brain size and intelligence. *Intelligence, 15,* 223–228.

Williams, K., Harkins, S., & Latané, B. (1981). Identifiability as a deterrent to social loafing: Two cheering experiments. *Journal of Personality and Social Psychology, 40,* 303–311.

Williams, R. D., & Long, J. D. (1979). *Toward a self-managed life style* (2nd ed.).

Boston: Houghton-Mifflin.

Windes, J. D. (1968). Reaction time for numerical coding and naming of numerals. *Journal of Experimental Psychology, 78,* 318–322.

Wohwill, J. F. (1970). Methodology and research strategy in the study of developmental change. In L. R. Goulet & P. B. Baltes (Eds.), *Life-span developmental psychology: Research and theory.* New York: Academic Press.

Wolf, M. M., & Risley, T. R. (1971). Reinforcement: Applied research. In R. Glaser (Ed.), *The nature of reinforcement.* New York: Academic Press.

Woods, P. J. (1976). *Career opportunities for psychologists.* Washington, DC: American Psychological Association.

Woolfolk, M. E. (1981). The eye of the beholder: Methodological considerations when observers assess nonverbal communication. *Journal of Nonverbal Behavior, 5,* 199–204.

Woolfolk, M. E., Castellan, W., & Brooks, C. I. (1983). Pepsi versus Coke: Labels, not tastes, prevail. *Psychological Reports, 52,* 185–186.

Wright, L. (1988). The Type A behavior pattern and coronary artery disease. *American Psychologist, 43,* 2–14.

Young, P. C. (1952). Antisocial uses of hypnosis. In L. M. LeCron (Ed.), *Experimental hypnosis.* New York: Macmillan.

Young, P. T. (1928). Precautions in animal experimentation. *Psychological Bulletin, 25,* 487–489.

Zajonc, R. B., & Marcus, N. (1975). Birth order and intellectual development. *Psychological Review, 82,* 74–88.

GLOSSARY

ABA and ABAB designs see *reversal design*

AB design a frequently used design in therapy in which a therapy (B) is instituted after measuring a particular behavior (A); a poor research design

Abscissa the horizontal axis (or *x*-axis) in a graph

Absolute threshold the average point on a sensory continuum (such as light intensity) at which an observer detects a stimulus

Abstract short summary at the beginning of a journal article that informs the reader about the results

Aftercare the need for experimenters to guard the welfare of their subjects subsequent to the research manipulation; especially important in drug research

Alpha level see *significance level*

Analysis of variance a statistical test appropriate for analyzing reliability from experiments with any number of levels on one or more independent variables

Anthropomorphizing attributing human characteristics or emotions, such as happiness, to animals

APA format the journal article format specified by the American Psychological Association (APA)

Applied research research whose focus is on solving a practical problem

A priori method according to Peirce, a way of fixing belief due to the reasonableness of the event (see *method of tenacity, method of authority,* **and** *empirical*)

Apprehensive-subject role a presumed role taken by a research subject who dislikes being evaluated; see *evaluation apprehension* and *reactivity*

Balanced Latin square counterbalancing scheme in which each condition is preceded and followed equally often by every other condition

Baseline the "normal" or typical behavior used as a standard of comparison in an experiment

Basic research research whose focus is on understanding rather than on the immediate solution to a problem

Behavior the basic dependent variable of psychology

Beta the criterion of the decision process in signal detection measured by the slope of the receiver-operating-characteristic (ROC) function at the point of interest

Between-groups variance a measure of the dispersion among groups in an experiment

Between-subjects design an experimental design in which each subject is tested under only one level of each independent variable

Blind experiment experiment in which subjects do not know whether or not they are in the treatment condition (see *double-blind design*)

Block randomization a counterbalancing technique in which the treatment orders are randomized in successive blocks of presenting those conditions

Carryover effect relatively permanent effect that testing subjects in one condition has on their later behavior in another condition

Case study intensive investigation of a particular instance, or cases, of some behavior; does not allow inferences of cause and effect but is merely descriptive

Ceiling effect see *scale-attenuation effects*

Cell an entry in a data table defined by a particular row/column combination

Central tendency descriptive statistics indicating the center of a distribution of scores; see *mean, median,* and *mode*

Computerized literature search a method of searching the data base in a library that uses a computer

Conceptual replication attempt to demonstrate an experimental phenomenon with an entirely new paradigm or set of experimental conditions (see *covering operations*)

Confidence level see *significance level*

Confidentiality information obtained about subjects should remain confidential unless otherwise agreed

Confounding simultaneous variation of a second variable with an independent variable of interest so that any effect on the dependent variable cannot be attributed with certainty to the independent variable; inherent in correlational research

Construct validity when several measures fit sensibly with other results, we are measuring an underlying psychological concept

Contingency table a relational research design in which the frequencies with which all combinations of two variables are assessed to determine the relationship between them

Control the technique of producing comparisons and holding other variables constant

Control condition the comparison condition in a within-subjects design (compare to *control group*)

Control group the group in a between-subjects experiment that receives a comparison level of the independent variable

Control variable a potential independent variable that is held constant in an experiment

Converging operations a set of related lines of investigation that all bolster a common conclusion

Correlation a measure of the extent to which two variables are related, not necessarily causally

Correlation coefficient a number that can vary from -1.00 to $+1.00$ and indicates the degree of relation between two variables

Correlational research relational research that shows both the degree and the direction of the relationship between two variables

Counterbalancing refers to any technique used to vary systematically the order of conditions in an experiment to distribute the effects of time of testing (e.g., practice and fatigue) so they are not confounded with conditions

Criterion an independent means of determining the validity of an observation, experiment, or judgment; and the decision point in a signal-detection experiment at which an observer decides to say yes or no

Critic a person who makes an informed judgment

Critical thinker a person who approaches scientific procedures and results with a critical attitude

Cross-lagged panel correlation calculating several correlation coefficients across time on the same participants to increase the internal validity of correlational research

Cross-over interaction when the effect of one independent variable on a dependent variable reverses at different levels of a second independent variable

Cross-sectional method taking a large sample of the population of various ages at one time and testing them (contrast with *longitudinal method*)

Cross-sequential design a quasi-experimental design used when age is a subject variable to try to control for cohort and time of testing effects; involves testing several different age groups at several different time periods (see *longitudinal method* and *cross-sectional method*)

d' the sensitivity of an observer in a signal-detection experiment; the distance between signal and noise distributions

Data the scores obtained on a dependent variable

Debriefing when subjects are told all details of an experiment after they have participated; an ethical obligation of the researcher

Deception a research technique in which the participant is mislead about some aspect of the project; may be unethical (see *double-blind design*)

Decision process evaluation of the sensory impression of a stimulus

Decision threshold the stimulus that elicits a response resulting from both the criterion and the strength of the stimulus (see beta and d')

Deduction reasoning from the general to the particular

Degrees of freedom the number of values free to vary if the total number of values and their sum are fixed

Demand characteristics those cues available to subjects in an experiment that may enable them to determine the purpose of the experiment, or what is expected by the experimenter

Dependent variable the variable measured and recorded by the experimenter

Descriptive observation a determination of the quantity (frequency, magnitude) of behavior resulting from observation, case study, survey, and testing methods

Descriptive statistics methods of organizing and summarizing data

Deviant-case analysis investigation of similar cases that differ in outcome in an attempt to specify the reasons for the different outcomes

Difference a basic property of all measurement scales, such that objects or their attributes can be categorized as different from each other

Difference threshold the average point at which two stimuli are judged to be different (half of the interval of uncertainty)

Diffusion of responsibility the tendency for individuals to assume less responsibility to act in a group situation

Directional/nondirectional statistical tests see *one-* and *two-tailed tests*

Direct scaling the observer applies his or her scale in assigning numbers (see *indirect scaling*)

Direct replication repeating an experiment as closely as possible to determine whether the same results will be obtained

Discounting cue a message, signal, or pertinent fact that makes you doubt the accuracy or credibility of a persuasive message

Dispersion the amount of spread in a distribution of scores

Distribution a set of values of a variable

Dolorimeter an instrument used to generate heat; used in psychophysical research to determine peoples' pain thresholds

Double-blind design experimental technique in which neither the subject nor the experimenter knows which subjects are in which treatment conditions

Ecological validity the extent to which a research setting matches the environment of the problem under investigation; a threat to the external validity of experiments

Einstellung the effect of expectancy on cognition; for example, if the people solve problems in one particular way, they will often approach new problems in the same way even when the original strategy is no longer effective

Empirical relying on or derived from observation or experiment

Equal interval a property of measurement scales such that a one-unit change is equivalent throughout the range of the scale

Ethogram a data sheet providing categories for making naturalistic observations

Ethology the systematic study of behavior; usually animal behavior in natural settings

Evaluation apprehension a source of reactivity in which subjects are uneasy about being evaluated in an experiment (see *reactivity*)

Experiment the systematic manipulation of some environment in order to observe the effect of this manipulation on behavior; a particular comparison is produced

Experimental control holding constant extraneous variables in an experiment so that any effect on the dependent variable can be attributed to manipulation of the independent variable

Experimental group the group in an experiment that receives the level of interest of the independent variable

Experimental reliability see *replication*

Explanation a causal statement about why or when a particular event occurs resulting from experimental methods (see *joint method of agreement and difference*)

Ex post facto literally, "after the fact"; refers to conditions in an experiment that are not determined prior to the experiment, but only after some manipulation has occurred naturally

External validity refers to the generality of research; externally valid research is representative of real life and does not distort the question under investigation

Factorial design an experimental design in which each level of every independent variable occurs with all levels of the other independent variable

Faithful-subject role when subjects do their utmost to follow the demands of the experimenter (see *reactivity*)

False alarm saying yes when a signal is not present (in contrast to a hit)

Falsifiability view the assertion by Popper that negative results are more informative than positive results

Fechner's law $\psi = K \log$ **stimulus** an ordinal scale specifying the relation between psychological judgment and stimulus intensity

Field research research conducted in natural settings in which subjects typically do not know that they are in an experiment

Floor effect see *scale-attenuation effects*

Forced-choice tests tests in which the participant must select between two or more statements; often used to control response styles

F **ratio** a ratio of between-groups variance to within-groups variance; forms the basis of the analysis of variance

Freedom to withdraw experimenter is ethically obligated to allow subjects to discontinue participation in the research

Frequency distribution a set of scores arranged in order along a distribution indicating the number of times each score occurs

Frequency polygon a frequency distribution in which the height of the curve indicates the frequency of scores (see *histogram*)

Generalizability the issue of whether a particular experimental result will be obtained under different circumstances, such as with a different subject population or in a different experimental setting

Good-subject role when a subject attempts to determine the purposes of an experiment and reacts accordingly (see *demand characteristics* and *reactivity*)

Hawthorne effect refers to conditions under which performance in an experiment is affected by the knowledge of participants that they are in an experiment (see *demand characteristics*)

Histogram a frequency distribution in which the height of bars in the graph indicates the frequency of a class of scores; also called a bar graph

History a possible confound in research that inadvertently takes place between measurements because of historical changes in the participant

Hit saying yes when a signal is presented (see *false alarm*)

Independent variable the variable manipulated by the experimenter

Indirect scaling the observer limits judgments to a small set of categories in order to scale the attribute in question (contrast with *direct scaling*)

Individual differences a problem that may confound the results of a between-subjects experiment

Induction reasoning from the particular to the general

Inferential statistics procedures for determining the reliability and generality of a particular experimental finding

Informed consent potential subjects must be in a position to decide whether to participate in an experiment

Institutional Review Board (IRB) a board in nearly every United States institution conducting research that oversees the protection of human subjects

Interactions experimental results that occur when the effects of one independent variable depend on the levels of other independent variables

Internal distribution the presumed sensory impressions in signal-detection theory

Internal validity allows straightforward statements about causality; experiments are usually internally valid because the joint method of agreement and difference is employed

Interobserver reliability the degree to which two or more observers can accurately categorize naturalistic observations

Interrupted-time-series design a quasi-experiment that involves examination of a naturally occurring treatment on the behavior of a large number of participants

Interval of uncertainty the difference between the upper and lower thresholds in the determination of a difference threshold

Interval scale a scale with equal intervals but without a true zero point (for example, temperature)

Intervening variable an abstract concept that links independent variables to dependent variables

Joint method of agreement and difference in Mill's system a situation, such as an experiment, in which X always follows A and never occurs when A is not present

Just-noticeable difference (JND) the smallest perceptible difference between two stimuli

Large-n designs designs in which inferential statistics are used to determine whether two or more groups differ reliably

Latin-square design a counterbalancing procedure in which each conditioning occurs equally often during each time period of the experiment (see *balanced Latin square*)

Longitudinal method testing one group of people repeatedly as they age (contrast with *cross-sectional method*)

Magnitude a property of measurement scales having to do with the fact that scale values can be ordered on the basis of magnitude—if A > B and B > C, then A > C

Magnitude estimation observers assign numbers to attributes usually without restriction except that the numbers be assigned proportionately to the judged magnitude (a ratio scale)

Magnitude of effect a calculation such as r_{pb} that reveals the magnitude of the effect of the independent variable—how wrong the null hypothesis is

Main effect when the effect of one independent variable is the same at all levels of another independent variable

Mann-Whitney *U* test a nonparametric test to determine whether the behavior of two independent groups is statistically different

Matched-groups design experimental design in which subjects are matched on some variable assumed to be correlated with the dependent variable and then randomly assigned to conditions

Matching see *subject variable* and *matched-groups design*

Maturation changes in people over time because of growth and other historical factors; may be a source of confounding in quasi-experiments

Mean measure of central tendency; the sum of all the scores divided by the number of scores

Measurement the systematic assignment of numbers to objects or attributes of objects

Measurement scales in order in increasing power; nominal, ordinal, interval, and ratio

Median measure of central tendency; the middle score of a distribution, or the one that divides a distribution in half

Method of authority a method of fixing belief in which an authority's word is taken on faith (contrast with *empirical*)

Method of limits a psychophysical procedure for determining thresholds in which ascending and descending sequences of stimuli are presented

Method of tenacity a way of fixing belief involving a steadfast adherence to a particular belief, regardless of contrary arguments (see *empirical*)

Mixed design an experimental design that contains both between-subjects and within-subjects manipulations of the independent variables

Mode a measure of central tendency; the most frequent score

Mortality a possible source of confounding in research resulting from subjects dropping out either because they will not participate or because they cannot participate

Motivated forgetting distortions of past events reported retrospectively because of the emotional nature of those events

Multiple baseline design a small-n design in which different behaviors (or different people) receive baseline periods of varying lengths prior to the introduction of the independent variable

Naturalistic observation description of naturally occurring events without intervention on the part of the investigator

Negativistic-subject role when a subject deliberately attempts to sabotage an experiment

Noise a random disturbance that can be confused with signals in a signal-detection experiment

Nominal scale a scale in which objects are named or categorized—the weakest measurement scale

Nonequivalent control group in quasi-experiments a control group that is not determined by random assignment but is usually selected after the fact and is supposed to be equivalent to the naturally treated group

Normal curve a distribution of events that, when plotted, results in a bell-shaped curve; in a normal curve the mean, the median, and the mode are all equal

Normal distribution one producing a symmetric bell-shaped curve

Nonparametric statistics statistical tests that do not make any assumptions about the underlying distribution of scores; ordinarily require just ordinal-level data (see *parametric statistics*)

Null hypothesis states that the independent variable will have no effect on the dependent variable

Null result an experimental outcome where the dependent variable was not influenced by the independent variable

Observation-treatment-observation a quasi-experimental design; usually includes a nonequivalent control group

One-shot case study (see *case study*) a quasi-experiment in which the behavior of a single individual is studied and "explained" in terms of life events (see also *deviant-case analysis*)

One-tailed test test that places the rejection area at one end of a distribution

Operational definition a definition of a concept in terms of the operations that must be performed to demonstrate the concept

Ordinal scale a measurement scale in which objects or attributes are ordered but in which the intervals between points are not equal

Ordinate the vertical axis (or y-axis) in a graph

Organize one function of a theory is to collect or organize what is known into a coherent statement

Parallel forms two alternative forms of a test

Parametric statistics statistic tests that make assumptions about the distribution of scores (e.g., normally distributed); require interval or ratio data

Parsimony a good, powerful theory should explain many events with few statements or explanatory concepts; thus, refers to simplicity

Participant observation an observation procedure in which the observer participates with those being observed; e.g., living with gorillas in the wild

Pearson r one form of correlation coefficient

Pearson's Product Moment Correlation Coefficient see Pearson's r

Personal space the "invisible bubble" surrounding a person

Pilot research preliminary research undertaken to discover problems of method and design for a subsequent full-scale project

Placebo effect improvement often shown in drug effectiveness studies in which patients believe they have received a drug when they actually received an inert substance

Point biserial r a correlation coefficient often used in two group experiments to determine the magnitude of effect of the independent variable

Point of subjective equality the mean of the upper and lower thresholds in a difference-threshold experiment

Population the total set of potential observations from which a sample is drawn

Power (of a statistical test) the probability of rejecting the null hypothesis in a statistical test when it is in fact false

Precision a good theory should be precise in its predictions

Prediction a specification of relationships resulting from correlational methods; also one aim of a theory

Predictive validity when a test can predict a particular outcome

Protection from harm ethical researchers protect their subjects from any harm

Protocol a recipe to be followed exactly in conducting a research project

Proximate cause the immediate causes of an event, such as the independent variable in an experiment (see *ultimate cause*)

Psychological Abstracts a journal produced by the APA that lists abstracts of most of the journal articles relevant to psychological topics

Psychophysical methods procedures such as the method of limits used to determine absolute and difference thresholds

Psychophysics judgment of stimuli along a known physical dimension; e.g., the perceived brightness of lights of different intensities

Quasi-experiment an experiment in which the independent variable occurs naturally and is not under direct control of the experimenter (see *ex post facto*)

Random assignment a crucial tool in experimentation whereby subjects are assigned to conditions in an unbiased fashion

Randomization see *random assignment*

Random-groups design when subjects are randomly assigned to conditions in a between-subjects design

Random sample a sample from a population that has been selected in an unbiased way

Random sampling (see *random sample*)

Range descriptive measure of dispersion; the difference between the largest and smallest score in a distribution

Ratio scale the highest form of scale in which there is a true zero and in which it is meaningful to consider multiplicative differences among attributes

Reactivity term to describe observations that are influenced by (or may be, in part, a reaction to) the detected presence of the investigator

Realism the extent to which a research procedure matches the characteristics of the real world (contrast with *generality of results*)

Receiver-operating-characteristic (ROC) a plot of hits against false alarms in signal-detection experiments

Regression artifacts an artifact in the measurement of change on a variable when groups of subjects who scored at the extremes on the variable are tested again (see *regression to the mean*)

Regression to the mean tendency for extreme measures on some variable to be closer to the group mean when remeasured, due to unreliability of measurement

Relational research research that tries to determine how two or more variables are related

Reliability refers to the repeatability of an experimental result; inferential statistics provide an estimation of how likely it is that a finding is repeatable; also refers to the consistency of a test or measuring instrument determined by computing a correlation between scores obtained by subjects taking the test twice (test-retest reliability), or taking two different parallel forms of the test, or scores obtained on each half of the test (split-half reliability)

Removing harmful consequences ethical researchers remove any harmful consequences that their subjects may have incurred

Repeated-measures design several measures are taken on the same subject, such as several learning trials or numerous psychophysical judgments; a type of within-subject experiment

Replication the repetition of an earlier experiment to duplicate (and perhaps extend) its findings (see also *systematic replication*)

Researcher bias deliberate or inadvertent bias in which data are misanalyzed or participants are differentially treated over and above any planned differences in treatment

Response acquiescence a habitual way of responding on tests that involves frequently responding "yes" (see *response styles*)

Response deviation a habitual way of responding on tests that involves frequently responding "no" (see *response styles*)

Response styles habitual ways of responding on a test that are independent of the particular test item (see *response deviation, response acquiescence,* and *social desirability*)

Retrospective in case studies when the person has to report on events that occurred in the distant past; subject to ordinary and motivated forgetting

Reversibility an assumption made in research that the characteristics of different populations and species of subjects have the same underlying process; the behavioral "equation" can be determined from the behavior that is observed

Reversal (ABA) design small-n design in which a subject's behavior is measured under a baseline (A) condition, then an experimental treatment is applied during the B phase and any change sin behavior are observed; finally, the original baseline (A) conditions are reinstituted to ensure that the experimental treatment was responsible for any observed change during the B phase

Sample observations selected from a population

Scale-attenuation effects difficulties in interpreting results when performance on the dependent variable is either nearly perfect (a ceiling effect) or nearly lacking altogether (a floor effect)

Scatter diagrams a graphical relationship indicating degree of correlation between two variables made by plotting the scores of individuals on two variables

Scientific method according to Peirce, this method fixes belief on the basis of experience (see *empirical*)

Selection bias occurs when subjects are not selected randomly (see *subject attrition* and *matching*)

Self-correcting science is self-correcting because it relies on public, empirical observation; old beliefs are discarded if they do not fit the empirical data

Sensory impression a hypothetical process that depends on the intensity of the stimulus in a signal-detection experiment

Setting representativeness see *ecological validity*

Significance level probability that an experimental finding is due to chance, or random fluctuation, operating in the data

Simulated experiment a fake experiment in which subjects are told to simulate the behavior of real subjects in a particular experiment

Skewed distribution a nonsymmetrical distribution

Sleeper effect an improvement in the effect of a persuasive message with the passage of time

Small-*n* design research design utilizing a small number of subjects

Social desirability a habitual way of responding on tests that involves making socially desirable responses (see *response styles*)

Social loafing the decrease in individual effort that sometimes occurs when other people are present and when group performance is measured

Social Science Citation Index a journal containing lists of articles that cite a particular author or work

Speciesism a term used to describe the view that animal life is qualitatively different from human life and, therefore, a form of bigotry

Split-half reliability determining reliability of a test by dividing the test items into two arbitrary groups and correlating the scores obtained on the two halves of the test

Staircase method an abbreviated version of the method of limits in which only stimuli around the threshold value are presented

Standard deviation descriptive measure of dispersion; square root of the sum of squared deviations of each score from the mean divided by the number of scores

Standard error of the mean the standard deviation of the distribution of sample means

Standard normal distribution a distribution of events that, when plotted, results in a bell-shaped curve; in a standard normal distribution the mean, the median, and the mode are all equal

Standard scores also called z scores; differences between individual scores and the mean score expressed in units of standard deviations

Statistical reliability rejecting the null hypothesis on the basis of a statistical test that yields an alpha level of less than .05

Stevens' law $\psi = k \text{ stimulus}^n$ the law derived from the method of magnitude estimation that says that psychological judgments grow exponentially with increments in stimulus intensity

Stratified sample an alternative to a random sample in which the population is divided into units and random sampling is done from the units.

Strong inference Platt's view that scientific progress comes about through a series of tests of alternative theoretical outcomes

Stroop effect difficulty in naming the color of an object when the color conflicts with the name of the object (when the word *blue* is printed in red ink)

Subject attrition when a subject fails to complete an experiment, which may destroy the basis of matching subjects across groups

Subject representativeness determination of generality of results across different subject populations

Subject roles how a subject reacts in an experiment (see *apprehensive-subject role, faithful-subject role, good subject role,* and *negativistic-subject role*)

Subject variable some characteristics of people that can be measured or described but cannot be varied experimentally (e.g., height, weight, sex, IQ, etc.)

Sum of squares (SS) sum of the squared scores used to calculate effects via analysis of variance

Survey research the technique of obtaining a limited amount of information from a large number of people, usually through random sampling

Synergism a term used in medical research to describe an interaction (see *interactions*)

Systematic replication repeating an experiment while varying numerous factors considered to be irrelevant to the phenomenon to see if it will survive these changes

Test reliability see *test-retest reliability* and *split-half reliability*

Testability a good theory needs to be capable of disproof

Testable hypothesis a hypothesis that specifies what can be measured and manipulated to test a theory

Test-retest reliability giving the same test twice in succession over a short interval to see if the scores are stable, or reliable; generally expressed as a correlation between scores on the tests

Theory a collection of ideas whose purpose is to describe and predict

Theory of signal detection states that sensory impressions and decision processes control our detection of signals

Threshold in psychophysics the hypothetical barrier a stimulus must cross to be detected

Time-lag design a quasi-experimental design used when age is a subject variable in order to control time of testing effects; subjects of a particular age (e.g., 19-year-olds) are tested at different time periods

Treatment × treatment × subjects design a within-subjects factorial design with two independent variables

True zero the absence of a physical property (zero weight in grams) as opposed to an arbitrary zero such as 0° Centigrade

Truncated range a problem in interpreting low correlations; the amount of dispersion (or range) of scores on one variable may be small, thus leading to the low correlation found

t **tests** parametric tests for testing differences between two groups

Two by two factorial design (2 × 2) a design in which there are two levels of each of two independent variables yielding four conditions

Two-tailed test test that places the rejection area at both ends of a distribution

Type 1 error probability that the null hypothesis is rejected when it is in fracture; equals the significance level

Type 2 error failure to reject the null hypothesis when it is in fact false

Ultimate cause the basic or final cause of an event, such as a "big bang" or evolution (contrast with *proximate cause*)

Unobtrusive measures measures taken from the results of behavior not the behavior itself

Unobtrusive observations observations not resulting in reactivity

Validity refers to whether an observation or procedure is sound or genuine

Variable representativeness determination of generality of results across different manipulations of an independent variable or different dependent variables

Variance measure of dispersion; the standard deviation squared

Volunteer problem volunteer subjects differ from those less eager to participate; may be a source of bias in research

Weber's law $\Delta I/I = K$ the just-noticeable difference is a constant fraction of the base intensity

Wilcoxon signed-ranks test a nonparametric test for two related groups

Within-groups variance a measure of the dispersion among subjects in the same group in an experiment

Within-subjects design an experimental design in which each subject is tested under more than one level of the independent variable

Workload the amount of attention-demanding effort imposed on a person

X^2 **test for independence** a test that is often used to determine the statistical significance of the relationship between variables in a contingency table

Name Index

SUBJECT INDEX